D0238632

# THE AFFAIR OF THE POISONS

To b

WITHDRAWN FROM
THE LIBRARY

UNIVERSITY OF
WINCHESTER

KA 0331150 3

*Also by Anne Somerset*

Elizabeth I
Unnatural Murder: Poison at the Court of James I
Ladies-in-Waiting: from the Tudors to the Present Day
The Life and Times of William IV

# THE AFFAIR OF
# THE POISONS

MURDER, INFANTICIDE AND SATANISM
AT THE COURT OF LOUIS XIV

## ANNE SOMERSET

Weidenfeld & Nicolson
LONDON

First published in Great Britain in 2003
by Weidenfeld & Nicolson

© 2003 Anne Somerset

All rights reserved. No part of this publication may be
reproduced, stored in a retrieval system, or transmitted,
in any form or by any means, electronic, mechanical,
photocopying, recording or otherwise, without the prior
permission of the copyright owner.

The right of Anne Somerset to be identified as the author
of this work has been asserted by her in accordance with
the Copyright, Designs and Patents Act 1988.

A CIP catalogue record for this book
is available from the British Library.

ISBN 0 297 84216 1

Typeset by Selwood Systems, Midsomer Norton

Printed in Great Britain by
Butler & Tanner Ltd, Frome and London

Weidenfeld & Nicolson

The Orion Publishing Group Ltd
Orion House
5 Upper Saint Martin's Lane
London WC2H 9EA

For Ella, with much love

# CONTENTS

# ILLUSTRATIONS

The author and the publishers offer their thanks to the following for
their kind permission to reproduce images:

1  Bridgeman Art Library
2  Hulton Getty Picture Library
3  Réunion des Musées Nationaux

# PRINCIPAL CHARACTERS

**Alluye, Bénigne, Marquise de**  Friend of Comtesse de Soissons who accompanied her on her visit to la Voisin. Fled France with Comtesse de Soissons January 1680

**Amy, Monsieur D'**  Officer in Provençal *Parlement*, posthumously alleged to have wanted to poison Colbert

**Aubray, Antoine Dreux d'**  Civil Lieutenant of the city of Paris. Father and first victim of Mme de Brinvilliers. Died 10 September 1666

**Aubray, Antoine d'**  Eldest brother and second victim of Mme deBrinvilliers. Succeeded father as Civil Lieutenant of the city of Paris. Died 17 June 1670

**Aubray, François d'**  *Conseiller* in Paris *Parlement*. Younger brother and third victim of Mme de Brinvilliers. Poisoned September 1670

**Bachimont, Roger, Seigneur de**  Alchemist and associate of Vanens arrested May 1678. Suspected of poisoning Duke of Savoy. Imprisoned for life

**Bachimont, Mme Marie de**  Wife to the above

**Barenton, Mathurin**  Accused of having traded in poisons and being involved in plot to poison King. Executed September 1681

**Belleguise**  Clerk of Pennautier and associate of Sainte-Croix. Went missing after the arrest of Mme de Brinvilliers, but arrested August 1676. Though he was widely suspected of having acted as an intermediary between Pennautier and Sainte-Croix he was convicted only of handling counterfeit money and banished for a short period

**Bellière, la**  Divineress. Allegedly Mme Chapelain had wanted to send her to the Caribbean to commune with the devil. La Bellière alleged that la Filastre had offered her large sum of money to deliver something to Mme de Montespan, but she had refused, fearing hanging

**Belot, François** Member of the royal guard, convicted of having tried to poison M. de Poulaillon's silver cup. Executed June 1679

**Bergerot, Martine** Illiterate divineress alleged to have arranged for pact drawn up by la Filastre for Duchesse de Vivonne to be signed by spirit

**Bertrand** Friend of Romani, alleged to have been his accomplice in plot to poison Mlle de Fontanges

**Bezons, Louis Bazin, Seigneur de** Commissioner of *Chambre Ardente* who served alongside La Reynie as investigating magistrate in the Affair of the Poisons, and *rapporteur* to the Chamber

**Blessis, Denis Poculot, Sieur de** Alchemist lover of la Voisin. In late 1678 the Marquis de Termes had detained Blessis in his chateau in hopes that Blessis would furnish him with the secret of the Philosopher's Stone. The petition which la Voisin sought to present to the King in March 1679 requested that Termes be ordered to release Blessis. Condemned to galleys by Chamber

**Bonnard, Pierre** Man of business to Maréchal de Luxembourg. In bid to recover documents for his master, employed Lesage to cast spells. Sent to galleys by Chamber, May 1680

**Bosse, Marie** Divineress arrested January 1679 after boasting at a dinner party that she had grown rich from supplying poison. Burnt May 1679

**Bossuet, Jacques Bénigne** Bishop of Condom, preceptor of Dauphin and celebrated preacher

**Bouillon, Marie-Anne, Duchesse de** Sister of the Comtesse de Soissons and wife of King's Great Chamberlain. Visited la Voisin and Lesage, and alleged to have expressed wish that her husband would die

**Briancourt, Jean-Baptiste** Tutor to Mme de Brinvilliers's children who became her lover. Subsequently testified against her at her trial

**Brinvilliers, Marie Madeleine, Marquise de** Murderess executed July 1676 for poisoning her father and two brothers

**Brissart, Mme Marie** Widow of *Conseiller* in *Parlement*. Alleged by la

Voisin to have wanted to poison her sister. Lesage performed magic spells on her behalf to enable her to capture the heart of Captain Rubantel

**Broglio, Mme de, formerly Marquise de Canilhac** Alleged to have poisoned first husband with aid of la Voisin. Never arrested as had left France

**Bussy, Roger de Rabutin, Comte de** Cousin of Mme de Sévigné exiled from Paris 1666 for having written scurrilous novel. Kept in touch with friends at court by letter

**Cadelan, Pierre** Banker associate of Vanens. Suspected of involvement in international poisoning conspiracy. Died in prison September 1684

**Carada, Anne** Executed June 1681 for having poisoned her lover's wife

**Cessac, Louis de Guilhem de Castelnau, Marquis de** Courtier who had to leave France after caught cheating at cards 1671. Returned to France 1674. Implicated in Affair of the Poisons after Lesage alleged he had sought to kill his brother so that he could marry his sister-in-law. Fled the country to escape trial. Permitted to return to France 1691

**Chanfrain, Jeanne** Mistress of Guibourg

**Chapelain, Mme Magdelaine** Divineress and former employer of la Filastre. Suspected of being responsible for several poisonings. Sent la Filastre to see Galet. Imprisoned for life

**Chasteuil, François-Galaup de** Major in White Cross Regiment at Turin. Referred to as 'the author' by Vanens, who said he knew secret formula for an oil which converted base metal into gold. Died before arrest of Vanens

**Cheron, Anne** Fruit seller alleged to have supplied toad to be used to poison cup belonging to M. de Poulaillon. Executed June 1679

**Choisy, Abbé de** Author of memoirs

**Colbert, Jean-Baptiste** Controller-General of Finance

**Cotton, Jacques** Priest who conducted black mass attended by la Filastre. Burnt October 1680

**Dalmas, P.** Blind associate of La Chaboissière, arrested February 1678

**Davot, Gilles**  Priest alleged by Lesage to have performed black masses for la Voisin. Executed July 1681

**Debray, Étienne**  Associate of Deschault who revealed details of plot to assassinate King. Executed September 1681

**Delaporte, Marguerite**  Divineress, alleged to have purchased poisons from Maître Pierre. Supposedly present at black masses celebrated in presence of Mme de Montespan. Imprisoned for life without trial

**Deschault, Jacques**  Shepherd alleged to have performed spells and supplied poison to Mme Carada. Executed June 1681

**Desmaretz, Mme**  Widowed client of Lesage who asked him to devise spells to persuade her lover Gontier to marry her

**Dreux, Mme Françoise de**  Client of la Voisin, arrested April 1679. Alleged to have sought to kill her husband and to have asked la Voisin to supply her with poisoned bouquet. Admonished by Chamber 1680 and freed. New warrant issued for arrest July 1681 after named as client of la Joly. Alleged she had sought to kill Duchesse de Richelieu. Fled country to avoid trial

**Duplessis, Claude**  Lawyer and legal adviser to Colbert who drew up memoranda defending Mmes de Montespan and de Vivonne

**Dusoulcye, Louise**  Mistress of Dalmas alleged to have poisoned a woman with plums

**Exili, Egidio**  Italian in service of Queen Christina of Sweden, arrested in Paris February 1663. In Bastille at same time as Sainte-Croix. Alleged to have been great expert on poisons

**Ferry, Mme**  Client of la Bosse and la Voisin. Executed May 1679 for having poisoned her husband

**Feuquières, Antoine de Pas, Marquis de**  Courtier alleged to have been client of la Vigoreux. Present at encounter between Luxembourg and Lesage. Alleged by Lesage to have sought death of a relative of a woman he wished to marry

**Filastre, Françoise**  Sorceress, aged thirty-five in 1680. She claimed to have drawn up satanic pact for Duchesse de Vivonne. At time of arrest planning to obtain position in household of Mlle de Fontanges. Under torture admitted having sacrificed her own child. Also confessed to having purchased aphrodisiacs and poisons on behalf of Mme de Montespan. Retracted claims before being burnt

**Fontanges, Marie-Angélique de Scorailles, Mlle de** Maid of honour to Duchesse d'Orléans, who became King's mistress probably late 1678. Had miscarriage January 1680 and never really recovered health. Created Duchesse de Fontanges, April 1680. Died June 1681. Some people suspected poison responsible

**Fontet, Marquise de** Hostess at whose Paris house Luxembourg and Feuquières met Lesage.

**Fouquet, Nicolas** *Surintendant* of Finance who was arrested by King 1661 and charged with financial corruption and treason. Imprisoned for life in fortress of Pignerol. Subsequently it was claimed that some years before had sent Christophe Glaser to Florence to research poison

**Galet, Philippe** Norman peasant alleged to have supplied la Filastre and Mme Chapelain with poisons and aphrodisiacs. According to la Filastre, Galet boasted that Mme de Montespan was a client of his

**Gassilly, Comte de** Client of la Bosse and la Vigoreux. Alleged to have requested Lesage to arrange death of his uncle. Never questioned by Chamber

**Glaser, Christophe** Swiss chemist who held positions of apothecary-in-ordinary to Louis XIV and the Duc d'Orléans, and resident lecturer at the Royal Botanical Garden in Paris. Alleged to have supplied Sainte-Croix with poison made to his own special formula. Exact date of death unknown but certainly died before Sainte-Croix's death in 1672

**Guesdon, Mme** At one point employed by Mme de Brinvilliers and Sainte-Croix. Imprisoned for life on suspicion of having poisoned M. Violet on orders of Maillard

**Guibourg, Abbé Étienne** Elderly priest who claimed to have performed black masses for Mme de Montespan. Confessed to having performed child sacrifice

**Joly, Marguerite** Divineress and alleged poisoner. Executed December 1681

**La Chaboissière** Name adopted by Jean Barthominat, valet to Louis Vanens. Arrested December 1677, he was the last person executed during the Affair of the Poisons, 16 July 1682

**La Chausée** Name adopted by Jean Hamelin, a barber and servant employed by Sainte-Croix and Mme de Brinvilliers. Infiltrated into service of Mme de Brinvilliers's younger brother, who lived with

Antoine d'Aubray and his wife. On orders of Mme de Brinvilliers and Sainte-Croix poisoned both brothers. Confessed after torture. Broken on wheel March 1672

**La Fare, Marquis de** Author of memoirs

**La Ferté, Madeleine, Maréchale de** Famously promiscuous court lady who gave evidence before Arsenal Chamber after being named as having visited a divineress

**La Grange, Magdelaine de** Divineress arrested February 1677 on suspicion of having poisoned her lover Jean Faurye and forged a marriage contract. While in prison warned La Reynie and Louvois that the King was at risk of poisoning. Hanged February 1679. Later alleged to have supplied la Voisin and la Bosse with poisons

**Lamoignon, Guillaume** *Premier Président* of Paris *Parlement* during trial of Mme de Brinvilliers. Died suddenly December 1677. Subsequently reported to have been poisoned

**La Reynie, Nicolas-Gabriel de** Lieutenant-General of the Paris Police, commissioner and *rapporteur* to Arsenal Chamber

**La Rivière, M. de** Self-styled 'Marquis' who was lover of Mme de Poulaillon. Left Paris after her arrest and became friend and correspondent of Comte de Bussy

**Latour** Stone mason and associate of la Voisin's. Alleged by Lesage to have been involved in plot to supply Mlle des Oeillets with poison to kill King

**La Vallière, Louise de, later Duchesse de Vaujours** Became mistress of King 1661. Entered convent 1674

**Le Boultz, M.** *Conseiller* in Paris *Parlement* and member of powerful legal dynasty. As the brother-in-law of Pennautier, Le Boultz was suspected of using his influence to secure Pennautier's release

**Leféron, Mme Marguerite** Wealthy client of la Voisin, arrested April 1679 on suspicion of having poisoned her husband, Jerome Leféron, in 1669. Tried April 1680, fined and banished

**Lepère, Catherine** Midwife who carried out numerous abortions for clients of la Voisin. Alleged by la Voisin to have supplied her with poisons. Hanged August 1679

**Leroux, Jeanne** Associate of la Voisin, executed April 1680 for complicity in death of M. Leféron

**Leroy, Catherine** Mistress of La Chaboissière. Confessed to having poisoned two women on his orders

**Lesage** Name adopted by Adam du Coeuret, formerly known as Dubuisson. Magician, sent to galleys 1668 for having committed impieties. Freed and returned to Paris, and resumed activities. Arrested again March 1679. Source of many accusations against people at Court

**Lescalopier, Mme** Suspected of having murdered her husband over ten years before the Affair of the Poisons. Fled country to avoid trial

**Le Tellier, Michel** Father of Louvois and Chancellor of France

**Lorraine, Philippe, Chevalier de** Favourite of Duc d'Orléans exiled from France 1670. Suspected of being responsible for poisoning Duchesse d'Orléans. Permitted to return to Court 1672

**Louvois, François-Michel Le Tellier, Marquis de** Minister of War who played an active part in the Affair of the Poisons

**Ludres, Marie-Isabelle, Mme de** Maid of honour and lay canoness of Poussaye Abbey who became King's mistress in 1677

**Luxembourg, François-Henri, Maréchal-Duc de** Distinguished general who had at least one encounter with Lesage. Lesage alleged that he sought death of various individuals, including his wife, and that he tried to poison a businessman who was seeking to renege on a property transaction

**Maillard, Jean** *Conseiller* in Paris *Parlement*. Client of Moreau. Suspected of involvement in plot to poison King. Suspected of poisoning Violet, the husband of his lover. Tortured and executed February 1682

**Maine, Louis-Auguste, Duc du** Eldest illegitimate son of King and Mme de Montespan

**Maintenon, Françoise Marquise de (formerly Mme Scarron)** Governess to King's children by Mme de Montespan. In 1680 became lady-in-waiting to Dauphine. After death of Queen in 1683 became King's morganatic wife

**Marie-Thérèse, Queen** Spanish princess who married Louis XIV in 1661. Died 1683

**Mariette, François** Priest who acted as Lesage's partner in Paris 1667–8. Arrested March 1668. Sent to monastery of Saint-Lazare but absconded. Arrested in Toulouse February 1680. November 1680 questioned about earlier dealings with Mme de Montespan. Died in Vincennes

**Montemayor, Vicomte de** Name adopted by François Boucher, personal astrologer of Maréchal de Luxembourg. Imprisoned for life without trial

**Monteran, Antoine** Servant of the Marquis de Termes suspected of trying to poison King. Died under torture without being tried, March 1682

**Montespan, Athénaïs de Pardaillan de Gondrin, Marquise de** Married mistress to King and mother of seven of his illegitimate children. Implicated in Affair of the Poisons

**Montespan, Louis-Henri de Pardaillan de Gondrin, Marquis de** Husband of Mme de Montespan

**Montpensier, Anne-Marie d'Orléans, Duchesse de** First cousin of Louis XIV and author of memoirs

**Montvoisin, Antoine** Husband of la Voisin

**Montvoisin, Marie** Daughter of la Voisin who made a series of devastating allegations

**Moreau, Christophe** Shepherd and magician convicted of having supplied poison to men who wished to kill King. Executed September 1681

**Mortemart, Gabriel de Rochechouart, Duc de** Father of Mme de Montespan appointed Governor of Paris 1669

**Nail, Abbé** Accomplice of Magdelaine de La Grange, hanged February 1679

**Oeillets, Mlle Claude de Vin des** Chambermaid of Mme de Montespan who had daughter by King c. 1675. Alleged to have been client of la Voisin's and to have plotted to murder and bewitch King

**Orléans, Elizabeth Charlotte, Duchesse de** German princess who in 1671 became the second wife of Louis XIV's brother the Duc d'Orléans

**Orléans, Henriette Anne, Duchesse de** English princess who married Louis XIV's brother in 1661. Died suddenly June 1670. Poison suspected by many people

**Orléans, Philippe Duc de** Brother of Louis XIV, known as 'Monsieur'

**Palluau, M.** *Conseiller* in Great Chamber of Paris *Parlement*, appointed as investigating magistrate in cases of La Chausée and Mme de Brinvilliers

**Pelletier, la** Divineress alleged by la Voisin to have been ready to supply Mme Brissart with poison. Alleged by Marie Montvoisin and Guibourg to have been present during black masses celebrated by Guibourg, and to have supplied babies for sacrifice

**Pennautier, Pierre-Louis Reich de** Immensely wealthy Receiver-General of the French clergy. Suspected of poisoning his predecessor in the post, M. de Saint-Laurens. Documents belonging to him were found in Sainte-Croix's casket after the latter's death in 1672. Arrested June 1676 after Mme de Brinvilliers wrote to him while awaiting trial. Discharged 23 July 1677

**Perceval, Jean** Executed September 1681 for involvement in plot to kill King

**Philbert, Mme (formerly Mme Brunet)** Wife of court musician, client of la Voisin and la Bosse. Arrested March 1679 for having poisoned her first husband. Executed June 1679

**Pierre, Maître** Herbalist alleged to have been expert at making poison

**Pinon du Martroy, Jacques** Client of Moreau who died some years before the Affair of the Poisons. Supposedly wished to poison King

**Pirot, Edmé** Jesuit professor of theology who was appointed confessor to Mme de Brinvilliers and accompanied her on her way to execution. Subsequently wrote account of her final hours

**Polignac, Jacqueline du Roure, Vicomtesse de** Client of la Voisin and Lesage, alleged to have sought to bewitch the King. Fled France to avoid arrest January 1680

**Poligny, Anne** Executed July 1681 for having aided Mme Lescalopier to poison her husband

**Poulaillon, Mme Marguerite de** Client of la Bosse and la Vigoreux arrested February 1679 on suspicion of having sought to poison her husband. 5 June 1679 judged by Chamber. Sentenced to banishment but confined in workhouse

**Primi Visconti, Giovanni-Battista** Italian visitor to court who arrived in France 1673. Acquired reputation for psychic powers. Wrote memoirs of his time in France

**Racine, Jean** Playwright, alleged by la Voisin to have poisoned his mistress Thérèse du Parc in 1668

**Romani** Friend of Blessis and la Voisin. Alleged to have planned to poison Mlle de Fontanges by disguising himself as silk merchant and selling her poisoned gloves

**Roure, Claude Marie, Comtesse du** Alleged to have been client of la Voisin and Lesage and to have sought death of Louise de La Vallière. Questioned by commissioners 1 February 1680. Discharged March 1680

**Saint-Maurice, Thomas Chabod, Marquis de** Savoyard ambassador to France 1667–73

**Saint-Simon, Louis de Rouvroy, Duc de** Author of memoirs and courtier

**Sainte-Croix, Gaudin de** Former army officer and lover of Mme de Brinvilliers. Helped arrange murder of her relations and supplied her with poison. Died of natural causes 30 July 1672

**Sandosme, Denise** Hanged July 1681 for having supplied Mme Lescalopier with poison

**Savoy, Charles Emmanuel, Duke of** Ruler of Italian state who died suddenly 12 June 1675

**Sévigné, Marie, Marquise de** Devoted mother and celebrated letter writer

**Soissons, Olympe, Comtesse de** Known as 'Mme la Comtesse'. Niece of Cardinal Mazarin, married in 1657 to Prince Eugene of Carignan-Savoy, a cousin of the Duke of Savoy who was subsequently created Comte de Soissons. Reputed to have been a lover of the King at one point. On the King's marriage she was appointed *Surintendante* of the Queen's household (equivalent to the English post Mistress of the Robes). In January 1680 she fled France after a warrant had been issued for her arrest. La Voisin had alleged that about fourteen years earlier the Comtesse had visited her and voiced threats against the King and Louise de La Vallière. Died 1708 in Brussels

**Soubise, Anne de Rohan-Chabot, Princesse de** Alleged by Saint-Simon to have been mistress of King

**Sourches, Marquis de**  Courtier who kept journal

**Spanheim, Ezechiel**  German diplomat who in 1690 wrote description of court for Elector of Brandenburg

**Termes, Roger, Marquis de**  Cousin of M. de Montespan who detained the alchemist Blessis in his chateau. Later arrested on suspicion of having tried to poison King

**Thianges, Gabrielle, Marquise de**  Eldest sister of Mme de Montespan

**Tingry, Marie Louise Charlotte, Princesse de**  Lady-in-waiting of Queen, alleged to have had an affair with her brother-in-law, the Maréchal de Luxembourg

**Trianon, Catherine**  Successful divineress and close associate of la Voisin. Alleged by Marie Montvoisin to have been involved in plot to murder King. Died early 1681 in Vincennes

**Trichâteau, Marquis de**  Friend and correspondent of Comte de Bussy

**Vanens, Louis**  Alchemist arrested December 1677. Suspected of having poisoned the Duke of Savoy in 1675

**Vassé, Marquise de**  Court lady alleged by la Bosse and la Filastre to have wanted to kill her husband. Never brought before Arsenal Chamber

**Vautier, and wife**  Associates of la Voisin alleged by Marie Montvoisin to have been involved in her mother's plot to kill the King

**Vertemart, Mme Marie**  Client of la Voisin who had come to her in hope that she could procure death of her husband. Subsequently emerged that she had asked la Voisin to obtain her a place in the household of Mme de Montespan

**Vigoreux, Marie**  Divineress arrested January 1679 on suspicion of supplying poisons. Died under torture May 1679

**Vivonne, Antoinette, Duchesse de**  Sister-in-law of Mme de Montespan who was alleged to have been a client of la Filastre and several other divineresses. Lesage claimed that la Filastre had aborted her child and offered up the foetus to the devil

**Voisin, Catherine**  Wife of Antoine Montvoisin. Leading divineress, arrested March 1679. Confessed to several murders and incriminated numerous associates. Burnt alive February 1680

# GLOSSARY

*Brodequins*
> Instrument of torture which crushed the legs of the victim between planks that were tightened by having wedges hammered in

*Chambre Ardente, also known as Chambre de l'Arsenal*
> Special commission established by the King in 1679 to investigate and judge cases of poisoning. Its sessions were held at the Arsenal in Paris

*Chambre des Comptes*
> Legal Chamber charged with overseeing the handling of the royal domain; also the chamber where documents relating to grants of nobility or pensions were registered

*Châtelet, the*
> Court of first instance for the Paris area. Its active head was the Civil Lieutenant of Paris

*Conseiller*
> See *Parlement*

*Cour des Enquêtes*
> See *Parlement*

*Intendant*
> Royal agent who performed many administrative tasks in the provinces

*Lettre de Cachet*
> Sealed letter enshrining direct expression of royal will. Most usually used to order the arrest of a named individual

*Maîtres de Requêtes*
> Judges whose jurisdiction related to execution of council decrees and appeals relating to council procedures. Often entrusted with extraordinary commissions by the King

*Parlement*
> Regional High Court. The *Parlement* of Paris had jurisdiction over one third of all France; the remaining areas of the country were covered by provincial *Parlements* such as the *Parlement* of Rouen. The Paris

*Parlement* had its seat at the Palais de Justice and was staffed by
approximately 200 officers. It was divided into several chambers, the
most ancient and prestigious of which was the *Grand Chambre*, presided
over by the *Premier Président* of the Paris *Parlement*. In addition the
Chamber had nine *Présidents à mortier*, twelve *Conseiller Clercs* and
twenty-five *Conseillers*. Besides this, there were in the *Parlement* of Paris
three *Chambres des Enquêtes* and two *Chambres des Requêtes*, each with its
own complement of *Présidents* and *Conseillers*. There were also
additional chambers, such as the *Tournelle* and the *Chambre des Vacations*,
which were staffed by rotation with officers from other chambers.

Only the *Premier Président* of the *Parlement* was appointed by the
King and could be removed from office. The other officers of
*Parlement* purchased their places, which then became their property. In
return for the payment of an annual fee to the Crown, the officers had
the right to transmit the places to their heirs. Partly in consequence of
their independence from royal control, the magistrates of *Parlement*
formed a wealthy and socially cohesive caste, who considered
themselves no less grand than the ancient nobility.

Criminal cases involving the aristocracy were heard directly by
*Parlement*. The highest in rank, such as dukes and peers and royal
officers, were entitled to be tried by the *Grand Chambre*. The cases of
lesser members of the nobility came before a joint session of the
*Grand Chambre* and the *Tournelle*. It was more usual, however, for
*Parlement* to act as the highest court of appeal.

Apart from its judicial responsibilities, *Parlement* had the right of
registering royal edicts. During the civil wars of the Fronde, the
*Parlement* of Paris had sought to exploit this and had become a source
of opposition to the Crown. However, once Louis XIV assumed
personal control of government, he acted to curb the power of
*Parlement*. Although he respected the magistrates' privileges as
hereditary office holders, he restricted their means of expressing
political dissent. Most notably, in 1673 he denied *Parlement* the right
of making any remonstrance before registering legislation

*Rapporteur*
    Judge who presented a summary of the evidence uncovered by the
    investigating magistrate to all the judges appointed to hear a case

*Sellette*
    Stool on which defendant sat during trial and final interrogation by
    judges

*Tabouret*
    Stool on which duchesses and other high-ranking ladies were entitled
    to sit in the presence of the Queen

# FOREWORD

The Affair of the Poisons was the name given to an extraordinary episode which took place in France during the reign of Louis XIV. In 1679 fears that poisoning had become widespread led to drastic action. What followed seemed to show that there was a serious problem, for an investigation suggested that many people were indeed using poison and black magic to rid themselves of enemies. Numerous arrests and executions resulted, with torture being widely used and suspects including distinguished individuals from the highest ranks of society.

The prelude to the Affair of the Poisons was the Brinvilliers murder case. In 1676 the Marquise de Brinvilliers was executed after being convicted of poisoning three members of her family. While there was satisfaction that this woman had been brought to justice, the case aroused fears that similar crimes were being committed by people of comparable social standing and that these were going undetected.

Shortly after this the authorities received information that Louis XIV himself was at risk of poisoning. Although these warnings came from a dubious source, they were taken seriously. Determined to protect the King from this hidden menace, the Chief of the Paris Police remained on constant alert for every sign of danger.

When two fortune tellers from Paris were arrested on suspicion of having supplied poison to wealthy clients, this was taken as confirmation that a network of poisoners was active in the city. On the King's orders a special commission was set up to bring offenders to justice and scores of disreputable characters from the Paris underworld were seized and questioned. Many of them had made a living by predicting the future, advising on love affairs or offering to use their magic powers by providing contact with the spirit world. It was suspected that a high proportion supplemented these activities by selling poison.

Under interrogation some of these people claimed that their services had been sought not just by rich middle-class ladies who had become dissatisfied with their husbands, but also by members of the high nobility. Determined to eradicate what he regarded as an intolerable evil, the King decreed that no one, no matter how grand, would be spared having to account for their conduct.

The royal court was thrown into disarray as prominent figures there were placed under arrest or called before the special tribunal for questioning. The Queen's Mistress of the Robes, the Comtesse de Soissons, fled the country to escape being charged with attempted murder. One of France's most distinguished generals, the Maréchal de Luxembourg, was imprisoned in the Bastille pending his trial for sorcery and poisoning.

However, despite his avowed intention to deal firmly with all suspects, the King was placed in a quandary when evidence emerged that incriminated Mme de Montespan, his mistress of many years. She was said to have engaged in vile Satanic rituals and to have sought to poison another woman who had become the King's lover. Uncertain whether to believe this, but realising that it would be impossible to establish the truth without irreversibly discrediting his mistress, the King was unsure how to proceed. As a result, the inquiry stagnated while the King and his police chief strove to resolve this dilemma.

When researching a subject, every historian is dependent on the quality of the sources and the Affair of the Poisons poses certain difficulties in this respect. Works such as the Memoirs of the Duc de Saint-Simon have to be used with caution, not least because Saint-Simon was only born in 1675 and was hence not at court during the Affair of the Poisons. Although he wrote about the events and personalities of the period, his comments were based on hearsay rather than personal observation. This did not stop him from expressing subjective judgements, or make him exercise any restraint in his opinions, but despite his assured tone the reader has to remember that his knowledge of what took place was circumscribed.

Letters written at the time of the affair are in some ways more reliable, but here, too, there are pitfalls. The proceedings of the special commission set up to deal with poisoners were in theory secret and sometimes when people managed to obtain news they thought it more prudent to pass it on verbally rather than write it in a letter. Inevitably, too, private prejudices sometimes distorted observers' judgement. The Comte de Bussy, for example, was incurably malicious, while even the shrewd and perceptive Mme de Sévigné was sometimes misinformed or mistaken. As for the letters of the Duchesse d'Orléans, these are wonderfully entertaining, but were often written years after the events she describes and are less than trustworthy.

Trial records or transcripts of interrogations can also be misleading. In many cases the evidence derives from people who were accomplished liars and who had a strong incentive to incriminate others in order to distract attention from their own misdemeanours. Testimony given under torture must likewise be treated sceptically. One historian has remarked that 'we have only to imagine the range of the Popish Plot in England in 1679 if every witness had been tortured'.[1] During the Affair of the Poisons, which took place at the same time in France, torture was used extensively. There can be no doubt that this complicated matters greatly and prolonged the inquiry.

Despite the fact that there are limitations to what can be known about the Affair of the Poisons, I have ended by reaching firm conclusions on various crucial matters. However, I am well aware that these judgements cannot be considered definitive and that other people inspecting the same evidence might interpret it differently.

When describing the profession of women like Catherine Montvoisin, Marie Vigoreux or Marguerite Delaporte, I have used the term 'divineress'. Every time I have done so, I am reminded by a wavy red line on my computer screen that the word is not to be found in the modern lexicon (though my French dictionary does translate '*devineresse*' as 'divineress', while cautioning that the term is rarely used). Nevertheless, I decided to retain the term, as all the possible alternatives seemed unsatisfactory. 'Fortune teller' was too limited, while the English seventeenth-century equivalents of 'wise woman' or 'cunning folk' were arch as well as archaic. My dictionary variously defines the verb 'to divine' as 'to predict or conjecture; to discover by guessing, intuition, inspiration or magic'. Since this precisely describes the activities carried out by these women, the noun 'divineress' seemed most appropriate.

When mentioning these women by name I have often adopted the French usage of prefixing it with the definite article, as in 'la Voisin', 'la Vigoreux' or 'la Delaporte'. Though Catherine Montvoisin's clients and acquaintances sometimes addressed her as 'Mme Voisin', she was more usually referred to as 'la Voisin'. In documents such as records of trial and interrogations this is the style invariably adopted for all female suspects who were not members of the aristocracy. I have emulated this. It is unfortunate, however, that the surnames of some of the characters in this book, such as Nicolas de La Reynie and Louise de La Vallière, begin with 'La'. I hope this does not cause confusion.

I have tried to supply references for every quotation in the book.

3

However, in order to reduce the quantity of numbered endnotes, I have generally only placed a single one in each paragraph. All the source references for that paragraph can be found grouped in order under the appropriate number in the endnote section at the back of the book.

There were several different units of currency employed in France at this period. Readers should note that in addition to the livre, which was the basic unit of currency:

$$1 \text{ écu} = 3 \text{ livres}$$
$$1 \text{ pistole} = 10 \text{ livres}$$
$$1 \text{ gold louis} = 24 \text{ livres}$$

Although the value of French money fluctuated in the course of the seventeenth century W. H. Lewis calculated the rate of exchange between England and France during the reign of Louis XIV as being 24 livres to £1 sterling.[2] To translate these sums into modern values is notoriously difficult, but the Bank of England estimates that £1 in 1680 would have been worth £82.66 in December 2002. According to these figures, 100 livres in 1680 would have been worth just over £4 in England at the time, which converts to just under £345 in today's money.

I should like to thank the staff of the following libraries who have helped me with my research in England and France: the Bibliothèque de l'Arsenal; the Bibliothèque de l'Assemblée Nationale; the Bibliothèque Nationale; the Bodleian Library, Oxford; the British Library; Imperial College Library; the Institute for Historical Research; the London Library; the Public Record Office; the Service Historique de l'Armée at Vincennes and the Wellcome Library.

Many individuals have helped me in the course of writing this book, but I have particular cause to be grateful to three men. With great generosity Geoffrey Treasure read the typescript for mistakes and made many invaluable comments and suggestions. Michael Crawcour took immense trouble going through the text and much improved it by altering some of my translations from French sources. My father-in-law, Raymond Carr, also read the book at an early stage and contributed much appreciated ideas and queries.

I should also like to thank Nick Ashley; Antonia Fraser; Jasper Guinness; Julian Hope; Linda Kelly; Antoine Laurent; Bill Lovelady; Sophie-Caroline and Gilles de Marjerie; James Milson; Andreas Philiotis; Stewart Preston; Guy Rowlands; Tally Westminster and

Cristina Zilkha. All have helped me in different ways while I have been working on this book in London and Paris. In addition especial thanks are due to Douglas Matthews for compiling the index.

My editor Ion Trewin, his assistant, Victoria Webb, and the copy-editor Ilsa Yardley have all been enormously helpful. As ever my agent Ed Victor has been a tremendous source of encouragement.

I should also mention the man who wrote to me (from Cambridge?) after the publication of my last book on the poisoning of Sir Thomas Overbury. He made a reference to Mme de Brinvilliers and it was this which gave me the idea to start researching this book. Unfortunately I have since lost his letter, so I cannot thank him personally.

As well as being wonderfully enthusiastic when he read an early draft of the book, my husband Matthew Carr has supported me in countless other ways. The book is lovingly dedicated to my daughter Ella Carr.

# ONE

# MME DE BRINVILLIERS

At seven o'clock in the evening of 17 July 1676 a small woman in her mid-forties was led out of the Conciergerie prison in Paris. A tumbril stood in the courtyard, waiting to take her to the Place de Grève, the usual site for public executions in Paris. The woman, whose hands were bound, was barefoot and clothed in the traditional garb of a condemned prisoner. A coarse linen shift concealed her trim figure and her chestnut hair was covered by an unbecoming hood fastened under the chin. Although she was to be beheaded, rather than hanged, a noose had been placed round her neck to symbolise the death sentence that had been passed on her.

Despite the oppressive heat, a huge crowd had massed in the prison courtyard, where they had been waiting for several hours. The entire route from the Conciergerie to the Place de Grève was likewise thronged with spectators intent on catching a glimpse of the prisoner as she passed. It was later estimated that 100,000 people had turned out to witness the spectacle. The mood of most of them was unmistakably hostile, for though the Parisian populace generally evinced compassion for offenders on their way to execution, this woman's crimes had inspired such repugnance that scarcely anyone felt any sympathy for her. Instead, she was reviled as an 'enemy of the human race' who deserved to be held 'in execration by all men'.[1]

At first sight the prisoner appeared an inoffensive person. She was tiny and slender-boned with huge blue eyes, which struck an observer as 'gentle and perfectly beautiful'. Her appearance was indeed so deceptive that one person commented that 'nothing proves better that . . . the science of physiognomy is false'. For, in fact, this innocuous-looking woman had slowly poisoned her father and two brothers, inflicting the most frightful sufferings on them before they died. Nor was this all. She had also administered poison to her husband and eldest daughter, though admittedly in both cases she had subsequently regretted her action and given them antidotes. She had furthermore intended to murder her sister and sister-in-law, who had only been saved because her crimes had come to light before she could effect her plans. In the words of a shocked contemporary, 'Medea did not go that far!'[2]

As if this was not bad enough, she was widely believed to have acquired her expertise in poisons by conducting a series of fiendish experiments. It was said that she had visited paupers in the public hospitals and, under the guise of charity, had fed them poisoned food. She had then observed the effects so as to be able to calculate precise dosages when murdering her family.[3] These stories, as it happened, were not true, but the fact that they were so widely credited naturally added to the hatred felt for her.

Even if one ignores these false reports, it is easy to understand why this case had created such a sensation. One aristocratic lady noted that for the past few weeks it had formed the sole topic of conversation in Paris, to the exclusion even of the war France was currently waging against the Dutch.[4] The gender of the accused in part accounted for the excitement, for the fact that a woman had committed mass murder was deemed peculiarly monstrous. The obsessive interest had been heightened by details relating to the murderess's sexual depravity. It was common knowledge that in a written analysis of her own shortcomings she had acknowledged gaining her first sexual experience at the age of seven and that, since that time, she had regularly committed adultery and incest.

The fact that poison was involved exacerbated the horror, for it was an accepted maxim that 'a man is more culpable when he poisons than when he kills by the blade'. As the accused woman's confessor had observed, when urging her final repentance, 'Poison is held in horror everywhere and … poisoners are abominated by all the world.' Needing guile and ruthlessness, rather than strength, poison was a weapon in some respects ideally suited to a woman and was the more to be dreaded on that account. It was true that in recent years there had been very few suspected instances of poison (the condemned woman's confessor had told her, 'Until now parricide has been very rare and poisoning almost unheard of')[5] but there was concern that this case might signify the start of an alarming trend.

There was another reason why this case had gained such notoriety. The condemned woman was no low-born wretch who had turned to crime to claw herself out of a desperate existence. She was, on the contrary, a person 'of birth and condition', a marquise, who had squandered a sizeable fortune and was related to some of the most influential people in France.

The woman's name was Marie Madeleine Gobelin, Marquise de Brinvilliers. Born in 1630, she was the eldest of Antoine Dreux d'Aubray's five children. In 1643 Dreux d'Aubray had been appointed Civil Lieutenant of the city of Paris, an immensely lucrative and powerful post. With his counterpart, the Criminal Lieutenant, the Civil Lieutenant was one of the two most important magistrates in the Parisian law courts, which were based at the Châtelet. Robed in scarlet, he presided there as a judge of appeal as well as adjudicating on other major cases. Besides this, he enjoyed various privileges and administrative responsibilities. These included the right to proclaim war and peace in Paris, and to oversee the provisioning of the capital in times of dearth. He was, in short, one of the most influential and highly paid officials in the country.

In 1651 Marie Madeleine d'Aubray was married to Antoine Gobelin. He was a descendant of the dye-manufacturing dynasty, which had established the Gobelin tapestry workshops. Having made a fortune several generations earlier, the family had abandoned industry and commerce to pursue more socially acceptable occupations within the administrative hierarchy. Antoine's father held the remunerative position of President of the Chamber of Accounts and, although Antoine was a younger son, he was extremely well provided for. He had an income of 30,000 livres a year and, since his bride brought with her a dowry of 150,000 livres – soon swollen by an inheritance of 50,000 livres from her grandmother – the young couple's joint wealth was considerable.[6] In 1660 their status was further enhanced when they entered the lower ranks of the nobility. Gobelin's fiefdom of Brunvilliers was elevated to a marquisate (in France titles were attached to properties rather than being conferred on individuals) but, because the scribe who recorded the details made a clerical error, Gobelin and his wife were henceforth known as the Marquis and Marquise de Brinvilliers.

We do not know if Marie Madeleine's inclinations were taken into account when a husband was selected for her. A defender of Mme de Brinvilliers later claimed that the early years of the union 'were marked by the greatest happiness and tenderness' but there is no way of verifying this. In 1658, however, Mme de Brinvilliers's destiny was transformed when she embarked on an affair with the man later described as her 'evil genius'.[7]

M. de Brinvilliers was an officer in the French army. Soon after his marriage he became colonel of the Normandy regiment and it was while on active service that he made the acquaintance of another officer named Gaudin de Sainte-Croix. Sainte-Croix was, by his own account, the illegitimate offshoot of an illustrious Gascon family. Presumably they had given him money to purchase a commission in the army, for he was a cavalry captain in the Tracy regiment. Sainte-Croix was an immensely attractive man. Handsome, witty and unscrupulous, he possessed a vitality and charm that many found irresistible. While entering with enjoyment into most forms of dissipation, he retained a capacity for serious conversation which gave the impression that he was an upright character. Unfortunately, 'beneath the appearance of a wise and good-natured man he concealed a most black and detestable soul'.[8]

M. de Brinvilliers liked Sainte-Croix so much that he invited him to stay at his house in the Rue Neuve Saint-Paul in Paris. This was a mistake. According to one account Mme de Brinvilliers was already dissatisfied with her husband as he had been unfaithful to her and thus proved highly susceptible to Sainte-Croix's 'artful and insinuating manners'. Before long Sainte-Croix's 'assiduities towards the husband were transferred to the lady'. Her discontent with M. de Brinvilliers reinforced the attractions of her admirer, ensuring that Sainte-Croix 'did not sigh for long'.[9]

M. de Brinvilliers was a somewhat lethargic man who appears to have made little protest about his wife's liaison with Sainte-Croix. Her family, however, were less supine about the attachment. Her two brothers made plain to her their disapproval and her father demanded that she break off the relationship.[10] When his daughter ignored him Dreux d'Aubray retaliated in the way open at that time to all persons in authority in France whose family honour was being undermined by troublesome individuals. He obtained a *lettre de cachet* – a sealed order issued in the King's name which enshrined a direct expression of the royal will – ordering the arrest of Sainte-Croix.

On 19 March 1663 Sainte-Croix was arrested in Mme de Brinvilliers's coach and taken to the Bastille. His confinement there was not particularly arduous. Prisoners in the fortress were generally well fed and cared for and, unless orders were given to the contrary, they were permitted to have books, to associate with other inmates and to play cards and chess. Furthermore, although the *lettre de cachet* had not specified the length of his detention, Sainte-Croix was freed after only six weeks, on 2 May. Even so, Mme de Brinvilliers was incensed by the manner in which her father had exercised his paternal authority. She later recorded that she had murdered him to gain revenge for her 'vexation at this man's imprisonment'. At another time she mused, 'One should never annoy anybody; if Sainte-Croix had not been put in the Bastille perhaps nothing would have happened.'[11]

It is possible that Sainte-Croix's stay in the Bastille had other unforeseen consequences. Mme de Brinvilliers later said that while there Sainte-Croix encountered Egidio Exili, an Italian who knew more about poison than almost anyone in the world. During one interrogation she said that after being released from the Bastille, Exili stayed in Sainte-Croix's house for six weeks. She also told a witness who subsequently testified against her that she had given Sainte-Croix a large sum of money to enable him to purchase Exili's secret recipe for poison.[12]

It is true that Sainte-Croix was imprisoned in the Bastille at the same time as Exili, who had been taken into custody on 2 February 1663, shortly after his arrival in France. Exili was in the service of the former Queen Christina of Sweden, who was currently on strained terms with the French court, and Louis XIV had ordered his arrest because he wanted to find out the reason for his presence in his kingdom. He remained in the Bastille till 27 June while enquiries were made about him, but there is no reason to think that these uncovered anything which suggested he might be a poisoner or, indeed, a criminal of any sort.

This does not exclude the possibility that Exili *was* knowledgeable about poison and he may have discussed the subject with Sainte-Croix while they were in the Bastille, but it would have been difficult for him to impart much highly specialised information without access to a laboratory. On Exili's release, orders were given for his immediate deportation and he was escorted to Calais so that he could sail to England. It is conceivable that he subsequently returned and went to stay with Sainte-Croix but we only have Mme de Brinvilliers's word for this and on balance it seems implausible.

Despite the paucity of the evidence, the claim that Exili was a key figure in the Brinvilliers murder case was readily accepted, for it accorded neatly with French prejudices. Within France there was a widely held preconception that the Italians were a devious and untrustworthy race who habitually despatched their enemies by covert means. One French pamphlet asserted that in Italy poisons were 'the surest and most common aids to relieving hatred and vengeance', and added that Italians mocked Frenchmen for being so simple as to kill people without the requisite degree of subterfuge, which invariably resulted in their being brought to justice.[13]

Italians were thought not only to be predisposed to employing insidious methods but were also regarded as experts on toxicology, a devastating combination in French eyes. Wildly exaggerated notions were held about Italian prowess in this field, for the French believed that their neighbours had developed secret formulas for poisons that worked through inhalation, or proved fatal if they came in contact with the skin. When Mme de Brinvilliers mentioned the subject of poison to one young man of her acquaintance he had remarked that, like most Frenchmen, he knew little about it, 'but it was said that in Italy there were many very subtle sorts of poison and that they poisoned using gloves and bouquets'. A tract issued shortly after Mme de Brinvilliers's trial likewise stressed that the Italians had an unrivalled mastery of poison and that 'by dint of hard work and study they have composed such subtle and well-disguised types of poison that they baffle the skill and capacity of doctors. Some are slow ... others prompt and violent, but none leave the slightest trace that might reveal their presence.' The statement typifies attitudes at the time and helps explain why the mythic status of 'a great artist in poison' was so readily conferred on Exili.[14]

When Sainte-Croix was released from the Bastille he shrugged off the interruption and renewed his links with Mme de Brinvilliers. However, despite his hedonistic existence, he still found time for other pursuits. At some point he rented a property in the Place Maubert, which he converted into a laboratory. This in itself was not necessarily suspicious for at the time, Paris abounded with workshops where individuals could carry out experiments. Sainte-Croix ostensibly used these premises for alchemical research, an activity which obsessed many of his contemporaries. At a time when the boundaries of knowledge were being constantly expanded it seemed perfectly possible that the secret of the Philosopher's Stone – a miraculous substance that would permit the conversion of base metals into silver or gold – would soon be discovered. Accordingly, a surprisingly large number of people were preoccupied by the search for it and Sainte-Croix was apparently among them.

Sainte-Croix encouraged the belief that he was close to making great discoveries in this field. He showed one person the results of an experiment which had supposedly caused mercury to solidify after being processed in a 'digestion oven'. It may be, however, that his professed interest in the subject was entirely fraudulent. There is some evidence that suggests that what he was really doing at the Place Maubert was counterfeiting coins. Alternatively, like many others who professed to know alchemical secrets, he may simply have aspired to persuade gullible people to part with large sums of money in the hope of making a handsome return on their investment. With hindsight, however, another possibility was put forward. Suspicions were later voiced that Sainte-Croix's alchemical experiments had merely formed a cover for more sinister activities and that he was using his knowledge of Exili's 'detestable secrets' to perfect new varieties of poison. One person suggested that this had always been his ultimate goal and that, as far as Sainte-Croix was concerned, 'the secret of the Philosopher's Stone was poison'.[15]

However, Mme de Brinvilliers would later allege that Sainte-Croix obtained his best poison from another source altogether, for shortly before her execution she claimed that a Swiss chemist based in Paris named Christophe Glaser had been Sainte-Croix's principal supplier. This was a startling claim, for Glaser – who had died some years before, possibly in 1672 – had been a scientist of some distinction. It was he who had identified impure sulphate of potassium and in recognition of his achievement this substance was always known as 'Glaser's salt' until the reform of chemical nomenclature. Furthermore, thanks to the patronage of the King's physician, Dr Vallot, by 1663 Glaser had not only become 'apothecary-in-ordinary' to both King Louis XIV and his brother, the Duc d'Orléans, but he had also been appointed resident lecturer at the Royal Botanical Gardens in Paris. These gardens were an impressive institution, which reflected the King's interest in scientific progress. Four thousand plant varieties were cultivated there, some of which, of course, were poisonous, though many others had therapeutic qualities. There was also a workshop where Glaser held chemistry classes for members of the public and it is possible that Sainte-Croix had attended these.

Some indication of Glaser's knowledge is given by his book on chemistry, which was published in France in 1663 and subsequently translated into English under the title *The Compleat Chymist*. This gave instructions for procedures such as the purification and calcination of metals and metallic elements like gold, silver, tin, lead and mercury, and also provided information on practical matters such as laboratory equipment and the construction of furnaces and stills. Besides this, the book contained recipes for various outlandish concoctions, which Glaser recommended for medicinal purposes such as a sal volatile prepared from 'the skull of a man dead of a violent death'. Glaser praised these salts for their 'very great virtues', extolling them for the way 'they penetrate to the places furthest removed from the first digestion and dissolve all viscous and tartarous matters, open all obstructions, heal all fever ... preserve from plague and strongly resist all putrefaction'. Other formulations that Glaser considered efficacious included a salt made from the flesh of disembowelled vipers and a solution distilled from the 'fresh urine of children from eight till twelve years of age', which he found excellent for alleviating stiffness of the joints and depression.[16]

As well as advocating the use of these curious preparations, Glaser's book contained information about how to fabricate well-known poisons such as vitriol, arsenic and corrosive sublimate. The section on arsenic noted that there were three kinds (white; yellow – known as orpiment – and red, or realgar) and that it could be produced in various forms such as oil, liquor or powder. Glaser was well aware that all these substances had to be treated with great caution. He warned his readers that while arsenical preparations were often 'used outwardly with happy success and some are bold to make use thereof inwardly', he advised against this, 'because nature furnisheth us with other remedies enough, less dangerous and more safe'.[17]

It would be misguided, however, to attach great significance to the fact that Glaser wrote about such matters, for this was hardly arcane knowledge. The poisons that he described had been in use for centuries and were readily available. Their sale was virtually unregulated in France, for though in 1642 a directive had been issued stating that apothecaries should not sell dangerous substances such as antimony, arsenic or sublimate to persons unknown to them or of doubtful honesty, this was laxly enforced. It would therefore have been simple for Sainte-Croix to obtain poisons such as these without recourse to Glaser.

However, Mme de Brinvilliers later claimed that Glaser had developed a unique formula, which was far superior to more readily available poisons and which Sainte-Croix had acquired from him. She was vague about its components, saying that she thought it consisted principally of refined arsenic and essence of toads, but she had been prepared to pay a large sum to buy some for her own use. In a letter she wrote to Sainte-Croix, which was later recovered and used in evidence against her, she declared that she was contemplating killing herself by taking 'Glaser's recipe, which you gave me at such a high price'.[18]

Shortly before going to her execution Mme de Brinvilliers provided more details about Glaser's researches into poison. She said Sainte-Croix had told her that at some time in the 1650s Glaser had gone to Florence to learn how to make 'the finest and most subtle poisons'. She maintained that Glaser had brought back from Italy some leaves that resembled those of a senna plant but which, if gathered in the month of March, were highly toxic. Furthermore, Sainte-Croix had led her to believe that Glaser's visit to Italy had been financed by M. Fouquet. At the time Fouquet had been Louis XIV's Surintendant of Finance, though he had since been imprisoned for life in the fortress of Pignerol after being arrested in 1661 on charges of malversation and treason.

Hearing that he had sponsored Glaser's trip to Florence, Mme de Brinvilliers said she had assumed that Fouquet had wanted to poison 'someone who was in the way'. She added that Sainte-Croix had also told her that from his deathbed Glaser had given him information about poisons which were 'so good and sophisticated that their results were infallible'.[19]

When all this emerged in the course of Mme de Brinvilliers's final interrogations it caused terrible consternation. The seventeenth century was a time of phenomenal technological advance when educated people's understanding of the world was undergoing profound modification. There had been significant discoveries in the fields of physics, mathematics, astronomy and medicine, and it therefore did not seem implausible that comparable advances had been made in toxicology. Understandably, therefore, the possibility that a brilliant and innovative man of science like Glaser might have been using his knowledge for perverted ends aroused intense disquiet.

Poison had of course been in use for centuries but it now seemed conceivable that all existing knowledge about it had been rendered obsolete. This meant that the threat it posed was greatly magnified, for criminals would have no fear of using it if they thought they could do so undetected. It was even possible that poisons had been developed that mimicked the effect of other illnesses. If so, doctors might have certified that people had died from natural causes when in reality they had been murdered. This led to retrospective speculation about deaths of prominent figures that had occurred in recent years but which at the time had aroused no suspicion.

The irony is that there is nothing to indicate that Sainte-Croix and Mme de Brinvilliers really did have access to poisons that were particularly novel or rare. Autopsies were performed on two of Mme de Brinvilliers's victims precisely because they had exhibited classic symptoms of poisoning. Although at the time it was not possible to reach precise conclusions about what had killed them, a twentieth-century doctor who read the post-mortem results deduced that the poison used had been some form of corrosive sublimate. Apart from the fact that the victims had blackened digestive tubes, one of them was said to have complained that a drink he had been served had a horribly metallic taste, which supports this diagnosis. Mme de Brinvilliers also claimed that milk worked as an effective antidote to the poison she employed, and it is true that the proteins in milk can prevent absorption of mercury-based poisons.[20] Sainte-Croix's assertions that Exili and Christophe Glaser initiated him into mysteries unknown to other practitioners of the art of poison should therefore be treated with caution. It may be that he made these inflated claims to Mme de Brinvilliers simply because he realised that if he convinced her that his skills as a poisoner were unrivalled she would pay more highly for his services.

Certainly, Sainte-Croix had always been intent on extorting as much money as possible from Mme de Brinvilliers. When he had joined their household in Paris, M. and Mme de Brinvilliers were still a wealthy couple. Even in 1662 their financial position was good enough to enable them to loan cash to an acquaintance. Soon afterwards, however, they started experiencing money problems, brought about, it would seem, through M. de Brinvilliers's extravagance and incompetence (his wife later described him as 'not at all capable'). By 1663 his family were so concerned by the way he was wasting his inheritance that they forced him to settle some of his patrimony on his children.[21] To prevent him from squandering her own money, Mme de Brinvilliers entered into an arrangement known as a 'separation of goods', which prevented a husband who had overspent from having access to his wife's wealth.

Unfortunately, the money which had been put beyond the reach of M. de Brinvilliers was not protected from the depredations of Sainte-Croix. The latter had sold his commission in the army after moving to Paris and ever since, despite having no visible source of revenue, had lived a life of 'frightful extravagance'. He gambled extensively, as well as employing two servants and maintaining a carriage for his private use. Much of this was financed by Mme de Brinvilliers, for she later noted bitterly that she had given him a great deal of money. She also relied on Sainte-Croix for financial advice with the predictable result that 'he completed the ruination of her affairs, which her husband had already done much to advance'.[22]

Besides resenting her father's treatment of Sainte-Croix, Mme de Brinvilliers now coveted his wealth and this provided her with an additional motive for murder. In the expectation that she would be a beneficiary of his will, she made methodical arrangements to kill him. In early 1666 she placed in her father's household a servant named Gascon whom Sainte-Croix had recruited for her and this man began the process of slow poisoning. A few months later Mme de Brinvilliers took control of the affair herself when she accompanied her father to his country estate at Offemont. She later confessed that, while there, she poisoned Dreux d'Aubray 'with her own hands twenty-eight or thirty times'. Poison was administered in both powdered and fluid form with the result that Dreux d'Aubray became 'tormented by extraordinary fits of vomiting, inconceivable stomach pains and strange burnings in the entrails'.[23]

By the time he returned to Paris, Dreux d'Aubray was mortally ill and on 10 September 1666 he died, aged sixty-three. Despite the curious nature of his last illness, foul play was not suspected. His doctors ascribed his death to a recurrence of the gout which had intermittently attacked him in past years. Ironically, one of his colleagues believed that his decline had been exacerbated by his grief at having recently been served a writ by another of his daughters who wanted a larger share of his wealth.[24] No one blamed Mme de Brinvilliers for his demise.

It did not take Mme de Brinvilliers and Sainte-Croix long to run through the money that came to her as a result of her father's death. By 1670 she was again in such financial straits that her carriage was repossessed and she was being harassed by numerous creditors. Her response was to resolve upon the murder of her two brothers. The elder of the two, Antoine, had succeeded his father as Civil Lieutenant of Paris, while the younger was a *Conseiller* in *Parlement*. Both were therefore prosperous men although their sister actually stood to gain little from their deaths. Neither of the two had bequeathed money to her in their wills, although it may be that she had not grasped this. At any rate, since both men had angered her by supporting her father's stand against Sainte-Croix, she considered she had ample justification for disposing of them.

Once again Sainte-Croix found a man who could be infiltrated into the unsuspecting victims' household. He was a former servant of Sainte-Croix's named Jean Hamelin, but known as La Chausée. He had already commended himself to Mme de Brinvilliers because of his aptitude for dressing her hair, but now he revealed talents of an altogether different order. Mme de Brinvilliers arranged for him to enter the service of the younger of her two brothers who, conveniently, was an unmarried man who lived with Antoine d'Aubray and his wife.

Once installed in their house, La Chausée began by targeting the elder brother. An early attempt on Antoine d'Aubray's life misfired when the latter complained that a drink served to him by La Chausée had a bitter and metallic savour. 'Your servant's trying to poison me,' he complained to his brother, whereupon La Chausée coolly suggested that someone else must have used that glass to take a purgative and removed it from the table.[25]

In April 1670 La Chausée and his master spent Easter at Antoine d'Aubray's country estate at Villequoy. During a paschal feast an elaborate raised pie was served, filled with cocks' crests, sweetbreads and kidneys in a rich cream sauce. Seven people who ate this subsequently fell ill, but the most severely affected was Antoine d'Aubray. After that, he never recovered his health and grew steadily thinner. Besides vomiting frequently, he was tormented by thirst and experienced a burning sensation in his stomach.[26] On 17 June 1670 he died.

Having fulfilled the first part of his assignment, La Chausée turned his attention to the surviving brother. At every meal La Chausée assiduously dosed his master, adding liquid poison to his wine and sprinkling it in powdered form on bread and meat dishes. Soon d'Aubray was afflicted by the identical symptoms as his late brother and entered upon a lingering but inexorable decline. In the weeks that preceded his death, La Chausée masqueraded as the most loyal of servants. As d'Aubray's condition deteriorated his body became 'so stinking and infected' that it was unendurable to enter his bedroom and the dying man's temper grew so atrocious that few people dared approach him. Only La Chausée showed himself ready to brave both the stench and d'Aubray's rages. With exemplary devotion he nursed the invalid tenderly and frequently changed his horribly soiled bedlinen.[27]

By September 1670 d'Aubray was so ill that Mme de Brinvilliers was informed she should go to Paris in order to be present when he died. She did so with some irritation, for she wrote from the deathbed that she was having a very disagreeable time. She complained that the house was full of pious people whom she found uncongenial and that she was worn out by the 'continual cares' her brother required.[28]

Much to the relief of his sister, d'Aubray did not last much longer, dying some time in September 1670. By this time suspicions were mounting that neither brother had died of natural causes. Towards the end of his life Antoine d'Aubray had himself voiced fears that he had been poisoned and as a result an autopsy had been carried out. Although in the seventeenth century there were no forensic tests that could establish the presence of poison in a corpse, the results of the post-mortem had given ample cause for concern. The officiating doctor reported that the dead man's stomach and liver were blackened and gangrenous, and the intestines were so dried out that they were starting to disintegrate. Although he could not absolutely rule out disease, he pronounced that the 'alteration and corruption of the aforesaid parts' could only have been caused by 'poison or by some extraordinarily malign humour', which had the same effects as poison. He noted that an illness of that sort was extremely rare,[29] so when the dead man's brother followed him to the grave in quick succession after manifesting the same symptoms, the likelihood of poison seemed even greater.

However, though it appeared probable that a crime had been committed, no one had any idea of who the perpetrator might be. Certainly there was not the remotest suspicion that La Chausée might be the culprit. In fact, his late master had felt such gratitude for the solicitous way his manservant had treated him during his last weeks that he bequeathed La Chausée one hundred écus in his will.[30]

Not content with having murdered her three closest male relatives, Mme de Brinvilliers next contemplated poisoning her sister. The latter was a devout spinster who had displeased her by making large donations to various religious foundations, thus diminishing the wealth which Mme de Brinvilliers considered should be passed on intact to her children. She also would have liked to poison her widowed sister-in-law, for she had inherited Antoine d'Aubray's fortune and in Mme de Brinvilliers's opinion this money was rightfully hers. She was trying to devise a way of placing someone in her sister-in-law's service to carry out her wishes when her plans were interrupted by the death of Sainte-Croix.

Sainte-Croix died on 30 July 1672. A myth subsequently developed that he had accidentally killed himself while concocting poisons in his laboratory. The story went that he had been wearing a glass mask to protect himself from the dangerous vapours given off during the manufacturing process. When this broke, he supposedly inhaled the noxious fumes and died instantly. In fact, his end was far more prosaic. He died after a long illness, having received the last rites and performed his final devotions with apparent piety.[31]

No one realised what terrible things he had done in his lifetime and these might never have come to light had his financial affairs been left in a better state. As it was, however, he died heavily in debt and seals were therefore placed on the doors of his lodgings in the Place Maubert so that his assets could be assessed for the benefit of his creditors. On 11 August, in the presence of various interested parties and their legal advisers, a commissary from the Châtelet started going through Sainte-Croix's belongings.

Quite early on in the proceedings a paper scroll was discovered, inscribed in Sainte-Croix's hand, 'My Confession'. Unfortunately, as Sainte-Croix was not then suspected of any crimes it was agreed that this was a sacred document, subject to the secrecy of the confessional, and it was burnt 'by common consent'. Soon afterwards, however, a casket was found, which had a note from Sainte-Croix attached. This was dated 25 May 1670 and stated that in the event of his death the casket should be given to Mme de Brinvilliers, as 'all that it contains belongs to her and concerns her alone'.[32] When the commissary peeped inside the casket he glimpsed numerous phials and packets filled with unknown substances. Finding this disturbing, he closed up the casket and entrusted it to the safekeeping of a sergeant until such time as its contents could be evaluated in the presence of an official from the public prosecutor's office.

Matters stood thus when La Chausée unwisely attracted attention to himself. He went to the commissary and said that Sainte-Croix had been looking after some money on his behalf and that he now wished to recover it. With breathtaking recklessness he added that his late employer, M. d'Aubray, had also owed him money and that confirmation of this would be found among Sainte-Croix's papers. However, when La Chausée heard about the discovery of Sainte-Croix's casket he became uneasy and hastily left the commissary's office without pressing his claims any further.

Mme de Brinvilliers also behaved in a highly suspect fashion as soon as she learned that the casket had been removed from the Place Maubert. At eleven o'clock that night she presented herself at the commissary's house, demanding that the casket be handed over to her. She had to withdraw when he explained that he no longer had custody of it but in the next few days she made several more attempts to secure it. All proved fruitless and only served to create suspicion.

The casket was finally opened on 18 August and its contents were carefully inventoried. The first thing it yielded was a bundle of passionate letters from Mme de Brinvilliers to Sainte-Croix, including the one in which she threatened to kill herself with Glaser's formula. Besides this, the casket contained a promissory note from Mme de Brinvilliers to Sainte-Croix for the sum of 30,000 livres. It was dated 20 April 1670,[33] which was significant as this was around the time when Antoine d'Aubray had become ill and the note could be interpreted as a promise to reward Sainte-Croix once the poisoning was accomplished.

More compromisingly still, the casket proved to be brimming with all sorts of poisons. There were several packets containing different varieties of corrosive sublimate, as well as vitriol, antimony and a little earthenware pot of opium.[34] Curiously, there was no arsenic, although Mme de Brinvilliers later said that that was the principal ingredient used by Sainte-Croix.

Though most of the drugs in the casket were recognised without difficulty, there were two phials containing liquids that could not be identified. These were handed to a physician named Dr Jean Moreau for testing. After conducting various experiments he pronounced himself defeated. 'This cunning poison evades all researches,' he reported, insisting that it differed from every sort he had previously encountered. Tests were then carried out on various unfortunate animals. A chicken, a pigeon and a dog were given some of the mysterious liquids and all died within a few hours. When the corpses were dissected the internal organs appeared unaffected, although there was a little curdled blood in the ventricles of one animal's heart. A cat who was fed some white powder found in the casket also died. The subsequent autopsy once again failed to establish the reason, as the only unusual finding was a little reddish water, which had been retained in the stomach. Dr Moreau clearly believed that his tests had confirmed that Sainte-Croix had perfected a revolutionary new poison but it would be unwise to accept this too readily. All that had really been established was that Dr Moreau had no idea what the liquid was. As one person sarcastically commented, 'You should believe the doctors... and always take their word for it when they admit their ignorance.'[35]

As soon as she was informed of these developments, the widow of Antoine d'Aubray rushed to Paris seeking vengeance for his murder. She lodged a formal complaint at the Châtelet, demanding that proceedings be instigated against La Chausée. Mme de Brinvilliers promptly fled the country. For a time La Chausée also went into hiding but at six o'clock in the morning of 4 September 1672 he was captured as he slunk down a Paris street 'with his nose in his overcoat'.[36]

La Chausée was imprisoned while evidence was gathered that could be used against him at his trial. The judicial process in seventeenth-century France differed from that in England in several important respects. In particular, there was no trial by jury, but this did not necessarily mean that the French system was more prejudicial to the interests of an accused person than was the case across the Channel. In France the Crown's case was pieced together by an investigating magistrate who interrogated the accused and interviewed other witnesses. The resulting depositions were subsequently laid before a panel of judges. The accused was also brought face to face with hostile witnesses, who repeated in his presence allegations they had made earlier. Although the defendant was never permitted access to legal counsel, during these confrontations he was entitled to challenge the witness's fitness to give evidence and to contradict specific pieces of testimony. The judges considered what emerged at these encounters before proceeding to the final stages of the trial when the accused appeared in court and was questioned while seated on the culprit's stool, or *sellette*. The judges then reached their conclusions, aided by the recommendations of the

Attorney-General, who had independently inspected the evidence and formed his own judgement.

The case against La Chausée was far from compelling. At the time of his arrest he was found to be carrying Cypriot vitriol, but he claimed that he used this in his professional capacity as a barber to treat clients cut while shaving. One witness came forward to testify that despite La Chausée's ostentatious attentions to his late master, in private he had displayed a callous indifference to his sufferings. When asked about M. d'Aubray's health La Chausée had allegedly responded, 'That bugger's taking his time! He's causing us a lot of trouble. I don't know when he'll die.'[37] However, this scarcely constituted proof that La Chausée had poisoned the d'Aubray brothers.

While reluctant to convict the defendant on such slender grounds, the judges accepted that the use of torture was warranted. This was unusual, for a suspect could only be tortured prior to conviction if the investigating magistrate could claim to have uncovered 'considerable proof' of culpability, but it was felt that in this instance the criteria had been fulfilled. However, there was no certainty that torture would force La Chausée to confess and the law stated that if a prisoner withstood the pain without incriminating himself he could not subsequently be convicted. There was, in fact, quite a strong likelihood that La Chausée would have managed to save himself in this way, for prisoners who knew that their lives hung in the balance could show remarkable fortitude under torture. Though there can be no doubt that victims of 'preparatory torture' were subjected to terrible pain, it would seem that the torture was applied somewhat less rigorously than in the past. In the fourteenth century virtually all torture sessions resulted in admissions but of the 101 cases where it was used in the year 1619–20, only three acknowledgements of guilt were secured.[38] And indeed, precisely because she was fearful that La Chausée would confound his interrogators, Antoine d'Aubray's vengeful widow now intervened to persuade the judges that it would be inappropriate to offer La Chausée any chance of escape. The judges decided she was right. Although they had only 'conjectures and strong presumptions' on which to base their decision,[39] on 24 March 1673 they pronounced La Chausée guilty of murder and sentenced him to be broken on the wheel after undergoing torture.

The object of torturing a condemned person after obtaining a conviction was to force the prisoner to name any accomplices who had connived in the crime. The First President of the Paris *Parlement*, Guillaume Lamoignon, had recently urged that the practice should be banned. This was not merely on humanitarian grounds but also because it produced such unsatisfactory results, for it was 'rare that it has extracted the truth from the mouth of a condemned man'.[40] It could even lead investigators astray, as would subsequently be demonstrated during the Affair of the Poisons. In a bid to relieve their agonies victims could say things which were completely misleading and excessive reliance on confessions obtained in this way had many dangers. Nevertheless, torture remained an integral part of the French justice system.

In La Chausée's case it appeared at first that nothing would be wrung from him by this means, but in the end torture did produce the desired results, He was subjected to the *brodequins*, a fearful instrument in which the legs of the victim were trapped between planks. These were progressively tightened as wedges were inserted, crushing the limbs and causing excruciating pain. Throughout the torture session La Chausée continued to protest his innocence and it was only when he was released from the ghastly contraption and placed on a mattress to recover that his resolve suddenly crumbled. Just as his interrogators were despairing, he volunteered a full confession acknowledging that he had murdered the d'Aubray brothers.

With his guilt established beyond doubt, La Chausée went to his execution. His sufferings were not over, for he was killed in the horrible manner known as 'breaking on the wheel'. After he had been spreadeagled on a cartwheel, his limbs and torso were struck repeatedly with iron bars, breaking his bones and damaging internal organs. He was then left to die in agony. An English traveller who saw a criminal being put to death in this way in Poitiers was shaken by the experience. On that occasion a degree of mercy was shown, as the victim was eventually put out of his misery by being strangled. Even so, the Englishman noted that 'seeing what this caitiff suffered made us conclude that it was a cruel death to be broken in that sort'.[41]

Meanwhile, even before La Chausée had been brought to trial, attempts were made to lay hands on Mme de Brinvilliers. In the autumn of 1672 it emerged that she had fled to England and the French at once sought to extradite her. Permission for this was granted, but the English declined to arrest the fugitive themselves, and the resultant delays gave Mme de Brinvilliers time to escape to the Continent. During La Chausée's trial she was pronounced in contempt after ignoring a summons to appear in court and for this the judges sentenced her to be beheaded. For several years, however, Mme de Brinvilliers remained beyond the reach of justice as she travelled war-torn Europe, never resting long in one place and eking out a penurious and wretched existence. Ironically, her main means of subsistence was a small allowance sent to her by the devout sister whom she had once plotted to kill. In August 1675 the sister died of natural causes, leaving Mme de Brinvilliers in a more precarious condition than ever.

Then, in the spring of 1676, Mme de Brinvilliers made the colossal blunder of renting a room in a convent in Liège. Liège at the time was an independent city state but it had become embroiled in the war between France and Holland, and a year earlier French troops had occupied its citadel. When her presence there became known the French applied to the city authorities for permission to arrest her and this was granted. On 25 March she was seized and taken to the citadel. The news was at once relayed to a delighted Louis XIV, who had shown a keen interest in her case and taken it 'very much to heart that Mme de Brinvilliers does not escape justice'.[42]

When her room at the convent was searched a document was found headed 'My Confession'. Unlike that written by Sainte-Croix, the paper was carefully preserved by her captors who saw that, provided it could be used in evidence against her, it contained extraordinarily damaging admissions. Most important, she acknowledged in it that she had poisoned her father and two brothers, and she also recorded that she had tried to poison her daughter and her husband, though in neither case had this proved fatal. In all, she had made five or six attempts on her husband's life, thinking 'to make myself more comfortable' by ridding herself of him, though she had subsequently thought better of it and nursed him back to health.

Other disclosures were startling in a different way, for she detailed a history of remarkable sexual depravity. She noted that three of her five children had not been fathered by M. de Brinvilliers, for two were the product of her fourteen-year union with Sainte-Croix and another was the offspring of an unnamed cousin. She would have had more illegitimate children had she not taken drugs to induce abortion. Besides taking lovers, she had 'committed incest three times a week, perhaps three hundred times' in all. She further claimed that she had lost her virginity aged seven and that she had been even younger when she had first had impure 'touchings' with her brother.[43]

One should perhaps be cautious about accepting all aspects of this confession as the literal truth. Mme de Brinvilliers herself would later attempt to discredit it by insisting that she had been of unsound mind when she wrote it and while it was obviously in her own interests to say this, parts of it invite scepticism. For instance, it is hard to know what to make of her claim that she had sinful contact with one of her brothers (the eldest of whom was two years younger than her) at such an early age. However, when knowledge of this confession seeped out, few people bothered with quibbles of this sort; the text was instead taken as confirmation that she had been predisposed to evil even as a child. Nowadays a different interpretation can be drawn from it for, if it was true that she was sexually abused as a very young child, this might explain, even if it cannot excuse, her extraordinary callousness and psychopathic tendencies.

Once a passport had been obtained, Mme de Brinvilliers was driven under military escort through the Spanish Netherlands to France. En route she made several suicide attempts, repeatedly swallowing glass and pins, and also attempting to impale herself on a sharp stick inserted into her vagina. Reports of the last incident were seized on with glee by a male correspondent of Mme de Sévigné, the widowed noblewoman whose own witty and insightful letters are such an imperishable source for the period. He affected to believe that, far from trying to harm herself, Mme de Brinvilliers had been seeking sexual gratification, for he wrote archly, 'She thrust a stick – guess where! Not in her eye, not in her mouth, not in her ear, not in her nose, and not Turkish fashion [i.e. up the anus]. Guess where!' During her trial Mme de Brinvilliers's judges were less inclined to be jocular about these suicide bids. One remarked that her attempts to kill herself represented a wilful rejection of the possibility of divine redemption and were hence her greatest sin of all.[44]

When Mme de Brinvilliers reached Mezières on the French borders an office holder from the Paris *Parlement* named M. Palluau was sent to interview her. Palluau had been the investigating magistrate in the proceedings against La Chausée and hence was already familiar with the essentials of the case. It was thought significant that the King had decided the preliminary part of the investigation should take place outside the capital, for already there were fears that the magistrates of the Parisian law courts were so closely related by blood and marriage to Mme de Brinvilliers that they would be prejudiced in her favour. It may seem strange that there could be concern on this point, for Mme de Brinvilliers's victims had also been members of the legal fraternity and one might therefore have thought that class solidarity would have encouraged those judging her to be particularly severe. On the contrary, however, it was felt that the magistrates might consider that her conviction would reflect dishonourably on their own profession and that on this account they would treat her too indulgently. Later it was even suggested that M. Palluau was swayed by considerations of this sort and that he had failed to pursue the case against Mme de Brinvilliers with the requisite energy.

By the end of April Mme de Brinvilliers had been transferred to Paris, where she was imprisoned in the Conciergerie. Palluau set about assembling evidence against the accused, but at first he uncovered nothing that established her guilt beyond doubt. La Chausée's testimony in the torture chamber was not particularly helpful for, while he had made it clear that he had murdered the d'Aubray brothers on the orders of Sainte-Croix, he had been ambiguous about the part Mme de Brinvilliers had played. At one point La Chausée had said that it was she who had supplied Sainte-Croix with the poisons used to kill her brothers, but he later contradicted himself by saying that Sainte-Croix had told him she had been unaware of his plans to poison the two men. The fact that Sainte-Croix had written that everything in his casket belonged to her was also far from conclusive, for his note was dated 25 May 1670 and it was arguable that the poisons had been placed in the casket after that.

Testimony gathered from witnesses was also not very impressive. A former servant girl of Mme de Brinvilliers alleged that her mistress had tried to poison her with gooseberry jam and ham, permanently affecting her health. Another maidservant testified that Mme de Brinvilliers had once ordered her to fetch a pair of earrings from her casket, and when she unlocked the box she had seen it contained pots of paste and powder. The maid said that, as the daughter of an apothecary, she had recognised these as forms of arsenic. She added that on another occasion, when Mme de Brinvilliers was plainly drunk, her employer had opened up her casket and said laughingly, 'This is what you need to revenge yourself on your enemies; it is full of inheritances!'[45] When she had sobered up, Mme de Brinvilliers had clearly regretted her indiscretion and had begged her servant not to tell anyone what she had said. Although the evidence against La Chausée had not been much more substantial, it needed weightier proof than this to persuade the judges to convict a woman of Mme de Brinvilliers's standing.

Under repeated interrogations Mme de Brinvilliers herself revealed remarkably little. She adamantly maintained her innocence, insisting that she had been wholly ignorant of Sainte-Croix's machinations against her brothers. She explained the promissory note in Sainte-Croix's casket by saying she had hoped to lodge money with him in order to safeguard it from her creditors. As for her written confession, she disowned it entirely, claiming that she had written it when delirious with a fever, which had filled her mind with 'reveries and suchlike extravagances'.[46]

The investigating magistrate did not accept her explanation but he was doubtful whether he could make use of her confession. If it was agreed that the document had been drawn up under the secrecy of the confessional, then it was by definition 'extra-judicial' and it would be sacrilegious to reveal its contents in a court of law. Concerned about the prospect of violating 'one of religion's most sacred mysteries', Palluau consulted a panel of senior judges. Several disagreed with Palluau's belief that the document was inadmissible, but the First President of the Paris *Parlement*, Guillaume Lamoignon, did not deny that the matter was 'highly problematic'. In the end the question was referred to a group of theological experts who pronounced that, in view of the fact that no priest had been present when the document was written, it was not a confession in the religious sense. Accordingly, it was permissible to use it as evidence.[47]

On its own her confession might not have sufficed to convict her, but on 13 July there was a major new development. In the autumn of 1670 Mme de Brinvilliers had employed as a tutor for her children a barrister in his early thirties named Jean-Baptiste Briancourt. Soon after entering her service he had become her lover. After Mme de Brinvilliers's arrest he had been imprisoned in hopes that he would testify against her, but so far he had said nothing incriminating. Now, however, he indicated to the Attorney-General that he was prepared to reveal all he knew.

On being taken before the court, Briancourt related that shortly after starting his job he had travelled with Mme de Brinvilliers to her country house in Picardy. Her younger brother had died fairly recently and during the journey she suddenly confided that she and Sainte-Croix had poisoned him. She described how they had used La Chausée to effect this, and later came close to admitting that she had killed her father and her other brother in the same way. Briancourt said that he had naturally been alarmed to discover what 'a strange woman' he had taken as his mistress, but that he was too infatuated to break off the relationship.

Briancourt had grown more uncomfortable when, after receiving a visit from Sainte-Croix, Mme de Brinvilliers started hinting to him that she wanted him to help her murder her sister and sister-in-law. Briancourt had indignantly told her that he would rather die than harm either of them, but he at once saw that this response had vexed Mme de Brinvilliers and made her distrustful of him. Shortly afterwards Mme de Brinvilliers had invited Briancourt to visit her at midnight in the bedroom of her Paris house. Before doing so, Briancourt had looked into the room through a window and to his horror had seen her assisting Sainte-Croix to conceal himself. Realising that Sainte-Croix was planning to attack him as he lay in his mistress's arms, Briancourt entered and, ignoring Mme de Brinvilliers's attempts to entice him into her bed, flushed Sainte-Croix from his hiding place. Sainte-Croix promptly fled, whereupon Mme de Brinvilliers leapt upon Briancourt's back like some crazed incubus. With difficulty he shook her off, but she then became hysterical and threatened to take poison. She only calmed down when Briancourt somewhat surprisingly promised to forgive her. Though he had genuinely hoped they were reconciled, within a few days Briancourt became convinced that Sainte-Croix was still trying to assassinate him. This had finally persuaded him that the situation was untenable and that he had no alternative but to quit Mme de Brinvilliers's nightmarish household.[48]

After Briancourt had finished giving evidence Mme de Brinvilliers was brought in for her confrontation with the chief witness for the prosecution. Her composure never faltered throughout this gruelling session, which lasted until eight in the evening of 13 July and then resumed early the next morning for a further five hours. She began by objecting that Briancourt was a drunkard whom she had dismissed from her household for disorderly conduct and that therefore no reliance should be placed on his testimony. When his allegations were put to her, she calmly rebutted them, sneering, as Briancourt began weeping, that this merely demonstrated his utter baseness and that he should be ashamed to make such an exhibition of himself before the judges. While not disguising her contempt for Briancourt, she remained throughout in complete control of her emotions, speaking calmly and showing great respect for the judges. The most senior judge present was simultaneously repelled and fascinated by her performance for, though chilled by her utter lack of remorse, he could only marvel at the steely resolve and self-possession of this 'intrepid or, rather, unfeeling soul'.[49]

On 15 July Mme de Brinvilliers underwent her final interrogation on the *sellette*. Once again she unflinchingly maintained her innocence but she did so in vain, for the judges had already made up their minds. Mme de Brinvilliers was then returned to prison so that they could record their verdict and decide on her sentence. On 16 July they pronounced her guilty and decreed that she should be tortured in the hope that she would name her accomplices. After that she would be beheaded, then her body would be burnt and the ashes thrown to the winds. In passing this sentence the judges were, in fact, being generous. In his report on the case the Attorney-General had recommended that, prior to execution, the prisoner should be punished for her parricide by having her right hand cut off at the wrist. The judges had overruled him and they had also shown leniency by specifying that she should be beheaded, when they could have condemned her to be burnt alive.

It was now necessary to find a confessor to minister to the condemned woman during her final hours. The man selected for the task was a Jesuit professor of theology named Edmé Pirot. In some ways it was a surprising choice for he had no previous experience of attending prisoners on their way to execution. However, as the First President of the Paris *Parlement* made clear to Pirot, it was not simply concern for Mme de Brinvilliers's immortal soul that had influenced the decision. There were fears at the highest level that she still harboured terrible secrets and it was felt that in order that 'her crimes die with her' she must be persuaded to divulge all she knew. Otherwise there was a danger that associates of hers would carry out similar crimes without being apprehended and in this way 'her poisons would serve her after her death'.[50]

Pirot saw Mme de Brinvilliers for the first time on the morning of 16 July. As yet she had not been notified of the judges' decision, but she told him she considered it inevitable that she would be found guilty, which meant that, within twenty-four hours, she would have to undergo torture and face death. Like the judges who had tried her, Pirot was amazed by the fact that she did not seem at all perturbed by the prospect. When she was given her midday meal she tranquilly requested that the soup served that evening should be more nutritious than usual, as the following day was likely to be 'very tiring for me'.[51] However, as the hours passed by, Pirot was able to penetrate her protective carapace by impressing upon her that even the vilest sinner could attain divine forgiveness through penitence. He was delighted to see 'the first signs of contrition and distress' as she began to weep, declaring it was fortunate that her crimes had not gone undetected, as this afforded her a chance to escape eternal damnation. Pirot urged her to summon the judges immediately and admit everything, but though she promised she would ultimately make a full confession to the Attorney-General, she said she did not wish to do this until the following day. She realised that if she delayed it would be assumed that her admissions had been coerced from her by torture, but she said that for the remainder of the day she wished to concentrate on the spiritual guidance Pirot could offer her.

Early the following morning, 17 July, Mme de Brinvilliers was formally informed of the verdict against her and the full sentence of the court was read to her. She was then taken to the torture chamber to be subjected to the water torture, an ordeal in some ways more terrible than the *brodequins*. It consisted of more than twenty pints of water being forced down the victim's throat and Mme de Sévigné heard that when Mme de Brinvilliers saw the three large buckets of water that she would be compelled to drink she exclaimed that the intention must be to drown her, as no one could suppose that a woman of her size could swallow such a huge amount. Pirot, however, was given a different account. He was told that when she sighted the buckets she remarked calmly, 'Gentlemen, that is needless; I will tell everything without being put to the question. It is not that I aspire to escape it; my sentence says that it is to be given to me and I believe that I will not be spared it. But I will declare everything beforehand.'[52]

As promised, she then unburdened herself to the Attorney-General, acknowledging freely that she had poisoned her father and two brothers. It was now, too, that she made her claims about Christophe Glaser having been sent to Florence by M. Fouquet to find out about poisons, though she stressed she was only repeating what Sainte-Croix had told her and that she did not know if there was any truth in what he had said. In some respects, however, her revelations fell far short of what had been hoped, for nothing was forthcoming about accomplices who remained at large and who might be plotting further homicides.

The torture was then inflicted but nothing further could be wrung from Mme de Brinvilliers. Later it was claimed in some quarters that because of her connections with eminent members of the judiciary, orders were given that she should only be subjected to mild torture and that she had been able to bear this without making further disclosures. A highly placed courtier recorded that the King himself believed she had not been pressed hard enough and that his displeasure with the *Parlement* for showing her such favouritism later led him to set up a commission which was outside *Parlement*'s jurisdiction to investigate other poisonings.[53]

One person who was sure that 'La Brinvilliers's torture was alleviated' subsequently pointed out that the crowds of people who saw her go to her execution could confirm that all her limbs were still functioning satisfactorily and such 'free and easy movements ... are incompatible with coercive and harsh torture'. It is clear from Pirot's account of her execution that after being tortured she was able to walk with relative ease, although he noted she had difficulty kneeling. However, torture was not intended to leave its victims permanently mutilated and one should therefore be cautious about accepting the allegations that she was given privileged treatment.[54] A doctor and surgeon were in attendance throughout the torture session, but this was a standard precaution designed to guard against the victim dying under interrogation and the written record of the proceedings certainly does not bear out the theory that she escaped lightly.

In preparation for her ordeal Mme de Brinvilliers was first stripped naked and then bent backwards over a wooden trestle. Her ankles were attached to a ring on the floor and her wrists fastened to rings set low on a wall. Her body was thus unnaturally distended and in a position of extreme discomfort even before the torture itself began. A cow's horn was then forced between her lips and eight *coquemards* of water (a *coquemard* was a unit of measurement equalling two and a half pints) were funnelled down her throat. After each *coquemard* had been administered there was a pause so that questions could be put to the prisoner and the answers noted down by the clerk in attendance.

From the outset Mme de Brinvilliers appears to have been in great pain, for as she was being stretched over the trestle she cried out, 'Oh, my God! They're killing me and yet I have told the truth!' As the first unit of water was poured into her mouth she spluttered 'You're killing me!' but even as she writhed and moaned, she insisted that she could not add to her story. The only thing that she called to mind was that she had once sold poison to an unnamed man who had wanted to poison his wife, but such vague information was of little interest. She refused to say anything further, pleading that it would burden her conscience if she falsely incriminated innocent people.

After she had been compelled to swallow ten pints of water the torture entered a new or 'extraordinary' phase, more severe still than the 'ordinary' form which had preceded it. The trestle on which she was supported was removed and replaced by another higher off the ground, so that her body became still more arched and contorted. As the ropes binding her ankles and wrists bit cruelly into her flesh, the wretched woman shrieked, 'Oh, my God! You're dismembering me! Lord forgive me! Lord have pity on me!' Despite her pleas and groans, yet greater quantities of water were forced into her, but without producing the desired result. With grim determination she told her interrogators that they could kill her if they saw fit, but she refused to forfeit her soul by telling lies.[55]

At last her tormentors accepted that it was futile to prolong her sufferings and she was untied and laid upon a mattress. This was an integral part of the torture ritual and, oddly enough, was often the most productive, for the overwhelming relief of being suddenly free of pain caused many hitherto obdurate prisoners to impart things of significance. Mme de Brinvilliers, however, remained silent even at this psychologically vulnerable moment. After a torture and interrogation session which had lasted a total of four and a half hours, she was permitted to rejoin her confessor in order to prepare herself for the final ordeal of execution.

For more than four hours Mme de Brinvilliers was closeted with Pirot

in the Conciergerie chapel. At length, just before seven, the executioner indicated that the final reckoning could not be postponed any
longer. As she was led down the passageway towards the prison door,
she had to pass a group of about fifty high-born people who, like
everyone else in Paris, were consumed with curiosity about this
prodigy of evil. They had exploited their privileged position at court to
station themselves where they could be sure of having a good look at
her.

Among those who watched her as she passed was the Comtesse de
Soissons, one of the grandest ladies at Louis XIV's court who, piquantly, would herself later be compromised in the Affair of the Poisons. At
the time of her disgrace it was even suggested that the Comtesse de
Soissons had been in some way linked with Mme de Brinvilliers's
activities, though no evidence was ever put forward to justify the
claim. Certainly if Mme de Brinvilliers had ever been acquainted with
the Comtesse de Soissons, she gave no indication of it as she passed the
well-dressed group who were 'devouring her with their eyes'. While
understandably disconcerted at finding herself the object of such ghoul-
ish scrutiny she confined herself to murmuring to her confessor,
'Monsieur, here is a strange curiosity.'[56]

In the gaol courtyard Mme de Brinvilliers was loaded on to a
tumbril and transported through the teeming streets to the Cathedral of
Notre-Dame. There she was required to perform a public penance:
bearing a lighted torch in her hand, she had to kneel outside the
church and ask pardon of 'God, the King and justice' for having murdered her father and brothers 'wickedly and out of vengeance and to
have their wealth'.[57] Then she was put back in the cart and driven to
the Place de Grève.

The windows of the houses in the Place de Grève were packed with
spectators who had paid high prices to observe the execution from a
prime vantage point. In the square itself the crowd surrounding the
scaffold was so dense that the cart driver had to lash out with his whip
to force through a passage. When Mme de Brinvilliers was finally able
to mount the scaffold, a new indignity awaited her, for she had to go
down on her knees while the executioner laboriously shaved her head.
All the while Pirot knelt by her side murmuring prayers, but his words
were often drowned out by the angry roars of the crowd.

Having finished his preparations, the executioner indicated that he
was ready to wield his sword and Pirot withdrew slightly. The blade
flashed so swiftly that for a moment Pirot thought that the executioner
had missed his mark, for Mme de Brinvilliers's head remained on her
shoulders. Then, as he watched, the head slowly toppled sideways.

Satisfied by the way he had proved his expertise, the executioner demanded complacently of Pirot, 'That was a good stroke, Monsieur, was it not?'[58]

'At last it is done; la Brinvilliers is in the air,' Mme de Sévigné informed her daughter later that night. Having described how 'after the execution, her poor little body was thrown on a great big fire and the ashes to the winds' she added playfully that now that 'we will be inhaling her' perhaps 'we will be taken by some kind of mood for poisoning which will surprise us all'.[59] She was, of course, being facetious (some might say tasteless) but events would show there were genuine fears that the 'mood for poisoning' was indeed rampant in France.

The trouble was that though Mme de Brinvilliers had been punished for her crimes and Sainte-Croix was dead, many people did not accept that the matter could be regarded as closed. It seems that among those who had doubts on this score was King Louis XIV himself, who had shown such concern about bringing Mme de Brinvilliers to justice that even while on campaign he had been sent regular reports about the progress of her trial.[60] Undoubtedly he had been pleased by its outcome, but he did not feel that it had been conclusive, for he was one of those who feared that this murder case had not been an isolated phenomenon. There was a widespread assumption that Sainte-Croix could not have worked alone. This meant that there was a possibility that others who were equally expert about poisoning and who shared Mme de Brinvilliers's predatory tendencies were still operating undetected. If so, it was dangerously complacent to assume that with the execution of Mme de Brinvilliers an evil had been eradicated.

Such concerns were heightened by the case of Pierre-Louis Reich de Pennautier, an immensely rich man who had been imprisoned a month before the death of Mme de Brinvilliers. For many years Pennautier had occupied the demanding but relatively unremunerative post of Treasurer of the Estates of Languedoc. In 1669, however, he had secured for himself one of the most coveted offices in the kingdom when he had succeeded M. Hannyvel de Saint-Laurens as Receiver-General of the French clergy. As such he had become a financier of the first importance, for he was not only entrusted with the collection of all ecclesiastical dues owed to the Crown, but he advanced the government loans on the anticipated revenues. The rewards of the position were commensurate with the responsibilities, for the job was estimated to be worth 60,000 livres a year.

When Sainte-Croix's casket had been opened in August 1672, one set of papers had been found there which did not concern Mme de Brinvilliers. The bundle was endorsed, 'Packet addressed to M. Pennautier, which must be given back'. When the contents of the casket were inventoried on 18 August it was officially recorded that the documents related to a loan Pennautier had made to M. and Mme de Brinvilliers in June 1668, which had been partially repaid in May of the following year. Pennautier was then summoned before the official who was compiling the inventory and, when shown the documents, acknowledged they were genuine.

Pennautier's transactions with M. and Mme de Brinvilliers appeared to have been legitimate but suspicions were still aroused. After La Chausée's execution in March 1673 Pennautier was questioned about his links with Sainte-Croix and Mme de Brinvilliers. On 22 April Pennautier deposed that he had known Sainte-Croix for ten or twelve years and that he had occasionally loaned him money. He also said that he had sometimes encountered Mme de Brinvilliers when visiting houses in the area of Paris where they both lived, but that in recent years he had hardly seen her.

Unfortunately, this accorded oddly with his admission that, when he had discovered that most of the papers found in Sainte-Croix's casket had related to Mme de Brinvilliers, he had attempted to visit her at her rented lodgings. When asked why he had wanted to see her, he said he had gone to pay his compliments out of 'pure civility', as slanderous things were being said about the lady and he had wished to demonstrate his support.[61] It was hardly a satisfactory explanation but, for the moment at least, the investigating magistrate had to accept it.

Mme de Brinvilliers's capture afforded an opportunity for the matter to be probed further. At her first interrogation in April 1676 she was asked whether Sainte-Croix and Pennautier knew each other well, and she did the financier no favours when she replied that the pair had been 'very good friends and had secret business'. In a bid to find out more a trap was set: once she was in prison in Paris, a supposedly obliging gaoler pretended that if she wished to contact anyone he would deliver letters. Falling for the ruse, Mme de Brinvilliers wrote twice to Pennautier, warning him that questions were being asked about him and urging him to do all he could to help her. In particular, she wanted him to ensure that an individual named Martin, who had been a known associate of Sainte-Croix's, should go into hiding, cautioning Pennautier that these 'things matter as much to you as to me'.[62] The letters were intercepted before Pennautier could receive them. It was decided that it was now justifiable to take him into custody. On 15 June Pennautier was arrested as he sat at his desk writing a letter, making matters worse for himself when he frantically tore up the paper before him and tried to swallow the pieces.

In subsequent interrogations Mme de Brinvilliers was questioned intensively about Pennautier but she said nothing to damage him. Even at the end, when she finally acknowledged her own crimes, she made no accusations against the financier. Under torture she was again pressed on the subject but she merely said that while she had sometimes wondered whether Pennautier and Sainte-Croix had had dealings about poison she had never seen any proof of this. She explained that while in prison, she had decided she had nothing to lose by writing to a rich and powerful man like Pennautier, implying that she could compromise him, but that in reality she knew nothing to his discredit.[63]

Those interrogating her were highly sceptical of this and an hour before she went to her execution the Attorney-General again tried to persuade her to inculpate Pennautier. Mme de Brinvilliers replied that, knowing she was about to be judged by God, she would not have protected Pennautier if she had believed him to be guilty of poisoning, but she had no grounds to accuse him of such a thing. Frustrated by her answer, the Attorney-General told Pirot, 'This woman's reducing us to despair,' but even then he had not given up all hope of learning what he wanted. At the very moment that Mme de Brinvilliers was about to mount the scaffold, a clerk of the court told her that if she had anything further to add to what she had said, she could be taken into the Town Hall, where two commissioners were waiting to see her. Mme de Brinvilliers indicated that she would like to make some minor amendments to her testimony, but it was clear that these did not concern Pennautier and her offer was dismissed. 'That's not what we're asking for!' the clerk said crossly and rode off in disgust.[64]

Once Mme de Brinvilliers was dead it was assumed that Pennautier was out of danger. The Minister for War, Louvois, told a colleague that he expected Pennautier would soon be freed and Mme de Sévigné commented sarcastically that he would doubtless emerge from prison 'whiter than snow' even if, in the eyes of the public, his innocence remained in doubt. However, on 26 July 1676 Mme de Saint-Laurens, widow of the man whom Pennautier had succeeded as Receiver-General of the clergy, made the dramatic move of issuing a formal accusation against him. She contended that Pennautier had not only poisoned her late husband but also that he had murdered his father-in-law and a former business partner named Monsieur Dalibert.[65]

In support of this she alleged that when Sainte-Croix's casket had first been opened, it had contained a promissory note of November 1667, written in Pennautier's own hand, in which he undertook to pay

Sainte-Croix 10,000 livres at some time in the future. Some substance was given to this claim by the fact that, when Pennautier had been called upon to authenticate his documents, he had agreed that one with that date had been among those found in the casket. Pennautier later explained that this had been caused by a simple misunderstanding, which had since been rectified, but Mme de Saint-Laurens provided a more sinister explanation. She suggested that Pennautier had bribed those in charge of the casket to remove the compromising paper, commenting portentously, 'Pennautier's fortune has perhaps brought off more difficult enterprises [than that].'[66]

Mme de Saint-Laurens pointed out that Pennautier had a clerk named Belleguise whom the authorities wished to locate so they could question him about his association with Sainte-Croix. She suggested that Pennautier had also had close links with 'Martin', another crony of Sainte-Croix. This was the man to whom Mme de Brinvilliers had referred in her letter to Pennautier, and whose whereabouts still remained a mystery. Mme de Saint-Laurens also drew attention to the fact that Sainte-Croix had spent lavishly despite his lack of income. She insisted that it must have been Pennautier who financed this profligate lifestyle.

According to Mme de Saint-Laurens, the reason why Pennautier had so far evaded justice was that he enjoyed the protection of high-ranking members of the judiciary. Pennautier was the brother-in-law of M. Le Boultz, and was hence allied to a powerful legal dynasty, for M. Le Boultz was himself a *Conseiller* in the *Parlement* and his father occupied a still more exalted position in the judiciary. Mme Saint-Laurens was sure they had done everything possible to aid Pennautier. She even alleged that, after Mme de Brinvilliers had undergone 'imaginary torture', M. Le Boultz had approached her while she lay on the mattress, thus distracting her during those 'happy moments' when the truth was most likely to emerge.[67]

Mme de Saint-Laurens was not the first person to voice such fears. Even before the execution of Mme de Brinvilliers concern about the activities of the Le Boultz clan was such that some people came to suspect that her confessor Pirot was their stooge and that, far from urging her to be frank about her accomplices, he had encouraged her to remain silent. The Attorney-General became so disturbed by these rumours that he actually confronted Pirot on the matter. The Jesuit protested that prior to being chosen as Mme de Brinvilliers's confessor he had never met any of the Le Boultz family. He did concede, however, that after he had accepted the task M. Le Boultz had sought him out and spoken of his fears that torture might provoke Mme de Brinvilliers to make false accusations against Pennautier. If so, he begged Pirot to persuade her to retract these by telling her that she could not die with a clear conscience if she had incriminated an innocent man.[68] Presumably the reason why Pirot subsequently wrote his account of Mme de Brinvilliers's final hours and deposited it in the Jesuits' library in Paris was that he knew his integrity had been questioned and he wished to establish that he had acted correctly.

Pennautier had other influential supporters besides MM. Le Boultz. They included the King's Controller-General of Finance, Jean-Baptiste Colbert (who was grateful for the way Pennautier had persuaded the Estates of Languedoc to grant large sums of money to the Crown), and the Archbishop of Paris, but the public merely assumed he had purchased their loyalty with his wealth. Though the vengeful Mme de Saint-Laurens did not dare impugn the honesty of these important figures, she named others who she considered had been remiss in their duty. In a petition to the King she reminded him that M. Palluau, the investigating magistrate in the Brinvilliers case, was 'an old and intimate friend' of MM. Le Boultz. She alleged that this had made him reluctant to uncover evidence which could have been used against Pennautier, as was shown by his unaccountable failure to press Pennautier as to why he had sought to eat the letter he had been writing at the time of his arrest.[69]

The King was by no means impervious to such concerns, for he too was worried that *Parlement* would fail to show the necessary vigour and impartiality when dealing with Pennautier. He had heard the rumours that 'strong solicitations' had been made to *Parlement* on his behalf and that a great deal of money was being spread about. He was determined that this should not affect the way Pennautier was treated. On 28 June he ordered that First President Lamoignon and the Attorney-General, Achille de Harlay, should be told that he required this investigation into poisoning to be conducted with the utmost diligence. He wrote, 'I expect that they will do everything that upright men like themselves ought to do to baffle all those of any rank whatsoever who are mixed up in such an evil trade.' The King may have been disappointed that his intervention did not prove more effectual, for he was later said to have observed that no man worth 4 million livres like Pennautier would ever be found guilty by *Parlement*. He also allegedly remarked, 'If I had a lawsuit against Le Boultz, I would lose it.'[70]

In early August Pennautier's missing clerk, Belleguise, was tracked down and many people thought that once he began to talk Pennautier would be fatally compromised. It was whispered that *Parlement* would have preferred it if Belleguise had remained at large and that it was only because the King had taken an interest in the matter that he had been detained. Mme de Sévigné believed the Attorney-General was doing his duty properly, but she felt sure that Pennautier's wealth had corrupted lesser members of *Parlement*. She heard that 100,000 écus had been distributed to make things easier for Pennautier and commented darkly that an innocent man would hardly need to be so lavish.[71]

To counteract the campaign waged against him by Mme de Saint-Laurens, Pennautier arranged for pamphlets to be issued protesting his innocence.[72] Apart from ridiculing the idea that he could have tampered with the contents of Sainte-Croix's casket, he put forward convincing arguments in his defence. He pointed out that it made no sense for Mme de Saint-Laurens to suggest that in 1667 he was already planning to murder her husband and that he had promised money to Sainte-Croix on that account. As he reminded his readers, at that date Saint-Laurens had not yet been appointed Receiver-General of the clergy, so Pennautier would have had nothing to gain by killing him. Even once Saint-Laurens had become the incumbent, a mere five weeks before he died, it could hardly have been foreseen that Pennautier would benefit from his death. Saint-Laurens had already designated another man as his successor and it was impossible to predict that this arrangement would be overturned. Furthermore, after her husband's death, Mme de Saint-Laurens had not only supported Pennautier's candidacy to become Receiver-General, but had also reached a deal with Pennautier, whereby he undertook to share the profits of the post with her. It was surely unthinkable that Mme de Saint-Laurens would have been ready to do business with Pennautier if she had grounds to believe he had murdered her husband. It was only after the arrangement had come to an end, in December 1675, that Mme de Saint-Laurens had begun voicing suspicions about Pennautier.

Above all, however, Pennautier was adamant that there was nothing to support the idea that Saint-Laurens had died as a result of poisoning. Because his last illness had been 'extraordinarily violent' and his tongue had turned 'black and livid' when he died, an autopsy had been carried out on him. Having found 'a great quantity of pus or floating matter in the intestines', the doctors had concluded that the cause of death was an abscess in the lower stomach, which had burst after Saint-Laurens had been jolted during a long journey on horseback. Despite Mme de Saint-Laurens's allegations, the doctors continued to stand by their original diagnosis.

(It should perhaps be mentioned here that three years later the fortune-teller Mme Voisin would suggest that M. de Saint-Laurens had been poisoned by his brother, the Chevalier de Hannyvel. However, her only reason for saying this was that Hannyvel, 'an impious person who was always seeking to speak with the devil', had subsequently talked of murdering his nephew and widowed sister-in-law so that he could inherit his brother's wealth.[73] No harm had ever ensued to them and on this evidence it would hardly be fair to reject the conclusion of Saint-Laurens's doctors that he had died of natural causes.)

Pennautier could not deny that he had known Sainte-Croix and loaned him money but he insisted that this was of no significance. 'With whom was this man not acquainted?' he demanded rhetorically, adding that it was absurd to think that just because he had advanced funds to someone who happened to be a poisoner he had committed the same crime.

Pennautier's case was finally heard on 20 July 1677. Once again he was required to explain why he had tried to see Mme de Brinvilliers after Sainte-Croix's casket had been discovered and he was also questioned about the letter he had been writing at the time of his arrest. When the torn-up pieces had been reassembled, it had transpired that Pennautier had been making arrangements to send an unnamed man to the country, but he denied that this was 'Martin', whose disappearance had been so desired by Mme de Brinvilliers. He insisted it was simple panic that had prompted him to try to prevent the letter being seized by the arresting officers, and that its contents were wholly innocuous. The court accepted these assurances and Pennautier was given an absolute discharge.

Pennautier had in theory been completely vindicated. He was left free to pursue his successful career, for he had retained his post as Receiver-General of the French clergy. He resumed his place in Paris society, acting as if he had never been suspected of murder. In reality, however, his reputation never really recovered and in fashionable circles his name still provoked sniggers many years after he had supposedly been exonerated. Mme de Sévigné was proved wrong when she prophesied that from now on no one would risk dining with Pennautier but, though people soon showed themselves ready enough to accept his hospitality, he was always regarded in a faintly macabre light. An observant Italian visitor to France named Giovanni-Battista Primi Visconti confessed that he felt uneasy when Pennautier came to court and stationed himself in the throng of courtiers who gazed on while the King had his dinner. He explained that he was sure the King was aware of the presence of this notorious figure and that this cannot have enhanced his appetite.[74]

Pennautier's clerk, Belleguise, was also tried in July 1677. Although at the time of his arrest there had been great expectations that he would turn out to have been a key figure who had formed a vital link between Pennautier and Sainte-Croix, his trial proved a great anticlimax. He admitted having visited Sainte-Croix's laboratory but said that this was because he had been interested in alchemical research. He categorically denied that he had ever seen anything to suggest that Sainte-Croix was producing poison. Without further evidence he could not be convicted of involvement in Sainte-Croix's crimes but he was not completely cleared, for there were better grounds for suspecting that he and Sainte-Croix had been jointly involved in a counterfeiting racket. The judges were satisfied that he had handled fake silver coins and accordingly they banished him from France for the period of three years, three months and three days.

The Brinvilliers murder case had been resolved but it had caused a lingering unease. Poisoning, which had previously been dismissed as the province of foreigners, no longer seemed an impossibly remote threat. Indeed, the danger it posed had penetrated the national consciousness to such an extent that it was close to becoming an obsession with the French. In one of the pamphlets written in his defence Pennautier had recalled how, after the execution of La Chausée, 'All the public was stirred up; in Paris all the talk was of bizarre deaths that had been witnessed. Everyone … went over the circumstances in their mind, everything dreadful that happened was attributed to poison.' In her pursuit of Pennautier, Mme de Saint-Laurens had done her best to exploit such fears, for she maintained that poisoners had claimed many victims without the cause of death being recognised. She confidently pronounced, 'Between 1667 and 1672 poison, disguised under the name of apoplexy, ravaged the whole of France with sudden deaths.'[75]

It was not just that poisoning was now supposed to be more commonplace than previously imagined. Mme de Brinvilliers's involvement meant that henceforth no one could be above suspicion, for her social position and female sex had not precluded her from committing the most iniquitous acts. While Mme de Brinvilliers was awaiting trial a lawyer named Maître Nivelle had written a pamphlet seeking to defend her; he had begun by urging that she must be innocent because her 'advantages of birth, rank and fortune' rendered it unthinkable that she could be 'capable of the horrible and cowardly crimes of which she is accused'.[76] The outcome of the trial, and Mme de Brinvilliers's subsequent confession, meant that such comforting assumptions could no longer be sustained.

This gave rise to the nagging fear that other outwardly respectable persons were engaged in equally despicable deeds. Some years later Louis XIV's Chief of Police in Paris, M. de La Reynie, would even claim that Mme de Brinvilliers had herself acknowledged this. He alleged that 'she was the first to say ... during the confrontations with witnesses and at other times, that there were many people engaged in this wretched trade of poison, including persons of high station'. La Reynie's statements about the Brinvilliers case are not always reliable, but there were other reports of her making similar comments. It was rumoured, for example, that when she realised, just before her execution, that she would not be reprieved, she had exclaimed, 'Out of so many guilty people must I be the only one to be put to death?' Her confessor Pirot insisted there was no truth in the story but it continued to be widely believed. The gaoler who had tricked Mme de Brinvilliers into writing to Pennautier added his contribution: he said she had boasted that if she chose, she could 'ruin half the people in town', but that she was 'too generous' to betray them.[77]

If it was true that such wicked people were still at large, not even the King could regard himself as invulnerable to their machinations. The Brinvilliers case itself had raised concerns about his safety. Christophe Glaser had, of course, been the royal apothecary and it was undeniably frightening that a man alleged to have supplied Sainte-Croix with poisons should have been responsible for preparing drugs for the King. Furthermore, it had been reported that towards the end of his life Sainte-Croix had boasted that he had plans to become one of the King's cabinet secretaries or, still more alarmingly, a royal cupbearer, serving the King drinks at meals. In her petition to the King Mme de Saint-Laurens implored him to consider the dangers he would have faced if such a sensitive position had been entrusted to a criminal of his calibre.[78] To obtain one of these posts Sainte-Croix would have needed the support of an influential person at court and, predictably, Mme de Saint-Laurens was sure this had been Pennautier. Once Pennautier had been acquitted this theory no longer seemed tenable, but there was still a possibility that Sainte-Croix had had other powerful protectors within the court. If so, the King might even now be nurturing monsters who were plotting to destroy him. All this gave rise to fear and suspicion, and ensured that the satisfactory resolution of the Brinvilliers case was not looked on as a cause for congratulation. Instead, it created the perception that French society was menaced by hidden dangers, all the more perilous for being unfathomable.

# LOUIS XIV AND HIS COURT

In July 1676, a week after she had seen the Marquise de Brinvilliers go to her execution (or rather, after waiting for hours on the Pont Notre-Dame in order to glimpse the tip of the condemned woman's hood) Mme de Sévigné paid a visit to Versailles. Despite the fact that France was at war, she found the court immersed in pleasure. Although his armies remained in the field against the Dutch and their allies, at the beginning of July King Louis XIV had taken a break from campaigning in order to enjoy a summer holiday at his favourite residence, Versailles. To mark his return, a succession of entertainments were devised, in which his courtiers enthusiastically participated. Every evening there were plays, concerts or carriage rides or, alternatively, a nocturnal gondola trip on the newly enlarged canal to the palace's western side might be followed by a torchlight picnic supper. In the afternoons the courtiers were kept amused by gambling sessions in the King's upper apartment, an imposing suite of rooms, which had only recently been completed. In these ornate surroundings they hazarded their luck at the newly fashionable game of *reversis* and, since the minimum stake was 500 louis, huge sums were won and lost.

Prominent at the gaming tables was the Marquise de Montespan, who had been the King's mistress for the past nine years and had already borne Louis five children. She was universally agreed to be a great beauty, but Mme de Sévigné noted that she had never seen her look better. She had recently lost weight after a visit to the spa town of Bourbon and was dressed in the height of fashion, wearing a gown lavishly adorned with exquisite lace. Her blond hair was arranged in a mass of curls, becomingly topped by black ribbons, and at her throat she wore jewels that might have been borrowed from the Maréchale de l'Hôpital, but which were finer than any the Queen possessed. 'In a word, a triumphant beauty' was Mme de Sévigné's admiring verdict. Concluding her description of her visit Mme de Sévigné reported, 'The court has never been so agreeable and everyone very much wants this to continue.'[1]

Seemingly, at least, the scene could not have been further removed from the grisly events enacted a few days earlier in the Place de Grève. Mme de Sévigné certainly had no inkling that within four years a significant number of the elegant and well-connected figures who graced the afternoon reception would face disgrace and ruin following allegations of poisoning. Still less did she imagine that the radiant and resplendent Mme de Montespan would herself be touched by the same scandal after she too was accused not just of poisoning but also of sacrilege, Satanism and infanticide.

In some ways the France of Louis XIV was an unlikely setting for the events that form the subject of this book. At the time, France was an assertive, self-confident nation, proud of its status as a great power and convinced of its superiority to its neighbours. The Affair of the Poisons challenged these assumptions and proved a humbling experience for a country accustomed to being the focus of envy and admiration.

It would also undermine the prestige of the court, which hitherto had been famed for its splendour and sophistication. The shocking and distasteful revelations that were a feature of the affair stripped the court of some of its lustre and made it seem decadent and tawdry. Members of the French aristocracy, proverbially arrogant and assured, were accused of terrible crimes and depicted as twisted and perverted. Even when it was impossible to prove that these people were truly wicked, the affair exposed them as being superstitious, backward and deluded. The story of the Affair of the Poisons is strange by any standard, but it becomes still more bizarre when placed in context.

In August 1678 the war with Holland, which had lasted six years, was ended by the signing of the Treaty of Nymwegen. With hindsight people saw this as the apogee of Louis XIV's reign. Abbé Choisy declared in his memoirs, 'In making the Peace of Nymwegen King Louis the Great had attained the summit of human glory.' Another courtier described Louis as 'master in Europe ... the arbiter of all in this part of our hemisphere'. After Louis's death Voltaire would echo this assessment, identifying this as the moment when 'the king was ... at the height of his grandeur' and noting that having been 'the terror of Europe for six years running', Louis had now established himself as the most commanding figure on the continent.[2]

The King could justly pride himself on having transformed France in less than twenty years, for it was only in 1661, following the death of Cardinal Mazarin, that he had assumed personal direction of his affairs. Since that time he had been aided in his task by a group of powerful and capable ministers, but though much responsibility was delegated to these individuals, final decisions rested with the King. By the end of the Dutch War, France possessed the most powerful army to have been seen in Europe since Roman times, numbering 200,000 men even in peacetime. The navy, which had been negligible in 1661, had been fashioned into a formidable fighting force. Between 1661–72 the King's net revenues had more than doubled, thanks largely to the efforts of his Controller-General of Finance, Colbert, although not even the crippling taxation imposed on France's peasant population had been able to prevent debts accumulating during the Dutch War. Colbert had also worked tirelessly to improve communications within France, to promote foreign trade and encourage manufacturing. Particular importance had been attached to the production of luxury goods for the court, partly because Colbert wanted to reduce imports but also because he believed that in themselves these high-quality goods promoted the 'grandeur and magnificence' of France.

The arts, too, were cultivated assiduously. The written word flourished to such a degree that Voltaire could declare of the period, 'In eloquence [and] in...literature...the French were the legislators of Europe.' As well as being a generous patron to artists and composers within France, the King signalled his devotion to the arts by conferring pensions on distinguished writers throughout Europe, establishing himself as the Maecenas of his age. However, art was not merely valued for its own sake, for it was expected to serve the purposes of the state by reminding observers of the King's power and prestige. When the King set up a school in Paris to provide instruction in painting and sculpture he did so not merely because he held both disciplines in 'singular esteem' but also because he believed that these were 'two arts which should pre-eminently contribute to the establishment of his fame and the transmission of his name to posterity'. Those who received royal patronage were mindful of their obligations. In 1677, when touring the workshops set up for the manufacture of Gobelins tapestries, John Locke was impressed by the 'very rich and good figures' in the designs, but he noted 'in every piece Louis *le grand* was the hero, and [in] the rest the marks of some conquest etc.'.[3]

As befitted a monarch who prided himself on ruling a modern and progressive state, the King took an interest in promoting science. At a time when the mysteries of the universe were being shown to operate in conformity with the laws of geometry and mathematics, it was feasible to assume that a similar logic and consistency underlay much of human existence. The results that could be attained through observation and experimentation were incalculable, and the King was determined that France would be well placed both to take advantage of recent scientific advances and to make new discoveries. In 1666 the Royal Academy of Sciences was founded in Paris with the aid of generous financial support from the Crown. The previous year the world's first scientific journal, the *Journal des Savants*, had appeared, enhancing the claim of Paris to be regarded as the scientific capital of the world. In 1667 work was started on a magnificent observatory, equipped at royal expense with a superlative telescope and other intruments designed to facilitate the study of astronomy and cartography. The King's personal enthusiasm for scientific enquiry was demonstrated in 1681 when the elephant in the menagerie at Versailles died and Louis was present when its vast corpse was dissected by the Academy of Sciences.[4]

According to Voltaire it was under Louis XIV that 'human reason in general was perfected', and the King himself was sure that his conduct as a ruler was consistently shaped by rational thought. He told his son that in discharging his responsibilities 'I ... governed myself in accordance with reason', 'using good sense' to resolve problems.[5] The Affair of the Poisons would nevertheless demonstrate that despite Louis's enthusiasm for technological progress and his avowed espousal of modernity, Reason was not so firmly in the ascendant in seventeenth-century France as its King liked to think.

The King believed that the enhancement of his '*gloire*' – a potent word which encompassed 'reputation' as well as its literal translation of 'glory' – was his overriding priority. He told his son that all else must be subordinated to this, for the acquisition of *gloire* was rightfully 'the governing and dominant passion' of all princes. In his eyes it was not enough merely to maintain France's position in the world; instead, it was incumbent on him to take every opportunity to increase his kingdom's power and prestige. As he explained, 'A reputation cannot be preserved without adding to it every day. Glory, finally, is not a mistress who can be neglected, nor is one ever worthy of her first favours if he is not always wishing for new ones.' This conviction had grave implications for the stability of Europe, for Louis was clear that 'war is undoubtedly the most brilliant way to acquire glory'. Because of Louis's 'thirst for *gloire*', France enjoyed only fleeting interludes of peace between 1661 and the King's death in 1715. A German diplomat would indeed claim that it was this 'boundless and inordinate passion for glory ... which dominates and possesses him even to excess' that lay at the root of 'the fatal events of our times'.[6]

The first war the King embarked on was a relatively painless affair, for after his 1667 declaration of hostilities against Spain the campaigns that followed in Flanders and Franche-Comté bore more resemblance to triumphal progresses than bitter conflict. Peace was restored in 1668 but the war against Holland, which broke out in 1672, was an altogether more formidable undertaking. At the outset it seemed that the French would win easily and in the summer of 1672 the Dutch sued for peace, offering exceptionally generous terms. However, when these were rejected the Dutch concluded that France was set on their annihilation, leaving them with no alternative but to resume the struggle. By cutting the dykes and flooding the land around Amsterdam the Dutch halted the French advance, but the country had been saved at a terrible cost. As the war dragged on, other European powers allied with the Dutch, concerned that if France crushed Holland her power would become overwhelming. In the course of the savage struggle that ensued the civilian population of Holland suffered terrible cruelties at the hands of French troops and though Louis XIV's Minister of War, Louvois, has customarily been blamed for this policy of 'frightfulness', Louis himself must bear the ultimate responsibility.[7]

When the war finally came to an end in 1678 the French could reasonably claim to be the victors, even though the terms obtained at Nymwegen were less favourable than those proposed by the Dutch six years earlier. Yet the victory had been costly, for casualties on all sides had been high. In September 1674, when France was celebrating its success at the battle of Senef, Mme de Sévigné noted ruefully, 'We lost so many at this victory that without the *Te Deum* and a few standards carried to Notre-Dame we would have believed that we had lost the fight.' More serious, however, was the fact that France had come to be viewed throughout Europe as an arrogant and exorbitant predator whose ambitions must be curbed. When Louis began exploiting legal ambiguities in Nymwegen and earlier treaties to lay claim to further territories, his determination to make 'peace a time of conquest' only reinforced the perception that France was a dangerous bully.[8]

A king so obsessed with his prestige required a fitting setting to emphasise his majesty, for Louis fully concurred with Colbert's dictum that apart from 'striking actions of war, nothing indicates the grandeur and spirit of princes more than buildings'. The King was particularly well endowed in this respect, for the wonderful palaces and chateaux he had inherited included Saint-Germain, Chambord, Fontainebleau, Vincennes and, in Paris, the Tuileries and the Louvre. The King used all these as temporary residences, and made significant alterations and improvements to many of them. His real passion, however, was Versailles and it was here that Louis indulged his love of building to transform an unassuming house originally used by his father as a hunting lodge into one of the most stupendous palaces in the world. Despite the unsatisfactory nature of the terrain and the lack of an abundant water supply, the King engaged the landscape designer André Le Nôtre to create the extraordinary gardens and park, with features that included a cruciform canal broad enough to accommodate a flotilla of sailing ships, and 1400 fountains. Well might the Duc de Saint-Simon write of Louis, 'It diverted him to ride roughshod over nature and to use his money and ingenuity to subdue it to his will.'[9]

In 1668 the King embarked on a major programme of construction, commissioning the architect Louis Le Vau to enlarge the original building. Le Vau's additions included a grandiose suite on the ground floor for the King's private use with rooms adorned by columns and statuary, culminating in a magnificent bathroom, whose centrepiece was a massive octagonal tub carved from a single block of marble. The King's upper apartment, which overlooked the gardens, was sited above these rooms and it was here that he entertained the court. 'Everything is furnished divinely; everything is magnificent,' Mme de Sévigné wrote appreciatively on first seeing it. In each room the door surrounds and window embrasures were enriched with a different coloured marble 'as fine as those formerly brought over from Italy or Greece', hewn from French quarries which had only recently been opened and exploited. As one passed in succession through the Salon of Venus, the Salon of Abundance, the Salon of Diana, the Salon of Mars, the Salon of Mercury and the Salon of Apollo, the interiors became progressively more elaborate and the decorative scheme was completed by ceilings 'enriched by paintings by the best painters of the Royal Academy'.[10]

By 1678 the King had resolved to make Versailles the permanent seat of court and government, and he addressed himself to beautifying it still further. The conclusion of the Dutch War meant that he could allocate twice the amount of money that had been spent at Versailles during the previous year to effect more improvements. Since Le Vau was now dead, Jules Hardouin Mansart was engaged to construct the Salons of Peace and War, and the monumental Hall of Mirrors, a dazzling conception which overwhelmed the senses as much by its sheer scale as by its visual splendour. Following its completion in 1684 a court lady confidently proclaimed this to be 'without doubt…the finest thing of its kind in the universe'.[11]

It is a truism that life at Versailles, so grand in many ways, was also pervaded by squalor. In an age of primitive sanitation this was, of course, a problem common to all large buildings where many people congregated. When touring Fontainebleau in 1677, John Locke noted that the back stairs leading to the apartments of the King's brother smelt like an urinal. In 1675 a report on the Louvre claimed that 'on the grand staircases... behind the doors and almost everywhere one sees there a mass of excrement, one smells a thousand unbearable stenches caused by calls of nature which everyone goes to do there every day'. As the description was penned by a man who was bidding for a contract to supply the Louvre with close stools and to dispose of their contents, he may have exaggerated. However, at Versailles problems of this sort were particularly acute. Once the court settled there permanently after 1682 it became more difficult to arrange for a palace which was so rarely left unoccupied to be thoroughly cleansed and aired. Sewage disposal was made more challenging because the building was not situated on a river. Courtiers also frequently referred to the 'bad air' of Versailles, which they generally blamed on the 'exhalations' that emanated from the vast masses of earth that were moved by hundreds of labourers during the landscaping of the gardens.[12]

Anecdotal evidence also suggests that some individuals at court were remarkably casual about the performance of natural functions. The King's sister-in-law, Elizabeth Charlotte, Duchesse d'Orléans complained in 1702 that 'the people stationed in the galleries in front of our room piss in all the corners. It is impossible to leave one's apartments without seeing somebody pissing.' It is true she was apt to exaggerate but other stories go some way to bearing out her claims. The Duc de Saint-Simon described an occasion when the eccentric Bishop of Noyon was overcome by such 'a great desire to piss' as he passed the chapel at Versailles that he entered the King's tribune and urinated over the balustrade, splattering the floor below. Some years earlier a correspondent of the Comte de Bussy reported that Mmes de Saulx and de Tremouille had caused outrage when they defecated in their box at the theatre 'and then, to remove the evil smell, threw everything into the pit'. Not unnaturally the audience shrieked abuse, obliging the two ladies to withdraw, but while the response makes it plain that such behaviour was considered neither normal nor acceptable, the incident helps explain how Versailles could have acquired its insalubrious reputation.[13]

The King had been supremely successful in ensuring that the life of the French aristocracy revolved around the court, even while he denied them a role in central government. Despite their effective exclusion from political power, other forms of advancement were open to the nobility and they pursued these assiduously. They came to court to negotiate advantageous marriages, or in hopes of obtaining preferment in the army and Church. Others craved positions in the royal household, which not only conferred prestige on the holder but brought with it tangible benefits. The King might reward loyal servants with financial favours such as pensions or grants of monopoly: during his visit to Paris in 1679, for example, John Locke noticed that bills had been pasted all over the city 'with a privilege for a receipt to kill lice whereof the Duke of Bouillon has the monopoly'.[14] Contact with the King afforded opportunities to present him with direct requests, as well as to intercede for others who did not enjoy such close proximity to the monarch. It was, of course, understood that if this was successful, the person who had approached the King would be rewarded for his efforts by the benefiting party. Others who did not have access to the King and who had devised money-making schemes that required his approval, found it impossible to implement them directly. Instead, they sold their ideas to more privileged courtiers who were better placed to exploit them.

Naturally the King was incapable of fulfilling the expectations of more than a tiny minority of those who came to court and he had to find ways of preventing disillusionment from becoming too widespread. According to Saint-Simon, 'He fully realised that the substantial gifts he had to offer were too few to have any continuous effect and he substituted imaginary favours that appealed to men's jealous natures, small distinctions which he was able with extraordinary ingenuity to grant or withhold.' Yet despite his skilful management, the King himself was acutely aware of how limited were the means at his disposal. He told his son, 'We...who see so many hopes before us every day...can thereby easily recognise how unwarranted they are and how much time is wasted upon them.'[15]

To try to stave off disappointment, the King deferred decisions for as long as possible, invariably answering 'I'll see' when suits were presented to him. He was conscious that even when he was able to grant requests, this stirred up resentment in other quarters. He was said to have remarked, 'Every time I award a vacant place I make a hundred malcontents and one ingrate.'[16] It was therefore a considerable achievement on the part of the King that people at court continued to see it as a place full of opportunity.

The reality was, however, that most of them had a dispiriting existence. Few were so clear-sighted about this as Mme de Maintenon (which was somewhat ironic, as her own career at court lifted her to extraordinary heights). She came to the bleak conclusion that 'to pay one's court entails much trouble, constraint, expense and boredom...In effect... one gets up early in the morning, one dresses oneself with care, one spends all day on one's feet awaiting a favourable moment to get oneself seen, to present oneself, and often one comes back as one went, except that one is in despair for having wasted one's time and trouble.'[17]

It is clear that in most cases the investment required to live at court far outweighed the gains. To keep up appearances it was necessary to lay out large sums on fine clothes, household expenses, servants and carriages, and all this at a time when the income from land (on which most aristocrats depended) was diminishing in real terms. The Italian observer Giovanni-Battista Primi Visconti realised that many of the nobility were being ruined by their extravagance and Mme de Sévigné professed herself mystified as to how people at court avoided total insolvency. Concerned at her daughter's expenditure, she wrote anxiously, 'There must be some kind of sorcery you practise in connection with... the high life you lead... I think you must resort to black magic, as must these impecunious courtiers. They never have a sou, but they go on royal tours, on every campaign. They dress in the height of fashion, take part in all the balls... no matter how bankrupt they are... Their lands decrease in value. No matter, they go on just the same.'[18] Her words had an eerie resonance for, during the Affair of the Poisons, it would appear that some people at court had indeed had recourse to black magic in hopes of improving their prospects.

Inevitably the court was beset by jealousy and spite. A Paris doctor named Gui Patin declared in 1664, 'The court is full of intrigue, ambition and avarice' and he stigmatised it as a place where people would rather repudiate their closest companions than to see them prosper. The Duc d'Antin confirmed this by observing that, at court, 'One should, as a fundamental principle, render ill services to everyone, for fear of seeing someone elevated.'[19]

The Marquis de Sourches recalled, 'As few people had money, everyone sought ways of getting it.' Whenever an attractive opportunity arose, people of both sexes at court could be utterly unscrupulous about pursuing it. In August 1671 the death of the King's principal physician, Dr Vallot, sparked a desperate struggle to succeed him, with rival courtiers supporting different candidates. Gui Patin reported that the whole court was 'dominated... by intrigues in which the ladies are much to the fore' and he heard that one doctor had promised 'a great lady' (thought to be Mme de Montespan) 30,000 livres if she bestirred herself to obtain him the post. In 1664 there had been similar excitement when it had been decided to supplement the number of ladies in the Queen's household. 'Almost all the ladies of the court are taking part and each one is intriguing for it,' the Duc d'Enghien disclosed to a correspondent. The sort of tactics to which the contestants could stoop is shown by Saint-Simon's description of what happened when a household was formed in 1696 for the Savoyard princess who married the King's eldest grandson. As he recalled, 'All the ladies of suitable rank and favour were actively canvassing for positions, often to one another's detriment. Anonymous letters flew about like flies, libels and denouncements were everywhere.'[20]

In one of his celebrated sermons the great preacher Jacques Bénigne Bossuet waxed eloquent on the envy and malice which consumed the court. 'O court!' he declaimed, '… If only I could see the collapse of the ambition which carries you away, the jealousies that divide you, the slanders that tear you apart, the quarrels that stain you with blood, the delights that corrupt you.' In 1682 the vindictiveness and spite which she encountered at court prompted the King's German sister-in-law, the Duchesse d'Orléans, to complain, 'Every day I hear innumerable calumnies with not a grain of truth in them, promises which are never kept and polite expressions which conceal thoughts of a very different nature.'[21]

Rank and precedence were of paramount importance in court society and provided fertile ground for quarrels. The passions stirred up by such matters may now seem strange but people at court were conscious that they provided the criteria by which they were evaluated. It was not vanity alone that led court notables to expend such energy on struggles over precedence, for their standing at court defined them in the eyes of the world. It even affected the prestige in which they were held in their local communities, for visitors who came to court from outlying areas were capable of judging the nuances of etiquette, and their esteem for individual nobles varied accordingly. In the words of the sociologist and historian Norbert Elias, precedence and etiquette were 'not mere externals … They were literal documentations of social existence, a notation of the place one currently occupied in the court hierarchy. To rise or fall in this hierarchy meant as much to the courtier as profit or loss to the businessman.'[22]

The King understood all this very clearly. He told his son, 'Those who imagine that claims of this kind are only questions of ceremony are sadly mistaken. There is nothing in this matter that is unimportant or inconsequential. Since our subjects cannot penetrate into things, they usually judge by appearances and it is most often on amenities and ranks that they base their respect and obedience.'[23]

Even if the King appreciated why it was that etiquette and precedence so preoccupied his courtiers, the bickerings and wrangles which resulted revealed human nature at its least attractive. Even when France was at war, or in the midst of some crisis, a disproportionate amount of the King's time was spent adjudicating on such questions. Distinctions such as the right to wear a hat in the presence of foreign ambassadors, or to kneel on a certain sort of hassock in church, gave rise to bitter controversy. Duchesses were entitled to sit on stools known as *tabourets* during audiences with the Queen, but many of them coveted the honour reserved for ladies of still higher rank, who could occupy a chair with a back or, better still, an armchair. Dukes and peers were accorded the jealously guarded privilege of having both double doors opened for them as they passed through rooms at court, while an elite few at the top of the social scale enjoyed 'the honours of the Louvre', which meant that the King addressed them as 'cousin' and permitted them to drive their coaches into his palace courtyards. When lodgings were allocated to courtiers who were accompanying the King on his travels the question of whether an official chalked on the door '*for* Monsieur or Madame X', rather than the name alone, was deemed of immense significance. The omission of this seemingly innocuous preposition could cause dreadful agonies.

Courtiers devoted intense effort to edging themselves higher up the pyramid of rank, engaging in elaborate manoeuvres to establish their superiority to people who considered themselves their equals. They operated on the principle that it only required one occasion when their pretensions went unchallenged to raise their status for ever. Ambitious individuals were thus constantly on the lookout for suitable opportunities, while maintaining constant vigilance against rivals who might hope to encroach on their privileges or otherwise undermine them.

In 1665, for example, a dispute over precedence sparked a quarrel between the Princesse de Bade and the Duchesse de Bouillon. Intending to deliver a snub to another court lady, Mlle Elboeuf, the Princesse unwisely suggested that the Duchesse should place herself next to her. To the Princesse's alarm, however, the Duchesse took advantage of this to seat herself on Princesse's far side, nearer the Queen, which implied that the Princesse was her inferior. Despite the Princesse's shrill protests, the Duchesse stubbornly declined to relinquish her *tabouret*. The following year there was a near identical disagreement between the Duchesse de Rohan and the Duchesse de Richelieu, who ended up screaming insults at each other while the Queen received the Polish ambassador.[24]

Three years later a similar dispute erupted between the Comtesse de Gramont and the Comtesse de Soissons. The Comtesse de Soissons had been seated by the Queen at a gaming table, but when she rose and left the room the Comtesse de Gramont hurriedly deposited herself in the vacated place. On returning, the Comtesse de Soissons demanded that Mme de Gramont surrender her seat, but the latter retorted fiercely 'We'll see about that.' The Comtesse de Soissons gave a disdainful laugh, whereupon the Comte de Gramont entered the fray on his wife's side by declaring, 'Madame, one does not nail down chairs here; my wife will remain there; we come from as good a family as you.' The matter was only resolved when it was brought to the King's attention and he forced the Gramonts to apologise.[25]

The King did not relish being called upon to intervene in such matters. Indeed, according to Saint-Simon, he 'vastly preferred to let everything fall into disorder...rather than hear disputes debated or, above all, be asked to decide them.' However, as the ultimate authority in such matters he could not always avoid becoming involved and, once he had given a ruling, there was no question of him revising it.

In February 1697 an argument broke out between the Bishop of Orléans and the Duc de La Rochefoucauld after the Bishop complained that Rochefoucauld had usurped his allotted place in the royal chapel. The Bishop protested so vehemently that Louis commented wearily, 'So, Monsieur, this affects you very deeply?' Without hesitation the prelate responded, 'Yes, Sire, this affects me so strongly it will be the death of me.' After considering the matter the King surprised the court by finding in La Rochefoucauld's favour, but after a time the Duc came to regret having antagonised the Bishop, with whom he had previously been friendly. La Rochefoucauld went to the King and said that he was prepared to concede the point but Louis, 'who did not like changing his decisions, much less to see them censured, not only held firm but added that, after what he had ruled, it was his own affair, and no longer that of Monsieur de La Rochefoucauld.' In conclusion he declared 'that if the matter was to be decided between Monsieur d'Orléans and a lackey, he would give the place to the servant rather than him.'[26]

La Bruyère, who wrote a series of pen sketches encapsulating life in Louis XIV's France, was responsible for the aphorism that 'The court does not make one happy; it prevents one from being so elsewhere.' Certainly, even those who were most critical of the institution found it hard to tear themselves away. According to Bishop Bossuet, court life was 'an enchanted brew which intoxicates the most sober, and the majority of those who have tasted it cannot savour anything else.' Having acknowledged that the dealings of people at court were constantly disrupted by 'self-interest, intrigues and faction', the Duc d'Antin (who had the reputation of being the most consummate courtier of his generation) added, 'It has to be admitted, however, that it is difficult to quit that place when one has spent part of one's life there.'[27]

One reason, of course, why people became addicted to life at court was because of the opportunities it afforded for socialising. D'Antin might complain that tender and sincere friendship was virtually unknown at court, but in an assembly where wit was supremely prized no one could complain that the company was dull. Gaiety was pursued with the utmost dedication. In February 1667 the Duc d'Enghien told a friend that there had been so many balls and fêtes at Versailles during recent weeks that everyone had been relieved when Lent started, and he added, 'These sort of things take up as much time as more serious matters, and are extremely tiring.' After a time this frenzied existence palled on some: Mme de Sévigné commented that at court there was 'a constant round of pleasure but not a moment of genuine enjoyment'.[28] She was unusual, however, for the majority of people caught up in this hectic whirl were incapable of making the distinction.

Besides the regular amusements which punctuated the court's social calendar, still more spectacular entertainments were periodically put on for the courtiers. These fêtes lasted several days and were of an opulence and extravagance that left observers gasping. Their object was by no means wholly frivolous, for the King believed they fulfilled a valuable propaganda purpose. He told his son that when foreigners saw that substantial sums were being lavished on 'expenses which can be considered superfluous', it 'made a very advantageous impression on them of magnificence, power, riches and grandeur'. As Théophraste Renaudot wrote in 1671 in the *Gazette de France*, a journal which documented events at court, the King's lavish hospitality 'served...as an example even to the most polished princes of his age', demonstrating that Louis was 'foremost in the fine manner of his entertainments as he was greatest in glory and power'.[29]

To convey this message to foreign monarchs the King took great care that ambassadors stationed abroad received detailed descriptions of events such as the series of entertainments he gave for the entire court over a six-week period in the summer of 1674.[30] Despite the fact that France was currently engaged in a savage European war, these festivities were of an unparalleled magnificence and luxury. They started on 4 July with a feast, which took place in a glade in the gardens of Versailles. As music played softly, guests took refreshments at marble tables that had been set up in leafy enclosures overlooking a specially constructed pond. In the centre of this was a realistic artificial tree cast in bronze, from whose branches water spurted. Jets also gushed from bronze bowls set in the centre of the tables, carefully designed to minimise splashing. Interspersed among the porcelain tubs full of flowers which surrounded the tables were ice figures of various shapes and sizes, a particularly impressive sight in high summer in an age where refrigeration was unknown. Having eaten their fill, the guests returned to the Chateau, where every window was illuminated with candles. A performance of *Alceste* then took place in the marble courtyard, converted for the evening into a sumptuous theatre, decorated with orange trees in tubs on marble pedestals and lit by crystal chandeliers.

Five days later a concert was held in the gardens of the Porcelain Trianon, an enchanting pavilion made of Delft tiles that the King had originally constructed for trysts with Mme de Montespan. On 28 July the King gave a supper for the ladies of the court in the octagonal menagerie and this was followed nine days later by an open-air feast in a specially constructed amphitheatre. The enclosure was bordered by grass terraces, ascending in tiers, and was bedecked with apple, pear and apricot trees in tubs, all laden with fruit out of season. A 'sumptuous collation' was provided, concluding with crystallised fruits and sorbets, with every sort of liqueur being served from crystal carafes. The evening terminated with an opera and a firework display over the canal.

The final offering in this triumphal cycle of entertainments took place ten days later in another grove in the gardens of Versailles. A circular table twenty-four feet in diameter had been set there with the usual array of delicacies. Around its circumference were placed pyramids of fruit, topped with golden balls and linked with festoons of flowers. Afterwards the King and Queen drove by carriage to see Racine's *Iphigenia* performed in the orangery, where a temporary – albeit exceptionally elaborate – theatre had been improvised. To approach this structure they passed down a path bordered with grottoes and fountains, and entered through a marble portico, supported by pillars of lapis lazuli. After the play, the guests again congregated in the gardens to see a firework display and illuminations on the canal.

For this final tableau vast figures, artfully lit, were placed on stone pedestals embellished with bas-relief friezes. On one of these, captives were depicted huddled at the feet of a triumphant Hercules, who was being crowned with flowers and laurels by little children. In his lyrical description of these festivities André Felibien explained that the children 'signified the love of the people who are crowning so many generous exploits' on the part of the King, and that they were binding the captives with garlands of flowers rather than chains to show that 'the domination of the prince who has vanquished them is glorious and sweet'. Whether the subjugated population of the occupied provinces of Flanders would have endorsed this interpretation is questionable. One wonders, too, whether the King's poorer subjects could have shared Felibien's enthusiasm for these sights. Rather, the fact that during the following year the oppressive weight of tax resulted in a series of revolts in various parts of France, tends to support the Abbé Choisy's observation: 'The people were in penury while we talked of nothing but fêtes, ballets and diversions.'[31]

Even Louis XIV could only provide entertainments on such a scale every few years, so the courtiers had to devise other means of passing the time. Throughout the reign gambling was one of the court's principal recreations and enormous sums changed hands daily at the tables. Saint-Simon went so far as to allege that the King 'used this means deliberately and successfully to impoverish everyone ... so that gradually the entire court became dependent on his favours for their very subsistence'. This was, in fact, unfair for the King himself was a man of great self-control who could not understand how others could let themselves be dominated by a passion for gambling. Furthermore, while it was widely believed that the King liked his courtiers to spend lavishly not just on gaming but also on clothes, carriages and household expenses, it does seem that the nobility were apt to use this as an excuse to justify their own extravagance. Certainly the Duc d'Antin recalled being told by false friends on his first coming to court that 'nothing pleased the King more than magnificence' in his courtiers and army officers, and it was only after he had incurred large debts that he discovered the King considered him a spendthrift.[32]

The games played at court in the King's reign were *hoca*, (a precursor of roulette) *reversis*, *basset* and *lansquenet*. The Lieutenant-General of the Paris Police, Nicolas-Gabriel de La Reynie, considered that *hoca* was especially pernicious as it afforded numerous opportunities for cheating. On his insistence in 1671 it was banned in Paris on pain of death but, as he lamented, the fact that it continued to be played at court meant that it was difficult to enforce this prohibition.[33]

Towards the end of the 1670s *basset* replaced *hoca* as the current craze, but its effects were scarcely less destructive. Indeed, it would seem that the reason why the King – who until that point had himself been a keen gamester – virtually ceased gambling was that he was sickened by the extent that people close to him became addicted to it. Not only was his mistress Mme de Montespan a frenzied gambler but in

1678 the King's brother, known as 'Monsieur', lost so much that he had to pawn his best jewels. At the time it was noted that the King appeared 'vexed by these excesses'. He was still more displeased when even the Queen, proverbially pious and dull, succumbed to the fever and one morning lost 20,000 écus after refusing to tear herself away from the tables in order to attend mass, which she normally did without fail. Alarmed at the prospect of her losses if she carried on at the same rate, her husband icily rebuked her, 'Madame, let's just calculate how much that is a year.'[34]

Curiously, it was not considered unacceptable to show wild excitement during gambling sessions. Those who maintained their dignity such as the Comtesse de Soissons or the Marquis de Beaumont ('who lost 10,000 pistoles and fell into poverty without uttering a single word'),[35] were the exceptions. Most people were completely uninhibited when playing: they swore, tore at their hair, pounded the table or stamped their feet, and the Duchesse de Bouillon, sister to the Comtesse de Soissons, would turn on onlookers, accusing them of bringing her bad luck.

At least one man behaved much worse than this. In March 1671 the King was playing cards with his Master of the Wardrobe, the Marquis de Cessac. On being called away, the King asked the Maréchal de Lorges to play his hand for him and, after a bit, the Maréchal came to the conclusion that Cessac was cheating. On investigation it turned out that Cessac had been playing with marked cards and the upshot was that the King banished him from court. Mme de Sévigné heard that Louis had been reluctant to dishonour a man of Cessac's high rank but, since Cessac's winnings in recent weeks amounted to 500,000 écus and since numerous people had been ruined playing with him, the King had little alternative. The Savoyard ambassador was relieved that severe action had been taken, for he was sure that cheating was all too prevalent.[36] However, Cessac's exile did not last very long. In 1674 he was permitted to return to court, only to be disgraced again within a few years during the Affair of the Poisons.

Gambling provided one absorbing occupation for the court's leisured elite, but time was still apt to lie heavy on their hands. As a result they were invariably on the lookout for novel diversions and were not always too particular about how they alleviated boredom. Fortune-tellers and those supposedly gifted with powers of divination offered excitements that many people at court found intriguing. There are several stories of quite eminent people at court being taken in by practitioners who were credited with the ability to conjure up spirits in a glass of water. The King's sister-in-law even claimed that after one such demonstration the Minister of War, Louvois, became convinced that a child brought to court had the gift of second sight. The Abbé Choisy described how, one night at the Comtesse de Soissons's, a little girl correctly predicted the death of the absent Comte de Soissons, and the Duchesse d'Orléans recalled that another fortune-teller conjured up a vision in a glass of water of Mme de Montespan giving birth to one of the King's children, which she described to the lady's niece in great detail.[37]

As Voltaire remarked of this period, 'The former habit of consulting diviners, to have one's horoscope drawn, to seek secret means of making oneself loved, still survived among the people and even in the highest of the kingdom.' Such credulity so angered Bishop Bossuet that he attacked it in one of his sermons: 'Who can guarantee our future?' he demanded scornfully. 'How I laugh at the vanity of these soothsayers who threaten whomsoever they please and fashion for us at will ill-omened years.'[38] It took more than these strictures to purge the court of such beliefs.

At one point Bossuet fulminated that 'these curious sciences ... serve as covers for spells and *malefice*' (i.e. doing harm through sorcery) but, prior to the Affair of the Poisons the King took a more indulgent view of the matter. According to his sister-in-law, Louis 'was not superstitious except in regard to religious matters such as the miracles of the Mother of God and such things' and it is clear that he personally had no faith in astrological predictions. Although at his birth a horoscope had been drawn up for him, he was the first French monarch for many generations who did not retain a court astrologer. Following the appearance of a comet in 1664, the King had commissioned the astronomer Pierre Petit to write a treatise explaining that there was no reason to interpret this as a presage of evil. Sixteen years later another astronomer remarked that he knew better than to speculate about what comets portended, for such 'vain presumptions' were the province of 'the vulgar' and were not acceptable to the King.[39] Nevertheless, until 1680, Louis seems not to have been particularly censorious towards people at court who dabbled in astrology, dismissing it as a harmless pastime which amused women and other silly people.

The King's relaxed attitude to astrology and fortune-telling is demonstrated by his treatment of Giovanni-Battista Primi Visconti, a young Italian who arrived at the French court in 1673. He soon acquired a reputation as a seer because, when an unknown person's handwriting was shown to him, he would make surprisingly accurate pronouncements about their life and character. He was able to do this by a combination of logical deduction, inspired guesswork and careful research into the backgrounds of people at court, but for a time belief in his powers became so fervent that he was 'literally besieged.' The seal was set on his success when he was taken up by the Comtesse de Soissons, and he recalled that there was one day when he counted 223 carriages waiting outside his lodgings. Visconti's clients included the Duchesse de Vitry, Mme de Thianges, the Duchesse de Montpensier, the King's brother the Duc d'Orléans and even the Queen. The King himself never consulted him, but after his cousin Mlle de Montpensier had raved about Visconti's abilities he said lightly to her one day, 'Cousin, there is the wonderful man.' This semi-ironical endorsement raised Visconti's stock still higher.[40]

The Marquise de Vassé was among those who eagerly sought Visconti's services, which was scarcely surprising, for her interest in the future was all-consuming. Visconti was aware that she had already employed two female fortune tellers 'one of whom traced geomancy figures and the other read lines on palms'. She had also engaged an Augustinian friar who claimed to be able to predict the future although, as Visconti drily noted, she had dispensed with his services after he foretold that her husband would outlive her. Later Mme de Vassé would feature peripherally in the Affair of the Poisons because several fortune tellers claimed that she had approached them in hopes of killing her husband, although Mme de Vassé herself never seems to have been questioned about this.[41]

Apart from his skill as a graphologist Visconti also claimed to be able to divine a person's disposition and outlook by studying their facial features. One day a court lady slyly asked him if he could derive the same insights from gazing at a woman's breast, rather than her physiognomy. Visconti instantly responded that doing so would bring 'still better' results, 'and if it was permissible to examine a naked body, I would acquire myself a reputation as a miracle worker.'[42] Visconti was joking but during the Affair of the Poisons it was seriously suggested that court ladies had been prepared to submit themselves to comparable indignities at the hands of much more sinister figures than he.

Visconti himself encountered people at court whose interest in the occult went further than his own. The Comtesse de Soissons's brother, the Duc de Nevers, and the Duc de Brissac told him that they wanted to see the devil but that, 'despite their extensive investigations, their invocations and their expenditures', Satan 'had never satisfied their curiosity'.[43] Later it would be alleged that they were by no means alone in dabbling in such matters.

It was, of course, a paradox that such primitive beliefs could find adherents in a court which prided itself on being the most sophisticated and urbane in the world. Louis XIV's cousin, Mlle de Montpensier, indeed described it as 'the most polished and refined court there has ever been', while it was the judgement of Voltaire that 'Europe owed its good breeding and social sense to Louis XIV's court.' It was only to be expected that French fashions should dominate the continent, but even in matters such as gastronomy a celebrated chef was confident 'that in that...France carries the day...over all other nations as it does in good breeding and a thousand other sufficiently well-known ways'.[44]

According to Voltaire the French court was characterised by a 'singular politeness', taking its tenor in this from the King who was described by one acquaintance as 'the most polite man in his kingdom'. At court the most intricate rules governed everyday social intercourse, which could be a minefield to the uninitiated. For example, it was considered a solecism on the part of a gentleman actually to kiss the hand of any lady below the rank of princess but on being presented to ladies of lesser status it was correct to utter the words 'I kiss your hands.' Those who fell foul of such arcane procedures found themselves mercilessly ridiculed. The unfortunate Marquis de Montbrun discovered this when he made the mistake of boasting that he was good at dancing and then performing gracelessly at a court ball. The other guests began hooting with laughter, making such an uproar that 'nobody has ever endured the like. And so he disappeared immediately after and did not show himself again for a long time.'[45]

The French court instilled in its inhabitants an overwhelming sense of superiority, for it was taken as self-evident that the world of Versailles represented civilisation at its height. The Abbé de Saint-Réal noted wryly, 'Their contempt for anything that is not of the court is unimaginable, and goes to the point of extravagance. There is nothing well said or well done except what is said or done among them.' In his opinion, however, the lustre of the court was largely superficial. He wrote caustically, 'The people of the court...are not all men of intelligence but they are possessed of an admirable politeness that serves them in its stead. They are not all worthy men but they have the air and manner that makes one think them such.'[46]

Certainly their surface polish could not disguise a fundamental lack of kindness and Christian feeling in many courtiers. The journal of the Marquis de Sourches provides an illustration: after suffering a stroke in 1687, Mme de Menesserre kept breaking into inane laughter for no reason, apparently without realising what she was doing. Sourches noted that this afforded the courtiers, who were 'not very charitable by nature', endless opportunities to make cruel jokes at her expense. Such incidents justify La Bruyère's dictum that the court was composed of men who, like diamonds, were 'very hard but highly polished', which led him to the conclusion that 'all this great refinement is nothing other than a vice called falsehood'.[47]

Although great importance was attached to correct behaviour, the courtly code of conduct was much less strict when it came to fundamental morality. La Bruyère commented that at court one saw 'vice reign equally with good breeding' and the curé of Versailles, Hébert, claimed that never before had there been a court 'so given up to every sort of vice'. The German diplomat Ezechiel Spanheim believed that the court of the Sun King was 'the most libertine court in Europe', while another foreign visitor, the Duke of Pastrana, was so amazed by the spectacle which greeted him when he first set eyes on the court that he exclaimed, 'Monsieur, this is a real bordello!'[48]

Primi Visconti was surprised to see that many aristocratic married ladies lived separate existences from their husbands, which he believed was conducive to 'a great liberty of morals'. Even in cases where marriages had not completely broken down, infidelity was rife. The King's German sister-in-law, Madame, stated, 'It is an acknowledged fact that men have affairs and scorn their wives,' and after studying the period Voltaire formed the impression that 'all the married women were permitted to have lovers.' The Savoyard ambassador sounded a note of caution when he told his master that the court was not nearly as promiscuous as scandalmongers claimed, but the force of this disclaimer is undermined by the fact that at other times his despatches provide confirmation that moral standards were poor.[49]

Ladies had to exercise care in committing adultery, for husbands whose wives too blatantly overstepped the bounds of decorum had the right to incarcerate them in a convent. In June 1671 the Minister for Foreign Affairs, Lionne, exercised this prerogative after he caught his notoriously promiscuous wife and their married daughter in bed together, 'with the Comte de Saulx between them'. Lionne himself was no paragon, for he interspersed his labours at the Ministry for Foreign Affairs with bouts of debauchery, but having previously tolerated his wife's misdemeanours he now decided she had gone too far. In the acerbic words of Mme de Sévigné, 'although her husband was accustomed to being cuckolded on his own account', he could not accept that his son-in-law should be exposed to similar humiliation.[50]

Despite the undeniable provocation, Lionne's action caused something of a flurry. Mme de Bouchet told her friend the Comte de

Bussy: 'Today everything is going topsy-turvy; husbands are in revolt and no longer wish to put up with anything from their wives. The poor ladies can no longer make cuckolds of them with impunity.' Bussy, however, replied that she was wrong to think that husbands had ever been more patient, for the real difference was that until recently lovers had been more discreet.[51]

While one has to be guarded about drawing general conclusions from particular cases, numerous examples can be cited of court ladies who were lacking in virtue. Of Cardinal Mazarin's five nieces, only the eldest, the Duchesse de Mercoeur (who died young), had an unblemished reputation. Saint-Simon remarked that it would be hard to decide which of her four sisters was the greatest libertine. The Comte de Bussy's mistress Mme de Montglas was dismissed by one observer as 'not much of a conquest' as she was known to have had so many lovers. The Princesse de Bade's own mother confided to the Savoyard ambassador 'that she was in despair about her daughter's intrigues at court' and that 'she brought her lovers back to the Hôtel de Soissons under her very nose'. After the Duchesse de Villeroy gave Mme de Sévigné's son venereal disease in 1680, Mme de Coulanges remarked that the Duchesse had now infected so many people that it would constitute 'cause for public rejoicing' if she were cured.[52]

The Maréchale de la Ferté and her sister, the Comtesse d'Olonne, were both 'notorious for their love affairs'. Although the Maréchale's husband was a famously 'hot-tempered man, he was perpetually gulled by her, or else he put up an excellent show of so being'. The Maréchale not only had numerous aristocratic lovers such as the Duc de Longueville (by whom she had a son) but, according to a scurrilous novel entitled *La France Galante*, she also had an affair with a Basque acrobat. He found her so insatiable that he declared it would be less tiring to perform all day long than to spend an hour with her. Her daughter-in-law, the Duchesse de la Ferté, was equally libidinous. One person later suggested that the Maréchale had deliberately chosen her as a bride for her son in the hope that the younger woman's appalling conduct would distract attention from her own sins.[53]

Some court ladies were so disreputable that women of good character shunned them, but lack of virtue proved no bar to preferment at court. After Mme Dufresnoy, mistress of the Minister of War, Louvois, was made a lady-in-waiting to the Queen, the Marquis de La Fare declared that this was indicative of 'the age's prostitution'. Voltaire observed of this appointment that 'in thus favouring his ministers' inclinations the King hoped to vindicate his own'.[54]

Despite the fact that sodomy was a capital offence, homosexuality was thought to be widely practised at court. Some people were sure this accounted for the growing number of anal fistula and haemorrhoid cases though others, it is true, blamed the rise on rich food and more comfortable upholstery in coaches. On hearing of an outrage perpetrated by a homosexual coterie, the Comte de Bussy commented, 'Our fathers were no more chaste than us, but they confined themselves to natural forms of debauchery; nowadays vices are embellished and refined.' A novel entitled *La France Devenue Italienne* (sodomy was known as 'the Italian vice') satirised the court for being infested with homosexuality. Its anonymous author blamed women for the development, asserting that the reason why homosexual debauchery 'reigned there more than anywhere in the world', was that 'the facility of all the ladies had rendered their charms... contemptible'.[55]

Throughout his life the King evinced what Saint-Simon described as 'a just but singular horror for all inhabitants of Sodom.' Nevertheless, however much he may have wanted to eradicate homosexuality at court, he was precluded from effective action because his own brother, Monsieur, was a notorious pederast. This flamboyant figure, who even went into battle heavily bejewelled and wearing make-up, took the Chevalier de Lorraine as his favourite. In early 1670 the King was furious when Monsieur demanded that he confer the revenues of two abbeys on the Chevalier. The King objected that Lorraine 'led too libertine a life to possess benefices' and let it be known that he believed that the Chevalier had committed 'the infamous crime of sodomy with the Comte de Guiche and even with men who had been burnt for that crime in the [Place de] Grève'. When Monsieur protested, the Chevalier was arrested and exiled, though within two years the King relented and permitted his return. Monsieur himself remained incorrigible. Primi Visconti heard that when in the company of the Duc de Créqui, the Marquis de La Vallière and the Marquis d'Effiat, 'they talked about young men like a group of lovers comparing the charms of young ladies.'[56]

The monarch at the centre of the court was a truly remarkable individual. Louis XIV had inherited the crown in 1643 when he was four years old. The early years of his reign had been troubled by a period of aristocratic insubordination and civil unrest known as the Fronde, but once this had been quelled the royal authority could hardly have been more comprehensively reasserted. By the time the King entered his forties his power was awesome and Primi Visconti was guilty of only slight hyperbole when he wrote, 'Both within and without the realm all were submissive to him. He only had to desire something to have it. Everything, down to the weather, favoured him... Besides this, he had money, glory and, above all, fine health; in short, he lacked nothing but immortality.' Somewhat surprisingly, however, this shrewd observer qualified this by saying that he did not envy the King 'for, in spite of all this, I am sure he was not happy'.[57]

In some ways this would appear a curious statement, for the King himself left testimonials that he found his life pleasurable and fulfilling. In his memoir, *Reflections on the Calling of a King*, he told his son that, providing one was up to the job, theirs was a 'grand, noble and delicious' occupation. Elsewhere he vividly described his exhilaration when he first immersed himself in royal business: 'I could almost feel my spirits and my courage rising...I discovered something new about myself and joyfully wondered how I could have ignored it so long...I knew then that I was King and born for it.'[58]

Saint-Simon noted that the King 'had a natural bent towards details', and worked extremely hard. He seemingly coped admirably with the pressure. After spending hours in council he amazed people by the apparent ease with which he threw off the cares of government and gave himself over to pleasure. Naturally, however, there were times when he found his work stressful. Even while enthusing to the Dauphin about the satisfactions his position could afford, the King acknowledged 'it is not exempt from troubles, fatigues and anxieties.' He even noted that on occasion uncertainty could induce feelings of despair. In private it seems that he intermittently succumbed to depression. A casual mistress of the King's, Mlle des Oeillets, related that, when with her, the King did not disguise that he 'had his troubles...Sometimes he sat for whole hours by the fire, very pensive and heaving sighs.' Her testimony could perhaps be discounted were it not for the fact that, much later in the reign, Louis's morganatic wife, Mme de Maintenon, said much the same thing. She told a confidante that it fell to her to soothe his 'griefs...his melancholy and his vapours; sometimes he is seized by sobs which he cannot master.'[59]

When France was experiencing difficulties during the Dutch War there were times when Louis fell prey to what might have been psychosomatic illnesses. In 1673 he was tormented by insomnia, and such sleep as he did have was disturbed by 'dreams, cries and agitations'. For the past four or five years he had also suffered from sporadic fits of 'the vapours', a new ailment, which became fashionable at court after the King was diagnosed as a victim. This vague term encompassed a wide series of disorders, which could take the form of headaches, digestive problems and general malaise, 'which constricts the heart and fogs the mind'. The royal physicians prescribed purgative broths and emollient enemas and, on the whole, these seemed to contain the problem, although in January 1675 the King was assailed by 'a violent vapour which made his head spin'. This soon passed but in late September the complaint returned in a much fiercer form. The King was plagued by severe headaches, shivering, hot flushes, shortness of breath, lack of appetite, depression, yawning fits, a sensation of weakness in the legs and 'dryness of stomach'. He did not have a fever, but when he managed to sleep he often woke drenched in sweat. He complained of having a permanently bitter taste in his mouth and the doctors noted that his tongue was heavily coated. Once again d'Aquin prescribed purgative broths and enemas, and insisted that the King must be bled, despite the fact that Louis maintained that this remedy did not agree with him.[60]

After six weeks the crisis passed. D'Aquin had no doubts as to what had caused the problem: he declared that these vapours originated from a melancholic humour in the spleen, as was shown by the fact that they were accompanied by depression and a desire for solitude. He explained that, from the spleen, 'They slide through the arteries to the heart and lungs, where they excite palpitations and anxieties ... Rising from there to the brain, they cause giddiness and head spinning by agitating the spirits of the optical nerves.' D'Aquin also believed that overwork had contributed to the attack, which had been exacerbated by the King's blood being overheated by 'the continual fatigues of war.'[61]

However, other explanations can be put forward for the King's ill health at this time. It is possible that the medical treatment he received actually undermined his constitution. Certainly, some people at court thought that Dr Vallot, who died in 1672, made the King take much too strong purgatives. In December 1673 there were concerns that d'Aquin was also overdosing him with laxatives. As d'Aquin indignantly noted, 'The natural goodness of the courtiers, and their remarkable capacity in all things, particularly medicine, made them say many things against this remedy, of which the King took little notice, and shut them up by saying that he found himself very well for it.'[62]

It is also possible that the King occasionally took substances which no doctor had prescribed and which had an adverse effect on him. Saint-Simon claimed that the reason why the King took 'a highly fashionable bath attendant of Paris' named Quentin Vienne into his service as a valet was that Vienne had supplied Louis with 'various drugs reputed to give opportunities of greater [sexual] satisfaction'.[63] Furthermore, during the Affair of the Poisons it was suggested that around this time the King's mistress had been feeding him love philtres, which she obtained illicitly. This gave rise to suspicions that the curious symptoms suffered by the King in 1675 had been caused by cantharides poisoning.

It was not just the conduct of state affairs that kept the King under pressure for, as he himself warned his son, 'Our work is sometimes less difficult than our amusements.' Louis could not but be acutely aware that there were very few moments in the day when he could escape the court's scrutiny and he regarded it as his duty to maintain an impeccably regal aura at all times. Primi Visconti observed that though the King occasionally appeared relaxed in private, he would instinctively straighten his bearing and assume a more dignified expression if he thought there was any chance he could be glimpsed through an open door. Courtiers were in attendance even as he dressed in the mornings or sat on the close stool, and a large crowd likewise watched him eat his dinner or retire to bed. Since the King knew he was the cynosure of all eyes his every gesture and look were carefully weighed and carried out with an immaculate poise which so impressed the Abbé Choisy that he declared it was no flattery to describe him as 'great even in the slightest things.' Even Saint-Simon, often so critical of the King, wrote admiringly of 'his polite chivalrous manner which he ... knew so well how to combine with stateliness and propriety'.[64]

However, the paradox was that although the King was in a sense on permanent display, his was in many ways a very isolated existence. Saint-Simon noted, 'The awe inspired by his appearance was such that wherever he might be his presence imposed silence and a degree of fear', and though one of Louis's generals claimed that he had the knack of putting people at their ease, it is clear that even quite experienced courtiers could be overcome by shyness in his company. The playwright Racine berated himself for the way he became tongue-tied in the royal presence, despite the fact that he saw the King quite often. In 1685 the wit and presence of mind of Mme de Sévigné's daughter counted for nothing when she was presented to the King, for she was so 'totally disconcerted by that awesome majesty of his' that she quite forgot everything she had intended to say.[65]

The King himself was generally somewhat taciturn, although he knew how to be a delightful conversationalist. The diplomat Ezechiel Spanheim said that the King 'spoke little but to the point' and that in his private conversation he contrived to blend majesty and affability in a manner that was neither too haughty nor informal. Mme de Maintenon's niece, Mme de Caylus, said that in a few well-chosen words the King could wrap up almost any subject that arose. When he talked seriously, people were impressed by his knowledge and charmed by the way he displayed it. When he discoursed in a lighter vein, it was 'with infinite grace, with a noble and subtle turn of phrase which I have never known in anyone but him'. His sister-in-law the Duchesse d'Orléans said he could be 'truly agreeable company' while Saint-Simon conceded, 'No man of fashion could tell a tale or set a scene better than he, yet his most casual speeches were never lacking in natural and conscious majesty.'[66]

Though the King was naturally drawn towards witty people, and though he was perfectly capable of acquitting himself well in such company, he knew he had to be exceptionally guarded in his social dealings. Louis was well aware of the harm that could be caused by apparently inconsequential remarks and when his son was very young he impressed on him the overriding importance of circumspection. 'It is not merely in important negotiations that princes must watch what they say; this is also true of their most ordinary and intimate conversations,' he cautioned.

> Unpleasant as this restraint may be it is absolutely necessary for those in our position to speak of nothing lightly ... Things that would be meaningless in the mouth of a private individual often become important when spoken by a prince. He cannot show the slightest disdain towards anyone without wounding him to the heart ... One of the best solutions for this is to do more listening than talking, because it is very hard to talk a great deal without saying too much. Even a pleasant conversation about seemingly unimportant things will sometimes lead to the most hidden ones ... Little harm has ever come from not having said enough ... but infinite misfortunes have resulted from having said too much.[67]

The King's reserve towards his courtiers was not dictated solely by a fear of causing offence, but also because he believed it essential to the preservation of his mystique. The Comte de Bussy declared, 'By nature the King loves society, but he holds himself back out of policy.' He explained that the King feared the French tendency to take advantage of attempts at familiarity, leading inevitably to their respecting him less. Comments by the King support this interpretation. He warned his son, 'Those who are closest to the Prince, being the first to know his weakness ... are also the first to abuse it.' When his grandson was setting out to assume the Spanish Crown, Louis issued the blunt prohibition, 'Never have an attachment for anybody.'[68]

The King's aloofness was doubtless encouraged by the fact that when he did permit himself to form close bonds with the Marquis de Vardes and the Duc de Lauzun, these two men let him down badly. After they proved unworthy of his affection, the King was said to have commented bitterly that 'he had looked for friends and found only intriguers'. Both men were punished harshly by Louis, whose anger at such misdemeanours was demonstrated by his remark to his son that 'my rebel subjects when they have had the audacity to take up arms against me have perhaps provoked me to less indignation than those who, while remaining close to me paid me more respect with greater assiduity than all the rest, when I was well aware that they were betraying me and had no true respect for me or true affection of the heart.'[69]

The King was so inscrutable that it was impossible for courtiers to tell from his exterior whether or not things were going well for him. During the Dutch war Primi Visconti noted, 'The King conducts himself in such a way that one does not know when he is victorious or when he loses. Since the start of his reign he has never been seen to be angry and he has never once sworn.' The curé of Versailles, Hébert, confirmed this when he praised the King's 'perfect equanimity' which gave no indication 'whether his affairs had succeeded or if they had had some disappointing outcome'. In 1687 it was considered extraordinary when the King emerged red-faced and angry from a meeting with the Papal Nuncio, and it was clear that something exceptional had occurred to put 'the most self-possessed prince in the world' so out of countenance.[70]

The King had certainly followed the advice of his late godfather, Cardinal Mazarin, to 'cultivate that kingly quality of dissimulation which nature has bestowed so lavishly upon you'. He was indeed so skilled at disguising his true feelings that courtiers had no way of knowing how they stood with him. The Marquis de Sourches commented, 'The King was the most difficult man in the world to know, often making much of people in public when he was dissatisfied with them,' and the result was that courtiers sometimes failed to realise they had displeased him until they fell irrevocably from favour. In 1693, for example, the court was amazed when the King suddenly dismissed his chief physician, d'Aquin, who until then had been regarded as 'the best courtier ever' and thought to possess 'infinite credit with his master'. Saint-Simon claimed that only the night before, 'the King had never talked so much to d'Aquin as at his supper...and had never seemed more kindly disposed to him.'[71] During the Affair of the Poisons there were other instances when the King behaved similarly. In particular, he continued to treat the Maréchal de Luxembourg with every appearance of cordiality until the very moment when he was ordered to prison on suspicion of sorcery and poisoning.

The King might take care that his courtiers could never tell what he was thinking but, conversely, he thought it desirable that they could keep little hidden from him. Colbert noted, 'All things, great and small, important and trifling, are equally well known to this prince, who never misses an opportunity to make himself acquainted with everything.' 'He wants to know everything,' wrote Primi Visconti, noting that Louis was not just tireless in collecting information from ministers, Presidents of *Parlement* and judges but also from his mistresses, who were expected to brief him on all the love affairs going on at court. Visconti concluded, 'In any one day little happens of which he is ignorant and there are few people whose reputation and habits he does not know. He has a perspicacious eye and knows the inmost life of everyone.'[72]

According to Saint-Simon, 'The King was even more interested in gossip than people imagined, although he was known to be vastly inquisitive,'[73] He claimed that Louis employed his palace guards to spy on courtiers and certainly private letters were intercepted by the postal service. If they contained anything of interest they were brought to the King's attention.

Far from being ashamed of such practices the King believed it essential that he remain abreast of even comparatively insignificant developments at court. He told his son that no ruler could underestimate the importance of 'keeping an eye on the whole earth ... of being informed of an infinite number of things that we are presumed to ignore, of seeing around us what is hidden from us with the greatest care, of discovering the most remote ideas and the most hidden interests of our courtiers.' He did not hide that he considered this one of his more 'pleasant duties', confiding with endearing honesty, 'I don't know, finally, what other pleasures we would not abandon for this one for the sake of curiosity alone.'[74] Nearly twenty years after writing this the King would be shaken to discover that despite the energy he devoted to keeping his courtiers under surveillance large numbers had engaged in dubious activities without his knowledge.

At times the fawning and sycophancy surrounding the King reached absurd levels. Once, when the Abbé de Polignac was walking with the King in the garden of Marly, Louis's private retreat near Versailles, it started to rain and the King expressed concern that the Abbé's cassock afforded him little protection. 'Sire, that makes no difference, the rain is not wet at Marly,' the Abbé simpered. The Duc d'Uzès professed an equally strong conviction that the forces of nature were in thrall to the King. When Louis asked him on what day his wife's baby was expected, he answered, 'Sire, the day it pleases your Majesty.' The Duc de Richelieu was scarcely less effusive, declaring on one occasion, 'I would rather die than go two months without seeing the King.'[75]

The King recognised the dangers of excessive flattery and advised his grandson to employ men who dared to tell him unpalatable truths, rather than seeking always to please. To his son he claimed that he sometimes tested his courtiers 'by encouraging them to praise me even for things that I believed I had done badly, only to reproach them for it immediately.' There is an anecdote of Primi Visconti that supports this: he relates that after biting into a nasty pear, the King teased 'the perfect courtier', the Maréchal de Gramont, by exclaiming, 'What a delicious fruit! Taste it, Monsieur le Maréchal!' The Maréchal fell into the trap, proclaiming it 'an exquisite fruit', whereupon the King burst out laughing and mischievously offered the pear to other courtiers for their appraisal.[76]

However, the King was not always so good at detecting sycophancy. One day he was playing backgammon when he made a move that might have been against the rules. The onlookers declined to settle the matter so, when the Comte de Gramont entered, the King appealed to him to adjudicate. Without hesitation Gramont ruled against the King, prompting Louis to demand how he could be so sure without knowing all the circumstances. The King was somewhat nettled when Gramont told him that it must have been absolutely clear that he was in the wrong, for otherwise the courtiers would have unanimously taken his side.[77]

All this meant that although the King was the object of extravagant adulation, he could never be truly confident that his nobility loved him. There was no doubt that he enjoyed their respect – Primi Visconti wrote, 'They are as afraid of the King as schoolboys of their master' – but the extent of their affection for him was debatable. Having noted that the courtiers were in a state of utter subjection to the King, the German Ezechiel Spanheim added, 'There are not many of them, perhaps, whose acclamations and homage are truly sincere and spring as much from heartfelt sentiments as from self-interest or fear. Without doubt respect has a greater part in it than inclination.'[78]

The King did not have a stronger bond with his poorer subjects, making little attempt to endear himself to the public. By the 1670s he rarely appeared in Paris and his attitude to his capital was one of marked ambivalence. He took satisfaction in being the ruler of one of the world's great cities, and lavished care and expense on urban improvement projects. But while he declared that he wanted 'to do for Paris what Augustus did for Rome', he had no love for the city and the Marquis de Sourches actually suggested that he had 'an extreme aversion' for it. In 1670 the Savoyard ambassador reported that the mere prospect of spending some time in Paris was enough to put the King in a bad mood; by 1687 it excited comment if Louis even travelled through the city, rather than following his usual practice of making a detour in order to avoid it.[79]

The King's distaste for his capital stemmed largely from his love of fresh air and outdoor pursuits, which were denied him in Paris, but he also did not forget that the capital had been disloyal to the Crown during the civil unrest that had occurred during his youth. His sensitivity on such matters is illustrated by the comments he made for the benefit of his son following the 1666 Great Fire of London. He observed that since London had sided against King Charles I during the English Civil War it might seem an obvious assumption that it was 'not a great misfortune' for the English monarchy 'to witness the ruin of a city' that had in the past been a source of opposition. However, while conceding that 'heavily populated cities have had their drawbacks and the very one in question was a ghastly case in point', he grudgingly concluded that the destruction of such an asset could not, on balance, be considered advantageous.[80] The Affair of the Poisons would provide the King with fresh evidence of the unruly spirit of Paris, for it showed that the city possessed a subversive subculture entirely independent of royal control. This only intensified the King's feelings of alienation and mistrust.

According to the Savoyard ambassador, the King had always believed there was a real possibility that he might meet a violent end and this nervousness was reflected in the strict security precautions which surrounded him at all times. The elaborate ritual that governed the serving of the King's food was partly designed to protect him from poisoners. When the King ate his midday meal, a table was set up near his own where the food was tasted before being offered to him. His Maître d'hôtel and *écuyer* also rubbed small pieces of bread on his napkin, plates and cutlery (not forgetting the royal toothpick), and then ate the bread to see if it had been contaminated by poison.[81]

When the King went hunting strict measures were employed to stave off assassination attempts. Several of the royal hunting forests were surrounded by walls and had guards posted at every gate. When the King wanted to use other areas of woodland for sporting pursuits, the local inhabitants were often denied access. The Marquis de Sourches suspected that such precautions were excessive, and that the King's guards deliberately misrepresented the dangers that threatened him in order to heighten Louis's dependence on them and to advance their own careers. Primi Visconti took the same view, complaining that the King's Captain of the Guard, the Duc de Noailles, kept his master in a state of perpetual agitation by claiming that 'he saw sinister figures everywhere'. Far from condemning Noailles as an alarmist, the King was annoyed that his other Captain of the Guard, the Duc de Rochefort, had a much more relaxed attitude. He upbraided Rochefort and was not reassured when the latter cheerfully replied,

'Fear not, Sire! Your subjects are good. The wicked ones are those who give you bad ideas.' When the Duc de Noailles's son succeeded his father as Captain of the Guard, he too believed that the dangers facing the King should not be exaggerated, telling Louis that it merely gave rise to the unfortunate impression that he was highly vulnerable. To this the King retorted frostily, 'Such should be the belief of those who guard me.'[82]

At various times in the reign plots against the King's life were uncovered, although it is difficult to gauge how much of a genuine threat they represented. In the summer of 1669 there was understandable concern when the Duke of York (brother of King Charles II of England) sent warning that an individual named Le Roux, Sieur de Marcilly had been overheard uttering threats against Louis XIV. Le Roux was shadowed when he left England and seized by French agents in Switzerland. He was taken to the Bastille where he tried to commit suicide by cutting off his own genitals but, amazingly, he survived long enough to receive a summary trial. Having been condemned to be broken on the wheel, he shouted such horrible imprecations against the King on the scaffold that he was gagged before being put to death. When informed, the King merely commented coolly, 'Monsieur le Lieutenant Criminel, see how we are rid of a wicked man.'[83]

In the spring of 1673 the Savoyard diplomat Saint-Maurice learned that three Dutchmen had been arrested after the King received a warning that they were conspiring against his life. It was reported that one of the trio had been found in possession of a flick knife, but when Saint-Maurice heard that they were being interrogated by the Minister of War, Louvois, he became sceptical. Suspecting that Louvois was manipulating the affair for his own ends, he noted sagely that such ploys were often used 'to envenom minds, prevent peace and make war more bloodthirsty'.[84]

Before the Affair of the Poisons there were also occasional references to plots to poison the King but it is even more difficult to tell if there was any substance to such stories. In 1664 a Burgundian was arrested after it was allegedly discovered that he had planned to poison Louis by feeding toxic substances to chickens, which he then sold to the royal kitchens for the King's consumption. In October 1672 Saint-Maurice reported that the sudden death of a royal cupbearer had caused panic for, when his body was searched, poison was found in his pocket. Unfortunately, after writing this, Saint-Maurice made no further mention of the incident, so there is no way of knowing whether there was legitimate cause for concern.[85]

Since the King's grandfather, Henri IV, and the latter's immediate predecessor, Henri III, had both been assassinated by solitary fanatics, it was understandable that there were fears that Louis himself might fall victim to a similar attack. However, the harsh treatment meted out to individuals who merely voiced sentiments hostile to the King excited some criticism. In July 1668 a woman whose son had been killed in a fall during construction work at Versailles presented the King with a blank petition and then started shrieking abuse. Startled, the King asked her if she was addressing him; when she said yes she was seized and condemned to be whipped 'with extreme rigour'. The senior judge, Olivier d'Ormesson, recorded, 'Many people have found fault with this severe punishment', for it was clear that the woman had been unhinged by grief. A few days later a man aged about sixty was arrested for having uttered 'similar extravagances', albeit not in the presence of the King. He had burst out that Louis was a tyrant and that France needed virtuous men like Ravaillac (the assassin of Henri IV) who could set matters right. He was sentenced to having his tongue cut out and then to serve in the galleys for the remainder of his life. This caused murmurs of disapproval for, though the customary punishment for blasphemers was to have a hole bored in their tongue, cutting it out altogether was not an established penalty. It was felt that in their eagerness to please the King the Grand Provost and his colleagues in the criminal courts had resorted to arbitrary measures.[86]

The King never managed to form a deep emotional bond with his Spanish consort, Queen Marie-Thérèse, whom he had married when he was twenty-one. Her appearance was not the problem: at the time of the marriage it was widely agreed that she was very pretty, although her blond hair and fine complexion were somewhat marred by a dumpy figure and poor teeth. Unfortunately, all at court, starting with the King, quickly concluded that she was extremely boring. It did not help that she never perfectly mastered French, pronouncing certain words with such a strong Spanish accent that it made purists wince. Her confessor was also partly to blame for he insisted that she shut herself away for large parts of the day to worship in her oratory. All too often she could be heard weeping and groaning as she prayed, and though the King might with justice have reflected that his own behaviour perhaps contributed to her grief, these pious excesses were held to have lessened his affection for her.[87]

In fact, it seems that the Queen's reputation for dullness was not wholly merited. Mlle de Montpensier sometimes quotes examples of her self-deprecating humour and notes that, if people at court had not been so dismissive, they would have discovered that she could be quite amusing. The Marquis de Saint-Maurice also recorded that she was much more intelligent than was commonly allowed and declared it unfair that her attributes went unnoticed.[88] As it was, however, the court treated her with the outward respect that the King desired, but otherwise took little notice of her.

The poor Queen could not even console herself with the pleasures of motherhood. Though she bore the King six children in all, only her firstborn, the Dauphin, survived to adulthood. Of the others the majority died shortly after birth, though Princess Marie-Thérèse lived five years, dying in 1672, and the Duc d'Anjou was aged three when he died in 1671.

As Mme de Caylus remarked, it was the Queen's misfortune that the King seemed to love all women save his own wife. Saint-Maurice declared that this was not just because they afforded him physical pleasure but also because Louis genuinely enjoyed their company. They in turn found him extremely attractive for, in the words of Mme de Caylus, the King was endowed with 'every pleasing quality.' Quite apart from his charisma and charm he was handsome, with fine legs and a well-modulated voice, and Saint-Simon had no doubt that 'had he been born into private life he would still have ... caused innumerable broken hearts'. Obviously, however, the real secret of his appeal lay elsewhere and there were few court ladies who could honestly say that they would not welcome his advances. Primi Visconti, for one, was quite sure that 'there is not one lady of quality who does not cherish the ambition of becoming the King's mistress.'[89]

With so many women vying for the same goal, the atmosphere at court sometimes became unpleasant. For example, in March 1667, when it was widely suspected that the King was tiring of his mistress, Louise de La Vallière, the Duc d'Enghien reported, 'There have been a thousand intrigues at Versailles.' He explained that while it was hard to make sense of the quarrels that had broken out between various ladies, the fundamental problem was that 'all are extremely jealous of Mlle de La Vallière and there are very few of them who do not feel great envy of her ... Being thus inclined it does not require much to exasperate them.'[90]

But it was not just the ladies who thought that a love affair with the King would be a rewarding experience. Primi Visconti declared, 'The worst thing is that their families, fathers, mothers and even certain husbands would take pride in it.' He insisted that numerous women, both married and single, had stated that, if they allowed themselves to be loved by the King, they would not be wronging their husbands and fathers, or even God himself. Visconti concluded, 'One must thus have some indulgence for the King if he falls in error, for he is surrounded by so many devils, intent on tempting him.'[91]

It is true that such complaisance on the part of husbands or family members was not universal, as the King found out to his cost. M. de Montespan objected strongly to his wife's liaison with the King and her brother, the Duc de Vivonne, was also said to disapprove, though his opposition was more muted. There are, however, plenty of examples to support Visconti's claims. The brother of the King's first acknowledged mistress, Louise de La Vallière, showed his enthusiasm for her association when he danced in a court ballet in 1664. His costume was adorned with a device depicting a phoenix illuminated by the sun (already recognised as the King's emblem) and bearing the motto 'It is fortunate to be scorched by such a fire.'[92] He was rewarded for his endorsement of the relationship when the King arranged for him to marry a rich heiress and then awarded him the command of the Dauphin's light horse.

In 1671 the King was thought to be attracted to Mlle de Grancey, a young lady who had recently arrived at court. At once her uncle, the Marquis de Villarceaux, volunteered his services as a pander. He told the King that if he found his niece appealing, 'he begged him to make use of him; that the affair would go better in his hands than in others'. The King was still too much in love with Mme de Montespan to avail himself of this offer, but even he was somewhat shocked by the proposal. He burst out laughing and said, 'Villarceaux, you and I are too old to pounce on young ladies of fifteen.'[93]

Behaviour of this sort would have made it easier for the King to believe certain allegations that were made during the Affair of the Poisons. He was told that the husband of the Vicomtesse de Polignac had been aware that she had been engaging in black magic in hopes of making the King fall in love with her. Far from trying to stop her, M. de Polignac had considered this an excellent plan, although perhaps he would have been less enthusiastic had he realised that his wife was also casting spells designed to bring about his death.[94]

Between 1661–80 the King always had a maîtresse-en-titre but he slept with many other women during those years. He had a voracious sexual appetite so it is impossible to estimate the total number of partners. The ladies whom he was said to have bedded included the Princesse de Monaco, the Comtesse de Gramont, Mme de Soubise, Mlle de Theobon, Mme de Roquelaure, Mlle des Oeillets and Mme de Ludres. Almost certainly he had in addition numerous casual encounters. The King's sister-in-law recalled, 'Often he took gallantry to the point of debauchery. Nothing came amiss to him as long as it was female –

peasants, gardeners' daughters, ladies of quality. They need only pretend to be in love with him.' According to her, 'He has slept with women he didn't know at all' and the Marquis de Saint-Maurice provides further insights on his promiscuity. Having informed the Duke of Savoy that the King had recently slept with Mme de Saint-Martin he confided, 'He uses those sort of women like post horses, that one mounts once and never sees again.'[95]

Some people believed there was little emotional depth even in the King's more lengthy attachments. Mme de Caylus thought that, though the King had many lovable qualities, he was not himself capable of real love. The Comte de Bussy was sure the King's relationship with both Louise de La Vallière and Mme de Montespan was driven primarily by lust. He took the view that 'What he felt for them was not passion, it was debauchery, and I think a good deal of habit also came into it. Those ladies are not, properly speaking, mistresses; they are the sort of women with whom their masters sleep.'[96]

The Queen was obliged to tolerate her husband's infidelities. She was not only required to receive the royal mistresses at court but on occasion had to visit them, and in due course their children by the King were paraded before her. On the whole she accepted the situation with what the Marquis de Saint-Maurice considered to be exemplary patience. He told the Duke of Savoy that though she despised the royal mistresses for their lack of virtue, she felt no hatred or jealousy. The most she permitted herself was to make occasional 'gallant little jokes' at their expense, 'which never cause offence'.[97]

If the Queen dared not voice any complaints about her husband's conduct, it was hardly to be expected that the courtiers would be more critical. The sole exception was the Duc de Mazarin, who in 1664 secured a private audience with the King and informed him that his infidelity with Louise de La Vallière was scandalising all France. The King had little difficulty ignoring the opinions of a man who was himself a notorious cuckold and whose eccentricities included protecting the milkmaids on his estate from impure thoughts by forbidding them to touch cows' udders, and believing that he was a tulip, who must be regularly watered and exposed to the sun. When the Duc had had his say the King demanded forcefully, 'Have you finished?' Then, tapping his forehead meaningfully, he told him, 'I have known for some time there's something wrong there.' When news of this exchange became known everyone at court agreed that the Duc had 'neither the authority nor the character' to raise such matters with the King. Mazarin found himself so mocked and ostracised that he had to withdraw from court.[98]

However, while there was little open criticism of the King's philandering, this does not necessarily mean it was viewed with universal approval. It has been suggested that if one compares the scurrilous rhymes circulated in the reign of Henri IV, Louis XIV's grandfather, with those current in Louis's day, it shows that, whereas the public had an amused tolerance for Henri's infidelities, the attitude towards Louis's extramarital activities was much more censorious. In 1668 the Marquis de Saint-Maurice wrote that the life the King led with his mistresses aroused much hostility against him, though he attributed this to the French tendency to 'complain about everything'. When Louis's younger son, the Duc d'Anjou, died in July 1671, Saint-Maurice further claimed that the public regarded this as divine chastisement on the King for his sins and that there was much murmuring against the fact that he continued to lead an immoral life.[99]

The King himself addressed the subject of his adultery in the *Memoirs*, which he compiled in annual instalments for his son when the latter was still a young child. He conceded that, ideally, 'Princes should always be a perfect model of virtue', particularly since their moral lapses could never be long concealed. However, 'if we should fall in spite of ourselves', the unfortunate consequences could be limited by taking two precautions. The first was to ensure that 'the time we devote to our love never be taken away from our affairs.' The second, and 'most difficult to put into practice', was to take care that 'we remain masters of our mind, that we keep the affections of a lover separate from the decisions of a sovereign and that the beauty who gives us pleasure never has the liberty to speak of our affairs or our servants.' He cautioned his son, 'Once you give a woman the liberty to speak to you of important things they are bound to make us fail.' Not only was 'no secret … safe with them', but their judgement was disastrously flawed, with 'the weakness of their nature often making them prefer trifling interests to more solid considerations.'[100]

Reading this passage, one could argue that the King believed his sins of the flesh were not truly pernicious and that, provided he observed the conditions he imposed on himself, indulging his desires was an excusable weakness. It would be wrong, however, to conclude that Louis's sexual transgressions left him untroubled by guilt, for in his own way he was a devout Catholic. It is true that the King's German sister-in-law derided him for being 'incredibly simple with regard to religious matters'. She claimed that he was ignorant of scripture and certainly he was not interested in theological debate, saying knowledge of such matters was not necessary for salvation. He arguably attached excessive importance to outward observance, attending mass every day and being punctilious about fasts, but devoting less time to private prayer and self-scrutiny. It was this which led one Bishop to complain in an anonymous letter of criticism (which the King almost certainly never saw) that Louis's religion consisted 'merely of superstitions' and 'little superficial practices'. Nevertheless, if the faith which his mother had inculcated in Louis as a child was based on instinct rather than reason, and if his devotion was, as Ezechiel Spanheim put it, 'blind... or at least scarcely enlightened', it was also central to his existence.[101]

In this he differed from many people at court who made a show of piety but were not true believers. Primi Visconti noted, 'Everyone here professes devotion, particularly the women, but all it consists of is observing the sins of others... People only become religious for worldly ends, the men for their advancement or following a disgrace, the women to show their discretion. From church one sees them returning very quickly to balls or places of ill repute.'[102]

It was indeed arguable that life at court could not be reconciled with true spirituality. When the Maréchal de Bellefonds withdrew from court in disgrace in 1674, the Abbot of La Trappe wrote to him, 'I should not be speaking to you sincerely if I said the news grieves me, being convinced as I am that God is neither known nor served in the world you are leaving.' The Abbot believed 'that to be occupied and employed in it offers as many obstacles and impediments to your salvation as a life of retreat offers means and facilities for achieving it' and he added that removing oneself from court was comparable to 'escaping from the midst of a shipwreck'.[103]

Some individuals were not worried that a court existence conflicted with the principles of true religion, preferring to believe that the Almighty himself subscribed to the values which prevailed there. When the famously dissolute Chevalier de Savoie died suddenly without receiving extreme unction, Mme de Meilleraye refused to accept that this inevitably meant that his soul was forfeit. Instead, she insisted, 'It is my considered opinion that where a man of that birth is concerned, God would think twice about damning him.'[104]

This was an error into which the King could never have fallen. His faith may have been unsubtle, but it was robust and he regarded himself as subject to God. Since he did not believe he was exempt from divine retribution, he was uncomfortably aware that indulging his lust carried a risk of eternal damnation.

In his twenties the prospect seemed so remote that for most of the time the King had little difficulty shrugging off this unpalatable thought. At Whitsun 1664, when the King's love for Louise de La Vallière was at its height, he was not only prepared to forgo the consolations of religion rather than renounce his mistress, but he scoffed at his brother, who apparently saw no contradiction in interspersing his bouts of sodomy with receiving the sacrament. Scornfully he told Monsieur that 'he would not play the hypocrite like him, who went to confession because the Queen Mother wished it.'[105]

However, he could not always sustain this brazen façade, for shortly after this he broke down when his mother upbraided him for his adultery. While he remained clear that, as yet, he lacked the strength to forsake the pleasures of the flesh, his answer showed that he was not untroubled by remorse. Tearfully he acknowledged 'that he knew his wrongdoing, that he felt at times the pain and the shame of it; that he had done what he could to restrain himself from offending God and from giving way to his passions; but that he was compelled to own to her they had now become stronger than his reason; that he could no longer resist their violence, nor did he even feel the desire to do so.'[106] In the years to come the King's recognition that he was a slave to sensuality when in all other respects he exercised an absolute mastery over himself could not but be a source of regret to him.

Although few people at court dared reproach the King for incontinence there was at least one brave churchman who did his best to awaken his conscience. In early 1662, a few months after Louis had started his affair with Louise de La Vallière, the great orator Bossuet preached a sermon before the King on the theme of David and Bathsheba. Later that Lent he told Louis in another sermon that it was essential that a sovereign should embrace both the royal and the Christian virtues. 'We cannot accept that he lacks a single one, no, not a single one,' he pointedly declaimed.[107]

At other times Bossuet inveighed in his sermons against false repentance. He reminded his audience that absolution of sin after confession was dependent on firm purpose of amendment and that, if this was lacking, it was sacrilegious to take communion. This would have touched a raw nerve in the King for, by the late 1660s, he was communicating regularly, despite his frequent adultery. In 1669 the King dealt with the problem by ceasing to attend Bossuet's sermons, but the following year he demonstrated his esteem for the Bishop by appointing him preceptor to the Dauphin.

Clearly, the King had not found it easy to forget Bossuet's admonitions and at Easter 1675 he experienced a major crisis of conscience. Despite the fact that he was still in love with Mme de Montespan he attempted to break with her although, in the end, he proved incapable of doing so. However, during the next four years their interludes of passion were disrupted by regular estrangements. Sometimes difficulties were caused by the King's attentions to other women, but at Easter different problems arose, for the knowledge that it was incumbent on him to confess and communicate meant that, around this time of year, the King became particularly conscious that his addiction to sensual pleasure was endangering his soul.

It is not clear how often during these years the King was able to persuade himself that he was in a sufficient state of grace to take the sacraments. His own confessor, Père de La Chaise, is reputed to have been fairly accommodating about this, although there is a story that in 1678 he feigned illness at Easter so that he would not have to hear the King's confession. When Père Duchamp took his place he told the King that he could not absolve him of his sins. According to another account, however, Louis voluntarily refrained from taking communion throughout this period, preferring to be censured for this rather than to risk profaning the holy mysteries. Whatever the truth of the matter, Holy Week was invariably 'a terrible week for Mme de Montespan', for, as the Comte de Bussy put it, 'With a lover whose conscience is so delicate as the King's, a mistress must always tremble at Easter.'[108]

When the King was troubled by pangs of remorse he could not fail to be aware that he was not only jeopardising his own soul but also setting a bad example to the court, and thus fostering immorality on a wider scale. The great preacher Père Bourdaloue once reminded the King in a sermon of the profound effect his behaviour had on the court and how beneficial it would be if he lived a better life. 'How many conversions, Sire, would your example bring in its wake!' he pleaded. 'What an incentive it would be to certain disheartened and despairing sinners when they said to themselves, "There is the man we have seen doing the same debauches as us; see him now converted and obedient to God".'[109]

As it was, if the King attempted to enforce higher standards of behaviour at court he risked being rebuffed on the grounds that he was in no position to preach. He had found this out in January 1670 when he had told his brother that it would be contrary to his conscience to confer the revenues of two abbeys on that notorious sodomite, the Chevalier de Lorraine. It subsequently reached the King's ears that Monsieur and the Chevalier had ridiculed his high-minded response, pointing out that his conscience was elastic enough where women were concerned.[110]

All this meant that when eminent people at court were implicated in the Affair of the Poisons the King had to contemplate the possibility that, indirectly at least, he was in some way responsible. His own carnality and sinfulness had contributed to the court's corruption and moral decay, undermining its spiritual welfare to a point where evil flourished.

# THREE

# SEX AND THE SUN KING

⸻⸱⸱⸱⸻

During the Affair of the Poisons it would be alleged that in the past twenty years several court ladies had conspired to poison or bewitch the King's earliest acknowledged mistress, Louise de La Vallière. A little later the Marquise de Montespan, who had succeeded Louise as royal mistress, was also named as a poisoner. She was said first to have established her hold over the King by using drugs and black magic. When these methods had failed her and the King had taken a young woman named Mlle de Fontanges as his lover, it was claimed that Mme de Montespan had taken steps to poison her rival. In addition, she had supposedly decided to punish the King for his infidelity by murdering him.

In many ways, therefore, the Affair of the Poisons revolved around the royal mistresses. In order to understand that episode, and to judge whether the allegations made in the course of it were true, it is helpful to know something about these women and to examine the course of the King's extramarital relationships.

It was during the summer of 1661, when his wife was pregnant for the first time, that Louis XIV started his affair with Louise de La Vallière. Louise, who celebrated her seventeenth birthday on 6 August, was a maid of honour to Henriette-Anne (known as Madame), the first wife of Louis's brother, Philippe, Duc d'Orléans. The King's love for Louise came about almost by accident: he only started flirting with her to distract attention from the fact that a mutual attraction had developed between him and his sister-in-law, but, against his expectations, this sham romance grew into a genuine attachment.

Some people were surprised that the 'very pretty, very sweet and very naive' Louise should have exerted so powerful an appeal. She was tall and blonde with beautiful blue eyes 'whose sweetness ravished one when she looked at you'. She appeared surprisingly modest and retiring for a royal mistress, although some people maintained it was her 'tender and reflective air' that formed an essential part of her 'indescribable charm'. Like the Queen's, her appearance was marred by poor teeth and she also had a slight limp, but 'that was not unbecoming to her', for it did not detract from her grace or prevent her from dancing well. Besides this, she was exceptionally thin, in an age when it was not fashionable to be underweight, and her bust was extremely small. When the distinguished judge Olivier d'Ormesson saw her for the first time, he was highly critical of her emaciated appearance, while in 1664 an Italian visitor to France declared that in his opinion the Queen was much prettier than Louise and the King's infatuation with her merely proved that 'sensuality blinds one'. Louise looked her best on a horse: not only was she an excellent rider who kept up effortlessly with the King on hunting expeditions, but riding habits were very becoming to her as the lace cravats worn with them enhanced her tiny bust.[1]

Louise did not strike people as being particularly intelligent or witty, although it is possible that she was more entertaining when she was alone with the King. Certainly, she later deplored the fact that through 'vivacity of mind' she had never scrupled to cause amusement by making malicious remarks at other people's expense. No one else, however, identified this as a failing of hers, and at least one person praised her for 'never doing harm to anyone and always doing all the good she can'. People were more inclined to criticise her for failing to exploit her position to the maximum. Mme de Lafayette complained, 'La Vallière's slight intelligence prevented this royal mistress from making use of her advantages and credit whereas anyone else would have profited from the opportunities afforded by such a grand passion on the King's part.'[2]

At first the King conducted his affair with Louise very discreetly. Their love burgeoned while the court was at Fontainebleau for the summer, but initially the King was careful not to see too much of Louise in the daytime. Instead, he waited until he and his entourage went on evening carriage rides, and then he would leave his own coach and stand for hours at the lowered window of Louise's carriage, talking intently. The relationship was reportedly consummated in the apartment of the Duc de Saint-Aignan, who from the first had acted as 'the confidant of this intrigue'. That autumn the court moved to Paris and, since Louise remained in the service of Louis's sister-in-law, the King was able to see his mistress when he visited Madame. One lady recalled that he and Louise would withdraw together to a small room and, though they never shut the door, it might as well have been 'barred with steel', for no one dared to enter. After a time Louise took to feigning illness and the King would visit her as she lay in her bedchamber.[3]

Initially, all this was kept from the Queen. While she did have fears that the King was being unfaithful, she was more inclined to suspect that he was having an affair with Madame than to guess the true state of affairs. However, for reasons of her own the Comtesse de Soissons, the most senior lady in the Queen's household, was determined to enlighten her. She leagued herself with her lover, the Marquis de Vardes, and tried to send the Queen an anonymous letter informing her of what was happening but the plan went awry when the letter failed to reach the Queen. A few months later, however, the Comtesse contrived to pass the news on orally to Marie-Thérèse and then pulled off the remarkable feat of persuading the King that it was the Duchesse de Navailles who had made the revelation. But the outcome of all this differed from the Comtesse's expectations. She had calculated that once the Queen knew about Louise, the King would either be forced to discard his mistress or, if he was determined to continue with the relationship, to enlist the Comtesse's aid when arranging assignations. In the event the King merely concluded that since his wife was now aware that Louise was his mistress there was much less need for secrecy. 'Instead of telling the Queen daily that he came from visiting Madame, he now owned freely that he had been elsewhere.'[4]

By the summer of 1663 Louise was pregnant and this meant she could not continue in Madame's household. The King installed her in a pavilion known as the Palais Brion in the grounds of the Palais Royal in Paris, and there she lived a fairly retired existence until the birth of her child. The baby arrived on the night of 18 December and was delivered by the celebrated obstetrician, Boucher, who had been sworn to secrecy. As prearranged by Colbert, Boucher then handed the child to a married couple named Beauchamp who had formerly been in domestic service with Colbert's family. They were told that the baby boy was the illegitimate offspring of one of Colbert's brothers although, since Olivier d'Ormesson heard that the King went regularly to see his child, they may have guessed the truth. Christened Charles, the baby died before his third birthday.[5]

Although the King had done what he could to hide the existence of his bastard son, he became much less guarded about flaunting his love for Louise. In May 1664 the court was invited to an entertainment lasting several days, the so-called 'Fête of the Enchanted Island'. Though these festivities were in theory put on for Marie-Thérèse and her mother-in-law, Anne of Austria, everyone present had no doubt that Louise was the real guest of honour. During the summer of 1664 the King was regularly seen out hunting with his mistress and in October the King prevailed upon his mother, who until then had been disapproving of her son's extramarital relationship, to receive Louise.

In January 1665 Louise gave birth to another son, Philippe, who, like his brother, was brought up secretly and died in infancy. By May she was once again regularly at the King's side when he went out hunting and the following year her presence became still more conspicuous. The King's respect for his mother had hitherto constrained him to show a degree of circumspection but Anne's death, in January 1666, removed such inhibitions. When Olivier d'Ormesson attended a requiem mass for the Queen Mother he noted that Louise was prominently placed near the Queen, who had been obliged to take her into her service.

It turned out, however, that Louise was not unassailable. In the autumn of 1666 she produced a daughter by the King, christened Marie-Anne, who survived to adulthood. By the following year Louise was once again pregnant but her hold over the King appeared increasingly precarious and informed observers detected unmistakable signs that Louis had grown tired of her.

Louise was supplanted by the Marquise de Montespan, a married woman whom she had considered a friend. Born in 1641, the Marquise was the daughter of Gabriel de Rochechouart, Duc de Mortemart. Her family lineage, which dated back to the eleventh century, was so illustrious that Mme de Montespan's sister liked to claim that the Bourbons were mere parvenus in comparison. Originally christened Françoise, as an adult she had abandoned this commonplace name for the more distinctive and flamboyant Athénaïs, which accorded better with her personality.

In 1663, three years after becoming a maid of honour to the Queen, Athénaïs had married Louis-Henri de Pardaillan de Gondrin, Marquis de Montespan. Since it was not a great match in material terms (Montespan already had debts, possibly from gambling) this might suggest that love had played a part in bringing them together. In theory Athénaïs had a dowry of 150,000 livres but at the time of her marriage her parents produced only 60,000. Even this sum was handed to Montespan's parents and the young couple were only permitted the income. The balance of 90,000 livres was not payable till Athénaïs's parents died, although she and her husband were entitled to the revenue from it. In theory they should have been able to manage on these amounts but they soon found themselves in financial difficulties and had to borrow money.

In early 1664, having already presented her husband with a daughter (a son followed in September 1665), Athénaïs was chosen to be a lady-in-waiting to the Queen. She soon became a favourite with Marie-Thérèse, who loved Mme de Montespan not only because she found her entertaining but also because she supposed her to be virtuous. This was not as naive as it may seem, for at the time others shared her opinion of Athénaïs's good character. When the Comte de Saint-Pol tried to pursue her in 1666 the Duc d'Enghien had no doubt that he was unlikely to succeed in so ambitious an enterprise.[6]

The Queen also approved of the fact that Mme de Montespan took communion regularly and, while one cannot rule out the possibility that this was a cynical exercise deliberately designed to commend her to her mistress, there is good reason to believe that Athénaïs had a strong underlying faith, which did not desert her even when her behaviour most flagrantly contravened Church law. There is a story that, once she had become the King's mistress, the Duchesse d'Uzès queried why, in her concern to maintain her Lenten fast, she even weighed her bread to ensure she did not eat too much. Athénaïs retorted that just because she was guilty of one sin, it did not mean she had to commit every other.[7]

Saint-Simon confirmed that she adhered to her religion with surprising tenacity. He recorded, 'She had never sinned carelessly, for often...she had left the King to go and pray in her closet. Nothing would have induced her to miss a meatless day or a fast. She kept her Lents strictly and was most scrupulous in fasting during the whole time of her evil living...never showing the least sign of religious doubt or impiety.'[8]

Saint-Simon, who was not even born at the time Louis started his affair with Mme de Montespan, asserted that she tried to resist the King's attractions. He claimed that as soon as she realised Louis was falling in love with her she pleaded with her husband to remove her from court, but Montespan failed to act on this. Things then progressed to a point where the temptation became too much for her. This seems implausible and conflicts with the recollections of others. Primi Visconti was told that Athénaïs set out to ensnare the King but that at first Louis was unimpressed, telling his brother, 'She does what she can but I want none of it.' Others maintain that Louise de La Vallière unwittingly brought ruin on herself. Believing that it would be a good way of keeping Louis amused, she arranged for Athénaïs to spend a great deal of time with them, with the result that the King ultimately came to prefer her company to Louise's.[9]

The first contemporary reference to the King being attracted to Athénaïs comes from the Duc d'Enghien, who noted in October 1666 that Louis was showing an interest in her. He added that there was probably nothing in it but 'to tell the truth she would well deserve it, because one could not be more witty or beautiful than her'.[10]

Enghien was not alone in considering Athénaïs a beauty, for everyone concurred that her looks were dazzling. Like Louise she was blonde with azure eyes, but her other features were far superior. She had what Primi Visconti considered 'a perfect face' with a nose that was 'aquiline but well shaped' and 'a small vermilion mouth with very fine teeth'. Her figure – which after multiple pregnancies ran to fat – was more voluptuous than Louise's and her shapely arms were also singled out for praise.[11]

But it was not just her beauty that made Athénaïs so exceptional. Elizabeth Charlotte of the Palatinate (the German princess who became Monsieur's second wife in 1671 and who was known, like her predecessor, as Madame) recalled, 'One was never bored with her,' while another person praised her knack of making 'the most serious subjects agreeable'. This was a trait she shared with her brother, the Duc de Vivonne, and her sister, Mme de Thianges. The three of them 'gave universal pleasure through their singular way of talking, a blend of jokes, artlessness and refinement which was called "the Mortemart wit".' Their utterances were gloriously unpredictable and at times seemed to take even them by surprise, for they had 'the gift of saying unusual and amusing things, always original, which nobody expected, not even themselves as they said them'. Athénaïs in particular had 'a witty languishing manner' that was wonderfully beguiling and possessed 'a special turn of phrase and a gift for selecting the apt word that was all her own'. 'It was enchanting to hear her,' Saint-Simon declared.[12]

Unfortunately, few examples of her wit survive. Her letters give little hint of her humour and she herself declared that she much preferred the spontaneity of conversation to the 'coldness' of the written word. It was the way she phrased her remarks, quite as much as their witty content, which made them so irresistible and besides this, her gaiety had an infectious quality. There is an account of her and Monsieur going into 'peals of laughter, which would have been audible at two hundred paces' when the Chevalier d'Arvieux regaled the King with an amusing account of his diplomatic mission to Turkey. She also had a keen sense of the ridiculous and the King loved the way she could deflate pomposity. According to Primi Visconti, when people talked to him in an affected manner he would later laugh about it with Mme de Montespan. At other times they shared silly jokes together. Mlle de Montpensier recorded huffily that on one occasion when the three of them were travelling in a coach together the King and Mme de Montespan woke her with a start by shrieking, 'We're overturning!'[13]

In addition she was a marvellous mimic. She made everyone laugh by imitating Mme de Mecklembourg's guttural way of speaking, which had acquired strange Germanic overtones after she married a foreigner. When the Savoyard ambassador Saint-Maurice was having an audience with the King in 1672, he noticed Mme de Montespan scrutinising him keenly and he guessed that this was so she could later 'tell some tale to make his Majesty laugh at my expense and to imitate me, for she makes use of everything to divert him'.[14]

Mme de Montespan was also a talented raconteuse who could spin 'a good yarn to make the King laugh'. Mlle de Montpensier fondly recalled Mme de Montespan relating how, during a grand wedding at court, there was a muddle and her dogs' cushions became mixed up with the hassocks. She reduced Mademoiselle to fits as she conjured up a picture of the bride and groom kneeling reverently on these canine accoutrements.[15]

Some people at court felt aggrieved that, in her determination to keep the King entertained, Athénaïs did not scruple to make fun of them. It seems she did not set out to cause trouble: the King's German sister-in-law (who in other ways was highly critical of Mme de Montespan) affirmed that neither she nor her sister, Mme de Thianges, were at all malevolent. While acknowledging that 'no one was sacred from their raillery on the pretext that it amused the King', she stressed that there was nothing spiteful about this, for 'when she had had her laugh at a person she was content and dropped the matter'. However, as Mme de Montespan herself admitted, there were times when she became so intoxicated by her own wit that she unintentionally caused offence. She ruefully admitted that in conversation, 'One is often carried away to say things one does not really think... In this way one makes enemies of people to whom one wishes no harm.'[16] Sensitive courtiers were conscious that they often became the butt of her mockery as they crossed the marble courtyard at Versailles (which was overlooked by her apartment) and they likened this to 'going under fire'.

As one court lady remarked, 'These things may be considered trifles and in effect so they are between private persons, but it's not the same when the Master is involved.' It was felt that these 'satiric barbs' could have a decisive effect on people's fortunes, for once the King had taken against an individual the prejudice was hard to shift. Years later Mme de Maintenon noted regretfully that when the King formed 'a disadvantageous idea of someone it is almost impossible to efface it' and the

Comte de Bussy was likewise sure that Louis 'gains poor impressions of people that others like to give him as easily as he gains towns'. Once instilled in his mind, these could only be dislodged with the utmost difficulty.[17]

Some people were apt to blame Athénaïs if the King seemed ill-disposed towards them when in reality she was not responsible. The Comte de Bussy, for example, developed a hatred for Athénaïs and her sister after he heard that Mme de Thianges had been saying disagreeable things about him to the King. However, at the time Bussy was already exiled from court for having written a scurrilous novel satirising prominent figures there and the King had been so furious about this that it was hardly fair to hold Athénaïs accountable for the Comte's continued disfavour. Nevertheless, despite the fact that the Marquis de Saint-Maurice was adamant that Mme de Montespan 'has never hurt anyone', she was viewed by many as a malign force and this was not easily forgiven. In the words of the great preacher Bossuet, 'To infect the ears of a prince, ah! It is a greater crime than poisoning the public fountains.'[18]

Some people maintained that Athénaïs was a shockingly callous woman. A possibly apocryphal story relates that one day she was riding in a coach with several ladies when it ran over a pedestrian. The other passengers were very upset by the incident, but Athénaïs was unmoved. Calmly she pointed out that such accidents took place every day without arousing their concern; why, then, should they worry simply because they had witnessed this one? Another example was cited by the Marquis de La Fare, who considered it reprehensible that Athénaïs failed to intercede when the Chevalier de Rohan (who was believed to have been a lover of Mme de Thianges) was condemned to death for treachery. Since Rohan's treason had been of a very high order, it is hard to believe that such a plea would have had any effect, but La Fare contended it was 'not the first time she displayed a hard heart, insensible to pity and gratitude'.[19]

It was hard for someone in Athénaïs's position to avoid such criticisms, whether merited or not, but other faults of hers are less open to dispute. She was by all accounts proud and imperious, and her temper, which had always been short, deteriorated as she grew older. Her increasing corpulence as successive pregnancies took their toll on her figure and possibly a tendency to drink to excess may have contributed to her bouts of ill humour but, certainly, her rages became more easily provoked and unpredictable. All too often the King was on the receiving end of her tirades and this ultimately played an important part in alienating him from her.[20]

The King's affair with Athénaïs is usually deemed to have started in 1667. Certainly, if one reads Mlle de Montpensier's account of what happened between the King and her that summer, the conclusion is inescapable that that was when they consummated their relationship. However, one should perhaps sound a note of caution, for such events can rarely be dated with utter certainty. As late as February 1668 the Marquis de Saint-Maurice reported 'the King loves Mme de Montespan and while she does not hate him, she is holding firm.' Athénaïs did not become pregnant by the King until the summer of 1668 and it was only then that M. de Montespan became jealous. All this means that one cannot wholly reject the claims put forward by the magician Lesage during the Affair of the Poisons. He alleged that in late 1667 Mme de Montespan came to him because she wished 'to attain the good graces of the King'. The implication is that at that point she and Louis were not on intimate terms and she wanted Lesage to use his occult powers to remedy the situation.[21]

In June 1667 Louis took the Queen and her ladies to see the army he had massed on France's northern frontiers in preparation for an attack on Flanders. Louise was left behind at Saint-Germain on the pretext that she was pregnant, although normally that never prevented the King from taking his mistresses on voyages. Before leaving, Louis created her Duchesse de Vaujours and legitimised their daughter, who from now on was known as Mlle de Blois. Ostensibly, these were marks of high favour but shrewd observers considered them to be more in the nature of parting gifts.

Poor Louise realised she was being discarded and did her best to retrieve the situation. In July, when the Queen and her entourage were staying at La Fère, prior to rejoining the King, Louise turned up uninvited. The incensed Queen gave her an icy reception and most of her ladies did likewise. Mme de Montespan was especially scathing and was heard to say sanctimoniously, 'God keep me from being the King's mistress! But, if I were, I would be very ashamed in front of the Queen.'[22]

Next day the Queen and her ladies drove to a review of troops, which the King was conducting at Avesnes. When their destination was in sight, Louise's coach suddenly overtook the Queen's, but though this breach of protocol enabled her to reach the King first, Louis was not at all welcoming. Shortly afterwards the wretched Louise had to return to Versailles, having succeeded only in making herself an object of scorn.

The King was now able to pursue Athénaïs without fear of being distracted by Louise's reproachful presence. At Avesnes Mlle de Montpensier noticed that only a short staircase separated Mme de Montespan's room from the King's bedchamber. At first this was guarded by a sentry but he was soon removed, making communication between the two rooms easier. The King spent a great deal of time in his bedroom and Mademoiselle noticed that Mme de Montespan was only rarely in attendance on the Queen during the day. She told Marie-Thérèse that she was exhausted and had to catch up on her sleep but, while the Queen accepted this, she expressed annoyance at seeing so little of the King. Later in the voyage she complained to him that he never came to her bedroom till four in the morning, and wanted to know what he was doing in the meantime. Louis – whose mood during these weeks was one of 'wonderful gaiety' – replied that he was busy reading and writing despatches, but Mademoiselle saw that as he said this he turned his face away so the Queen could not see the sly smile playing across his features.[23]

The Queen still had no idea that Athénaïs had become a rival. Since she was so fond of her company she was delighted when the King suggested that Mme de Montespan should join them when they travelled in a coach together, superseding ladies of higher rank. Even when she was sent an anonymous letter warning her that her husband was having an affair with Athénaïs, the Queen flatly refused to believe it. It is not known how long it took for the unpalatable truth to penetrate, but once the situation became clear to her she had no alternative but to accept it.

Perhaps her only consolation was that the same show of resignation was required from Louise. In October, after the court had returned from its travels, Louise gave birth to the King's son, the future Comte de Vermandois. Thereafter she, the King and Athénaïs formed a curious trio. For much of the time they were inseparable: in fine weather the two ladies were regularly to be seen accompanying the King on carriage rides in the gardens of Versailles and in due course Louise and Athénaïs shared an apartment at court with every appearance of amity. The Savoyard ambassador assumed that for a time the King divided his sexual favours between the two women and at one point Saint-Maurice understood that Louise was expecting another baby. As she never actually produced another child it is not clear whether he had been right about this. However, by March 1671 even he was sure that Mme de Montespan 'would no longer tolerate' the King sleeping with Louise.[24] Despite this, Louise remained a fixture at court, loving the King too much to summon up the resolve not to see him and thus prolonging her own agony.

If the King went on voyages during the summer, both mistresses went too. Sometimes they shared a coach with the Queen, to the amazement of watching peasants, who marvelled at the passage of 'three queens'. If this proved an ordeal, accompanying the King in his coach was scarcely preferable, for Louis was notoriously inconsiderate to travelling companions. As Saint-Simon put it, 'Pregnant, sick, less than six weeks after labour, otherwise indisposed, no matter, they had to be fully dressed, bejewelled, tight-laced into their bodices, ready to travel to Flanders or further ... to be cheerful and good company, move about, seem not to notice heat or cold or draughts or dust, and all punctual to the moment, giving no trouble of any kind ... As for the needs of nature they could not be mentioned ... To feel sick was an unforgivable crime.'[25]

Mme de Scudery described Louise's life at court during these years as 'a martyrdom' and Madame claimed that Mme de Montespan did all she could to add to Louise's misery. 'She used to mock at her publicly and treated her very badly,' Madame informed a correspondent. Furthermore, she 'made the King act in the same way' and Louise had to endure the humiliation of watching Louis pass through her own bedroom on his way to sleep with Athénaïs.[26] Madame's allegations have to be treated with caution, but there can be no doubt that throughout this period Louise suffered terribly.

While it can be safely assumed that this bizarre ménage-à-trois imposed strains on both ladies, from the point of view of Louis and Athénaïs, Louise's presence at court had one undeniable advantage. It distracted attention from the fact that the King's relationship with Athénaïs, a married woman, came into the category of a 'double adultery', a much worse crime in the eyes of the Church than his affair with the single Louise. To complicate matters further, not only was the burden of sin greater, but the King had to deal with an angry husband intent on causing maximum disruption.

Described as wild and witty by his cousin, Mlle de Montpensier, M. de Montespan came from Gascony, a region renowned for unruly characters. At first it had not appeared he would pose the King much of a problem. When Louis was falling in love with Athénaïs during the summer of 1667, Montespan was conveniently engaged in military service on France's southern border, campaigning in the Roussillon against the Spanish. Precautions were taken to keep him in good humour: he was supplied with money to maintain a company of soldiers, even though in theory commanders were meant to pay these expenses themselves, and in November he was sent a letter congratulating him on the King's behalf after he and his men were involved in a minor skirmish. When he returned to court in January 1668 it appeared he was still on good terms with his wife. In March of that year a legal document states that they were living together in rented accommodation in Paris and, before rejoining his men, he empowered her to take care of their financial affairs, which suggests there had not yet been a breakdown of trust between them.[27]

Montespan then went back to the Roussillon, but a few months later he applied for permission to return to Paris. This was granted without demur, but when he reappeared at court in the late summer it turned out that it had been a grave miscalculation to assume he would prove a *mari complaisant*. Although he had had amorous adventures of his own while on active service, his wife's infidelity now roused him to fury. More than one contemporary insisted he was motivated largely by mercenary considerations and that, far from being genuinely jealous, he was merely incensed that his acquiescence so far had not been more generously rewarded.[28] This may, however, have been too cynical an interpretation.

At any rate, Montespan proceeded to cause a tremendous fuss. In September 1668 he stormed to Saint-Germain and subjected the King to a vehement 'harangue', in the course of which he alluded to David and Bathsheba, warned Louis that he faced divine retribution and demanded that his wife be returned to him. Next he confronted the Queen's principal lady-in-waiting, Mme de Montausier. Believing that she had encouraged and abetted his wife in her adultery, he was so grossly abusive to her that she was left in a state of complete prostration. Saint-Simon alleged that he also physically attacked Mme de Montespan and it does seem likely that he was violent towards her, either now or at some other point in their marriage, for the document formalising their subsequent separation refers to ill-treatment against her person.[29]

The King was not prepared to tolerate such conduct. On 22 September Montespan was arrested and sent to For l'Évêque prison in Paris. A fortnight later he was freed but ordered to withdraw to his father's estates in Guyenne, which he was forbidden to leave without the King's 'express permission'. Even in rural exile, however, Montespan demonstrated a continued capacity to cause embarrassment. To show that his wife was dead to him he put his children in mourning and held a mock funeral for her. On visiting a local church he insisted on going through the main door, explaining that the side entrance was too low to accommodate his horns.[30] As he had calculated, these escapades were soon the talk of Paris.

Few people had any sympathy for Montespan. When he was sent to prison Saint-Maurice reported, 'The court and all Paris censure his conduct...Nobody pities him.'[31] Nevertheless, the Marquis posed a real threat to Athénaïs and the King. As a husband Montespan had strong legal rights and since it appeared he would not passively accept being deprived of his wife the implications were alarming. Of particular concern was the fact that Montespan not only automatically gained custody of the two children he and Athénaïs had had together but he was also entitled to claim as his own any children that the King fathered on his wife. Since Athénaïs was already bearing the King's child when Montespan was sent to prison, this was a serious matter.

In a bid to prevent the pregnancy from becoming common knowledge, Louis rented a house near the Tuileries for Athénaïs. When she did come to court she and the King led a much quieter existence than usual. At night the King visited her as discreetly as possible, gaining access to her by slipping up a hidden staircase which had been clandestinely constructed.[32] When Athénaïs's child was born in March 1669 it was at once spirited away from court and brought up in the utmost secrecy.

The young Secretary of State for War, Louvois, finally quelled the obstreperous Montespan. In 1669 the latter had been permitted to rejoin his troops in the Roussillon. It came to Louvois's ears that when Montespan and his company had been billeted in the town of Ille, Montespan had tried to force a local girl to come and live with him. To fend off his advances, her parents had placed her in the care of a local official, but Montespan had then confronted this man, pistol in hand, and addressed him in the most threatening and abusive terms. When the girl was removed to a convent, some of Montespan's men tried unsuccessfully to drag her out by force; a few days later Montespan himself appeared and insulted the Mother Superior.

Montespan had committed a similar outrage at Perpignan in 1667, but at that time Louvois and the King had been at pains to humour him. The incident had therefore been overlooked. However, now that Montespan was making a nuisance of himself, his oppressive treatment of the civilian population became a matter for official concern.

On 21 September 1669 Louvois wrote ordering the *Intendant* of Roussillon to make a full investigation of both incidents. He suggested that Montespan's men should be arrested in the hope they would implicate him in their misdeeds, enabling him to be cashiered 'with an appearance of justice'. If Montespan could be charged with sufficiently grave offences to warrant summoning him before the region's sovereign council, 'this would be a good thing', although Louvois made it clear that he would also consider it a desirable outcome if Montespan were terrorised into leaving the country.[33]

All went as Louvois had hoped. Realising that he had no chance of receiving a sympathetic hearing, Montespan fled to Spain in December 1669. When he failed to appear before a court in Pignerol, he was condemned as contumacious in his absence. About three months later he sued for pardon, presumably indicating that he would be more tractable in future. In April 1670 Louvois instructed the *Intendant* of Roussillon to drop proceedings against Montespan. Four months later a royal pardon was issued, although the text of this document recorded the details of his past transgressions, possibly to ensure that, if Montespan again proved troublesome, further sanctions could be brought to bear. Montespan was permitted to return to France but was forbidden to enter Paris unless he could prove his visit was essential.

In July 1670 the King instituted proceedings at the Châtelet to bring about an official separation between Montespan and his wife. Even the King, however, could not expedite the cumbersome legal process and it was four years before the case was finally settled. In the interval there were still fears that Montespan could make difficulties for Louis and Athénaïs. In late 1671, for example, it was rumoured that Montespan had leagued himself with the Comte de Lauzun to arrange the abduction of his wife and while the story was almost certainly false, it demonstrated the extent to which Montespan was still perceived as a danger.[34]

Because the legal situation remained so sensitive, Athénaïs's children by the King had to be kept hidden. Her eldest child by Louis – a girl – died in March 1672, but by that time Athénaïs had produced a son, Louis Auguste, born in March 1670, who later became the Duc du Maine. He was joined in June 1672 by a brother, subsequently created Comte de Vexin, followed almost exactly a year later by a sister, Louise Françoise, born at Tournai during the King's summer campaign. All these children had to be brought up away from court and Mme de Montespan needed to find someone reliable, virtuous and above all discreet who could assume charge of them. It was when pregnant with her first child by Louis that Athénaïs had hit on what seemed the inspired idea of entrusting the childcare arrangements to Mme Scarron, an impoverished but respectable widow she had met in the salon of her cousin the Maréchal d'Albret.

Known to history as Mme de Maintenon, Mme Scarron's maiden name was Françoise d'Aubigné. In 1635 she had been born in the most unpropitious circumstances, starting life in the Conciergerie at Niort which adjoined the prison where her scapegrace father had been imprisoned for debt. Rather than enter a convent, aged sixteen the penniless girl opted to marry an invalid in his early forties, the play-wright Paul Scarron, who was so severely crippled by rheumatoid arthritis that it is unlikely the marriage was consummated. Although always short of cash, Scarron presided over a witty and eclectic salon frequented by freethinkers. It was here that his young wife developed her conversational skills, though without acquiring a reputation for levity.

Scarron died in October 1660, bequeathing only debts to his widow. She was rescued from indigence when the Queen Mother, Anne of Austria, was induced to give her a small pension. Having rented cheap lodgings in a Paris convent, she was soon moving in elevated social circles. She made herself indispensable to several aristocratic ladies, rising at six to oversee the redecoration of Mme d'Heudicourt's house, and doing the accounts for Mme de Montchevreuil. She soon became an habituée at the Maréchal d'Albret's salon, commending herself to his dull wife − whom most of the guests avoided − by being unfailingly attentive.[35]

It was here that she made the acquaintance of Mme de Montespan and the two ladies were instantly drawn towards each other. As Mme Scarron later recalled, they became 'the greatest friends in the world. She was greatly taken with me and as for me, simple as I was, I entered into this friendship...she talked to me with great confidence and told me everything she was thinking.'[36]

It was not surprising that Athénaïs took so readily to this new acquaintance, for Mme Scarron was a woman of immense charm and discernment. There was nothing showy about her but, in the same way as she contrived to look elegant in plain but well-cut black dresses, which suited her better than bright silks, her conversation was always stimulating and original without being in any way improper. Saint-Simon recorded, 'When she spoke it was quietly and correctly, using excellent French, always brief and eloquent...Her every action was performed with incomparable grace and ease.' Though rarely flippant, she had a dry sense of humour, which somehow never descended into frivolity. While ready to enter into light-hearted discussions, she could also be fascinating on more serious subjects. Mme de Sévigné, who found her 'delicious company', described an evening when she was in particularly entrancing form, during which the topics covered ranged from court gossip to philosophical reflections. 'These discussions are far-reaching...sometimes Christian and sometimes political,' she told her daughter.[37]

Mme de Montespan concluded that this cultivated and well-bred woman was the ideal person to look after her children by the King. Mme Scarron had already proved herself not only diligent and capable but also ready to carry out comparatively menial tasks without complaining that this impaired her dignity. Given her lack of money, it was logical to assume she would welcome paid employment and she could be relied upon to perform her duties in an inconspicuous fashion. To complete her qualifications, she had practical experience of childcare, for she had not only frequently looked after Mme de Montchevreuil's children but had also taught them to read and learn their catechism.[38]

Athénaïs's appointment of Mme Scarron as her children's governess turned out to be the worst mistake of her life but initially it seemed that the choice could not be faulted. At the outset the children were farmed out to wet-nurses but Mme Scarron closely supervised their welfare, visiting them daily to ensure that all their needs were provided for. After a time the King purchased a house in an outlying area of Paris, the Rue Vaugirard, where his growing brood by Athénaïs could be united under one roof. There Mme Scarron devoted herself to their interests, living largely in seclusion because of the need for secrecy. On the rare occasions she did see old friends she preserved a rigid silence about her occupation.

Although the existence of a refractory husband complicated their relationship, in some ways the King manifested his love for Athénaïs far more overtly than had been the case with Louise. As early as 1668 Athénaïs was credited with having persuaded the King to appoint the Duc de Montausier as governor to the seven-year-old Dauphin. While this was a disaster for the child – for Montausier was a horrible bully who thrashed the little boy for the most minor infractions – it much impressed the court, who noted that Louise had never managed such a striking achievement.[39]

In January 1669 Mme de Montespan's father, the Duc de Mortemart, was appointed to the prime position of Governor of Paris, somewhat to the irritation of Colbert, whose own candidate was overlooked. Athénaïs's brother, the Duc de Vivonne, was believed to be critical of her liaison with the King but in March 1669 he too received promotion. He was made General of the Galleys, an important post, which had the additional advantage of removing him to Marseille, where he could not make his disapproval so plain. In August 1670 Athénaïs's younger sister was made Abbess of Fontrevault, a prestigious position in the past reserved for princesses of the blood royal. It was an extraordinary honour for a twenty-five-year-old nun without a vocation, but she acquitted herself with great distinction, translating Homer and Plato in her spare time and exhibiting formidable talents as an administrator. Athénaïs's achievements for her family were crowned in 1670 when she arranged a marriage between her niece and the immensely wealthy Duc de Nevers. These successive feats moved Mme de Sévigné to exclaim, 'Mme de Montespan is performing marvels all over the place.'[40]

The situation of Louise de La Vallière was, in contrast, utterly pitiful, but in the end her faith redeemed her. As she herself declared, even while she had been leading 'a wholly profane life, full of pride and sensuality', her piety had never deserted her for she was 'always troubled by the prospect of my crimes and my remorseful conscience'. Then, at the end of 1670, or just afterwards, she had a very serious illness. She later recalled lying in bed as 'the doctors on one side, and the priests on the other, were speaking with as little certainty for my life as for my soul, and where I, like a poor beast, could do nothing for my salvation'.[41] This marked the beginning of her conversion.

In February 1671 Louise fled to the convent of the Filles de Sainte-Marie de Chaillot on Ash Wednesday, apparently determined to withdraw permanently from court. To the puzzlement of many people who assumed that by this time the King regarded Louise as something of an unwelcome encumbrance, Louis evinced 'the greatest affliction in the world' at her departure. He enlisted the Comte de Lauzun and the Maréchal de Bellefonds to persuade her to reconsider and, when that failed, sent Colbert with orders to bring her back. The courtiers whispered that he and Mme de Montespan 'had had a big row about that as she was not at all willing to permit the other's return'. When Louise obeyed the King's summons, Louis was transparently overjoyed and Athénaïs too put on a good show, going to meet Louise 'with open arms and tears in her eyes'. However, people assumed that this friendly reception was deceptive and that whereas the King had shed tears of joy at Louise's return, Athénaïs had wept with frustration.[42]

Amidst general mystification that he should have exhibited such an 'extraordinary tenderness' towards Louise, the King resumed his curious tripartite love life. 'All this makes no sense,' Mme de Sévigné declared flatly. Court observers were left unable to decide whether the King had been motivated by genuine fondness for Louise or whether he was merely a creature of habit who disliked having his routine disrupted. One lady gushed that the episode showed that the King was 'praiseworthy even in his abandonments', but cynics had a different explanation. They believed that there were fears that M. de Montespan might once again turn awkward and the King needed Louise to remain at court as a sort of decoy.[43]

Some people thought that after her return Louise's standing with the King was better than it had been before. Others despised her for her weakness. 'Like an idiot she came back,' was the comment of Mlle de Montpensier, who thought that Louise ought to have extracted a promise that the King would treat her more kindly before coming out of retreat.[44] Louise rationalised her conduct by persuading herself that it was not inconsistent with her faith to resume her place at court for, by inflicting on herself the pain and humiliation of seeing Louis and Athénaïs together, she would atone for her former misconduct.

Louise later explained to Madame that during the next three years 'she suffered the tortures of the damned', but she 'offered all her misery up to God as an expiation of her past sins'. In a prayer composed at this time she told God, 'If, to impose on me a penitence that in some way accords with my offences, you wish that...I remain in the world to suffer on the same scaffold on which I transgressed,' she was ready to submit to this. All she asked was that God should give her the strength to avoid being corrupted by the vanity of the court and to 'shield me from being poisoned by the infectious air that one incessantly breathes there'.[45]

At the end of 1673 Louise finally concluded that it would be acceptable to God if she ceased tormenting herself in this way and withdrew from the world. Not only did she decide to become a nun but, instead of choosing a fairly comfortable convent of the sort that not uncommonly provided a refuge for aristocratic ladies, she resolved to join the Carmelites, a particularly severe order whose occupants never touched meat and practised numerous austerities. While it is clear that she was responding to a sincere religious impulse, it seems probable that she derived some satisfaction from the reflection that this very public way of renouncing sin would be a good way of embarrassing Athénaïs. Certainly Mme de Montespan appeared worried that it would reflect badly on her if Louise adopted a saintly way of life. While she had no objection to Louise retiring to a reasonably relaxed convent (indeed, she would probably have welcomed it), she tried to deter her from entering the Carmelites by covering the idea in ridicule. This prompted Bishop Bossuet to intervene and Athénaïs was forced to desist after he warned her that she must not shake Louise's resolve.[46] As for the King, he put up no resistance to Louise's departure for, though she had dreaded informing him of her decision, he had reached the stage where he could not be bothered to dissuade her.

For Athénaïs the weeks leading up to Louise's departure from court were very trying. Although as a mistress Louise had been notably shy and self-effacing, she insisted on staging her withdrawal from the world in the most conspicuous fashion. In front of the entire court she threw herself on her knees before the Queen and tearfully begged Marie-Thérèse to forgive her for the pain she had caused her. When the Maréchale de La Mothe remonstrated that such self-abasement was uncalled for, she said that, as her crimes had taken place in public it was right that her penitence should be equally well observed. Understandably, all this 'very much wearied Mme de Montespan'.[47]

In 1674 the King said goodbye to Louise in private before setting off on his spring campaign against the Dutch. Afterwards it was noted that his eyes were rimmed with red.[48] Athénaïs followed him on his travels but those at court who did not go to the war attended the ceremony on 19 April when Louise was received into the convent. Just over a year later she took her final vows.

The King had no difficulty forgetting Louise. Saint-Simon claimed that he later said that, from the day she had taken the veil he had looked on her as dead and certainly he acted as if this were the case. When her brother died in 1676 he sent her a polite message that, if he had been a good enough man to see so 'saintly a Carmelite' he would have offered his condolences in person, but as it was he thought it best to stay away.[49]

Louise's commitment to her enclosed order never wavered. During the rest of her long life, she subjected herself to still greater mortifications than was normal, fasting on bread and water, and depriving herself of sleep so she could spend more time at prayer. However hard her existence, she claimed she found it more restful than the years when she had lived in permanent dread of damnation, for 'now I sleep in peace without fearing apoplexy'.[50]

Whereas Louise's presence had once provided a useful screen which deflected attention away from the King's relationship with Athénaïs, this was no longer necessary, for by the time Louise retreated to a nunnery the threat posed by M. de Montespan had been at least partly negated. The King had found a way of legitimising his children by Athénaïs, taking as a precedent a decree passed by *Parlement* that a son produced by the Maréchale de La Ferté was the legitimate offspring of the Duc de Longueville, who had been killed on active service in 1672. In the deed certifying this, the name of the child's mother was not mentioned, thus overcoming the danger that her husband could claim the boy as his own. The King now adopted the same arrangement. On 23 December 1673 his three surviving children by Athénaïs were legitimised and the titles of Duc du Maine, Comte de Vexin and Mlle de Nantes were conferred on them. The children no longer were kept hidden away in the Rue Vaugirard. Courtiers started to catch tantalising glimpses of the Duc du Maine when he was brought to see his parents, and within a few months he and his siblings had been installed at court with their governess.

Athénaïs's separation from her husband, which had taken so long to resolve, was also finally formalised. On 4 July 1674 the courts pronounced on the matter in a ruling that had disastrous implications for Montespan. He was required to repay with interest the 60,000 livres of dowry that Athénaïs's father had handed over when he married her, despite the fact that the money had gone to Montespan's parents. Athénaïs was freed from responsibility for debts they had jointly incurred and Montespan was required to pay her maintenance of 4000 livres a year. He was also denied access to her, being forbidden from now on 'to haunt or frequent' his wife.[51]

When it became clear that Montespan was not going to fulfil the financial obligations imposed on him, Athénaïs sent bailiffs to seize furniture from the rented lodgings he had taken while in Paris for the case. Facing complete ruin, Montespan was obliged to seek an accommodation, pleading that his children by Athénaïs would suffer unless the terms of separation were modified. A fortnight later a new settlement was reached, deferring repayment of Athénaïs's dowry until after Montespan was dead and accepting that the allowance earmarked for her could be used for their children's education.

Montespan had seemingly been subdued but in years to come the King remained concerned that he would cause fresh problems. Although Montespan had no further legal dealings with his wife (to whom, of course, he remained married, despite their separation), he was by nature litigious. When cases that concerned him were being heard in the Paris courts it was not possible for the King to exclude him from the capital, but Montespan's proximity always made the King uneasy. In May 1678, for example, he was so alarmed to hear that Montespan was in Paris on legal business that he instructed Colbert to have him placed under observation. 'He is a madman, capable of great extravagances,' the King declared roundly, ordering that he be kept informed of Montespan's conversations and the company he was keeping. The King suggested that pressure should be exerted on the judges to hear Montespan's case as soon as possible so that he no longer had an excuse to remain in town. This seemed still more desirable when Louis discovered that Montespan was indulging in indiscreet outbursts and even threatening to see his wife. 'Since he is capable of it and the consequences are to be feared I rely on you to ensure that he does not appear,' the King told Colbert.[52]

In the event the threat was averted but it was many years before Montespan lost his capacity to unsettle the King. Only after his wife left court was he permitted to return to it. According to Madame, in his later years he would sometimes come there to play cards with the daughters Athénaïs had produced by Louis, of whom he at one time could technically have claimed paternity. Madame stated that while he always treated them with exaggerated respect, 'it used to amuse even himself, and he always turned round and smiled slightly'.[53]

Once Mme de Montespan's separation from her husband had been regularised the King could be more expansive about demonstrating his love for Athénaïs. In 1674 work was started on a residence for her at Clagny, a property to the east of Versailles, which the King had purchased some years earlier. As originally designed by Antoine Le Paultre, this was to have been a fairly substantial long, low building. It had a domed central section with a triangular pediment and a modest upper storey, but Athénaïs soon professed herself dissatisfied. When she and the King inspected the building works in March 1675 she is said to have told him that the result would be fit only for a showgirl and the King accepted that she deserved something much grander.[54]

Le Paultre was replaced with Jules Hardouin Mansart, the architect who would go on to design the Galerie des Glaces at Versailles. He adapted the original plans to produce a palatial 'house of delights', far more imposing than its predecessor. Not only did it have a much more lofty first floor, but the dome was now enlarged and flanked by *oeil de boeuf* windows and the façade was punctuated by slightly projecting pavilions. The finished 'Hôtel de Vénus' had a magnificent gallery on the ground floor adorned with numerous sculptures and paintings on the theme of Dido and Aeneas. It was lit by thirteen windows and its barrel-vaulted ceiling, enriched with painted panels and gilded coffers, anticipated the glories of the Hall of Mirrors. The house was set in magnificent gardens designed by André Le Nôtre and in 1676 alone 1300 narcissus bulbs and 5600 hyacinths were planted there.[55]

Clagny was a magnificent testimonial of the King's love for Athénaïs, but that love would soon be shaken. Until this point the King appears to have been remarkably successful at suppressing feelings of guilt about his adultery but at Easter 1675 things changed. Exactly what prompted this is unclear. It is usually claimed that in April, when Athénaïs went to confession in preparation for receiving the sacraments, the curé of

Versailles refused to give her absolution. Furious, she complained to the King, who consulted the Duc de Montausier and Bossuet. Both men were adamant that the curé had been absolutely correct, forcing the King to confront his own sinfulness. Unfortunately, the most detailed description of these events is to be found in a letter attributed to Mme Scarron, which is of questionable authenticity.[56] It is, however, clear that something of the sort did occur and persuaded the King that he and Athénaïs must part.

According to the same somewhat dubious source, Athénaïs withdrew to the house in the Rue Vaugirard that had been purchased for her children. There, she locked herself away and sat alternately raging and scribbling letters, which she soon afterwards frenziedly destroyed. Even if this account is not genuine, there can be no doubt that the King's renunciation of her caused her dreadful anguish. The King, too, was deeply distressed and was seen at court with red eyes.[57]

Not only was he personally wretched but he felt guilty for having ruined her life and did his best to make amends for this by ensuring that her status at court did not suffer. Before leaving for the war on 16 April, he visited her twice at Clagny but there was no lapse of decorum: their 'long and sad conversations' were conducted behind glass doors and were supervised by various court notables stationed just outside. Even when he went on campaign it was clear that Athénaïs was constantly in his thoughts, for he talked about her all the time and wrote to Colbert urging him to see that work on Clagny continued. He even drew consolation from the fact that its costs were so high, perhaps reasoning that this was his sole means of compensating her.[58] The poor Queen was also required to emphasise that Mme de Montespan was not an outcast by going to see her and taking her on outings. The King tried to ease things further by asking prominent court ladies to entertain Athénaïs at their houses.

Bossuet, meanwhile, was doing everything he could to encourage both parties to follow the path of virtue. At the King's request he visited Mme de Montespan as often as possible and he wrote reassuring Louis that he had found her in a 'fairly tranquil' frame of mind, although it was clear she had shed many tears. He reported with satisfaction that she was keeping herself busy with good works and that she had been 'very moved by the truths which I put to her'.[59] In a bid to fortify the King's will Bossuet warned him,

> Your heart will never belong peacefully to God while this violent love, which has separated you from him for so long, reigns there...
> How difficult it is to withdraw from so fatal and unfortunate a

connection. However, Sire, it is necessary, or there is no salvation to be hoped for. Jesus Christ … will give you the strength for this, as he has already given you the desire. I do not ask, Sire, that you extinguish so violent a flame in an instant; this would be to ask the impossible; but, Sire, try to diminish it little by little.[60]

Bossuet's admonitions ultimately proved in vain. It had been assumed that, if the King was serious about renouncing Athénaïs she would have to vacate her court apartments. However, when he returned from the war in July 1675, Mme de Montespan was in her usual rooms at Versailles and the King at once went to see her. It is, admittedly, not absolutely certain that the affair resumed immediately. On his return Louis tried to convince the Queen that he had not abandoned his resolution to lead a purer life and told her that she could say as much to others. The Duchesse de Richelieu also promised the Queen that whenever the King visited Mme de Montespan she would be present and act as a chaperone. This arrangement certainly did not prove effective for very long – after Mme de Montespan had given birth to two more children by the King the Queen would say wryly, 'There are the witnesses to this guarantee' – but it is possible that it delayed a reunion for some months. In October 1675 Mme de Richelieu insisted that she could vouch that Mme de Montespan was not living in a state of sin when a priest expressed reservations about receiving her confession.[61] The fact that the King performed his Easter duties in April 1676 has also been taken as an indication that even then, he was refraining from sexual relations with his mistress.

Whatever the truth of the matter, most people at court were sure that he and Mme de Montespan had wasted no time resuming their relationship. In late July 1675 the King was dining at Clagny when a message arrived that the great French general, Turenne, had been killed. Pious people 'immediately attributed the bad news to the resumption of sin'. The next day eight new field marshals were created, including Mme de Montespan's brother. His military record justified the appointment on merit, but this did not stop wags saying of the new promotions, 'Seven had been made marshals by the sword, and one by the scabbard.'[62]

Nor was it surprising that it was so widely assumed that Athénaïs and Louis were again committing adultery, for the attraction between them was manifest to all. 'The attachment is still extreme,' Mme de Sévigné told her daughter on 31 July, although she at least was prepared to admit the possibility that, although the King was 'doing enough to annoy the curé and everyone else', he was not doing as much as Athénaïs would have wished.[63]

There can be no disputing that the King's resistance did not last. The strength of Athénaïs's hold over him was demonstrated in July 1676, when he returned from campaigning. He was having a reunion with the Queen and the Dauphin – whom he had not seen for weeks – when news came that Mme de Montespan had arrived back from Bourbon, where she had been taking the waters. Louis at once rushed off to see her, leaving the Queen in tears.[64] It was shortly after this that Mme de Sévigné came to court and wrote her rapturous description of Athénaïs in her full glory. Within a month of the King's return, Athénaïs had conceived another child by him.

The King had proved incapable of giving up Athénaïs, but he did not remain faithful to her. A month after she had seen the exultant Mme de Montespan queening it at Versailles Mme de Sévigné reported, 'Fresh blood is smelt in Quanto's* domain.' The King was paying marked attention to the Princesse de Soubise, an elegant strawberry blonde in her late twenties who had been named as a possible rival to Athénaïs as early as November 1668. The following autumn she had again been linked with the King and her family were said to be very excited about her prospects. Some people were sure that she had already granted Louis the final favour, naming the time and place, but it is not clear whether their information was accurate. At any rate, at that point Athénaïs had swiftly regained her ascendancy. Despite subsisting on a rigorous diet 'so as to preserve the brilliance and freshness of her complexion', Mme de Soubise always lost her looks when pregnant. In the course of the next few years she had produced several children in succession and during that time had posed little threat to Mme de Montespan.[65]

In August 1676, however, Mme de Soubise re-emerged into the spotlight when the King's liking for her again became apparent. It is impossible to tell whether the relationship was consummated. The German diplomat Ezechiel Spanheim was certain that as a 'virtuous woman…who loved her husband', she rejected Louis's advances. Saint-Simon was equally positive that she did not. He claimed that the Maréchale de Rochefort told him that Mme de Soubise used to wait in her apartment for the royal valet, Bontemps, so that he could conduct her by back passages to his master's bedroom, but this may not have been true.[66]

Certainly the Prince de Soubise evinced no jealousy of the King. Saint-Simon claimed that this was because he was devoid of honour

*Quanto was Mme de Sévigné's nickname for Athénaïs.

and that he was prepared to accept 'a humiliating and only half-concealed affront' in the belief that this was the best way of advancing the family fortune. If so, his calculations proved correct, although Saint-Simon sniffed that the riches which subsequently accrued to him from royal largesse were 'the fruits of discretion such as few would care to imitate'.[67]

Mme de Montespan was very upset by the King's dalliance with Mme de Soubise. On 11 September Mme de Sévigné reported that Athénaïs was displaying the usual signs of jealousy – tears, affected gaiety and sulks – but that it was doubtful whether these displays of pique would be effective. Shortly afterwards Athénaïs appeared to rally, for she was at the King's side when he appeared at the gaming tables, leaning her head ostentatiously on his shoulder. Within days, however, it seemed that she was once again in danger of being eclipsed by Mme de Soubise. As always, Mme de Sévigné's assessment of the situation was shrewd: she remarked that even if the King's feelings for Mme de Soubise were not very serious, 'She is someone else and that means a lot.' His affection for her might well prove transient but 'she would open up the path to infidelity' and serve as 'a way to other women who were younger and more savoury'.[68]

So it proved. Before long Mme de Soubise's attractions were diminished by the loss of a front tooth and though she remained in favour with the King his interest in her became less pronounced. By this time, however, Athénaïs was six months pregnant and so not at her best. The result was that the King looked elsewhere.

In early 1677 Louis started an affair with Marie-Isabelle de Ludres, an unmarried girl who was an altogether more alarming rival for Athénaïs than Mme de Soubise. Now nearly thirty, she was known as Madame de Ludres on account of being a lay canoness of Poussaye Abbey in her native Lorraine. When she was no more than fifteen the Duke of Lorraine, then aged over sixty, had fallen in love with her on a visit to Poussaye. There are conflicting accounts as to what happened next. According to some sources he took her as his mistress and then grew tired of her. Alternatively, he may have tried to marry her, so alarming his family and long-established mistress that they prevailed on her parents to remove her. At any rate she moved to the French court and in 1670 became a maid of honour to Monsieur's first wife.

Following Madame's death on 29 June, she transferred to the Queen's household. Before long the King was showing signs of being attracted to her, perhaps seduced in part by her distinctive lisp, which other court ladies delighted in parodying. Shortly afterwards all the

Queen's maids of honour were dismissed and replaced by married ladies-in-waiting. This was ostensibly at the wish of Marie-Thérèse, but it was generally assumed that the change had been engineered by Athénaïs. She was said to have decided that, collectively, these young women were like a hydra and no sooner had she seen off one, than another would start encroaching on her territory.[69] However, Mme de Ludres did not have to leave court for in late 1671 the Duc d'Orléans had married his second wife, Elizabeth Charlotte of the Palatinate, and she invited her to become one of her maids. Having been provided with this haven, five years later Mme de Ludres became the King's mistress.

Not long after embarking on her affair with the King, Mme de Ludres let it be understood that she was expecting his child. Her standing at court at once became higher, even though it ultimately transpired that she had mistaken her condition. As she entered a room, duchesses and princesses now rose to their feet, only sitting down when she gave the signal. Since such treatment had hitherto been reserved for Mme de Montespan, this alerted the Queen to the fact that her husband had taken a new mistress. By now she was so 'used...to these infidelities' that she showed little concern, remarking imperturbably that it 'was Mme de Montespan's business'. Athénaïs, in contrast, was roused to fury by the interloper. Her sister, Mme de Thianges, did her best to support her. At the Tuileries Primi Visconti saw her exchange 'basilisk looks' with Mme de Ludres and every encounter between the two ladies led to an exchange of insults.[70]

On 28 February 1677 the King left to join his army. While he was away Mme de Ludres went to stay at the country house of a rich financier. Mme de Montespan also retired to the country and on 4 May was delivered of another daughter, christened Françoise Marie. By the time the King returned to court at the end of May she had recovered from the birth and was ready to trounce Mme de Ludres. Though people had looked on it as a foregone conclusion that she would be discarded (the Comte de Bussy had even composed a formal letter condoling her on her fall, though in the end he thought better of sending it), it soon emerged that, now she was no longer encumbered by her pregnancy, she had not lost her ability to captivate Louis. She was aided by the fact that he had by now become somewhat irritated by Mme de Ludres's presumptuous demands on him and the ostentatious way she flaunted their relationship. When he started treating Mme de Ludres more coldly, few people had much sympathy, for she had 'played the sultana too much' for their liking.[71]

Mme de Sévigné visited court that summer and found Mme de

Montespan reinstated. 'What a triumph at Versailles!' she told her daughter on 9 June. 'What redoubled pride! ... What a renewal of possession.' On paying a visit to her bedroom, Mme de Sévigné found Athénaïs looking resplendent. She was reclining on her bed, exchanging sarcastic remarks with her sister at Mme de Ludres's expense, and Mme de Sévigné reported, 'One breathes here nothing but prosperity and joy.'[72]

For the wretched Mme de Ludres the outlook was much bleaker. She had retained her position as maid of honour but that no longer gave her satisfaction. Occasionally the King still showed her some kindness but when he did so he at once incurred the wrath of Athénaïs and made her angrier still with Mme de Ludres. In June 1677 the King attempted to pay off Mme de Ludres by offering her a pension, but she rejected this, apparently still hoping that their affair had a future. The Comte de Bussy commented that if this prompted the King to return to her he would applaud her decision; if not, he would remember the maxim that honourable people often had to go without shoes.[73]

After a few more months of misery Mme de Ludres accepted that her position at court was intolerable and decided to enter a convent in Paris. Monsieur asked the King if he would object to her retiring there, to be met with the response, 'Isn't she there already?' Once she left court Mme de Ludres was forgotten so completely that it was 'as if she had perished in the flood'.[74] In October 1680 she swallowed her pride and accepted a pension of 2000 écus. She then withdrew to a convent in Nancy, where she lived for many years.

Athénaïs's victory had been convincing but it did not make her secure. Her hold over the King had been revealed as precarious and she now lived in perpetual fear that he would take another lover. The Comte de Bussy remarked that such uncertainty was a worse torment than actually losing the King and her temper became more volatile under the strain. Throughout the autumn of 1677 Louis kept flirting with other ladies, provoking an outburst of 'pure jealousy' from Mme de Montespan.[75]

In early 1678, despite being heavily pregnant, she accompanied the King on the final campaign of the Dutch War. The conditions were particularly gruelling: the ladies often had to sleep in their carriages, which kept getting bogged down in the mud, and at one point Athénaïs went down with a fever. She had put on so much weight during the pregnancy that she was no longer fit enough to endure such rigours and she was clearly very relieved to return to court after the war ended.[76]

In early May Mme de Montmorency reported that Athénaïs's downfall was considered imminent, although for the moment the King clung to her purely out of habit. Since she was 'in no state to serve the King', Athénaïs withdrew to the country to await the birth of her baby and Louis did not seem sorry to see her go.[77] On 6 June 1678 she was delivered of a son, who was subsequently created Comte de Toulouse. This was her last child by the King (she had borne him seven in all, of whom four survived to adulthood) and some people maintained that after this point he never slept with her again.

Certainly, her looks were not what they were, for after this birth, she did not regain her figure. On one occasion Primi Visconti saw her getting out of her carriage and was shocked by how ungainly she had become. Having caught a glimpse of her thigh, he claimed that it was the same size as his waist though, 'to be fair', he admitted he was now very slim. Perhaps in the hope of being pummelled into shape, Athénaïs had daily massages during which she was rubbed with scented pomades, but unfortunately the King was allergic to perfume and found the smell offensive. After her return to court it was noted that he now seemed reluctant to take her in his carriage.[78]

It was therefore not surprising that when there appeared at court 'a beauty far superior to any that had been seen for a long time at Versailles', the King proved highly susceptible. She came from the Auvergne and was the seventeen-year-old daughter of the Comte de Roussille. Her name was Marie-Angélique de Scorailles, though she was known as Mlle de Fontanges. She had blond hair with a slightly reddish tinge and was lovely 'from head to foot', according to Madame, who took her on as a maid of honour in October 1678. Though she was neither intelligent nor amusing – in the Abbé Choisy's words, she was 'beautiful as an angel, stupid as a mule' – her physical attractions sufficed to enrapture the King.[79]

Mlle de Fontanges had probably become the King's mistress by early 1679 but Athénaïs did not at once realise that she had acquired a rival. At the time her energies were being absorbed by frantic gambling, for every day she hazarded grotesque amounts at *basset*. It was usual for her to lose 100,000 écus a night, though on Christmas Day 1678 her losses amounted to seven times that. Mme de Montmorency mistakenly thought that the King's readiness to countenance her running up such debts showed that she was higher in favour than ever, when the real reason for his forbearance was that he welcomed the fact that her obsession distracted her from monitoring his activities.[80]

However, after Athénaïs had lost a total of 3,400,000 livres,* he became guilty that so much money was being squandered at a time when many of his subjects were oppressed by heavy taxation. He now virtually ceased to gamble, but Athénaïs's excesses continued. In early March she lost 4 million livres in one sitting but insisted on playing on through the night. By 8 a.m. she had won it all back and when the bank tried to end the game, she insisted she needed time to recover a further 100,000 pistoles, which she had lost on a previous occasion. Only after regaining this money did she finally retire to bed.[81] Having decided that matters had now gone too far, the King announced that he would pay her outstanding gambling debts but that *basset* could no longer be played at court.

By this time Athénaïs had become aware that Louis had taken a new mistress. The King had tried to be secretive, enlisting the aid of the Prince de Marcillac who, despite being one of Athénaïs's oldest friends, had done all he could to facilitate Louis's affair with Mlle de Fontanges. Accompanied only by a few bodyguards, the King would travel to Paris under cover of darkness for assignations with Mlle de Fontanges at his brother's town house, the Palais Royal. However, his attempts to be discreet did not succeed: his movements were observed and Athénaïs was alerted to what was happening.[82]

At first she did not appear to mind very much but then, on 4 March, it was reported that there was mounting tension between 'the two sultanas'. The Comte de Bussy prophesied that 'jealousy will embroil the seraglio' and, sure enough, after a row with the King, Mme de Montespan stormed from court on 15 March and went to Paris. Some people assumed that because Easter was approaching the King had suggested she retire for a time, but others were sure that it was her jealousy of Mlle de Fontanges that had prompted her departure. The King's disgust at her frenzied gambling was thought to have exacerbated the estrangement, while heightening his ardour for his new mistress.[83]

The next few weeks were tempestuous as an angry Athénaïs flitted back and forth between Paris and the court. Since she was being so awkward it was thought that the King would soon oblige her to leave the court permanently but in mid-April an accommodation was reached, which apparently resolved the situation. Although Athénaïs had ceased to be the King's mistress, Louis thought it fitting that 'in recompense for past services' she should be offered a position of great status. For years Athénaïs had coveted the post of *Surintendante* of the

---

* To put this in context, the annual income of the French crown has been estimated at approximately 80 million livres.

Queen's household, an office which entitled its holder to be ranked as an honorary duchess, bringing with it such privileges as the right to sit on a *tabouret* in the Queen's presence. Since 1660 the post had been held by the Comtesse de Soissons, who had defied all Athénaïs's earlier attempts to dislodge her, but the King now summoned the Comtesse and ordered her to relinquish the position. She had no alternative but to obey and was compensated for her loss with a payment of 200,000 écus.[84]

Athénaïs declared herself satisfied with the way things had turned out. To emphasise his regard for her, the King still paid her brief visits after mass and after supper although, to avoid unpleasantness, he was always accompanied by his brother. Athénaïs told her old friend the Duc de Noailles that this suited her very well. 'Everything is very calm here...It is much better to see each other seldom and on easy terms than frequently and with awkwardness.'[85]

For a time it seemed that everything would be civilised. The King was said to be frantically in love with Mlle de Fontanges but he took great pains to conceal it. In public he took no notice of her, reserving his affection for their private meetings. To ensure these went undetected, a small suite of rooms was constructed for Mlle de Fontanges above the King's bedroom at Saint-Germain, connected by a hidden staircase. Few people were aware of this until, bizarrely, two pet bears belonging to Mme de Montespan found the door open and 'avenged their mistress' by devastating the apartment.[86]

Meanwhile Mme de Montespan was apparently deriving consolation from religion. She 'went alone to churches' and had conferences with the King's confessor, Père de La Chaise, and another priest named Père Cesar. The Queen, at least, was impressed by what she took to be sincere contrition, though cynics believed that Mme de Montespan was hoping to recapture the King's heart by this moving display of devotion.[87]

A year later allegations would be made suggesting that Athénaïs had been making more sinister use of her time. One suspect arrested during the Affair of the Poisons would imply that during these months Mme de Montespan met with a woman in Paris named Magdelaine Chapelain. Her intention, it was claimed, was to arrange for a servant to be placed in the household of Mlle de Fontanges in order to poison the young woman.

Athénaïs's attempts to convey the impression that she had accepted her altered situation were not wholly successful. It was reported that she frequently broke down in tears and at times she abandoned all pretence of Christian resignation. Apparently without being conscious of any irony, she would rant 'against the great sin committed by Mlle de Fontanges'.[88]

At the end of August 1679 the Electress of Hannover attended the marriage by proxy of Monsieur's daughter to the King of Spain, which took place at Fontainebleau. She was interested to see that Mme de Montespan and Mlle de Fontanges were seated in the same row of the chapel. She noted that the former 'seemed sullen and to regard with mortification the triumph of her young rival, who was in full dress and apparently in high spirits'. Athénaïs's dejection was understandable, for the King 'looked with far greater devotion at Mlle de Fontanges than at the altar, raising his head frequently to look at her in her raised tribune'. A month later Mme de Montespan and the King were overheard having a furious argument in the orangery at Versailles, in the course of which Louis grumbled 'that he was being tormented excessively and he was sick of it'.[89]

That autumn arrangements were made for Athénaïs to set up gaming tables in her court apartments. The courtiers commented that she would be well advised to immerse herself in gambling and leave the King in peace. Mme de Scudéry remarked, 'Provided that she can do without love she will be treated with consideration by the King. That's all an upright gentleman can do when he is no longer in love.' To add to Athénaïs's pain the King was becoming less reticent about showing his passion for Mlle de Fontanges. Work started on a magnificent house for the young woman, and a detachment of guards now escorted her when she travelled from palace to palace. All this led observers to conclude that the King's love for her was growing stronger every day.[90]

On New Year's Day 1680 Mlle de Fontanges appeared at a celebratory mass attended by the King wearing magnificent jewels and looking 'like a goddess'. It seemed that she and the King were now set on flaunting their love, for her dress was made of the same material as his coat and both outfits were trimmed with blue ribbons. Later that day she confidently presented Mme de Montespan with a New Year's gift in the shape of an engagement diary studded with precious stones. The Comte de Bussy commented, 'I doubt whether that brings her her friendship.'[91] In view of the fact that Mlle de Fontanges was no longer kept hidden away, there was general surprise a fortnight later when she did not appear at the wedding of Mlle de Blois (the King's daughter by Louise de La Vallière) to the Prince de Conti. It soon transpired that she had had a miscarriage and, though it was assumed that she would swiftly recover, this turned out to have very serious consequences.

On 22 February 1680 the King left Saint-Germain to travel in slow stages to meet the Princess of Bavaria who had been chosen as a bride for the Dauphin. Mlle de Fontanges was deemed strong enough to go too and set off in a magnificent carriage, pulled by eight horses. It was rumoured that the King had sent her a generous cash endowment prior to departure. This can only have been welcome for, as her magnificently attired servants in grey liveries testified, she was spending at a lavish rate.[92]

On 27 February Monsieur gave a ball in the King's honour at Villars Cotteret and Mlle de Fontanges attended, looking marvellous. Astonishingly Mme de Montespan deserved some of the credit for this: she had helped Marie-Angélique to get dressed, a curious echo of the days when Louise de La Vallière had waited on her like a chambermaid. It was clear that Mlle de Fontanges's health remained delicate, for though she looked lovely she was too weak to do much dancing. However, her love for Louis was undimmed. At another ball a few days later she entered and then approached the King directly, 'looking neither to left nor right' as she traversed the ballroom. She had to be prodded into acknowledging the Queen, whose presence she had ignored. Though the King seemed a little embarrassed by his mistress's blatant display of adoration, onlookers could tell that it also gave him pleasure.[93]

On 6 April Mlle de Fontanges was created Duchesse de Fontanges and endowed with a pension of 80,000 livres. Athénaïs was furious that her young rival should enjoy an honour which, during the lifetime of her husband, could never be conferred on her. 'Yesterday she wept a lot,' reported Mme de Sévigné. 'You can imagine what a martyrdom her pride is suffering.' However, some wise observers considered that the ennoblement of Marie-Angélique 'smells of dismissal'.[94] Before long, events proved them right.

There were various reasons why the King's passion proved so transient. At the start of the affair the Comte de Bussy had presciently observed, 'Wit is necessary to make love last; and Fontanges is very young to have it.' She was far too insipid to amuse a man who was so easily bored as the King and one source claimed that her stupidity was such that Louis was actually ashamed when other people heard her speak. As for her physical allure, that had been diminished by her failure to recover from her miscarriage. Louis should have been sympathetic on the grounds that this was 'a wound received in his service', but he was always intolerant of ill health in others. The fact that she was suffering from 'a very stubborn and disobliging loss of blood' seriously incommoded him, for sleeping with her became problematical. Worse still, after a time her body began to swell and her beautiful face became slightly puffy.[95]

There were also spiritual pressures on the King. Once again Easter was approaching, so it was the season for the King's annual attack of guilt. This year his conscience may have been particularly sensitive, for it was whispered that the Pope himself was trying to reform his morals, having apparently sent instructions that the King's confessor, Père de La Chaise, must resign if Louis continued his affair with Mlle de Fontanges.[96] Besides this, in the past three months the Affair of the Poisons had devastated the court, as numerous grand people there had come under suspicion of poisoning and involvement in occult practices. This perhaps inclined the King to ponder matters such as sin and redemption rather more deeply than was usual for him. The long conversations he was having daily with his children's governess, Mme de Maintenon (the former Mme Scarron), may also have encouraged serious reflections.

Shortly after being created a duchess, Mlle de Fontanges left court to spend Easter at Maubuisson Abbey, where her sister was abbess. While she was away she was treated by the prior of Cabrières, a holy man who claimed to be able to cure persistent ailments and who currently was held in high repute. For a time it seemed that he had worked wonders, for when Mlle de Fontanges arrived back at court on 2 May she appeared fully recovered. On her return the King visited her immediately, all his scruples seemingly having been dispelled now that she was once again in 'a condition to please'.[97] However it turned out that she was only in temporary remission and by the end of the month she was as ill as ever.

On 3 July it was reported that the King now regarded her with 'extreme indifference' and that the poor young woman was often in tears as she knew she had lost his love. Since her sister had recently been transferred from Maubuisson to take up the position of Abbess of Chelles, on 17 July Mlle de Fontanges set off to visit her there. Her departure underlined the fact that she had achieved a great deal in material terms, for she travelled in an impressive cavalcade of six coaches, none pulled by fewer than six horses. However, as Mme de Sévigné observed, in other ways the scene was so poignant as to inspire compassion: 'The beauty losing all her blood, pale, altered, overwhelmed with sadness, thinking nothing of forty thousand écus of income and a *tabouret*, which she has, and desiring health and the King's heart, which she does not.'[98]

She was no better by September, and Mlle de Fontanges now began to voice dark suspicions. Claiming that she must have been poisoned, she requested the King to provide her with guards for her own protection.[99] However, nothing could halt her decline, which relentlessly continued. When she returned to court at the end of the month she spent most of the time languishing in her room, where the King paid her only fleeting and infrequent visits.

These developments should have favoured Mme de Montespan, but her fortunes showed no sign of reviving as Mlle de Fontanges's sank lower. Athénaïs's relations with the King had, in fact, been tense for most of the year. On 30 April the Comte de Bussy had reported, 'Mme de Montespan has fallen to a point which is scarcely credible; the King does not look at her and, as you may imagine, the courtiers follow his example.' The following month the King had a furious altercation with her while they were driving from Saint-Germain to Fontainebleau in the Queen's carriage. It started when he made a fairly mild protest about her reeking of scent, which, as usual, made him feel sick. Athénaïs at once flared up, whereupon the King lost his temper and an unpleasant row ensued.[100]

People predicted that if she remained on such poor terms with the King, Athénaïs would have to leave the court but Colbert (whose daughter had recently become betrothed to Mme de Montespan's nephew) did his best to smooth matters over. In late May he persuaded the King to follow his usual practice of taking *medianoche* (a midnight feast consumed at the end of fast days) with her. Though Louis grudgingly complied, he insisted that many other people must be present.[101]

All this meant that there was little likelihood of Mme de Montespan capitalising on the decline of the Duchesse de Fontanges. What really blighted her prospects, however, was a development that no one had expected. Even in the months when Louis had been most passionately infatuated with Marie-Angélique, he had been simultaneously forming a deep attachment to his children's governess, Mme de Maintenon. This was now assuming an ever greater significance, leading Mme de Sévigné to write on 9 June 1680, 'Mme de Maintenon's favour is still growing while that of Mme de Montespan is visibly diminishing.'[102]

Initially it had seemed that Athénaïs's choice of Mme Scarron (as she then was) to look after her children had been an unmitigated success. Mme Scarron proved to be a conscientious woman who was devoted to the welfare of her charges and justly prided herself on her talents as a teacher. She particularly doted on the Duc du Maine, whom she described as 'the prettiest creature in the world who surprises one twenty times a day with his wit'.[103] Aged three, the child had caught what was probably polio, which left him permanently lame, but his disabilities were offset by the most winning manner, which captivated all who encountered him. The King came to adore him and their shared affection for this enchanting child was undoubtedly a factor in bringing him closer to Mme Scarron.

Unfortunately, although her relationship with Mme de Montespan seems to have remained satisfactory while she and the children were living in the Rue de Vaugirard, it deteriorated once they were legitimised and Mme Scarron moved with them into Athénaïs's lodgings at court. One reason for this was that Mme Scarron was so passionately devoted to the children that she resented their mother's attempts to control their upbringing. Her lack of professional detachment caused many problems and at times even she admitted that it was unwise of her to be so possessive. When the Duc du Maine fell seriously ill in July 1674 she feared that he would die and leave her as bereft as she had been after the death of his elder sibling, two years earlier. Chiding herself for her weakness she wrote, 'There is nothing so stupid as to love to excess a child who does not belong to me.'[104]

Mme Scarron persuaded herself that Mme de Montespan wanted to institute practices that were actually injurious to the children's health and, in these circumstances, it amounted to a sin on her part not to protest. In particular, she and Mme de Montespan had conflicting ideas about child nutrition. At this distance it is difficult to judge who was in the right. For example, Mme Scarron complained that Mme de Montespan insisted that the Duc du Maine must eat dry bread at teatime rather than a heavier meal.[105] The governess claimed that this hurt his teeth, but while there may have been some truth in this it is hard to believe that it could have caused him serious harm.

Nevertheless, Mme Scarron felt very strongly about such matters. At one point she raged that the children were being 'fed as badly as it is possible to be' and in September 1674 she told her confessor, 'These poor children are being killed before my eyes without my being able to hinder it.' She continued,

> The tenderness I have for them makes me unbearable to those to whom they belong and the impossibility of hiding what I think makes me hate some people with whom I spend my life, and whom I would not want to displease even if they were not who they are ... Sometimes I am resolved not to put any effort into what I do and to leave these children to the conduct of their mother, but then I am assailed by scruples about offending God by this abandonment and recommence my efforts.[106]

It is clear that friction usually arose not because Athénaïs was indifferent towards her children but because she had strong views about infant welfare which differed from those held by the governess. However Mme Scarron's comments and sources such as the memoirs of her niece★ Mme de Caylus (who presumably derived her information from her aunt) all give the impression that Mme Scarron regarded her employer as a bad and unfeeling mother. It is worth considering the evidence for this because, if it is true that Athénaïs showed no love even towards her own children, it becomes easier to accept that, as was later alleged, she had a stranger's baby sacrificed in her presence.

Mme de Caylus implies that in her determination to restore to health the Comte de Vexin (who was a sickly child from birth, plagued by spinal problems) Athénaïs recklessly inflicted on him painful medical treatments, which did him no good. While it may be true that the poor boy suffered at the hands of doctors, his mother doubtless authorised this for the best motives and it is hardly fair to criticise her for it. A letter that she wrote in July 1675, when the three-year-old Vexin was recovering from a serious illness, testifies to her sincere concern for his well-being. Having said that she would have gone mad if he had died, as had seemed probable at one point, she writes that she will not complain if he takes a long time to recover, provided his life is spared.[107]

Mme Scarron herself raised no objection to the experimental treatments which were devised for the Duc du Maine in hopes of strengthening his withered leg. She took him to Antwerp to see a doctor who tormented the poor child to no avail and also accompanied him twice to the spa town of Barèges, in 1675 and 1677. For a time it seemed that this had helped him, and Mme Scarron was happy to take some of the credit for this. In the summer of 1681 Maine again went to Barèges, though this time with his tutor. In July Mme Scarron was proclaiming her belief in the efficacy of the waters, but two months later she became incensed when she learned that Mme de Montespan wanted him to stay longer in the town. Furiously she wrote that it was ridiculous that Mme de Montespan should meddle in a matter of which she knew nothing.[108]

Mme de Caylus later claimed that when Mme de Montespan's first child by the King died in 1672, the baby's governess had been far more distressed than the child's own mother. In September 1681, following the death of Mlle de Tours, Athénaïs's fifth child by the King (who had been born in 1674), Mme de Maintenon wrote a letter hinting at the

★ Mme de Caylus was actually Mme de Maintenon's cousin but because of the generation gap is usually referred to as her niece.

same thing. She confided to her confessor, 'The King has been very moved by this [the child's death] and I defer telling you what I know about the pain of Mme de Montespan.' However, Mlle de Montpensier noted in her memoirs that Mme de Montespan was 'very afflicted' by the child's loss and a letter that Athénaïs penned shortly after the death bears this out. She writes that ever since receiving the news she has been in a deep depression and that whenever she sees a place frequented in the past by her daughter, it adds to her grief.[109]

When the Duc du Maine was in his mid-teens he became somewhat alienated from his mother, but letters he wrote as a seven-year–old to Athénaïs (or his *belle Madame*', as he calls her) suggest that at that point he adored her. The letters refer to his immense tenderness for her and are full of passionate protestations that he is 'the man who loves you most in the world'. The letters were composed under the supervision of his governess and it is possible that he wrote these endearments at her instigation, but there is a spontaneity and warmth to them which gives them great conviction. The letters also contain references to presents that Athénaïs sent her son and to games she played with her children. This, coupled with Madame's statement that 'the children were always present' with Mme de Montespan, indicates that, by aristocratic standards of the time, she was by no means inattentive to them.[110]

There can be no question that Athénaïs was a very difficult employer who was often inconsiderate and whose tendency to fly into rages could make life uncomfortable for those around her. On the other hand, Mme Scarron was not without fault herself. One may surmise that, having moved with Athénaïs in salon society on a footing of equality, she found her transformation into a servant difficult to swallow. She nurtured every grievance with a brooding intensity but overlooked all Athénaïs's kindnesses and acts of generosity. This makes it easier to accept Mme de Sévigné's contention that it was Mme Scarron's 'pride' which disrupted the governess's relationship with Mme de Montespan and that, while she did all she could to please the King, she was reluctant to defer to Athénaïs's orders.[111]

There was a certain irony about this for, initially, the King had had grave reservations about Mme Scarron. She herself later recalled that he objected to her intellectual pretensions, complaining that she was interested only in 'sublime things'. At first, when disagreements had broken out between her and Mme de Montespan, the King had naturally supported Athénaïs.[112] Gradually, however, this changed as he became better acquainted with the governess and developed a growing esteem for her.

At the end of 1674 Mme Scarron received a cash grant of 200,000 livres from the King. This allowed her to buy the chateau and estate of Maintenon, a 'beautiful and noble' property whose possession not only yielded an annual income of 10,000 livres but entitled her to style herself the Marquise de Maintenon. It may be that she had Mme de Montespan to thank for the fact that she had been able to make so substantial a purchase. Originally she was to have received only 100,000 livres and Saint-Simon claimed (though long after the event) that it was Athénaïs who persuaded the King to double the amount.[113] If so, it failed to sweeten their relationship.

In February 1675 Mme de Maintenon reported to her confessor, 'Terrible things are happening here between Mme de Montespan and myself.' However, she took evident satisfaction in the fact that the King had witnessed one of their arguments the previous day, evidently hoping that from now on she could count on his support. When she accompanied the Duc du Maine to Barèges the following May, the King kept in regular contact with her by letter and by August Mme de Sévigné had heard that Mme de Montespan was annoyed that her governess was going to great trouble to keep the King informed of the Duc du Maine's progress while ignoring her. Mme de Sévigné believed that by now the two women were on terms of settled antipathy but that, though Mme de Montespan was indignant that the King now showed such partiality to Mme de Maintenon, she could not alter his sentiments. In May 1676 Mme de Sévigné reported that Mme de Maintenon was becoming an important personage at court and the following July she wrote that she was in greater favour than ever.[114]

Over the next few years Mme de Maintenon remained an unobtrusive presence at court but all well-informed people were aware that the King held her in the highest esteem. In August 1676 he sent André Le Nôtre to design her gardens at Maintenon, a sure sign of how greatly he valued her, and the following month Mme de Sévigné noted, 'Her favour is extreme.' In June 1677 it was rumoured that the King had presented her with precious stones worth 200,000 écus and although this may have been a false report, the fact that it was so readily believed is indicative of her standing. From now on she was regarded as a figure of consequence: when the King awarded her old friend M. de Montchevreuil the revenues of a rich abbey in May 1678, it was Mme de Maintenon who was credited with having secured this.[115]

In late 1679 Mme de Maintenon's situation at court underwent a transformation. The Duc du Maine now reached an age where his education had to be entrusted to male tutors, and since Mme de Maintenon had not taken charge of Athénaïs's two youngest children by the King there was no pressing reason for her to remain in Mme de Montespan's household. The Dauphin, now aged eighteen, had recently been betrothed to Princesse Marie Anne of Bavaria and in December it was announced that Mme de Maintenon had been selected as one of her ladies of the bedchamber. It was an unprecedented honour for a woman who, though of respectable birth, had not married into the aristocracy.

Mme de Maintenon was delighted, not least because, since she was now granted court lodgings of her own, she no longer had to live in Mme de Montespan's apartment. Ignorant courtiers assumed that it was Mme de Montespan who had prevailed on the King to provide for a woman who had accorded long and faithful service, but Mme de Sévigné knew better. She told her daughter that Mme de Maintenon's advancement 'will not be on account of Quanto'. She had no doubt that the pair now held each other in mutual detestation and that Mme de Maintenon had secured the honour on her own merits.[116]

In January 1680 Mme de Maintenon set off to meet the new Dauphine on the French borders so that she could escort her to her new home. By March she was back at court with her new mistress and, since the King went out of his way to be welcoming and attentive to his daughter-in-law, Mme de Maintenon saw a good deal of him. By this time Mlle de Fontanges's poor state of health was beginning to cool his affection for her and the King now devoted the hours which in former days he would have passed with Mme de Montespan on visits to the new Dauphine. These courtesy calls were more agreeable to him because they afforded him plenty of opportunities for conversing with Mme de Maintenon.[117]

Mme de Montespan was incensed at finding herself relegated to the sidelines. Her fury when Mlle de Fontanges was created a duchess was exacerbated by the fact that this coincided with the time when the King's attentions to Mme de Maintenon were growing ever more pronounced. On 25 March the Comte de Bussy declared, 'Nobody, without exception, is on better terms with the King than Mme de Maintenon.' The court's wonder at this increased when he began to call on her in her own rooms, rather than meeting in the Dauphine's apartment. Every evening he would spend two hours chatting animatedly to her with so 'free and easy an air that it makes this the most desirable place in the world'. This continued throughout the summer of 1680 although by June their evening tête-à-tête, which now lasted from 6 p.m. till ten at night, was taking place in the King's private apartments.[118]

Whereas a few weeks earlier the King had used his visits to the Dauphine as an excuse to see Mme de Maintenon, now the Dauphine almost felt like an intruder on the occasions when she joined them. She invariably found them seated opposite each other in comfortable chairs (in itself an extraordinary violation of the rules of etiquette) and, though they greeted her politely, it was evident that they were longing for her to leave so they could resume the thread of their conversation. No wonder that, by late June, the Duchesse de Fontanges believed herself superseded and was frequently seen weeping. As for Mme de Montespan, she had realised, far too late, that the challenge posed by the King's 'flash of passion' for Marie-Angélique was negligible compared with that which she now faced.[119]

Mme de Sévigné commented that the King's conversations with Mme de Maintenon were 'of a length to make everyone wonder', and people have been speculating ever since as to the exact nature of the relationship. Mme de Sévigné was inclined to believe that the secret of her appeal lay in the fact that the King felt absolutely relaxed and open with this woman who commanded his respect and whose sincerity he admired. She explained, 'She introduces him to a new world, hitherto unknown to him, of friendship and unrestrained conversation, free of chicanery. He appears charmed by it.'[120]

Abbé Choisy also believed that the King was attracted by what for him was a delightful novelty: despite his extensive experience of women, she was the first 'who talked to him only of virtue' and, furthermore, she could do so without being in the least boring. The German diplomat Ezechiel Spanheim likewise thought the King was drawn to her by 'a pure esteem', and he stressed that at this point it was generally accepted that their attachment was based on friendship and trust rather than proceeding from 'a more tender passion'.[121]

Others sought alternative explanations for the King's perplexing predilection for this middle-aged lady who was so completely different from the women who had gained his love in the past. Primi Visconti recalled, 'Nobody knew what to make of it, for she was old. Some regarded her as the confidante of the King, others as a go-between [with other women]; others still as a clever person whom the King was using to draw up the memoirs of his reign.'[122]

Inevitably, however, some people were sure that sex provided the key to it all. Rumours began to circulate that Mme de Maintenon's past history was not as virtuous as she liked to imply and that, though her marriage to Scarron may have been unconsummated, she had had affairs in early widowhood. The notorious rake the Marquis de Villarceaux was named as one of her lovers and there were exciting reports that she had been seen in his bed dressed as a page. However, having noted that Mme de Montespan was in the forefront of those who sought to cast aspersions on Mme de Maintenon, Primi Visconti decided there was no truth in these stories.[123]

Even if Mme de Maintenon had led a completely chaste life prior to her arrival at court this does not, of course, rule out that she surrendered herself to the King. Many historians have accepted that, from the moment she first acquired the King's favour circa 1675, she began sleeping with him. A letter which she supposedly wrote in 1673 is often cited in support of this. In it she refers to the King making advances which she has managed to spurn without disheartening him.[124] However, this document is of dubious authenticity and cannot be relied on. Even so it is sometimes still maintained that she and Louis became lovers long before his admiration for her was recognised. What is more, it is suggested that she did so in the conviction that she was following God's wishes.

There can be no doubt that Mme de Maintenon was a deeply religious woman, for the preoccupation with salvation that forms a theme of her correspondence cannot be dismissed as mere posturing. Nevertheless, it is contended that she was able to square what was ostensibly a grave sin with her conscience by persuading herself that she was sacrificing her virtue for a higher purpose. Her ultimate and paradoxical aim – so the argument goes – was to restore the King to a pure way of life by lessening his dependence on other mistresses. Furthermore, she acted with the blessing of her confessor who persuaded her that by this means she could bring the King to a spiritual awakening and save him from damnation.

There are, of course, many difficulties about accepting this hypothesis. Quite apart from the level of sophistry and elasticity of outlook it presupposes in both Mme de Maintenon and her confessor, it would have been a tremendous gamble on their part to believe that all would turn out as planned. It needed powers of supernatural foresight to anticipate that she could have conducted a casual affair with the King for many years without forfeiting his respect, and that her hold over him would subsequently tighten to a point where she could exert moral guidance. Furthermore, though she was known to be in favour, there is no hint that, prior to 1680, anyone at court remotely suspected that she had ever had sexual relations with the King.

It is, of course, much easier to believe that Mme de Maintenon succumbed to the King at some point in 1680. By that time his liking for her had matured into an overwhelming attraction, while his love for Mlle de Fontanges was fading. Arguably, indeed, it is inconceivable that a man of the King's known appetites would have been prepared to spend hours closeted in conversation with a woman he found alluring unless she was offering him sexual satisfaction. Some have believed him incapable of forming a profound attachment to a member of the opposite sex without attaining carnal knowledge.

Against this, it should be noted that once the King had ceased sleeping with Mlle de Fontanges his behaviour towards the Queen underwent a marked alteration. Mme de Caylus later recalled that he began showing her 'attentions to which she was unaccustomed. He saw her more often and sought to amuse her... She attributed the happy change to Mme de Maintenon.' When the court was touring the borders of Holland and Alsace-Lorraine in August 1680, Mme de Sévigné heard that the Queen was in unusually good form, and that the King was treating her very kindly. He also began having sexual relations with her much more frequently. The number of times he did this could be accurately charted because the Queen always took communion the following morning. Furthermore, according to Madame, 'She was so happy when that had happened that one saw it straight away; she liked it if one joked with her about it, and then she laughed and winked and rubbed her little hands.' In December 1680 M. de Trichâteau told the Comte de Bussy that the King was doing everything possible to furnish the Dauphin with a brother and 'the Queen has not had such fun for a long time'.[125] It seems plausible that Louis's sudden and uncharacteristic uxoriousness was caused by his having to seek a legitimate outlet for his passions now that he was no longer gaining sexual release through extramarital affairs.

Such an interpretation is supported by the fact that he made no attempt to be discreet about his meetings with Mme de Maintenon. Instead, every evening she was ceremoniously conducted to and from the King's rooms by the Dauphine's Master of the Household 'in the sight of all the universe.'[126] This forms a complete contrast to his almost obsessive secrecy when he started his liaison with Mlle de Fontanges. Unless one accepts that the King had suddenly become completely shameless, the only explanation is surely that Louis took real pleasure in being able to flaunt a relationship with a woman about which he had no cause to reproach himself.

The few surviving letters written by Mme de Maintenon at this period testify to her happiness, but this cannot be taken as proof that she and the King had become lovers. The knowledge that she was admired and esteemed by him was plainly a source of satisfaction, but for her the real triumph lay in the fact that she had achieved this without compromising her virtue. She now exerted her influence to extricate the King from a state of sin, in the belief that, having done so, she could effect a conversion and attain his salvation.

Mme de Maintenon later claimed that she would have left court long before this had it not been for her confessor's insistence that she remain there. Though at first she had been puzzled by his orders, after a time she saw their wisdom. As she recalled, 'I began to see that perhaps it would not be impossible for me to be of some use in the King's salvation; I began to be convinced that God had only kept me there for that.'[127]

Exactly when this revelation came to her remains unclear. One later statement of hers shows that for several years she considered that it was not incumbent on her to voice any disapproval of the King's way of life with Athénaïs. 'I never entered into his relations [with her],' she declared. 'They were already far advanced when he made my acquaintance and they did not take me into their confidence.' On the other hand a letter she wrote to her confessor, Abbé Gobelin, on 5 April 1675 suggests that even then she was starting to exert moral pressure on the King. She told Gobelin she had spoken to Louis the previous day and that Gobelin should 'fear nothing; it seems to me that I spoke to him as a Christian and as a true friend of Mme de Montespan'. Possibly, therefore, she played a part in bringing about the King's Easter separation from Athénaïs. Apart from this, we know of only one instance where she upbraided Louis, which she later described to her secretary, Mlle Aumale. She recalled that, one day when she was walking with the King at a court reception, she had observed that if he had discovered that one of his musketeers was conducting an affair with a married woman he would have drummed the offender out of the palace. The King sheepishly concurred with this indirect reproof.[128]

Presumably she put forward other arguments during their numerous private conversations. Certainly, Mme de Maintenon later came to think that her role had been crucial in bringing the King to forsake a sinful way of life. She acknowledged that in doing so she had undermined the position of Mme de Montespan, who in many ways had been her principal benefactor, but she insisted she felt no guilt on this score. She later mused, 'Was I wrong to have given him good advice and to have tried as far as I could to break off his relations [with Athénaïs]?' She then answered her own rhetorical question by declaring that Mme de Montespan would have had more cause to reproach her if she had encouraged the King to prolong the affair.[129]

It also appears that Mme de Maintenon did her best to put a stop to the King's affair with Mlle de Fontanges, though it is not clear if she confronted Louis himself on the matter. In March 1679, when the relationship came to light, she begged her confessor 'to pray and have others pray for the King, who is on the edge of a great precipice'. She also later confided to some girls at Saint-Cyr that the King had once sent her to reason with a furious Mlle de Fontanges, who was upset by the way he was treating her. She reminisced, 'The King feared an outburst and had sent me to calm her; I was there two hours and used the time to persuade her to leave the King and to try and convince her that this would be fine and praiseworthy. I recall that she answered me with vivacity, "But Madame, you talk to me of ridding myself of a passion as if it was like divesting myself of a chemise!"'[130]

The inexorable rise of Mme de Maintenon (now called Mme de *Maintenant* by knowing courtiers) meant that, despite the declining fortunes of the Duchesse de Fontanges, the summer of 1680 was a grim time for Mme de Montespan. That July the King travelled through Flanders, and along the borders of Holland and Alsace-Lorraine. Prominent among the ladies who accompanied him was Mme de Maintenon. Athénaïs trailed along too, taking with her her seven-year-old daughter, Mlle de Nantes, but this merely served to emphasise that she was now excluded from the King's innermost circle. In contrast to the rapturous letters penned by Mme de Maintenon enthusing about her treatment on the voyage ('Nobody at court is better served than I am'), communications from Athénaïs make it clear that she was leading a miserable existence. At one point she and her daughter were reduced to sleeping on a pile of straw and everyone around her fell prey to ailments. 'I was as ill as the others,' she lamented, confiding that a bad attack of the vapours had nearly killed her. A letter to her old friend the Duchesse de Noailles makes plain her sense of alienation. She wrote glumly, 'I don't have the heart for anything. At court one is still leading the same life. I am informed about it as little as I can be, and in effect that's very little.'[131]

Clearly she was deeply depressed, but things were about to deteriorate further. Since January 1680 the court had been convulsed by the Affair of the Poisons, which had resulted in the arrest and interrogation of numerous prominent people on suspicion of witchcraft and attempted murder. In July Mme de Montespan's name had begun to feature in the confessions of various unsavoury individuals who were currently imprisoned in the Château de Vincennes in connection with this matter. Their allegations gave rise to fears that Mme de Montespan was herself guilty of terrible crimes and that she too was part of the dreadful web of evil which had enmeshed so many court figures.

# FOUR

# THE FIRST ARRESTS

The Affair of the Poisons can be said to have started with the arrest in February 1677 of Magdelaine de La Grange. At the time this had seemed an event of little significance. Later described by the Chief of the Paris Police as 'the cleverest and most wicked woman in the world', Magdelaine de La Grange was the thirty-six-year-old widow of a tax collector who had been hanged for receiving stolen goods. Like many others in Paris at the time, she operated as a fortune-teller or 'divineress' and claimed to have predicted successfully developments in the Dutch War and the timing of the Queen's pregnancies. She also exploited people's fears by suggesting to clients in poor health that they had been poisoned and offering to provide an antidote.[1] However, it subsequently emerged that her knowledge about poison was more extensive than that.

For eight years Mme de La Grange had 'lived like a queen' in the house of an elderly lawyer named Jean Faurye. At the end of this time – according to her – he had decided to make her his wife. On 17 August 1676 she had visited a notary's office, accompanied by a man who identified himself as Faurye. After the couple had showed the notary their marriage certificate, the purported Faurye instructed him to draw up a marriage contract arranging that all his wealth should pass to his new wife in the event of his predeceasing her. Shortly after this Faurye had, in fact, died. His relations, who had counted on inheriting his estate, were naturally upset at having their expectations overturned. They lodged a formal complaint at the Châtelet and as a result an investigation was mounted. This led the Criminal Lieutenant of Paris to conclude that Mme de La Grange's marriage certificate was a forgery and that the gentleman who had gone to the notary's with her was in reality Abbé Nail, the priest who supposedly had conducted the marriage. Furthermore, there were grounds for suspecting that Faurye had been poisoned. Consequently, Magdelaine de La Grange and Nail were arrested, and confined in separate prisons to await trial on charges of forgery and murder.

In February 1677 Mme de La Grange sent a letter from prison to the Marquis de Louvois. She intimated that she had discovered that one of her fellow prisoners was a spy and she had uncovered information from him which had the gravest implications for national security. Taking this very seriously, Louvois at once arranged for Mme de La Grange to be taken to his Paris house so he could question her in person.

The involvement of Louvois was an extraordinary development, for he was one of the most powerful men in France. Born in 1639, he had since his early youth been groomed by his father, Michel Le Tellier – who himself had become Secretary for War in 1643 – to serve the King. In 1662, aged only twenty-two, he had won the right to style himself 'Secretary of State' and to deputise for his father when the latter was absent or ill. During the next few years he and his father had together carried out the major reforms which transformed the French army into the most formidable fighting force in Europe. Though Le Tellier in theory remained Secretary for War until 1677, by 1670 Louvois was probably more active in the War Department than his father and his contribution to France's ultimate victory in the Dutch War was immense. Having been promoted to a Minister of State in 1672, Louvois would be formally created Minister of War in October 1677, following Le Tellier's appointment as Chancellor. His power was further enhanced by various lesser positions, including that of Superintendent of the Postal Service, which enabled him to intercept and read all private correspondence that passed through France.

Louvois drove himself very hard and laboured indefatigably on the King's behalf. 'I've never known a man work so much,' the Marquis de Saint-Maurice declared in 1667. He was also a natural bully who did not consider politeness a priority. Even the King, who valued Louvois as an indispensable servant, would declare, once he was dead, that Louvois had been 'an unbearable man' and among those who had less cause to be grateful to him he excited feelings of intense dislike. The King's sister-in-law, the Duchesse d'Orléans, subsequently recalled, 'Louvois made himself hated by everyone on account of his brutality and coarse speech. He had no refinement and was a detestable man.' He was physically unattractive, with a corpulent figure and jowly face, and his manners were extraordinarily brusque. Describing him as 'mordant and peremptory in command, demanding complete submission to his wishes', the Venetian ambassador noted that Louvois not only ignored the complaints of subordinates but was less than deferential to some of the principal personages at court.[2]

Besides inspiring hostility, Louvois was ruthless about pursuing vendettas. His greatest rival was the Controller-General of Finance,

Colbert. While there could be no question of Louvois unseating a man who enjoyed the King's complete confidence, the friction between the two was palpable. In 1671 Michel Le Tellier remarked sadly that, though he had tried to cultivate amicable relations with Colbert, his son seemed set on warring with him. Louvois had still fewer reservations about antagonising other important figures. During the Dutch War he inspired fury among high-ranking officers with his insistence that they conform to his will, and even came into conflict with the great generals Condé and Turenne. Later it would be alleged that Louvois used the Affair of the Poisons – in which he played an active role from the start – to pursue 'personal enmities' by encouraging the persecution of individuals who had annoyed him or who were affiliated to Colbert.[3]

Having interviewed Magdelaine de La Grange, Louvois notified the King, who ordered that she should be transferred to the Bastille for further questioning. Louvois then instructed the Chief of the Paris Police, M. de La Reynie, to assume personal charge of the interrogations. While acknowledging that de La Grange might be lying in order to delay her forthcoming trial, Louvois explained that it was impossible to be too careful when it came to the sort of matters of which she had spoken.[4]

There could be no doubting the efficiency of Nicolas Gabriel de La Reynie, the taciturn and sombre figure who had been Chief of the Paris Police for the past ten years. Now aged fifty-one, La Reynie had started his career serving in provincial government before purchasing a post as a Maître de Requêtes in the Paris *Parlement*. As such he had both served as an appeal court judge and had given legal advice to the Crown, tasks he had carried out so ably that he had attracted the notice of Colbert. The latter had, indeed, been on the verge of putting him in charge of admiralty reform and harbour regulation when La Reynie had been entrusted with a still greater challenge. In his capacity as a crown lawyer he had attended the meetings held in 1666 to discuss the policing of Paris and there it had been decided that a new post, the Lieutenant-General of the Paris Police, should be created. On 15 March 1667 La Reynie was given this position by the King, who declared he had chosen him because he did not know 'a better man or a more hardworking magistrate'.[5]

The King made it clear that he would do everything possible to uphold the new Police Chief's authority. He wrote to Colbert, 'I shall submit *myself* to the rulings of this police and I intend that all shall respect and obey them as I will.' Such royal support was vital, for the task that confronted La Reynie was daunting. Colbert commented to

the King that the Police Chief would have to be 'unflinching as a magistrate and intrepid as a soldier. He must not pale before the river in
flood or plague in the hospitals any more than before popular uproar or
the threats of your courtiers, for it must be expected that the court will
not be the last to complain of the useful rigour of a police, carried on in
the interests of the well-being and security of all.'[6] These were
prophetic words, for La Reynie's handling of the Affair of the Poisons
would indeed bring him into confrontation with some of the most
high-born and influential figures in the country.

La Reynie's responsibilities were multifarious and extended to many
areas which today are not regarded as the province of a police force. It
has been suggested, indeed, that in some ways his role was more akin
to that of a modern mayor or chief executive of a great city than a
present-day chief of police.[7] Great importance was attached to the
control of public order by prohibiting the unauthorised carrying of
weapons and suppressing civil disturbances, but La Reynie was also
charged with dealing with emergencies such as fire and floods. Besides
this, it fell upon him to monitor the capital's food supplies and prices in
times of scarcity, repress vagrancy and prostitution, regulate the traffic,
institute precautions against the plague and enforce censorship. In addition he oversaw numerous administrative tasks, such as improving
hygiene in streets and public places, inspecting hostelries, inns and
taverns, and ensuring that commercial regulations were observed.

La Reynie had achieved an enormous amount in a short time and in
some respects had transformed Paris. Prior to his appointment Paris had
the reputation of being the filthiest city in the world, clogged by stinking mud that made walking an ordeal and stained clothes indelibly. La
Reynie effected a marked improvement, partly through the simple
expedient of forcing householders to clean the space in front of their
property. He lessened the risk that Paris might be consumed by a catas-
trophe on the scale of the Great Fire of London by obliging householders to maintain their backyard wells in good working order.
Perhaps most commendably of all, he introduced an extensive system
of street lighting, arranging in 1667 that 6500 lanterns should be strung
across the city streets. This was not merely a desirable amenity but dras-
tically reduced nocturnal crime. Primi Visconti noted that, whereas
before Paris was looked on as 'a nest of thieves and murderers', by 1676
it was considered safe to move about it at two in the morning.[8]

In addition to all this, in 1674 the King had put La Reynie in charge
of the special commission that had investigated and tried a treasonous
conspiracy led by the Chevalier de Rohan, and Louis had been much
impressed by the efficient way La Reynie conducted the case. At the

time La Reynie had told Colbert that he had made it a priority to punish only the most important culprits, rather than to pursue all the ramifications of the affair. He explained that while he had been careful not to overlook anything of importance, he had become concerned that if the prisons of Paris were filled with too many suspects, people would begin to think that the innocent were being caught in the net along with the guilty.[9] It would, perhaps, have been desirable if La Reynie had kept these precepts in mind when he came to deal with the Affair of the Poisons, for the inquiry into that became alarmingly diversified, with a consequent loss of focus.

La Reynie has invariably received favourable treatment from historians. This is partly on account of his undoubted achievements but also because he was eulogised in the memoirs of Saint-Simon. When La Reynie retired in 1697 Saint-Simon praised him for the equity and impartiality he had always shown, noting that while he had always performed his duty with the utmost exactitude, he had harmed people as little and as rarely as possible. In conclusion, Saint-Simon declared that he was 'a man of great virtue and capacity who ... should have attracted the hatred of the public, but who acquired universal esteem'.[10]

This panegyric was not strictly accurate for, during the Affair of the Poisons, La Reynie was regarded with loathing by many people at court. This, of course, can be taken to demonstrate that his unflinching integrity led him to do his duty even in the face of opposition in high quarters, but one should be cautious of assuming that La Reynie had right on his side at all times. Some of those who came under suspicion during the affair claimed that he distorted evidence against them and put pressure on witnesses to incriminate them, and these allegations cannot be automatically dismissed.

It should be borne in mind that Saint-Simon was particularly favourably disposed to La Reynie on account of the fact that the latter was an executor of a contested will of which Saint-Simon was ultimately a major beneficiary. During the Affair of the Poisons La Reynie may also have been influenced by political considerations. At the time of his appointment he was looked on as a protégé of Colbert's but in the intervening years he had drawn closer to Louvois and he undoubtedly considered it desirable to uphold the latter's interests. One cannot even exclude the possibility that at times during the affair he was pursuing an agenda of his own. Following his second marriage, La Reynie had become embroiled in a legal dispute with the Bouillon family over his wife's inheritance and it is permissible to wonder whether this affected his treatment of the Duchesse de Bouillon.[11] While this can never be more than a suspicion, it is indisputable that La Reynie's personal prestige became bound up with the outcome of the Affair of the Poisons and there were times when this clouded his judgement.

As Louvois requested, La Reynie questioned Mme de La Grange at the Bastille. Moving beyond her earlier claim that she knew about an espionage ring that threatened France, she now started implying that both the King and the Dauphin were in danger of assassination. She produced little evidence for this but stated that her lover, Faurye, had been poisoned (though not by her) for 'secret reasons' connected with the royal family's safety.[12] Despite their flimsy nature, her warnings were passed on to the King. He found them disturbing, but when she failed to reveal anything more under repeated probing he lost patience. In June Mme de La Grange was transferred back to the Conciergerie to await trial. From there she continued to write to Louvois but her letters were ignored.

Then, at the beginning of October, an anonymous letter was found in a Paris church, which seemed to confirm that the King or the Dauphin was in danger. It was apparently written by a widow to an admirer who had told her of his intention to place a 'white powder' on the napkin of an important person. The writer feared this would be the undoing of them both, for she could not believe that such a deed would escape detection. She lamented that her own downfall would come about simply because she had been aware of her admirer's plans, for while with all other crimes one had to be an accomplice before one could be punished, with 'this one', mere knowledge was sufficient to secure a conviction.[13] Since this only applied in cases of treason, the implications were alarming.

Although there was obviously a possibility that the letter had been deliberately planted in order to ensure that Mme de La Grange's warnings were taken seriously, dismissing it as a hoax might have fearful consequences. Accordingly, de La Grange and her clerical associate Nail were repeatedly questioned about the letter but they both insisted they knew nothing about it. Their denials made it pointless to delay their trial any further and later that autumn their case came before the Châtelet. Having been found guilty on all charges, Mme de La Grange and Nail were sentenced to torture and execution. However, as was normal in such cases, both defendants lodged appeals. While they were waiting for their case to be heard by a higher court, fresh developments occurred, which seemingly underlined that powerful figures were vulnerable to poisoning. Because it was arguably imprudent to execute two people who might hold the key to the mystery, de La Grange's and Nail's appeals were delayed.

Matters had taken a new direction with the arrest of Louis Vanens, one of the most intriguing and enigmatic figures to feature in this affair. A thirty-year-old who originated from Arles, Vanens was of sufficiently high social status to be officially classified a 'gentleman', although he preferred to style himself the Chevalier de Vanens. He was not initially suspected of involvement with poison and even today it remains impossible to determine whether he was a killer or merely an accomplished conman.

On 5 December 1677 Vanens was seized in an early-morning raid. Louvois had ordered his arrest after receiving intelligence that after boasting he knew how to formulate gold, Vanens had been seen in possession of a bill of exchange worth the enormous sum of 200,000 livres. Various associates of Vanens were also taken into custody, including his manservant, Jean Barthominat (known as La Chaboissière) and a forty-year-old banker named Pierre Cadelan, in whose name the bill of exchange had reportedly been drawn.

When questioned about his dealings with Vanens, Cadelan explained that Vanens had come into his life by selling him some home-made medical remedies. Once they were acquainted, Vanens had persuaded him that he had a secret method of making gold. The manufacturing process involved the distillation of herbs on a massive scale, and Cadelan had assisted Vanens to obtain equipment for this and to set up furnaces. Cadelan denied that he had furnished Vanens with more than everyday expenses but he agreed that he had made arrangements whereby a large sum could be deposited in a bank account set up in his name at Venice. He said he had done this because Vanens had told him that another friend who knew how to make gold needed to transfer funds to Italy but, in fact, the money had never materialised. However, Cadelan's interrogators were sceptical that 'an intelligent man of business' would have invested so much effort in so fanciful a scheme and were sure that 'some other matter' must be at the root of it.[14]

Cadelan's story was undermined by the fact that Vanens was meanwhile maintaining that large sums had indeed been deposited in Venice and had then been withdrawn on Cadelan's instructions. This seems unlikely to have been true: Louvois ordered the French ambassador in Venice to look into the matter and he could find no record of these transactions. Vanens also claimed that at the time of his arrest he had been carrying a bill of exchange for 20,000 livres from Cadelan, which he had destroyed in panic. While this was a much lesser sum than the 200,000 livres originally mentioned, it was still a significant amount. If Cadelan had been prepared to part with it, it was undeniably mysterious.

Meanwhile Vanens's servant La Chaboissière was making alarming statements. On 13 April 1678 he told his interrogators that, provided he was offered a pardon, hc had 'important things to say which concerned the King' and which might 'save the life of fifty people a year'.[15] It was an echo of the sort of thing that Magdelaine de La Grange had been saying and which had been considered so ominous.

More members of Vanens's circle were now taken into custody. These included a thirty-five-year-old blind man named Dalmas, who had reportedly lost his eyesight conducting alchemical experiments, and his mistress, Louise Dusoulcye. La Chaboissière's girlfriend Catherine Leroy was also arrested and, under questioning, these two women became extremely voluble. Catherine Leroy said she had seen La Chaboissière boiling up herbs in a great cauldron to which he had added mysterious powders. This had produced a solution which had been bottled in phials and sent abroad. La Chaboissière had later told Catherine that Cadelan had been well paid for this.

Still more worryingly, La Chaboissière had said that as a result of their activities 'a big cheese' from abroad 'had gone to carry letters to the late King'.[16] M. de La Reynie (who was co-ordinating the inquiry) deduced from this that Vanens and La Chaboissière had been commissioned to manufacture poison for Cadelan, who then sold it to foreigners so they could assassinate major political figures.

Further testimony suggested that, not content with being at the centre of an international poisoning network, Vanens had been in the habit of eliminating people who were unwise enough to cross him in daily life. A former employee of Vanens, Petit Jean, and another acquaintance named the Abbé Chapelle, had both died unexpectedly; in 1676 a former landlady of Vanens who had been indiscreet about his activities had perished, along with five members of her household, in an unexplained tragedy. When questioned about this Vanens protested that Petit Jean had died of the pox, while his landlady had poisoned herself by unwisely adding a secret solution to sour wine in the hope of making it drinkable. This failed to allay the suspicions against him.

According to Catherine Leroy, practically everyone who associated with Vanens had an equally cavalier attitude to the sanctity of human life. She claimed that La Chaboissière had been so fearful that she would betray his secrets that he had once tried to poison her by tricking her into taking some greyish and black grains, which had made her very ill. Despite that, she had not only continued to live with him but had herself murdered two women on his orders. The first was a seller of eau-de-vie named la Regnault whose dish of skate and eggs had been poisoned by Catherine Leroy when they dined together; the other was a Mme Carré, who died four days after Catherine had fed her poisoned wine and poisoned jam. Furthermore, at the behest of Dalmas, Louise Dusoulcye had killed a woman called la Levasseur by giving her plums dipped in poison.

It is certainly odd if Catherine Leroy was making all this up but on the other hand her testimony cannot be accepted uncritically. La Regnault had died three or four months after their dinner together, so it is by no means clear that poison was responsible. As for Mme Carré, she was a frail woman of eighty whose death was so clearly imminent that it was surely unnecessary to hasten it by poisoning. Yet to M. de La Reynie this did not seem significant. Instead, he was appalled by the glimpses he had gained of a world where poison formed part of the culture and where murder was routinely perpetuated without fear of retribution.

Catherine Leroy gave additional tantalising hints that in between doing away with these lowly individuals Vanens and La Chaboissière had targeted more eminent victims. She reported that after the death of Chancellor d'Aligre in October 1677 an unidentified relation of the Chancellor had paid La Chaboissière 300 livres. Could this have been a reward for hastening d'Aligre's end? At the time d'Aligre's death had been attributed to apoplexy and had not been considered suspicious – which was scarcely surprising as he had been aged eighty-five – but this new information aroused belated misgivings. Catherine Leroy also said that La Chaboissière had had meetings with the Comte de Saint-Maurice who in 1675 had been sent to France on a special embassy to announce the death of the Duke of Savoy. This strengthened the perception that Vanens and his band were engaged in commerce with important foreign clients.

To compound the unease, Catherine Leroy repeated several disquieting statements uttered by La Chaboissière. He had often declared that 'la Brinvilliers was not dead...She had left behind heirs.' He had also boasted that Vanens had the ability to kill people in a week, a fortnight or whatever period he chose. If time was at a premium, he could murder them very speedily with a bouquet of poisoned flowers.[17]

As concern mounted over Vanens's activities, everyone known to have consorted with him came under scrutiny. Some years before, Vanens had spent a great deal of time with Robert, Seigneur de Bachimont, and his wife, Marie. On learning that this couple were now living at Ainyé Abbey, near Lyon, Louvois ordered their arrest. He believed there was ample reason to investigate them: not only had Mme de Bachimont's first husband died in mysterious circumstances, but his mother and sister had followed him to the grave in quick succession. Besides this, Mme de Bachimont had been suspected (though never convicted) of coining false money.[18]

By 17 May Bachimont and his wife had been put in prison in Lyon, and there they were questioned intensively. Bachimont explained that he had befriended Vanens in 1674, drawn together by a mutual interest in alchemy. For years Bachimont (who then lived in Paris) had dreamt of attaining the Philosopher's Stone, so he had been intrigued when Vanens had told him he had a secret formula to transmute copper into gold. Vanens had promised that if they worked together they would make 3 million livres and Bachimont had become convinced of this after he and his wife had been privileged to witness Vanens converting base metal into gold.

Mme de Bachimont gave a detailed description of the way in which Vanens had performed this miracle. First he had boiled together bunches of vermicular, groundsel and broom and then, having sprinkled in a mysterious red powder, he evaporated the liquid, leaving behind a residue of white sulphate. Next he blended copper with arsenic and saltpetre, put this into a goatskin, and added the white sulphate and some mercury to the mixture. Then he filled a cauldron with vinegar, a little nitric acid and a secret ingredient which he called 'oil of petroleum'. When this brew was boiling, he immersed the knotted goatskin in it. Once its contents had been thoroughly heated, Vanens removed the goatskin and allowed it to cool. When it was untied, it was found to contain grey powder. Having combined this with molten silver, Vanens fashioned an ingot. Bachimont took this to the mint in Paris, where the officials pronounced it to be pure gold and exchanged it for cash on that basis.[19]

Following this impressive demonstration, Bachimont had set about assembling the ingredients that Vanens said he needed to repeat the process. A man had been sent to Provence to find the bulbs called onions of Scylla, which Vanens listed among his requirements. However, it proved difficult to acquire one important item, for Vanens explained that the formula for the oil of petroleum was in the hands of a mysterious figure whom he referred to as 'the author'.

Vanens told the Bachimonts that the author (whose real name was François Galaup de Chasteuil) owed him an immense debt of gratitude. According to Vanens, after leading a series of picaresque adventures Chasteuil had, some years earlier, become prior of a Carmelite monastery in Marseille. When the young girl he had kept as his mistress had become pregnant, Chasteuil had strangled her, but after being caught trying to bury the body in the abbey's crypt he had been sentenced to death. Vanens, who was serving at the time on a galley in the Mediterranean, had been prevailed upon to rescue Chasteuil from the scaffold and smuggle him to safety. In return Chasteuil had taught Vanens how to make gold but, though he had given him a small quantity of oil of petroleum, he had never imparted the formula for it. Since Chasteuil was now living in Turin, where he served as a major in the White Cross Regiment,★ Vanens suggested that they should all go there to see if Chasteuil would give them a fresh supply of this vital substance.

Vanens and the Bachimonts had travelled to Turin in the spring of 1675 and they stayed there nearly four months. Vanens declined to introduce the Bachimonts to Chasteuil, saying it was best if he had sole contact with him, but their patience was rewarded when Vanens told them that Chasteuil had handed over sufficient quantities of his precious elixir to enable them to return to France and resume gold production. While they were finalising their travel arrangements, the Duke of Savoy had fallen ill, but they had seen no reason to delay their departure on that account. On 10 June 1675 they had left Turin; two days later, the Duke of Savoy had died, aged only forty.

The Bachimonts only went as far as Lyon but Vanens journeyed on to Paris, promising to rejoin them shortly. In fact, he spent three months at their Paris house running up enormous bills, and then disappeared. Distraught, the Bachimonts contacted Chasteuil in Turin and were horrified when he told them that he knew nothing about the miraculous oil of which Vanens had spoken. He had, however, offered to help the Bachimonts, so in the autumn they had gone back to Turin in the hope of producing gold with Chasteuil's aid. After all their experiments failed the Bachimonts had forlornly returned to Lyon. After a time they were driven by debt to leave the hotel where they had rented lodgings and to take up residence in Ainyé Abbey. There Bachimont had set up the furnaces and stills required for alchemical procedures and, 'hoping to arrive at the secret through his own industry', had continued his obsessive quest to make gold.[20]

Such, at least, was the story that the Bachimonts now unfolded but unfortunately their account was not accepted. Their description of their pursuit of the Philosopher's Stone was dismissed as 'gibberish with which they are trying to cover up what they are doing'.[21] To their interrogators it seemed highly significant that the Bachimonts' first visit to Turin had coincided with the Duke of Savoy's fatal illness. At the

★ François Ravaisson asserts that Chasteuil was preceptor to the Duke of Savoy's son but he is never described as such in any of the documents printed in *Archives de la Bastille*.

time, it was true, this had been attributed to a fever but with hindsight it seemed permissible to entertain the possibility that Vanens, Chasteuil and Bachimont — who admitted having visited the royal Palace as a tourist while in Turin — had poisoned him. If so, Bachimont's second visit in the autumn could have been to try to secure a reward for his services.

However plausible this theory seemed in the febrile atmosphere engendered by Mme de La Grange's warnings, it is extremely hard to credit. There is no denying that Vanens was a suspicious character who may have used poison to settle personal vendettas, though the evidence for that is decidedly weak. He would later be linked with other poisoners who operated in Paris and it is clear that he regularly handled cantharides and other poisonous substances. As for Bachimont, he did not deny that at various times he had purchased arsenic and sublimate, and small quantities of these were found in his workshop in Ainyé. On the other hand these were standard ingredients used in chemical experiments, so possession of them was not in itself incriminating.

While there were some inconsistencies in Bachimont's account of his activities, the effort of imagination required to accept that he poisoned the Duke of Savoy is truly stupendous. It must be emphasised that when the Duke had died no one had mentioned the possibility that he might have been a victim of foul play.* Furthermore, the symptoms of his last illness were not indicative of poisoning: having fallen ill on 4 June 1675, he had died eight days later after enduring bouts of fever and severe headaches.[22]

Even if one accepts the premise that Vanens and Bachimont could have poisoned the Duke, the identity of the person who commissioned them to carry out the crime remains a complete mystery. It is true that the Duchess of Savoy had often been irritated by her husband's infidelities and was sufficiently ambitious to relish the prospect of becoming Regent. Once the Duke was dead she had several affairs, including a relationship with the Comte de Saint-Maurice. He was the person who in June 1675 was sent to France to convey news of the Duke's death and the fact that he was then reported to have had dealings with La Chaboissière is certainly an arresting coincidence. However, it would be rash to extrapolate too much from this.

The only evidence that in any way corroborates the hypothesis that Charles Emmanuel of Savoy was murdered came from Bachimont's

---

* Intriguingly when this Duke of Savoy's father, Victor Amadeus of Savoy, had died in 1637, after attending a banquet given by the French Maréchal de Créqui, it was rumoured he had been poisoned.

manservant, Nicholas d'Hostel. He was arrested at the same time as his master and spent the next few months in prison. After being repeatedly questioned, he was asked whether he had ever heard his employers discussing the Duke of Savoy's death. He obligingly replied that shortly before leaving Turin in June 1675, he had heard Vanens say that when the Duke had changed his clothes after becoming overheated out hunting, he had been given a poisoned shirt.[23] Since we now know that in the seventeenth century it was not possible to kill someone using garments impregnated with poison, this is hardly conclusive.

The Bachimonts' story was certainly strange, but it was not altogether incredible. As Bachimont himself belatedly came to realise, Vanens was 'a great liar and a great actor', and the prowess with which he tricked the Bachimonts into believing that he had fashioned a gold ingot from humble materials suggests that he was also an expert conjurer. For someone with skills of this order, convincing gullible individuals that he was an alchemical adept who had penetrated the secret of 'the Great Work' would not have posed an insuperable challenge. The dividends to be reaped could be considerable: Bachimont estimated that in the course of his association with Vanens he had spent 10,000 livres supporting him. Even after spending nearly two years in prison, Vanens was confident that he could use his powers of persuasion to extricate himself from trouble. In September 1679 he contacted Louvois and coolly offered to reveal to the King his knowledge of the Philosopher's Stone.[24]

Obviously, today it seems crazy that anyone could have been duped into believing that a process which amounted to little more than extracting an essence from herbs could produce gold, but this was consistent with a theory current at the time that metals were living organisms, which could grow like plants. Ideas of this kind had considerable antecedents: in the fifteenth century Thomas Norton wrote in his *Ordinal of Alchemy* of a man who had 'laboured in the fire' for fifty years, using herbs, gums, roots, grass, wax, honey, wine, quicklime and other ingredients in his quest for his goal. Norton frankly admitted that most alchemical receipts better deserved the name 'deceipts', but the deluded nature of such activities has only become apparent in retrospect. At a time when the nature of matter was only imperfectly understood, the possibilities inherent in such processes as calcination, sublimation and purification seemed immense. Drawing on an impressive body of literature devoted to Hermetic lore, the alchemist sought, by repeatedly dissolving and reconstituting material, to free the 'quintessence' that resided within all objects and gain access to the 'inner spirit' at their core.[25] Once this had been attained, the Philosopher's

Stone itself should be within his grasp, promising not only untold riches but the key to life itself.

Although the Bachimonts' interrogators expressed scepticism that they could really have believed that Vanens was engaged on a legitimate enterprise, the couple were far from unique in subscribing to the sort of ideas he promulgated. The quest for the Philosopher's Stone remained a widespread obsession: in England alone it numbered Robert Boyle and Isaac Newton among its adherents, and it has been shown that more books on alchemy were published there in the years 1650–80 than at any period before or since. As for Paris, a Sicilian visitor to the city said that as many alchemists lived there as cooks. Among those taken in by these charlatans were some surprising people. In 1664 the Sieur de Louvet informed Colbert that he knew of a surgeon who had successfully turned copper into gold and suggested that 'it would enrich his Majesty' if he made use of this expertise. In 1708 one of Colbert's successors as Controller-General of Finance, Michel de Chamillart, had such faith in a man who claimed to have found the Philosopher's Stone that he furnished him with a furnace and all the materials he said he needed to perform this feat. It was only after this individual had lived in comfort for two months that he was exposed as a fraud and sent to prison. Anecdotal evidence confirms that other well-educated and wealthy persons fell victim to the craze. Saint-Simon claimed that the Dauphin's physician Boudin spent a fortune seeking the Philosopher's Stone and the Comtesse de Gramont's father was said to have ruined himself by his addiction to alchemy.[26]

Against this background it would not have been impossible for a man of Vanens's ingenuity to exploit the prevailing credulity and entice rich men to invest in his schemes. Deception on such a scale required guile, audacity and inventiveness, but Vanens possessed these qualities in abundance. While not entirely free of risk, this would certainly have offered an easier way of making a living than co-ordinating an international murder ring specialising in assassinating heads of state.

The probe into Vanens's activities, coupled with the mystery of the anonymous letter, had left Louvois and La Reynie full of trepidation. At the end of 1678 a new development occurred, which convinced them that they were right to be concerned. In December a lawyer named Maître Perrin attended a dinner party given by Marie Vigoreux, the wife of a ladies' tailor. Now aged forty, she had at one time been a wet-nurse to members of the aristocracy, but had abandoned that trade to set herself up as a fortune-teller. She had done very well at this and had acquired a sizeable clientele from every stratum of Paris society.

Primi Visconti had come across la Vigoreux when the Marquise de Vassé had engaged her to tell fortunes at one of her parties and he had been very impressed by her powers. Describing her as 'very knowledgeable about palmistry', he insisted that when she read his hand, the most learned of men could not have given such a well-reasoned exposition on his future.[27]

The other guest at Mme Vigoreux's dinner party was a stout and powerfully built woman in her forties named Marie Bosse. The widow of a horse dealer, she had been briefly imprisoned for coining three years earlier but had been thriving ever since her release. As the meal wore on she became somewhat drunk and astonished Maître Perrin when she suddenly declared that things were going so well for her that once she had poisoned three more people, she would be able to retire.

Maître Perrin reported this conversation to the police, with the result that orders were given for the two women's arrest. On 4 January 1679 Mme Vigoreux and Mme Bosse (together with la Bosse's two sons and a daughter) were seized. They were taken to the Château de Vincennes, a royal fortress on the eastern edge of Paris. There they were confined in the fifteenth-century keep, which would be the place of custody for all suspected poisoners arrested in Paris over the next three years.

The arrest of la Vigoreux and la Bosse focused scrutiny on the numerous fortune-tellers and 'divineresses' who were currently active in Paris and who for the most part had been carrying on their activities without any interference from the authorities. Mme Vigoreux herself suggested that in the capital there were more than 400 people (the majority of them women, for fortune-telling remained a predominantly feminine occupation) who made their living in this way,[28] and her estimate was probably on the low side.

When clients came to them asking to have their futures foretold, the divineresses sometimes made predictions after drawing up a personal horoscope. They also practised physiognomy (the art of telling someone's destiny by examining their facial features) and palmistry. Though some had no education to speak of (Mme Bosse only knew how to write her name, while the divineress la Bergerot was completely illiterate), others were remarkably erudite in their approach. The redoubtable la Trianon, for example, was said to have more learning 'in the tip of her finger' than others could hope to acquire in a lifetime. She prided herself on being expert in 'magical science, following the natural magic calendar' and, upon her arrest, was found to possess a library of twenty-five manuscript volumes on occult subjects.[29]

However, their activities were much more diverse than this for, as la Vigoreux herself pointed out, 'Reading palms is not all they do.' In many cases the divineresses also acted as pharmacists and beauticians. They supplied their clients with home-made remedies for minor ailments such as corns and toothache. In addition they sold cosmetics such as 'talc' and herbal lotions for the complexion, made according to their own recipes.

They might also offer to use their powers of divination to locate lost or stolen property. They did a brisk trade attempting to direct clients towards hoards of abandoned treasure, which had supposedly been buried long ago and never reclaimed. A surprising number of people had great hopes of growing rich in this way and one divineress was under the impression that 'all Paris is searching for treasure'.[30]

One could argue that, while utterly futile, all this was essentially harmless, but M. de La Reynie came to have a different view of the matter. At the end of the Affair of the Poisons he looked back over what he termed an 'abyss of crime' and declared that these 'apparent simplicities of mind' invariably had a pernicious outcome. Clients who approached divineresses on such 'vain and ridiculous pretexts' as wanting to know what the future held, or seeking buried treasure, went on to raise other matters. Then, by an inevitable progression, 'terrible bargains were concluded'.[31]

Oddly enough, in taking this harsh view he was merely echoing the words of Marie Bosse, who at one point surprised her interrogators by uttering a sweeping condemnation of all the fortune-tellers who worked in Paris. She insisted that the best course would be to exterminate them all, for they had brought ruin on women of high and low rank. She explained that they could wreak such harm because clients revealed their weaknesses during palm-reading sessions. Having exposed themselves in this way, they were easier to manipulate.[32]

Much of the divineresses' time was taken up by advising their clients on love matters. They were consulted by ladies whose lovers were proving reluctant to marry them, or whose families were preventing them from making a match of their choice. A large proportion of their clientele, however, was comprised of unhappily married women who came to them for counsel. A few of them hoped that some way might be found to make their husbands treat them more kindly. Sometimes the divineress recommended rubbing one of their husband's shirts against an image of St Ursula or, alternatively, the client might be enjoined to embark on a nine-day cycle of prayer known as a Novena. If the client considered this too arduous, poor women could be found who, for a fee, would perform the orisons for them.

A significant number of clients despaired of ever finding happiness with their husbands. Discontented wives would often want to know whether their husbands would die in the near future and it did not require a gifted clairvoyant to know that they were hoping for an affirmative answer. For example, when an unhappily married woman called Mme Darsis had her palm read by Mme Vigoreux she queried hopefully whether the fortune-teller could see 'the mark of a coffin in her hand'. Much to her disappointment, la Vigoreux told her she could not.[33]

Sometimes a client would admit that she longed for her husband to die and the divineress was invariably sympathetic. A young woman called Mme Vertemart told the notorious divineress Mme Voisin that she wanted to be rid of her husband so that she could spend more time with her lover, and la Voisin assured her that this could be brought about by prayer. When Mme Vertemart said she found it difficult to believe that God would grant such a request, Mme Voisin told her that to achieve this it was 'necessary to live like her and to have as much experience as she had in this kind of thing'. Mme Vertemart remained sceptical, pointing out that since her lover had a wife, she would not be able to marry him even if she were widowed, but Mme Voisin promised to take care of everything. 'Don't pry!' she chided her client, 'I don't like little women who are so penetrating; suffice to say that for me nothing is impossible ... I've made other women happy; just bring the money.'[34] Mme Vertemart accepted these assurances but other women who came to Mme Voisin with similar problems were not content to rely on prayer alone to resolve their difficulties.

Sometimes magic and spells were used to assist clients. Drawing on old superstitions, the divineress might perform a ritual such as 'burning the faggot', in which an incantation was chanted over a flaming log. The log was said to represent the body, blood, soul and mind of a named person, who would enjoy no peace till he had accomplished the celebrant's desires. There were other forms of magic employed to incite love. When that doyenne of divineresses, Mme Voisin, was requested by a M. de Prade to bring about a marriage between him and the wealthy widow, Mme Leféron, la Voisin fashioned a wax figurine of de Prade and buried it in Mme Leféron's garden. With a woman called Mme Cottard, who wanted her lover Forne to marry her, la Voisin took a different approach. She supplied Mme Cottard with a powder to smear over her hand and said that when she next touched Cottard he would be unable to resist her.[35]

Marie Bosse believed that burying used bed sheets or samples of menstrual blood was a good way of promoting love, while urine specimens were better suited to harmful spells. Mme Voisin apparently concurred with this: when a woman called Mme Brunet applied to her in hopes that she would rid her of her husband, la Voisin instructed her to supply her with some of his urine, as well as the discarded shells of eggs that he had eaten.[36] It was only when spells using these items failed to have any effect that la Voisin adopted more extreme measures.

Pigeons' or sheep's hearts could feature in spells and sometimes even parts of the human body were used as adjuncts to sorcery. The magician Lesage admitted employing a dead man's bone in one ritual, while the formidable la Trianon went further. Not content with having a human skeleton hanging in her consulting room (when questioned about this she would claim it enhanced her piety to have an image of death constantly before her) she asked Mme Voisin to obtain the fingertips of a hanged man from her neighbour, the public executioner. La Voisin declined to carry out the errand, whereupon la Trianon herself allegedly cut the hand from a felon who had been broken on the wheel and whose decomposing corpse had been exhibited on the highway. When her house was inspected following her arrest, its contents included not only poisons such as arsenic and cantharides but also 'the finger of a dried hand'.[37]

In theory those who engaged in occult practices were subject to the severest penalties, but the law was seldom enforced. An eminent lawyer noted that 'in the Faubourg Saint-Antoine and other quarters of Paris' one did not have to look very hard to see people who 'publicly professed' that they knew 'secret ways of attaining success at gambling and good luck in lawsuits and love matters'. He commented that anyone who saw these people about their business would surely conclude that their activities were not 'worthy of reprehension', as for a long time now they had operated 'with impunity ... in full sight of the magistrates'.[38]

It was true that if sacrilege was deemed to have been committed it was regarded as a very serious matter. In August 1677 a priest named Bernard Tournet had been burnt alive after being convicted of 'sacrileges and profanation of the holy sacrifice of the Mass itself, invocation of the devil and the seduction of several persons whom he abused under false pretexts of making them find treasure by means of evil spirits'.[39] However, provided they were not suspected of defiling the holy mysteries, the majority of those in Paris who preyed on the superstitions of others were able to do so without encountering much harassment.

Those who confined themselves to practising astrology could do so without fear of the consequences, for drawing horoscopes had never been outlawed. This was in spite of the fact that in 1586 and again in 1631 Papal bulls had been issued condemning astrologers. Even the most eminent French churchmen had blithely overlooked the bull of 1631, while that of 1586 had been completely misinterpreted. It had been stated there that any attempt to predict the future was the work of the devil, but in 1640 no less an authority than the General of the Paris Oratory produced an officially commissioned study in which he assured his readers that the Pope condoned some forms of astrology. It is true that more recently, churchmen like Bossuet had openly condemned astrologers on the grounds that their work was impious. However, the Church was powerless to enforce sanctions against astrologers, for since 1628 responsibility for policing their activities had been entrusted to the secular authorities.[40]

The scientific revolution of the seventeenth century had had surprisingly little effect on belief in astrology. By the second half of the seventeenth century few men of learning still subscribed to Ptolemy's theories regarding the disposition of the planets, but the full implications of a heliocentric universe were imperfectly understood. Hardly anyone disputed that the stars had an effect on people's physical well-being and on the earth's climate, and in consequence astrology was still taught in faculties of medicine and even Jesuit training colleges.[41]

It is true that there was some attempt to differentiate between 'natural' astrology – which studied the effect of the stars on terrestrial bodies – and 'judicial' astrology – which sought to predict the future. Several authorities condemned this as undesirable, but even here astrologers enjoyed some latitude. Provided they maintained that the stars merely influenced men's behaviour, rather than controlling their destiny (which smacked too much of the Calvinist theory of predestination), objections to their activities were muted.[42]

The distinction between 'natural' and 'judicial' astrology was not enshrined in law. Legislation concerning astrology had not been updated since 1628, when predictions relating to states and important people had been outlawed. Since that time only one astrologer had been prosecuted under this law, and this was on purely political grounds, for he had come dangerously close to committing *lèse-majesté* by prophesying the death of the King.[43]

Since even learned opinion was hesitant to condemn astrology and the law was rarely invoked against it, it is hardly surprising that it still had a huge following. However, while astrologers could try to read the heavens without fear of molestation, divination through the use of magic was plainly condemned as diabolical. There can be no doubt that some of the activities practised by divineresses in Paris could be defined as witchcraft, and in theory this remained a capital offence. Quite apart from the fact that the divineresses carried out their ceremonies in secret, though, the legal position regarding witchcraft was confusing. In Paris, at least, the crime of sorcery was no longer actively persecuted. The last witch to be executed by decree of the Paris *Parlement* had been Catherine Bouillon in 1625. Since that date the *Parlement* had over-turned all death sentences imposed on witches by subordinate courts that came within its jurisdiction, though usually the penalty had been commuted to banishment rather than being waived altogether.[44]

There were other sovereign courts in France such as the *Parlement* of Rouen, which took a less lenient approach to witches. At Rouen death sentences for witchcraft continued to be upheld throughout most of the seventeenth century. However, in 1670 the modernising First President of the Rouen *Parlement* had asked Colbert to intervene after numerous people sentenced to death for witchcraft by lower courts in Normandy had their cases referred to Rouen. He told Colbert that the evidence against them was unsatisfactory and that there was no proof they were guilty of any wrongdoing, and a decree was accordingly sent out altering the sentences from execution to exile. Indignant at this infringement of their prerogatives, the Rouen *Parlement* protested to the King, reminding him that the evil effects of sorcery included deaths and mysterious illnesses. They insisted that there could be no doubt as to the existence of witchcraft, for it was referred to in the Bible, and phenomena such as people flying were attested to by numerous eyewitnesses.[45]

As late as 1718 the Duchesse d'Orléans reported that in Rouen people still feared witches, though she added that in Paris nobody now believed in them. However, it had taken a long time to reach that point and too much significance should not be attached to the absence of formal legal proceedings against witches. In particular, one must beware of assuming that the reluctance of the Paris *Parlement* to burn witches stemmed from a refusal to accept their existence. In 1643 a member of *Parlement* noted that he disliked convictions for witchcraft because the standard of proof in such cases tended to be unsatisfactory. When it could be demonstrated that witches had done verifiable harm it was better to prosecute them for those crimes, without becoming embroiled in uncertainties. But he added that while he suspected that some of his colleagues 'believe neither in God nor the devil', for his part he had no doubt that 'the Church and holy scripture teaches us … that there are magicians and sorcerers.'[46]

In the intervening years attitudes had changed further, but a remark of the Comte de Bussy's at the time of the Affair of the Poisons shows that even then, educated people had an ambivalent attitude to witchcraft. After the Maréchal de Luxembourg was arrested in 1680 on suspicion of having forged pacts with the devil, Bussy reported that Luxembourg's friends were ridiculing the charges and reminding everyone that the *Parlement* of Paris no longer condemned people to death for the crime of witchcraft. Bussy commented, 'It's true; but... Monsieur de Luxembourg *would* be put to death if he has killed anyone through sorcery.'[47] The fact that even a cynical sophisticate like Bussy believed that Luxembourg might have been able to harm anyone in this way is indicative of the state of opinion at the time. Although no one tried during the Affair of the Poisons was charged with sorcery, there can be no doubt that a residual fear of witchcraft was partly responsible for the scale of the persecution and the way matters escalated.

While not extinct, by 1679 belief in witchcraft was on the decline in sophisticated circles, but perceptions of the devil remained extremely vivid. To the preacher Bossuet, for example, the reality of the devil was very evident. In one of his sermons he stated firmly that it was a universally acknowledged truth, upheld by scripture, that there 'are in the world certain sorts of malicious spirits whom we call demons'. On another occasion he declared that the devil had always had his own 'altars, temples, mysteries, sacrifices' where his disciples congregated. Bossuet thundered that the evil one gloried in the 'impure ceremonies' that were celebrated by his ministers and which, though based on Christian forms of worship, were really a foul parody of it.[48]

The devil dominated people's consciousness in a way that today we can hardly grasp. More than one of Louis XIV's contemporaries wrote of the way his 'fear of the devil' influenced his behaviour[49] and the dread inspired by Satan was all-pervasive. The counterpart to living in an age of faith, when religion afforded comfort to so many, was that the devil was not conceived of as some remote entity, but rather as a malign being who could be visualised with horrible clarity.

Therefore, when it emerged that divineresses and other members of the Paris underworld were offering to conjure up evil spirits for clients or to forge pacts with the devil, it did not seem entirely fanciful to accept that communications of this sort might be possible. In 1680, when numerous people were arrested at court because they had consulted divineresses, the Maréchal de Villeroi commented 'These gentlemen and ladies believe in the devil and do not believe in God.' Perhaps he was right, but it does not follow that the two were mutually exclusive. Certainly, Louis XIV's faith in God did not preclude him from being 'dreadfully afraid of the devil'.[50]

Even people who were not particularly superstitious, and who would have repudiated the notion that spells and sorcery could yield results, harmful or otherwise, would have been open to the idea that those who dabbled in the occult could represent a menace to society. Through the ages witchcraft and poisoning had been held to be naturally affiliated, with many authorities maintaining that the devil enhanced witches' power to do harm by supplying them with deadly powders. Mme de Brinvilliers's confessor had told her that the two activities were so inextricably intertwined that in the Bible the word 'witch' was synonymous with 'poisoner'.[51] The Affair of the Poisons would reinforce the perception that a strong connection existed.

During that episode several cases would come to light when attempts to practise magic had ultimately led to much worse things. Few people came to the divineress with the express intention of purchasing poison. On the whole, they began by complaining of their husband or some other individual who irked them, and the divineress would hold out the hope that their death could be brought about by supernatural means. It was only when this failed to achieve the desired result that they became ready to countenance murder, for the spells that had proved so harmless to the intended victim invariably had a corrupting effect on the perpetrators. Having already parted with a great deal of money, and unwilling to endure disappointment, the client found it easier to take on board that poison could provide an acceptable solution. Thus, merely by consulting the divineress the client had set in motion a cycle of moral degradation, which led to crimes that would once have seemed unthinkable.

For this reason even those who did not believe that 'witches' possessed magical powers had no doubt of their capacity for evil. The Duchesse d'Orléans, who prided herself on her robust common sense, commented that it was obviously wrong to burn reputed witches for having 'flown down the chimney mounted on a broomstick', but all too often serious crimes could be laid at their door. In such cases harsh treatment was in order and if it could be shown that they 'had handled poisons or committed sacrilege they cannot be punished too severely'.[52]

M. de La Reynie was convinced that the arrest of Mme Bosse and Mme Vigoreux would prove pregnant with consequence. He was not surprised when preliminary interrogations indicated that la Bosse and Magdelaine de La Grange were known to each other, and had sometimes worked together. Furthermore, Mme de La Grange appeared to have had contacts with Vanens and his servant La Chaboissière who, prior to his own arrest, was reported to have visited the priest Nail in prison.[53] To La Reynie's mind all this confirmed that a network of poisoners was active in Paris and that they were operating in concert with one another. As yet, he was groping for details but he believed that, if she chose, Mme de La Grange could help him to find the missing piece of the jigsaw.

Since the discovery of the anonymous letter in the autumn of 1677, Magdelaine de La Grange had been regularly questioned, but her answers had always been infuriatingly obscure. She had explained that while she had a strong feeling that the King and the Dauphin remained in danger, her clairvoyant powers would not work while she was in prison. Only if she was moved to somewhere with a more 'free and serene' atmosphere would she be able to function satisfactorily.[54]

La Reynie had not fallen for this, but he was sure that, provided he waited long enough, Mme de La Grange would give him the information he wanted. However, although he would have liked to postpone the execution of both her and Nail until the moment when he could feel confident they had yielded up all their secrets, this proved impractical. In November 1678 the Controller-General of Finance, M. Colbert, had begun to complain that it would be an abuse of the legal process if their appeal were put off any longer. By early 1679 the pressure to resume proceedings had become irresistible.[55]

On 4 February the appeal of Nail and Mme de La Grange was heard by *Parlement*. That body upheld the lower court's verdict of guilty and confirmed that the pair should be hanged after enduring torture. Still anxious about the prospect of her being silenced for ever, the King, Louvois and La Reynie decided that, contrary to normal practice, an interval should elapse between Mme de La Grange's torture and execution. This would enable the King to study the written record of her interrogation. If under torture she said anything that suggested she and Vanens were leagued together in a conspiracy, a confrontation must be arranged between the two of them prior to her hanging. Because the information that might come to light as a result was likely to be so sensitive the King decreed that, in another departure from convention, no commissioners from *Parlement* should be present at this meeting. Instead, M. de La Reynie was entrusted with the responsibility of monitoring proceedings.[56]

After all these precautions, Mme de La Grange's end was something of an anticlimax. Under torture she revealed nothing of interest, insisting that Vanens was unknown to her and that she could cast no further light on the anonymous letter. Nail was equally unforthcoming, even though he was tortured so severely that at one point he lost consciousness and had to be revived before fresh torments could be applied.[57]

La Reynie did not give up hope, reasoning that one of the prisoners might start to talk as they were taken in tumbrils to the place of execution. If it appeared that either had anything significant to say, they could even then be diverted to the Town Hall for a confrontation with Vanens. However, to La Reynie's regret, as they were taken to their deaths, neither of the prisoners proved particularly communicative. On the way to the Place de Grève, Mme de La Grange did suddenly volunteer that her marriage certificate had been forged and that she had duped the notary who drew up her marriage contract. Nail admitted that he had impersonated Faurye, but their acknowledgement of these commonplace crimes fell far short of what La Reynie wanted. Enigmatic to the last, on the evening of 8 February 1679 Magdelaine de La Grange and Nail were hanged by torchlight.[58]

The pair had died with their secrets still intact, but while this was a setback for La Reynie he did not despair. By now there were other prisoners in custody on suspicion of poisoning and he was confident that, though so far the truth had eluded him, he was on the verge of making important discoveries. While Magdelaine de La Grange had ultimately frustrated him, it was to be hoped that Marie Bosse and Mme Vigoreux would prove more enlightening.

# FIVE

# LA VOISIN

Following the arrest of Mme Vigoreux and Marie Bosse in early January 1679 their houses had been searched. Substances discovered there were taken away to be analysed and suspicions mounted against Marie Bosse when a casket belonging to her was found to contain not only disturbing items such as nail clippings and samples of menstrual blood, but also arsenic, cantharides and nitric acid.

Things looked even worse when Mme Vigoreux disclosed that Mme Marguerite de Poulaillon was a client of hers and la Bosse. La Vigoreux maintained that this lady, who came from a good family in Bordeaux and was married to a well-to-do bureaucrat, had come to them to have her fortune read and to borrow money. However, it seemed likely there had been more to it than that, for Mme de Poulaillon had recently been put in a convent by her husband after he had been warned that she was trying to kill him.

Further interest was aroused when Mme Vigoreux revealed that la Bosse was on friendly terms with a woman called Mme Philbert. The latter was now the wife of a court musician, but some years ago her first husband, M. Brunet, had died in suspicious circumstances. La Vigoreux also provided the first intimation that people at court might be implicated in the affair when she mentioned that the Marquis de Feuquières had asked her to devise a way of protecting him against being wounded in battle. Sensing that this would be the forerunner of more significant disclosures, on 6 January 1679 M. de La Reynie requested the King's authorisation to take personal charge of the inquiry. This was speedily granted.

On 1 February Mme de Poulaillon was arrested and taken to Vincennes. A former servant of hers, Perrine Delabarre, was also taken into custody and before long poured forth a wealth of compromising information about her employer. It emerged that Mme de Poulaillon had been having an affair with the self-styled Marquis de La Rivière, an immensely charming adventurer who supported himself by preying on susceptible women. People had attempted to alert M. de Poulaillon to what was going on, but he did not listen, for he doted on his attractive young wife to such an extent that 'one kind word' from her was enough to keep him happy.[1]

Unfortunately, M. de La Rivière was so expensive to maintain that Mme de Poulaillon had found herself in constant need of money. If her husband gave her a new dress, she at once pawned it to raise cash for her lover, but the sums raised in this way were soon dissipated. Desperately she had formed plans to break into her husband's study to steal a valuable pair of hangings and even had a key cut to enable her to take money out of his strongbox. However, after a series of farcical mishaps, all these schemes had come to nothing.

By now Mme de Poulaillon had begun having consultations with Mme Vigoreux and, after hearing her plight, la Vigoreux sent her to see Marie Bosse. Matters had then taken a grimmer turn. After paying several visits to Mme de Poulaillon's country house, la Bosse had instructed her to furnish her with one of M. de Poulaillon's shirts, together with some arsenic which Mme de Poulaillon had originally purchased to use as rat poison. La Bosse had then combined the arsenic with soap and washed the shirt with it, claiming that when M. de Poulaillon next wore the shirt his lower parts would become painful and inflamed. Mme de Poulaillon may have been led to hope that the effects would prove fatal, although she later claimed that she had simply intended to rob her husband's strongbox while he was bedridden with this complaint. It is, in fact, doubtful that M. de Poulaillon would have been harmed by wearing the shirt (though la Bosse assured her client that she had achieved excellent results in the past) but in the event this was never put to the test. After being treated by la Bosse, the shirt acquired such a noticeably brownish tinge that Mme de Poulaillon decided it was impossible to use it.[2]

However, far from giving up altogether, Mme de Poulaillon twice gave her servant Perrine Delabarre phials of liquid and ordered her to add the contents to her husband's wine. On both occasions the frightened servant poured the liquid away, so M. de Poulaillon came to no harm. But towards the end of 1678 he received several anonymous warnings that his wife had attempted to murder him and this eventually persuaded him that his own safety demanded that he should place her in a convent.

Even this did not stop the determined Mme de Poulaillon. In December she left her convent to visit Marie Bosse and Mme Vigoreux in Paris, and they agreed that a final effort must be made to poison Poulaillon. Accordingly, Mme Bosse had enlisted the services of a fruit seller, Anne Cheron, and François Belot, a member of the royal guard. Belot had boasted that he had a secret way of poisoning silver cups, so infallible that 'if fifty people drank out of it, even after it had been washed and rinsed, they would all die'. At the very beginning of January 1679 la Cheron had supplied Belot with the live toad he said he needed, and at la Bosse's house they had together set about torturing the poor animal to render it in the right condition for their purposes. After it had been beaten, they forced arsenic into its mouth on the assumption that if the creature urinated during its death throes, its piss would prove highly toxic.[3] A cup supplied by Mme de Poulaillon was then treated with this noxious fluid. However, before the utensil could be used, Marie Bosse and Mme Vigoreux had been arrested on 4 January.

As La Reynie amassed more information, so the number of people in custody grew. François Belot and Anne Cheron joined Marie Bosse at Vincennes. On 1 March orders were given for the arrest of Mme Philbert, for there were now strong suspicions that she had murdered her first husband, M. Brunet. A woman called Mme Ferry, whose husband had died shortly before la Bosse's arrest, after an illness lasting three weeks, was also detained.

By 8 March it seemed clear that there would have to be numerous trials to bring these and other malefactors to justice. After consultation with Louvois, the King decided to form a special commission to hear all the cases. Fourteen commissioners from the higher ranks of the legal hierarchy were chosen by the King to serve as judges on this tribunal, which had its own president, attorney-general and recorder. M. de La Reynie was named as one of the commissioners, but besides this judicial role he also remained in charge of the investigation into poisoning. In addition he was appointed *rapporteur* to the commission, which meant that once he had amassed evidence against defendants he outlined the case to his fellow commissioners. In effect, therefore, he acted as a detective, prosecutor and judge.

Another commissioner, Louis Bazin, Seigneur de Bezons, was selected as an auxiliary *rapporteur*. This former *Intendant* had already established a fruitful working relationship with La Reynie when he had served alongside him on the commission that dealt with the Chevalier de Rohan's treason. The Marquis de La Fare later alleged that Bezons had trapped Rohan into admitting his guilt by falsely promising him a pardon. There would be claims that during the poisons inquiry, Bezons would be equally unscrupulous about obtaining convictions, and Primi Visconti went so far as to call him 'the Judas of the assembly'.[4]

One reason for forming the commission was that the King did not want the regular courts – which were overburdened with business as it was – to become clogged up with poisoning cases. Besides this, however, Louis wanted to prevent details of the investigation from becoming public and he strongly urged the commissioners to divulge nothing about their proceedings to outsiders.[5] It is clear that although no high-ranking people had yet been implicated as poisoners, it was anticipated that this would be an inevitable outcome of the current inquiry. When that happened, the King wanted secrecy to be preserved as far as possible. It was also assumed that in such circumstances a special commission would prove less vulnerable to pressure from interested parties than would be the case if the matter came before *Parlement*.

As Mme de Scudéry commented, the formation of the commission constituted an implicit rebuke to *Parlement* for the way it had handled the cases of Mme de Brinvilliers and Pennautier. The Venetian ambassador heard that the President of the Paris *Parlement* protested to the King that the bypassing of the established legal system represented a slur on the 'immaculate justice' always provided by *Parlement*. Despite his pleas that this venerable institution be spared an unmerited affront, he could not prevail on the King to reconsider.[6]

La Reynie was not yet ready to submit cases for judgement, so the letters patent which brought the commission into being were only signed on 7 April 1679. Countersigned by Colbert, in his capacity as the Minister with responsibility for the *département* of Paris, they stated that the commission should judge crimes of poisoning and other related offences committed in Paris and its environs.[7] It was agreed that the commission would hold its sessions at the Arsenal, near the Bastille. For this reason it was often called the *Chambre d'Arsenal*, but it was also referred to as the *Chambre Ardente*, or 'Burning Chamber'. This was a throwback to the sixteenth century, when a similar special tribunal had been established to judge cases of heresy. It, too, had sat at the Arsenal, in a room hung with black cloth and lit with torches.

In the weeks before the commission assembled, La Reynie doggedly pursued his enquiries. It had not escaped his notice that in her depositions Marie Bosse had frequently mentioned another divineress, Mme Voisin. La Bosse said that she was the person who had first introduced her to Magdelaine de La Grange and that Mme Voisin had also been consulted by Mme Ferry, who was currently under arrest on suspicion of murdering her husband. La Bosse went on to say that Mme Voisin had been intimately acquainted with another imprisoned suspect, Mme

Philbert, and when questioned about her own dealings with pregnant women she sought to divert suspicion by declaring that it was Mme Voisin who practised abortion. M. de La Reynie became still more interested when la Bosse stated that an unnamed 'lady of rank' had been to see Mme Voisin and that this woman – whose identity Mme Bosse had never discovered – had offered the divineress 6000 livres if she could bring about the death of her husband.[8]

On 12 March 1679 Catherine Montvoisin, known as 'la Voisin', was arrested as she came out of her local parish church where, as was her custom, she had attended mass. Now forty-two years old, she had been honing her skills in astrology, palmistry and physiognomy from the age of nine. Having devoted herself ever since to 'cultivating the knowledge God had given her', she had pursued her calling with remarkable dedication and prided herself on providing an excellent service. On one occasion when she was having difficulty concluding a marriage desired by a widowed client, she fretted that this would deal such a blow to her reputation that she would have to leave the country. A colleague of hers had to point out that in view of the huge quantity of work she took on, the occasional setback was inevitable.[9]

La Voisin appears genuinely to have believed in the power of magic but she combined this with an outward profession of piety. As the circumstances of her arrest suggested, she was a regular churchgoer, and her answers to her interrogators would abound with devout sentiments and respectful invocations of the 'Good Lord'. When she finally began to make significant revelations she would claim that she was doing so 'for the glory of God', who had commanded her to heed His will as she knelt in prayer. Earlier in her career her readiness to imply that she was in tune with the workings of providence had stood her in good stead, for clients were comforted by her apparent belief that her professional activities were compatible with Christianity. It may be that Mme Voisin herself was scarcely aware of any contradiction. Once, having assisted at an abortion, she was said to have wept tears of joy when the midwife in attendance baptised the foetus. Far from being troubled at having terminated the unborn child's existence, she exulted in having been instrumental in securing its salvation.[10]

La Voisin's renown as a divineress had made her prosperous. One acquaintance claimed that 'all the world came' to see her and Primi Visconti likewise believed that 'most of the ladies in Paris had visited her'. Marie Bosse suggested that Mme Voisin had earned a total of 100,000 livres 'from her evil dealings'; another estimate put her income at 10,000 livres a year. While it is impossible to know if these figures are accurate, she certainly lived in some style. Her house in the Rue

Beauregard was in a suburb of Paris outside the city walls called the Villeneuve. When her clients came to visit, she saw them in a little pavilion in the garden. According to one account, she was never short of business. After noting that 'la Voisin had as much money as she wanted', an envious colleague described how 'before she got up every morning, there were folk waiting to see her, and throughout the rest of the day she was with more people; after that, she kept open house in the evening, with violins playing, and was always making merry'.[11]

During these convivial evenings she developed a pronounced fondness for wine and several witnesses described occasions when she became visibly inebriated. Alcohol was apt to make her garrulous and in company she would sometimes speak more frankly of her activities than was wise. Perhaps because her interrogators hoped to take advantage of this tendency, she was not forced to moderate her intake in prison. In fact, Primi Visconti heard that she was drunk whenever she was interrogated.[12]

La Voisin's husband, Antoine Montvoisin, had at different times been a silk merchant and a jeweller, but his businesses had all gone bankrupt. Consequently la Voisin had to support him and all her children, and perhaps it was the pressure of having 'ten mouths to fill' that spurred her into crime. When a midwife she employed had expressed qualms about performing another abortion, Mme Voisin had retorted, 'You're mad! Times are too hard! How do you expect me to feed my family and children?'[13]

Her husband showed scant gratitude for the way she kept him, for she complained he became vicious when drunk and treated her badly. La Voisin had never made a secret of the fact that she longed to be rid of him. One of her admirers later recalled that upon encountering la Voisin, the standard form of polite greeting was to enquire whether her husband had yet died.[14] La Voisin herself would later tell M. de La Reynie that numerous people had urged her to kill Montvoisin, while maintaining that she had rejected their advice. Abundant evidence would eventually suggest that she had, in fact, made several attempts on his life, though none had succeeded. Perhaps she had been constrained by the need for caution, for her husband was on good terms with Samson, the public executioner. He had told Montvoisin that in the event of his dying suddenly he would arrange for an autopsy to be carried out on him.[15]

Mme Voisin's marriage may have been unhappy, but an active love life afforded some solace. Despite the homely features portrayed in the only known engraving of her, she clearly exerted a powerful sexual allure. Her lovers included magicians and alchemists such as Lesage,

Blessis and Latour, as well as the tavern keeper M. Herault, who promised to marry her if her husband died. She even had a brief affair with a member of the aristocracy, the Vicomte de Cousserans, to whom she had given lessons in palmistry.[16]

At one point Mme Voisin had operated in partnership with Marie Bosse and had sent clients to her when she judged it appropriate. However, no trace remained of their former friendship for, years before, they had quarrelled over money. As would ultimately become clear, la Voisin had suspected that Mme Bosse had denied her a full share of the proceeds deriving from the murder of M. Brunet, for which his widow had paid generously. The antagonism between the two women now proved helpful to M. de La Reynie, for each proved anxious to denigrate the other.

Mme Voisin was interrogated for the first time on 17 March.[17] Her strategy was to deny that she had ever done any harm, while throwing as much suspicion as possible on Marie Bosse. She admitted that several years earlier (the date was probably 1673) the then Mme Brunet had come to her complaining about her husband. Mme Voisin had sent her to see Marie Bosse and (so she claimed) from that time the pair had conducted their business without any reference to her. La Voisin said that, knowing that Mme Brunet had a great aversion for her husband, she had urged la Bosse to do nothing detrimental to 'the glory of God and their salvation', but she feared Mme Bosse had not heeded her words. This was because she knew that la Bosse had asked Mme Brunet to supply her with one of her husband's shirts and she said she was also aware that in the years since Brunet's death his widow had made regular payments to Mme Bosse.

La Voisin continued that her anxieties had increased when, in 1676, Brunet's widow − by this time remarried to the flautist M. Philbert − had come to see her. Mme Philbert had confessed that something was preying on her mind and, when la Voisin had read her hand, what she saw had been far from reassuring. La Voisin had told her client that she could tell that many disappointments were in store for her, and had then unsettled her further by remarking that the late M. Brunet's strange demise had inspired a lot of adverse comment.

When asked about Mme Ferry, la Voisin adopted similar tactics. She said that shortly after the arrest of Mme Bosse, Mme Ferry had paid her a visit. She was wearing mourning for her husband, who had died not long before. The young widow was obviously in a state of great anxiety, prompting la Voisin to ask 'whether she had done something unfortunate on la Bosse's advice'. Mme Ferry had denied this, but when her hand was read by la Voisin she kept asking nervously if there was any indication that she would soon be embroiled in legal proceedings.

Mme Voisin had done her best to deflect suspicion on to her rival, but her composure was shaken when she was asked about the lady who had offered her 6000 livres in order to be rid of her husband. It was also put to her that one of her grander female clients had sent her a bouquet of flowers to be treated in some unspecified manner. Plainly disconcerted, la Voisin blustered that she had often received flowers from people of rank.

Worse was to come, for the following day Mme Voisin and Marie Bosse were brought together for a confrontation.[18] Furious at la Voisin's attempts to blacken her, Mme Bosse made a series of strident accusations. Refuting Mme Voisin's claim to have had only minimal dealings with Mme Brunet, la Bosse insisted that la Voisin had met regularly with that lady in Notre-Dame Cathedral. She alleged that la Voisin had once tried to sell Mme Brunet a powder supposedly consisting of finely ground diamonds which, if ingested, would shred the intestines. However, the price had been exorbitant and since Mme Brunet did not believe that the powder was really made of diamonds she had declined the offer. Nevertheless, the pair had continued to meet and Mme Brunet had paid for la Voisin's services by giving her 400 livres in cash and a diamond cross.

La Bosse repeated her earlier claim that an unidentified lady of rank had offered to pay la Voisin 6000 livres if she killed her husband. It was this same lady who had asked la Voisin to poison a bouquet of flowers. Once the flowers had been treated, they were to be sent to another woman who had made the client jealous. Furthermore, la Voisin had been involved with another well-born lady, whose name la Bosse had never managed to discover, and she too had lost her husband after enlisting the aid of Mme Voisin. As soon as the period of mourning was over the gratified widow had visited la Voisin and given her the black clothes she had been wearing in memory of her husband.

La Bosse continued that Mme Voisin had repeatedly tried to murder her own husband. More than ten years before, she had tried to bewitch him with the aid of the magician Lesage. Lesage, who himself planned to marry la Voisin once her husband was out of the way, had buried a sheep's heart in la Voisin's garden. This, he said, would have a fatal effect on Montvoisin, although in the end the intended victim had realised that Lesage and his wife were up to something and had threatened retribution. As a result, Mme Voisin had lost her nerve and had forced Lesage to dig up the heart.

For her next attempt la Voisin had obtained some black grains from a sinister figure called the Chevalier d'Hannyvel. Having steeped them in wine to obtain an infusion, she gave a phial of it to Marie Bosse. She asked la Bosse to pour its contents into her husband's wine, but in the event la Bosse was overcome by 'some sort of scruple' and had only added a few drops. Even so, Montvoisin had fallen sound asleep once he had drunk the doctored wine. Mme Bosse had no doubt that if she had put in the entire phial it would have killed him.

La Bosse concluded her attack by claiming that the remains of countless aborted infants could be found buried in la Voisin's garden. The terminations had been carried out by a midwife named Mme Lepère, who used a metal tool for the purpose.

Clearly flustered by this comprehensive indictment, Mme Voisin protested that she had never sought to sell ground diamonds to Mme Brunet. She did, however, go some way towards acknowledging the truth of other allegations. She conceded that on more than one occasion she had been given powders by acquaintances who knew how wretched she was with her husband, though she insisted she had always thrown these away. Furthermore, she confirmed la Bosse's story about Lesage burying the heart in her garden. La Voisin explained that soon after the interment, her husband had been struck down by a stomachache and this had troubled her conscience. Accordingly, she went to church and, having confessed and received absolution, she had instructed Lesage to undo his spell on Montvoisin.

More compromisingly still, la Voisin agreed that she had been approached by a well-born lady who had wanted her to poison a bouquet of flowers. She also did not dispute that another – likewise unnamed – lady of rank had made her a gift of her mourning clothes. She recalled that the widow had pressed these garments on her with the kindly words, 'Mme Voisin, perhaps this will bring you luck and, if God permits that your husband dies, you can use them.'

On 20 March more details were teased out of la Voisin.[19] She gave a fuller account of her dealings with Mme Brunet, admitting that they were more extensive than she had earlier pretended. She explained that Mme Brunet had taken Philbert as her lover while her first husband was still alive. Unfortunately Brunet, unaware of the true situation, had taken a liking to the personable flautist and had decided to offer Philbert his daughter's hand in marriage. To Mme Brunet's despair, Philbert had been willing to accept this proposal.

La Voisin had revealed the motivation that could have driven a besotted woman to murder and in the next few days Mme Bosse edged closer to describing how Brunet had been killed. On 23 March she admitted that, with la Voisin's encouragement, she had supplied the distraught Mme Brunet with a liquid. What was more, she said she had obtained this from Magdelaine de La Grange, thus vindicating La Reynie's hunch that that woman had been guilty of a series of crimes.[20]

Four days later la Bosse confirmed an earlier admission of Mme Philbert (whose interrogations are unfortunately missing) that this liquid had been given to Brunet in an enema. Presumably this had been done with his consent, after he had been duped into thinking it would be good for him. On this occasion nothing much happened, for the liquid — which contained nitric acid — had been too weak to be effective. La Bosse recalled how surprised she had been when some days later she had seen Brunet in the street, still perfectly healthy. Next time, however, Brunet was less fortunate. Though the details as yet remained hazy, on the eve of her execution la Bosse would confess under torture that he had subsequently been dosed with another liquid and that had killed him.[21]

When interviewed on 20 March, Mme Voisin had not yet been ready to admit that Brunet had been murdered. However, there had been startling progress when she had named the lady who had bestowed on her her widow's weeds. La Voisin identified her as Mme Marguérite Leféron, a woman who until this moment had been considered a figure of the utmost respectability. Now aged sixty-five, she had been born into the moneyed oligarchy that dominated the upper echelons of the French judiciary. Her marriage to Jerome Leféron, President of the Second Chamber of Inquests had raised her still higher in the ranks of this bourgeois élite, and was a union only slightly less prestigious than that of her sister with M. Novion, who currently occupied the position of First President of the Paris *Parlement*. Despite the precedent afforded by Mme de Brinvilliers, the notion that someone with these impeccable connections might be a poisoner was singularly shocking.

When M. Leféron had died on 8 September 1669 it had aroused no suspicion, for he had been elderly and his health less than robust. His wife had apparently been grief-stricken, though she had confided to Mme Voisin that she had found it a great strain to keep up this show of sadness. In fact, the marriage had been far from happy. The couple had not shared a bed for the last fifteen years and Mme Leféron had found it intolerable that her husband was exceptionally cautious with money. Her bereavement had, of course, removed these constraints on her spending. She had carefully cultivated the image of a virtuous matron who performed good works and had donated funds to build a chapel in the local convent. In reality, however, she rejoiced in her new freedom.[22]

Less than three years after the death of M. Leféron a fortune hunter named M. de Prade had determined to marry this rich widow. In order to ensnare his prize he had turned to Mme Voisin and had drawn up a formal contract, promising to pay her 20,000 livres if she brought about the union. La Voisin set to work and cast various spells designed to make Mme Leféron hopelessly enamoured. Sure enough, in 1672 Mme Leféron married her suitor, though she did so in such complete secrecy that even la Voisin was unaware of what had happened. By the time she did find out, M. de Prade had reneged on his bargain. Although a promissory note in la Voisin's favour had been lodged with a lawyer, he had cunningly persuaded Marie Bosse to retrieve it for him, and had then destroyed it.[23]

In the end, however, M. de Prade's trickery did him little good. Although he had played no part in M. Leféron's murder, he had been aware of it and had not cared. He had professed himself untroubled by the possibility that Mme Leféron might treat him in the same way, saying that he knew how to look after himself and would kill her before she killed him. However, after only ten months of marriage, he and Mme Leféron were on very bad terms and de Prade grew uneasy for his safety. He became nervous of eating at home and decided to leave her. He never returned and, though La Reynie would have very much liked to interview him, his current whereabouts were unknown.[24]

The full truth about Mme Leféron would only come out gradually. From the first la Voisin acknowledged that Mme Leféron had come to her complaining about her husband and that the lady had made it clear that she wanted to poison him. At this stage, however, she maintained that she had done nothing to further these plans. The most she would admit was that, tempted by a payment of 300 livres, she had supplied Mme Leféron with a harmless opiate, which Mme Leféron had rejected as unsuitable for her purposes.[25] M. de La Reynie nevertheless had no doubt that, in time, Mme Voisin would reveal more.

On 22 March Mme Voisin created another sensation when she named the lady who had wanted her to produce a poisoned posy. This turned out to be Mme Françoise de Dreux, an extremely attractive thirty-year-old who lived in the Rue des Tournelles on the Île de la Cité. She was married to a Maître de Requêtes and numbered among her relations numerous other office holders and members of the judiciary. Indeed, M. d'Ormesson, one of the commissioners of the *Chambre Ardente*, was a cousin.[26]

The King's court was also swarming with her family and friends.

Her brother, M. Saintot, was a key figure there, for he was in charge of protocol whenever foreign diplomats presented their credentials. The Duc de Richelieu was another influential adherent of Mme de Dreux, for it was no secret that the two had been lovers for years.

It came as a great shock to the King when he heard that Mme de Dreux had been named by la Voisin. Before authorising her arrest he asked to be informed in more detail of the accusations against her.[27] Further interrogations of la Voisin over the next fortnight satisfied him that there were genuine grounds for suspicion. On 9 April Mme Leféron was arrested and taken to prison. Two days later Mme de Dreux followed her to Vincennes.

The arrest of these respected and well-bred women inevitably caused consternation. La Reynie had been aware that his actions were bound to cause resentment and as early as 20 March it had been agreed that he should never travel to Vincennes without a sizeable escort of guards. Now the English ambassador to France reported in wonderment to Secretary of State Coventry, 'The multitude of distinguished people arrested for poison grows every day.' He found it extraordinary that at the moment 'the most slight incidents are attributed to poison', while others hardly knew what to make of the latest developments. The Comte de Bussy was told by a friend at court, Mme de Scudéry, 'We talk of nothing but people being detained for poison,' and she added that the Duc de Richelieu was 'in despair about Mme de Dreux's ill fortune'.[28]

Not everyone was critical of these measures. When the Comte de Bussy (who may, it is true, have hoped that his letters would be intercepted and his approving comments noted) was told that 'a cruel war is being waged against poisoners' he responded that 'purging the earth of these monsters' was more praiseworthy than the labours of Hercules. He did, however, express puzzlement that the fate of Mme de Brinvilliers had not acted as more of a deterrent, for he was sure that some of those currently in difficulty had witnessed her execution.[29]

Already, however, there was a feeling in some quarters that the campaign against poisoners was going too far. The Marquis de Trichâteau tried to lighten the mood with a few jokes in bad taste. He pouted that it was dreadful that Mme de Dreux should be so humiliated as she 'is, apart from poison, one of my greatest friends and one of the prettiest women in France'. Mme de Scudéry was slightly more serious, confiding to the Comte de Bussy that Mme de Dreux's arrest 'scares everyone'. She added that at least she personally was in no danger as 'thank God, I have never purchased cosmetics or had my fortune told'.[30]

On 10 April 1679 the *Chambre d'Arsenal* sat for the first time. Its proce-dure mirrored that of normal courts of law. The judges considered the evidence presented to them by the *rapporteurs* before themselves inter-rogating defendants on the *sellette*. When reaching judgement, they took into account the opinion expressed by the Attorney-General on each case, but they were not obliged to abide by it.

The trials began on 4 May 1679. In the course of that one day Marie Bosse, Mme Vigoreux and their client Mme Ferry were examined on the *sellette*. Two days later all were sentenced to death and the Chamber ordered that la Bosse and la Vigoreux should be tortured prior to execution.

Under torture la Bosse clarified the methods used to kill M. Brunet. In addition she made some new allegations, the most important of which was a claim that the Maréchal de Luxembourg – one of France's foremost generals – and the Marquis de Feuquières had wanted to summon up the devil. La Vigoreux, in contrast, told her examiners little of substance. This was certainly not because they handled her gently. On the contrary, the agony of her legs being crushed in the *brodequins* proved too much for her and at 4 p.m. she died from what was officially described as 'an abscess of the head'.[31]

On 10 May the executions took place. Mme Ferry, who had con-fessed to poisoning her husband, had her wrist cut off outside Notre-Dame and was then taken to the Place de Grève to be hanged. Marie Bosse's eldest son was also hanged for having by his own admission assisted his mother to prepare poisons. His mother's crimes were deemed so heinous that she was burnt alive, a fate la Vigoreux would have shared had she not already died. By decree of the commission, Marie Bosse's fourteen-year-old daughter was brought to see her mother perish in the flames in the hope that the spectacle would have a salutary effect on her character.

For the moment, at least, Mme Voisin was spared execution, for La Reynie had no doubt that there was much still to be learned from her. Among other things he wished to question her about whether she had arranged abortions, for la Bosse had been emphatic that this had formed an important branch of her business.

At the time abortion was a capital offence, with both the mother of the aborted child and the midwife who performed the act being liable to the death penalty. This does not seem to have been an effective deterrent, not least because the crime usually went undetected. There were, of course, occasional exceptions. In 1660 there had been a terri-ble scandal when a member of the Condé family, Mlle de Guerchi, had a secret abortion after being impregnated by her lover, the Duc de Vitry. The matter had come to light after she suffered complications (haemorrhage and septicaemia were risks inherent in the procedure) which killed her. After the cause was determined, the curé of Saint-Eustache refused to bury her in consecrated ground. Mlle de Guerchi had to be consigned to a pit of quicklime in the garden of the Hôtel Condé and the midwife who had carried out the abortion was hanged. Years later Mme de Maintenon would hold up the case as a terrible warning to unmarried girls, pointing out that by her action Mlle de Guerchi had not only forfeited her own soul and that of the midwife, but had condemned her unborn child to everlasting damnation.[32]

Although cases of this kind usually escaped exposure, this did not mean there was a low incidence of abortion. Following the death of Mlle de Guerchi, senior churchmen warned *Parlement* that during the past year alone, 600 women in Paris had revealed in the confessional that they had rid themselves of unwanted babies. There is no reason to suppose that in the nineteen years that intervened between that incident and la Voisin's arrest the situation had greatly altered. Indeed, Primi Visconti would declare with regard to abortion that 'all the realm was infested with it'.[33]

When questioned on the subject, la Voisin was evasive, though she did admit that once Mme de Dreux's period had been late and that she had given her something to induce it. La Reynie fared better when he interviewed Catherine Lepère, an aged midwife who Marie Bosse said had carried out abortions on la Voisin's orders. Now aged seventy-eight, Mme Lepère had delivered some of la Voisin's own children and since that time had performed a variety of other tasks for her.

At first la Lepère insisted that she had done nothing to contravene the oath taken by certified midwives in Paris. She agreed that la Voisin had sent unmarried girls to her but maintained that, after examining them, she had always sent away the pregnant ones. Those who were not pregnant were given a douche of pure water, though la Lepère could offer no explanation as to what this was meant to achieve. When pressed, she claimed that many of the girls sent by Mme Voisin thought they had conceived babies but, on examination, they turned out to be virgins. She said she had protested to la Voisin that it was wrong to exploit their naivety in this way, to which la Voisin had answered with a shrug, 'Since they declared themselves to be whores, she really had to believe them.'[34]

On 27 May, by which time she had been in custody more than two months, Mme Lepère made much fuller admissions. She acknowledged for the first time that she had the knack of 'voiding' pregnant women, though she still insisted that the technique she used was not at all invasive. She explained gravely that she performed the operation with water rather than a hooked instrument and that 'everything depends on the manner of syringing'.[35]

By her own account she had profited little from these skills, for la Voisin had always fixed the price with the client and had only given Mme Lepère a small percentage. Mme Lepère even tried to make out that for many years she had been performing a public service: by saving ladies of rank from embarrassing pregnancies, she had succeeded in conserving their honour. She took pride, too, in recalling that when she performed abortions on women who were so far advanced in pregnancy that the infant showed brief signs of life she would baptise the little creature, securing its salvation. Having saved its soul, she would take the tiny corpse in a box to the local gravedigger who, for a paltry bribe, would be prepared to bury the pathetic bundle in a corner of the cemetery. It may be doubted, however, whether all the aborted infants came to rest in consecrated ground. La Bosse had alleged that large numbers of them were buried in la Voisin's garden (there is no mention, oddly, of it being searched for human remains) and other sources claimed that la Voisin disposed of bones and waste material in a small stove in her consulting room.

Neither la Voisin nor la Lepère appear to have been pressed to reveal the identities of the women who came to them for abortions, which gives some credence to Primi Visconti's claim that the King discouraged this aspect of the inquiry from being taken further. However, as the days went by Mme Voisin gave the names of a significant number of clients who, she said, had approached her in the hope that she could hasten the death of another person. Among them was Mme Brissart, the widow of a *Conseiller* in *Parlement*. According to la Voisin, she had first contacted her because her love life was going badly, but she had then asked if anything could be done to rid her of her sister, who had displeased her by contracting an unsuitable marriage. Mme Brissart was consequently detained at Vincennes, though she protested that her sister's death five years earlier had been caused by smallpox rather than as a result of her intervention. Mme Vertemart was also arrested after it emerged that she had consulted la Voisin on the advice of her aunts because she longed for her husband to die. Mme Roussel was another woman said by la Voisin to have had 'wicked designs' on her husband and she was taken into custody in early July.[36]

Some of those named by la Voisin were no longer available for questioning. Mme de Saint-Martin, who was said to have yearned for the death of her husband, had herself been dead for some years. Others who were still alive could not be located. In June 1679 la Voisin began giving an account of how, years before, the Marquise de Canilhac had visited her with her lover, M. de Broglio. The couple had started by asking whether Mme Voisin could provide them with some remedy which would make the Marquis de Canilhac drink less for, when drunk, he behaved 'worse than a pig and brute beast'. When the potion supplied by la Voisin failed to lessen his consumption, the lovers had demanded something more lethal. La Voisin had gone to Mme Lepère, who gave her a water which she said 'would put the husband to sleep for ever'. Sure enough, Canilhac had died shortly after being given this liquid and his widow had married M. de Broglio. However, the pair had since left the country and, though Louvois tried hard to track them down, he never managed to do so.[37]

La Voisin would later allege that this was not the only time that Mme Lepère had supplied her with poison, for she said the midwife had once given her something with which to kill her own husband. Mme Voisin had put this in her husband's broth but he had come to no harm because their servant, suspecting something was amiss, had thrown the soup away.

It was not only la Voisin's clients who now came under scrutiny. She and all the others taken into custody in the early stages of the inquiry were questioned exhaustively about their associates and this led to a spate of new arrests. On 24 April the commissioners of the Chamber decreed that fifteen more people should be taken to Vincennes. They included the divineress la Jacob who, Anne Cheron said, had expressed interest in purchasing a secret formula for poison; la Hébert who was 'blacker than a coal' and sold lotions to Mme Voisin; Jeanne Leroux, suspected of complicity in the murder of M. Leféron; Mme Vautier and her husband, who did distillations for la Voisin; and la Deslauriers, who had boasted to Anne Cheron that she knew 'the secret of la Brinvilliers'. Also arrested at this time was the mysterious Latour, a former stonemason who had persuaded la Voisin to part with large sums of money in the belief that he would use his magic powers to assist her clients.[38]

These people incriminated others in their turn and the list of prisoners at Vincennes grew steadily longer. By May Catherine Trianon, a fifty-two-year-old widow who was held in awe by other members of her profession and who had often drawn up horoscopes for clients of la Voisin, was in confinement. When her house was searched, many 'powders and suspicious drugs' were found in her casket, notably white arsenic, realgar, orpiment, powdered glass and cantharides.[39]

She was joined in the cells by Marguerite Delaporte, the sixty-nine-year-old widow of a master baker. Her speciality was reading the future in a glass of water and she admitted that in order to make her visions materialise, she uttered incantations. She insisted, however, that she had never done anyone any harm and that, when her clients asked her to predict the deaths of their husbands, she annoyed them by replying that she left that in God's hands. This did not fit with evidence from another source that, like la Voisin and la Trianon, la Delaporte had often purchased poisons from the herbalist Maître Pierre, 'the greatest and most skilled poisoner in France'.[40]

La Pelletier was another woman who had done a lot of work for la Voisin. She was said to know a great deal about the properties of dried herbs and had once supplied la Voisin with a powerful love potion, which was supposed to be applied to the palm of a hand. La Voisin claimed that when Mme Brissart had expressed a desire to kill her sister, she had sent her to discuss the matter with la Pelletier.[41]

As the numbers at Vincennes swelled relentlessly, La Reynie was filled with horror by what he was learning. It was his impression that the lives of an entire sector of the Paris population revolved around poison, and that a frightening amount of effort was devoted to its purchase, sale and manufacture. Poison was so much a part of these people's existence that they accepted as an occupational hazard that they themselves might fall victim to it. Sometimes this could be accidental, for the fact that so many of them dabbled in alchemy meant they were often exposed to dangerous chemicals. However, when unpleasant incidents occurred they were much more likely to ascribe the cause to deliberate attempts at murder. For example, Anne Cheron recalled an occasion when she and François Belot had fallen ill when drinking with a woman called la Montigny. Leaping to the conclusion that she had poisoned them, they had at once taken orvietan, a fashionable compound believed to be an antidote. On another occasion la Montigny herself had had an unpleasant experience when she had visited la Cheron's house. When she had wiped herself with a handkerchief left behind by Marie Bosse, her face had begun to swell, which she thought was because the handkerchief was impregnated with some toxic substance. La Cheron had saved the day: she urinated in her shoe and persuaded la Montigny to drink the contents, causing her to vomit.[42]

On 5 June 1679 Mme de Poulaillon was tried at the Arsenal. It was a significant test for the commission, as it was the first time it had been required to judge a well-born defendant. After examining the evidence the Attorney-General of the Chamber had recommended that, like Mme de Brinvilliers, Mme de Poulaillon should be tortured, then beheaded. The commissioners took a different view. When the prisoner sat before them on the *sellette*, her penitent demeanour, coupled with her grace and charm, made a very favourable impression. Mme de Poulaillon disarmingly admitted that she merited severe punishment for having sought to drug and rob her husband, while maintaining that she had never attempted to kill him. After she had been taken back to prison, the commissioners debated for four hours what penalty was appropriate. At first it seemed that a majority of the judges favoured a death sentence. However, some of them were mindful of the implications this would have on the treatment of Mmes de Dreux and Leféron, and were therefore predisposed to leniency. They proved singularly persuasive and M. Fieubet in particular spoke so eloquently in the prisoner's defence that he won over three of his colleagues. In the end the commissioners decreed that Mme de Poulaillon should be banished rather than executed.[43]

La Reynie, who clearly had been among the minority who voted for a death sentence, subsequently stated that Mme de Poulaillon herself considered that she had been shown undue compassion. He said that, when informed she would not be called upon to expiate her crime with her blood she had appeared inconsolable. She had pleaded that instead of being left free to roam abroad, she should be confined somewhere secure, for otherwise she could not guarantee that she would not commit fresh offences. If she really expressed herself thus, she subsequently had cause to regret it, for her wishes were fulfilled all too exactly. She was locked up in a forbidding 'house of correction' for fallen women in Angers and for eighteen years she eked out a sad existence in this grim institution. Finally, in May 1697, she petitioned that she might be permitted to retire to a convent where conditions would be less austere. Her request seemed likely to be granted until it was referred to M. de La Reynie. By that time on the verge of retirement, he showed that age had not in any way softened his rigour. He declared himself implacably opposed to her release, pointing out that she herself had warned that, if freed, she would be a menace to society. The result was that Mme de Poulaillon remained incarcerated in her horrible workhouse for the remainder of her days.[44]

Mme de Poulaillon can hardly be said to have evaded punishment. On the other hand she had been handled more gently than prisoners who came from a less privileged background. The outcome of the trial suggested that the King had been misguided to hope that, when called upon to deliver judgement on members of their own class, the commissioners of a special tribunal would be less partisan than *Parlement*. Plainly regretful that his colleagues had been swayed by such considerations, the Recorder of the Chamber noted that on this occasion the commission had failed to show 'the vigour which the public expected of it'.[45]

Events soon showed that the commissioners did not shrink from severe measures when they judged individuals with whom they could not so readily identify. On 10 June Mme Philbert was hanged for the murder of her first husband, having previously had her right hand amputated.★ The guardsman François Belot was hanged with her for trying to poison M. de Poulaillon's cup. Even under torture he had protested that he had not really known how to do this and that his real aim had been to steal the silver tankard. This earned him the concession of being strangled before being broken on the wheel. A week later his confederate Anne Cheron was hanged after admitting under torture that she had devoted great efforts to developing new poisons made from the juices of dead toads.[46]

The abortionist Mme Lepère was tried on 11 August. She was convicted of 'having abused her skill as a sworn midwife' by having 'brought to bed before their term several girls and women... causing the deaths of the children they were carrying'.[47] The next day she was placed in the *brodequins* although, in a rare instance of mercy, the torture was not actually applied on account of her advanced age. The grisly charade achieved nothing and she went to the gallows without revealing anything of substance.

Throughout the summer the grim toll mounted, but while this represented progress of a kind, La Reynie was not at all complacent. He did not flatter himself that the execution of these insignificant offenders would eradicate the scourge of poisoning, which was too virulent to be allayed so easily. He was sure that many crimes remained to be uncovered and that la Voisin's clientele was far more distinguished than she had yet admitted. While he had no doubt that this would be a slow process, he believed that with patience and perseverance he would eventually learn everything and that the information would be drawn either from Mme Voisin herself or from the prisoners locked up with her.

★ Her second husband, the flautist Philbert, was tried for the same crime the following April but was acquitted.

SIX

# THE MAGICIAN LESAGE

On 12 September 1679 Mme Voisin gave her fullest deposition to date.[1] Perhaps she hoped that if she co-operated, mercy would be shown her; alternatively she may merely have wanted to delay her trial and realised that her captors would not institute proceedings against her while they believed they could learn important things from her. At any rate, she explained that she had hitherto refrained from telling them all she knew because she had been reluctant to cause anyone distress. Now, however, she wished to clear her conscience, hoping that since she had entrusted herself to God's care and protection 'the King would out of his goodness wish to have pity on her and her family'.

She then provided a much more detailed account of her dealings with Mme Leféron. She described how Mme Leféron had come to her to have her palm read and had almost at once wanted to know if there was any likelihood that she would soon become a widow. Once 'accustomed to talking on this subject, little by little' Mme Leféron had progressed to asking whether it might be possible to poison her husband. She and la Voisin had then discussed the feasibility of sending someone to Italy to obtain powdered diamonds, or a perfume with a deadly fragrance, but ultimately these options were dismissed as impractical. Instead, la Voisin had obtained from Magdelaine de La Grange a phial of arsenic and distilled sublimate, which was delivered by a third party, a woman called la Leroux. When the phial was given to Mme Leféron she protested that it would be difficult for her to put it in her husband's broth as his servant was suspicious of her and watched her closely. However, it seems that an opportunity had presented itself for, three weeks later, M. Leféron had died. Subsequently the joyous Mme Leféron had paid a visit to la Voisin, saying that it was a relief to see someone with whom it was unnecessary to feign grief at her bereavement. Initially she had maintained that she had not given the liquid to her husband but she had soon dropped this pretence. When la Voisin had asked if she believed it was the effect of the poison that had killed him, Mme Leféron had cheerfully replied, 'Effect or no…she was rid of him thank God!'

Having unburdened herself about Mme Leféron, la Voisin next turned her attention to Mme de Dreux. She confirmed that Mme de Dreux had given her a diamond ring as a down payment for poisoning a bouquet of flowers. These were to be sent to a woman who had made Mme de Dreux jealous, though la Voisin insisted she had not carried out the commission. Mme de Dreux had also discussed procuring the death of her husband and had indicated that she would pay la Voisin 2000 écus on completion of the task. However, though she was impatient to be rid of him, she was fearful of being prosecuted for murder. She therefore hoped that his death might be effected by occult means rather than poison. She had suggested that la Voisin should arrange for a Novena to be said, praying for the death of M. de Dreux, but she had made difficulties when la Voisin said that for that she would need one of M. de Dreux's shirts, which his wife said would be hard for her to obtain.

Mme Voisin declared that she herself had never actually supplied Mme de Dreux with poison. However, she did not fail to point out that Mme de Dreux had had separate dealings with Marie Bosse and she made it clear that she could not answer for what had been agreed between them. Furthermore, la Voisin alleged that Mme de Dreux had told her she had already poisoned two men whom she had once loved but had grown to hate, although she was vague about the identity of the two victims.

As a result of these revelations a confrontation was arranged between la Voisin and Mmes de Dreux and Leféron.[2] In the face of their indignant denials, la Voisin repeated all she had earlier said, refusing to withdraw any of her accusations. Mme Leféron insisted that she had been slandered, recalling that when la Voisin had first told her she saw death marked in her hand, she had assumed it was her own demise that was imminent rather than her husband's. She raged that now la Voisin was taking advantage of her misfortune to insult her and was not at all mollified when la Voisin began weeping. Furiously Mme Leféron sneered that la Voisin was only crying in the hope of investing her claims with a spurious credibility. With dignity la Voisin answered that she had been moved to tears because God had excited in her an awareness of her faults.

La Voisin had declared that it pained her to betray her clients in this way, but her revelations did not end here. On 16 September 1679 Louvois excitedly informed the King, 'La Voisin's really beginning to talk.'[3] The statements she had made the day before precipitated the inquiry into a new phase as, for the first time, she had mentioned the name of the Duchesse de Vivonne, sister-in-law of Mme de Montespan. The precise allegations la Voisin made against her are unclear, as the record of that interrogation is missing. However, from Louvois's account it would seem la Voisin stated that Mme de Vivonne had wanted to kill her husband and that she had applied to the magician Lesage for help with this matter.

La Voisin's allegations ensured that attention focused more closely on Lesage who had been arrested on 17 March after Marie Bosse had described him as a dangerous man who put 'wholly pernicious' ideas in women's minds.[4] Initially he had been regarded as a figure of secondary importance but now this extraordinary individual assumed a much more prominent role in the inquiry. At times, indeed, he came close to dominating it.

The real name of the self-styled Lesage ('the wise one') was Adam du Coeuret and he came from Normandy. Now aged nearly fifty, he was physically a far from imposing figure. He habitually wore grey, with a reddish wig providing the only touch of colour,[5] but his drab appearance did not detract from his charisma. He described himself as a wool merchant, but though he had occasionally invested money in speculative ventures in the cloth trade, his primary means of making a living had never been commerce.

Lesage had already had an eventful career. He had first come to Paris in the late 1660s, though at that time he called himself Dubuisson. Before long he had met up with la Voisin and become her lover, forming such a close attachment to her that he had even attempted to send her husband into a fatal decline by burying a sheep's heart in her garden. In 1667 la Voisin had introduced him to François Mariette, a twenty-seven-year-old priest who proved a willing collaborator. For a time the trio had worked in partnership, with la Voisin providing the two men with a steady flow of customers. After a bit, however, Mariette and Lesage had decided they could make more money by operating independently. To la Voisin's chagrin, her business began to suffer as they enticed clients away from her. Furious at this betrayal, la Voisin engaged in angry recriminations, but this merely attracted unwelcome attention to the activities of Mariette and Lesage, and in March 1668 the pair were arrested.

That June they were tried at the Châtelet and the following September their appeals were heard by *Parlement*. They were charged with the serious offence of committing impieties but unfortunately the records of their trial are not very informative about the evidence gathered against them. Lesage was asked whether he had said prayers over the corpses of flayed frogs, but he denied this, saying he had only ever used frogs to create an oil to whiten the complexion. Mariette admitted that clients had visited him in his lodgings and that he had recited extracts from the gospels over their heads as they knelt before him. While this sounded innocuous, the suspicion may have been that he was quoting scripture backwards, an inversion of holy writ that was thought to be pleasing to the devil. He confessed, too, that he had conferred benedictions on certain books and perhaps this included a volume of incantations called the *Enchiridon*, which featured as an exhibit at Lesage's trial. Mariette was also asked whether he had passed notes under a chalice, another way in which orthodox Christian ritual could be adapted for illegitimate purposes.[6] At the time he said he had not but years later, when these events came under fresh scrutiny, he agreed that he had performed that and other deviant practices. With hindsight, however, the most striking thing to emerge from the hearings was that Mariette told the court at the Châtelet that the Marquise de Montespan (who had either just embarked on her affair with Louis XIV, or was on the verge of becoming his mistress) was a client of his.

At the time it is true that no one seems to have shown any interest in this statement, for no steps were taken against those named as customers by Mariette and Lesage. The two men were both found guilty, but there was a wide disparity in their punishments. Mariette was a cousin of the magistrate who had first investigated the case[7] and this family connection ensured that when sentence was passed he was condemned only to nine years' banishment. Even this was not properly enforced, for after a short spell in a corrective institute for wayward priests he left without permission and then withdrew to the country. Lesage fared much worse. Lacking Mariette's influence with the judges, he was sentenced to the galleys in perpetuity.

Serving in the galleys was a dreadful fate imposed on many convicts at a time when the expansion of the navy and the demands of war had created an insatiable demand for slaves to man the Mediterranean fleet. Because of the high mortality rate caused by harsh conditions and overwork, vacancies had constantly to be replenished and orders had been sent out that perpetrators of offences such as bigamy, which previously had incurred a mandatory death sentence, should instead be punished by being forced to man the galleys. Life in the galleys was deemed such an appalling prospect that some prisoners preferred to incapacitate themselves by mutilating limbs. In a bid to stamp out this vexatious practice a royal decree was issued in 1677 declaring that in future anyone who adopted this 'easy method' of evading service would be put to death.[8]

Louis XIV

The Marquise de Brinvilliers on her way to her execution after being tortured. She had confessed to poisoning her father and two brothers. On the right of this drawing by Charles Lebrun it is just possible to make out the profile of Father Pirot, the Jesuit priest who took her final confession.

TOP: A depiction of the water torture, a particularly horrible form of torment inflicted on Mme de Brinvilliers. The victim was forced to drink more than twenty pints of water, causing excruciating pain. Some people alleged that because of her connections with the judiciary Mme de Brinvilliers was subjected to milder torture than was usual in such cases, but this was probably untrue.

BOTTOM: A seventeenth century execution in France, a scene similar to the beheading of Mme de Brinvilliers in the Place de Grève in Paris in July 1676.

Louise de La Vallière, who became the mistress of Louis XIV in 1661. Later it would be alleged that several court ladies had sought to poison her out of jealousy.

OPPOSITE PAGE: The King's mistress, Mme de Montespan, reclining in front of her gallery at Clagny. In 1680 it was alleged that she had sought to poison the King and Mlle de Fontanges and that she had participated in satanic rituals and child sacrifice.

Marie-Angélique de Scorailles, Mlle de Fontanges, the beautiful teenage mistress of Louis XIV. When she fell ill after suffering a miscarriage in January 1680 she suggested that poison might be responsible.

A depiction of a victim being broken on the wheel, the 'cruel death' inflicted on
Mme de Brinvilliers's henchman La Chaussée and several others convicted by the *Chambre Ardente* .

The 15TH Century keep at the Chateau de Vincennes, the royal fortress to the east of Paris where suspects in the Affair of the Poisons were imprisoned pending trial.

Louis XIV's Minister of War, the Marquis de Louvois, who played an active part in the campaign against poisoners. It was said that the establishment of the *Chambre Ardente* afforded this 'malignant and hate-filled man… a fine opportunity to ruin whomsoever he wished'.

The Lieutenant-General of the Paris Police, Nicolas de La Reynie, who conducted the investigation into the Affair of the Poisons and served as a commissioner of the Arsenal Chamber. Horrified by the allegations that emerged during the affair, at one point he complained of being surrounded by 'impenetrable darkness'.

The Comtesse de Soissons, who until 1679 served as the Queen's Mistress of the Robes. After la Voisin alleged that she had planned to poison the King and Louise de La Vallière, the Comtesse fled France in January 1680. By an irony she is painted here on horseback in front of the Chateau de Vincennes, where she would almost certainly have been imprisoned had she not avoided arrest by leaving the country.

M. La Contesse De. Soisson

The Duchesse de Bouillon, younger sister of the Comtesse de Soissons. Following allegations by the magician Lesage that she had wanted to kill her husband, the Duchesse was summoned before the Arsenal Chamber, where she answered the commissioners' questions in a 'laughing and disdainful' manner.

The Maréchal Duc de Luxembourg, the distinguished general who Lesage alleged had signed a pact with the devil and had sought to murder his wife. After several months imprisonment in the Bastille, he was tried by the Arsenal Chamber in May 1680.

The King's Controller-General of Finance, Colbert. Alarmed by the way in which the Arsenal Chamber was instituting proceedings against individuals who were closely allied to him, in February 1681 he wrote a memorandum defending Mme de Montespan.

LE PORTRAIT DE LA VOISIN.

Engraving of the celebrated divineress, Catherine Montvoisin, known as 'la Voisin'. It was said that 'most of the ladies in Paris had visited her'. Under interrogation she incriminated many underworld figures and admitted having supplied the poison used in more than one murder. It was later alleged that Mme de Montespan had been one of her clients.

Even when offenders were sentenced to a fixed term in the galleys, it was common practice not to free them at the end of their time and they usually remained chained to their oar until death released them from enslavement. Most untypically, however, Lesage was freed after serving only a few years in the Mediterranean. This caused great puzzlement when he again came to the notice of the authorities. It was conjectured that an influential client of his must have interceded on his behalf, securing his early release. In 1679 Mme Leféron was asked if it had been she who had performed this feat, but she denied this, and other enquiries by Louvois failed to reveal who was responsible. There has been speculation that, in fact, it was Mme de Montespan who exerted herself to free Lesage, so that she could resume her consultations with him, but this now seems unlikely. Research by Jean-Christian Petitfils has shown that in June 1673 the Minister for the Marine sent instructions to the *Intendant* of the galleys to free fifteen French galley slaves who had distinguished themselves in an action against the Genoese. Lesage was probably among this contingent.[9]

Lesage (as he now called himself) promptly returned to Paris and, apparently undeterred by the frightful punishment he had received, resumed his former line of business. He soon re-established himself as 'a very great magician' who was held in the highest repute by others who practised his trade. Despite their earlier disagreement, Mme Voisin had missed him during his absence and had regretfully told one client that it was unfortunate he was not on hand to aid her.[10] Upon his return she settled her differences with him and was soon offering him fresh employment.

Lesage was nothing if not versatile. He dabbled in alchemy, hinting that he knew how to convert silver into gold and that he had found a way of solidifying mercury. He also sold skin preparations and beauty aids, making lotions to his own recipe. As he modestly put it, he also 'knew something about the stars' and drew up a chart for one client trying to select an auspicious day on which to undertake an important enterprise.[11] These, however, were the sort of skills which numerous other members of the Paris underworld were ready to offer their clients, whereas Lesage had additional talents that made him unique.

Lesage set out to convince his clients that he could communicate with the spirit world and could mediate on their behalf with its inhabitants. In order to promote this illusion he had perfected a conjuring trick of his own invention, which he performed – as he himself proudly noted – with incomparable 'subtlety and skill'. No one else in Paris knew how he did this and Lesage jealously guarded the secret, being careful to leave no clues that might reveal his technique. When clients came to him he would ask them to set down their desires in writing, then to fold and seal the list without showing it to him. Having embedded the paper in a wax ball, Lesage would cast this into the fire. As soon as it touched the flames the ball would explode with a resounding noise, disintegrating so completely that not even tiny fragments could be retrieved. In fact, however, Lesage had cleverly substituted the original ball with another, filled beforehand with saltpetre so that it would detonate on contact with fire. He then took the first ball away so he could extract the paper and, having read what his clients had written, he decided how to proceed. Sometimes he returned the paper to the clients, who were invariably amazed that a document they had seen destroyed before their very eyes should be restored intact and undamaged. Lesage would then tell them that their wishes had been made known to the spirits and that, if he was suitably rewarded, there was a good chance their desires would be granted. Alternatively, if Lesage saw that the client had written something compromising, he would indicate that he now had the paper in his possession and that they must pay him generously if they did not want its contents revealed.[12]

Lesage was considered to be unrivalled when it came to concluding marriages. He claimed he could invoke supernatural forces to bring about events he desired and if la Voisin had a case that was proving particularly intractable she was apt to enlist his aid. For instance, when a well-to-do widow named Mme Desmaretz came to la Voisin in a panic after being impregnated by her lover, M. Gontier, la Voisin assured her that Lesage would have no difficulty ensuring that Gontier honoured his earlier promise of marriage. Sure enough, Lesage's intervention proved decisive. He began by pronouncing orisons in Mme Desmaretz's bedchamber and followed this up with a variety of unconventional procedures. Chanting '*Per Deum Vivum, Per Deum Verum, Per Deum Sanctum*', Lesage repeatedly tapped a hazel wand on the bed the couple had shared, assuring Mme Desmaretz that this would have the effect of unleashing Gontier's love for her. On another occasion when la Voisin was present Lesage enacted a more sinister ritual with overtones of Satanism. He had instructed Mme Desmaretz to provide him with a pot of Gontier's urine and to this he added pigeon's blood and the heart of a sheep. Then, as Mme Desmaretz knelt before him, he again flourished his wand and called on Lucifer, Beelzebub and Astaroth to help her. Having done this he assured Mme Desmaretz that if she deposited the pot with its stinking contents in her cellar, Gontier would not enjoy a moment's repose until he had pledged himself to her'.[13]

All went according to plan, for shortly afterwards Gontier had taken Mme Desmaretz as his wife. Following Lesage's arrest, however, the methods she had used to ensnare her husband were exposed to humiliating scrutiny. In late August 1679 Mme Desmaretz was summoned before the *Chambre Ardente* to give an account of her actions. Presumably it came as an unpleasant shock to M. Gontier to learn of the manner in which he had been manoeuvred into marriage, but the commissioners were not too hard on her and let her off with a modest fine for profanity.

Mme Brissart was another of la Voisin's clients whose romantic aspirations were furthered by Lesage. She yearned for an army officer named Captain Rubantel who, before going on campaign, had happily spent her money to fit himself out with military accoutrements, but since then had treated her coldly. Once again Lesage resolved the situation by performing a solemn ceremony. Having struck the ground with his wand, he called on Rubantel, in the name of the 'all-powerful one' to cease neglecting Mme Brissart, who henceforth would possess his heart and body. This, too, yielded results, for Rubantel soon became more attentive, though Lesage himself would later give a prosaic reason for his success. He explained that Mme Brissart had initially wearied her lover by showing herself too eager, but when she followed Lesage's advice and became more distant, Rubantel's interest was reawakened.[14]

Matters relating to love and marriage formed a fair part of Lesage's business, but for him death, too, was a saleable commodity. Admittedly, when people came to him in the hope that he could arrange for a death to take place, he never sought to facilitate crude acts of homicide. Mme Voisin herself would ultimately exonerate him of this, for her final words on Lesage were that while he had proved to be 'no friend of hers', she did not believe he had ever been involved in any form of poisoning.[15] Instead, Lesage convinced his clients that he could procure deaths by casting spells and that this was an infinitely more sensible way to proceed than resorting to poison, with its inherent risk of detection.

It was not until some months after his arrest that details of all this began to emerge. Lesage had doubtless hoped that such matters could be kept hidden but gradually it became plain that they had taken up much of his time. He admitted, for example, that the Comte de Gassilly, a former client of Marie Bosse and Mme Vigoreux, had come to him because he wanted his uncle to die. Lesage had instructed the Comte to furnish him with some human bones and had then performed some 'monkey tricks' with them, which satisfied Gassilly that his uncle would not live much longer. On another occasion a cook named David and his friend Chaix had informed Lesage that they wanted to murder M. Poncet, a *Conseiller d'état*. Lesage then performed a series of spells featuring arsenic, telling them that this obviated the need of actually administering the poison to Poncet.[16]

Lesage did his best to make out that his conduct was not worthy of serious censure. Unlike other members of his profession, he did not really believe in magic and had merely cynically imposed on the credulous in order to make money. While he could hardly deny that his activities had been fraudulent, he sought to portray them as essentially harmless. He even argued that he had actually saved lives by luring clients away from the likes of la Bosse, la Voisin and la Vigoreux, for they would have advocated the use of poison to resolve difficulties, to which he was resolutely opposed. He therefore deserved credit for having persuaded 'Gassilly and the others to abandon the route of poison' by convincing them that he could help them attain their wishes with complete safety. Citing another case where he had persuaded the divineress Mme Chapelain to enlist his aid rather than kill someone through her own efforts, he noted proudly that 'by his monkey tricks he persuaded her he knew much more about poisoning people through magic' than she could achieve with more conventional methods. He claimed that there had been many times when, by 'similar contrivances' he had 'prevented...pernicious designs' from being executed.[17]

Despite his efforts to present his actions in a favourable light, Lesage had better reason than anyone to be aware that they were liable to incur savage retribution. Nevertheless, he clung to the hope that if he furthered the inquiry without incriminating himself too much he would be shown mercy, and he did everything he could to achieve this result. He had no qualms about denouncing others, overwhelming them with a torrent of accusations, which he steadfastly maintained in the face of their shrill denials. As a practised and polished liar who was accustomed to living on his wits, Lesage had no difficulty mingling truth and falsehood in the most plausible fashion, and he was determined that through his adroit manipulation of the evidence he would manoeuvre himself into a much more advantageous position.

Lesage's relations with la Voisin had by no means always been harmonious but they had acknowledged each other as masters in their field and la Voisin had never quite overcome her fascination for him. It appears that following his return from the galleys, she had continued to be strongly attracted to him, though Lesage had not reciprocated her feelings as warmly as she would have liked. At one point la Voisin had tried to remedy this by paying her neighbour, la Pelletier, to perform a

Novena on her behalf in the hope that this would make Lesage fall in love with her. When this had failed, la Voisin had tried another tactic, telling Lesage that she had given birth to his child and that he must support it. However, since Lesage suspected – rightly, as it turned out – that the child was supposititious, he refused to acknowledge it as his own. He told her he considered her too old to conceive a baby and that unless he received independent evidence that she had given birth – such as proof that she was lactating – he would not contribute a sou to the child's upkeep.[18]

Now, however, that both were in custody there was no question that memories of their past affection would make them try to protect each other. La Voisin herself recognised well enough that she could expect no loyalty whatever from Lesage. When they were brought together for a confrontation on 19 May she commented bitterly 'that he had always betrayed her' to which Lesage retorted that, on the contrary, it was she who had always cheated him. Certainly, on his arrest Lesage had wasted little time heaping calumny on his former lover. During his very first interrogation on 22 March he had described la Voisin as 'a wicked woman whom God will punish', and he would later refer to her as 'a veteran poisoner'.[19]

In the months after his arrest Lesage would testify that la Voisin had on more than one occasion tried to poison her own husband. He even claimed that after a quarrel between them he himself had come close to being poisoned by her. Hearing that he was ill, la Voisin had sent the herbalist Maître Pierre to his bedside but Lesage said that the supposedly therapeutic plasters that Maître Pierre had applied had made him so ill that he would have died had he not promptly removed them.[20] However, his allegations against la Voisin were far more extensive than this, for he accused her of multiple murders, which no one else attributed to her and for which she never admitted responsibility.

Among those whom Lesage listed as victims of la Voisin was a M. Le Roule, whose wife had supposedly sought la Voisin's help in eliminating him and who had been killed with poisons supplied by Maître Pierre. According to Lesage, la Voisin was also behind the death of the Comte d'Argenton. His widow had subsequently remarried but had then taken against her second husband and had approached la Voisin to see if he, too, could be poisoned. In addition, a man called Nesle had given la Voisin a pearl necklace because he wanted to poison somebody. When la Voisin was told of this accusation against her, she agreed that Nesle had been a client of hers but said he had come to her simply because he wanted her to further a marriage for him.[21]

Lesage further alleged that a woman called Mme Yvon had prevailed upon la Voisin to poison her husband. Some years after his death Mme Yvon had asked la Voisin to provide the same service for a daughter of hers named Mme Leroy, whose marriage was unhappy. On being challenged about this during a confrontation with Lesage, la Voisin protested that she had had nothing to do with Yvon's death and had never even met with Mme Yvon in the lifetime of her husband. It was true that Mme Yvon had later brought her daughter to see her but this was simply because they wanted la Voisin to devise a way of arranging that M. Leroy's niece should leave his household.[22]

Lesage supplemented this by accusing la Voisin of having enabled Mme de Montmort to kill her husband. When this was put to la Voisin she was adamant that Mme de Montmort had only wanted her assistance to recover a lost casket. Another person who had allegedly sought la Voisin's assistance in a murder was the German Mlle de Bribach, who had wanted to marry a man named M. de Montauban. Fearing that Montauban's sister would obstruct the union, she had sent a servant to obtain a liquid from la Voisin to resolve the matter. Lesage admitted he did not know whether the intended victim had lived or died, whereas la Voisin denied that murder had ever been contemplated. She admitted that Mlle de Bribach had hoped to marry M. de Montauban but said that all she had done for her was to provide her with a love potion made from the dried corpse of a mole.[23]

La Voisin was by no means the only person against whom Lesage testified, for he proved eager to blacken a significant number of his former associates. At his very first interrogation he had been scathing about Marie Bosse ('She's the worst, that one,' was his comment) but he followed this up with attacks on numerous other denizens of the Paris underworld who had hitherto escaped suspicion. It was he who first named the herbalist Maître Pierre as an accomplished poisoner, claiming that he was an expert on preparing deadly enemas and toxic infusions. He said la Voisin purchased many of her poisons from him, but la Bosse, la Trianon and la Delaporte were also his devoted customers. Blessis and Latour, two other men who were much in la Voisin's company, were 'very wicked persons'. Blessis, who was one of Mme Voisin's lovers, was not only a forger but was probably the person who had taught her how to poison linen and perfumes. For good measure Lesage added that he understood a man called Boucher, whom he had never actually met, had not only poisoned his own wife but had worked in conjunction with the divineress Mme Chapelain. Together they had practised magic and made poisons, and he believed them to have been guilty of 'great abominations'.[24]

On 23 June Lesage had announced that he had 'important things to declare ... which he was ready to do for the discharge of his conscience', as it was 'a question of duty, above all regarding the King'. What he had to say related to Louis Vanens and Cadelan, who had never been charged since their arrest in 1677 but were still in prison on suspicion of serious offences. Without advancing any proof, Lesage stated that he knew Cadelan had poisoned his wife's first husband, a rich man named Rondeau. More worrying still, he revealed that Vanens, Cadelan and Bachimont had entered into a grand conspiracy with a pirate captain named Baix and Dr Rabel, a fashionable physician who was currently living in England. Lesage remained vague as to their objectives, though he hazarded it had something to do with making gold, and that there was some Italian link, as all the protagonists had travelled extensively in that country. Lesage stressed that it was of 'great consequence for the King's service' that Baix should be located, as he was 'very dangerous'. Lesage was far from clear as to the privateer's whereabouts, suggesting that he might now be living in Dunkirk, Sweden or even Transylvania; nevertheless, urgent (though unsuccessful) efforts were at once made to find Baix.[25]

Since so much of Lesage's information was ill defined and insubstantial it is curious that he commanded so much attention. Strictly speaking, indeed, no account whatever should have been taken of his evidence, for the law stated that as a convicted criminal he was ineligible to testify against others. Yet Louvois made it clear that he considered him a particularly valuable witness, enthusing that despite the fact that Lesage himself had never been implicated in any poisonings, he knew all about those committed in recent years. Lesage did not fail to take advantage of such twisted logic and was determined to exploit every opportunity afforded him of talking his way out of trouble. Articulate and wily, and highly attuned to what his interlocutors wanted to hear, he was able to play upon their fears in the most masterly fashion. Possessing those essential attributes of the skilled liar, a fertile imagination and a retentive memory, he had the knack of enlivening his stories with such vivid detail that even his most brazen inventions acquired a spurious verisimilitude. Encouraged by the reception accorded to his words, he soon progressed from making accusations against former colleagues to attacking the reputation of much more eminent persons and it was largely due to him that the scope of the inquiry became so much wider. Having been put on trial as a result of Lesage's denunciations, the Maréchal de Luxembourg would bitterly point to him as the true 'author of this whole web of perfidy and iniquity'.[26]

On 15 September la Voisin had suggested that Lesage knew damaging things about the Duchesse de Vivonne. For a time Lesage dodged responding to this directly but two days later he counter-attacked by alleging that la Voisin herself had had links with people at court, which merited investigation. Precisely what he said cannot be established, but from the notes La Reynie jotted down it would seem Lesage indicated that in 1675 Mme Voisin had paid frequent visits to the royal palace of Saint-Germain. She had delivered powders to clients there and Lesage said these had contained cantharides. At the time she had been engaged in some project which her husband had considered extremely risky and had prophesied would bring disaster on her. La Voisin, however, had expected it would make her rich and had plans to leave the country once she had been paid the enormous sum of 100,000 écus. Several associates of la Voisin had been privy to the conspiracy, including Latour, Marie Bosse, la Vigoreux and the divineresses la Petit and la Bergerot.[27]

What was more, la Voisin had had some form of connection with Mme de Montespan's household. According to Lesage, one of Mme de Montespan's servants, a woman named Cato, had secured her job through la Voisin's influence. In addition the flighty young Mme Vertemart, who had originally consulted la Voisin in the hope of being freed from her husband, had also asked la Voisin to obtain for her a position with Mme de Montespan. More worrying still, Mlle des Oeillets, who had formerly occupied a position of some importance in Mme de Montespan's service, had had frequent dealings with la Voisin. Though Lesage probably did not appreciate the full significance of what he was saying, this was a devastating allegation, for Mlle des Oeillets had been a sexual partner of the King's, as well as an employee of Mme de Montespan's.

By 1679 Claude de Vin des Oeillets was in her early forties and was no longer resident at court.[28] The daughter of a successful actress, she had decided against emulating her mother's stage career and instead, at some time prior to 1669, had begun working for Mme de Montespan. Exactly when she became one of the King's casual sleeping partners is not clear. In January 1670 the King awarded her the estate of a foreigner whose wealth had been forfeited to the Crown and, almost three years later, this was followed by a more substantial endowment when he gave her a plot of property in the vicinity of Clagny, conveniently close to Versailles. There she built a house, which she rented out, though she retained a pavilion at the site for her own use. One might deduce from this that she had already shared the King's bed but if so, this does not seem to have created difficulties between her and Mme de Montespan.

In 1675 Mlle des Oeillets came to see Primi Visconti, who was at that time highly esteemed as a clairvoyant. She asked him to elucidate a dream Mme de Montespan had had about losing all her hair, though whether she was acting at the request of her employer or was curious on her own account is unclear. Visconti described her as a 'trusted chambermaid' of Athénaïs, apparently seeing no contradiction in the fact that Mlle des Oeillets also informed him that she had slept with the King on several occasions. Utterly unruffled by this perplexing state of affairs, Visconti commented serenely in his memoirs that Mlle des Oeillets was 'not beautiful but the King quite often found himself alone with her when her mistress was busy or ill'.[29]

Mlle des Oeillets indicated to Visconti that she had already had children by the King and we know that he was the father of a baby girl she produced around 1675–6. The child was given the name Louise de Maisonblanche and was probably raised by foster-parents. When she grew up the fiction was maintained that she was the daughter of a cavalry captain and his wife but, although elaborate precautions were taken to ensure that her real parentage remained secret, the King did not disown her entirely. Upon her coming of age she was provided with a modest dowry and married to Bernard de Prez, Seigneur de La Queue. For the most part she lived a retired existence in the country, but there were occasions when she was permitted to hover on the fringes of the court. One account mentions that she and her husband at one point occupied a house near the stables of Versailles, though before being allowed to come there she had to give an undertaking that whenever she went outside she would be veiled. Presumably this was to prevent her resemblance to the King from being noted.

Since Mlle des Oeillets did not leave Mme de Montespan's service till 1677[30] one can only assume that she either successfully concealed from Athénaïs that the King had fathered a child by her or else that Mme de Montespan was not put out by her intermittent liaison with Louis, deeming it of no importance. When Mlle des Oeillets finally did retire, she settled in rented accommodation in Paris. Her circumstances appear to have been comfortable for she accumulated a respectable collection of furniture, paintings and tapestries. One source does suggest, however, that having foolishly cherished hopes that the King would one day make her his acknowledged mistress, she was embittered that he had abandoned her.[31] Whether or not there was any truth in this, she would soon be accused of having plotted to enact a spectacular revenge on him.

Increasingly disquieted by the direction the inquiry was taking, the King took steps to ensure that unless he desired otherwise, knowledge of what was happening need never reach the public. On 21 September he issued orders that when certain prisoners were interrogated on matters summarised in an adjoining memorandum (unfortunately not preserved), their answers were to be written down on separate sheets of paper, rather than being inscribed as usual in bound volumes. Already, therefore, Louis was making contingency plans, which would facilitate the removal of particularly sensitive pieces of information from the official record.[32]

On 22 September la Voisin was interrogated once more. She did her best to dispel the notion that she had ever been involved in some sinister enterprise, which had entailed frequent visits to Saint-Germain. She also denied having exerted her influence to place clients in Mme de Montespan's service. She agreed that Cato had once asked her to secure her a position in Athénaïs's household, but said that she had done nothing more than to offer up prayers that the young woman might be taken on as a servant. When Cato was, in fact, given a job by Mme de Montespan, she had sent la Voisin an écu and a cheap ring by way of thanks. Since then, la Voisin had not seen her.

La Voisin conceded that Mme Vertemart had once told her that if she succeeded in placing her in Mme de Montespan's household, she would reward her with a pearl necklace. La Voisin said she had declined to act on the proposal as she considered Mme Vertemart to be such a loose woman that she was unfitted for such advancement. As for Mlle des Oeillets, la Voisin insisted that she had never had any contact with her at all.[33]

Nevertheless, when Lesage was questioned again on 26 September, he not only stuck to his story but even expanded it. He urged that a divineress named Françoise Filastre should be taken into custody for, once she was interrogated, 'one would learn some strange things'. After repeating that Mlle des Oeillets was well known to la Voisin, he made the new allegation that la Voisin's attempts to install Mme Vertemart in Athénaïs's household had come about in consequence 'of an affair which la Voisin had undertaken for Mme de Montespan'.[34] Thus, for the first time it had been hinted that Mme de Montespan was in league with la Voisin.

The following day Louvois wrote to the King. He made no mention of Lesage's imputation against Mme de Montespan, but he made it clear that other aspects of Lesage's testimony had worried him. He remarked that Lesage appeared confident that other witnesses would verify what he had said about la Voisin's visits to Saint-Germain and it was therefore hard to believe that the whole story was invented. On the other hand, in view of the fact that la Voisin had taken so many people into her confidence, it seemed unlikely that she had gone there to carry out some fearsome criminal enterprise. Louvois was more inclined to think it would ultimately turn out that la Voisin had been engaged in some superstitious nonsense, which need hardly be taken very seriously. Furthermore, the War Minister was sceptical that Mlle des Oeillets could have been guilty of grave wrongdoing. Obviously well aware of the King's fondness for her (and clearly discounting the possibility that she had harboured any kind of grudge against Louis), Louvois suggested that if Mlle des Oeillets had ever consulted la Voisin the likelihood was that it had been for some innocuous purpose.[35]

Lesage had created quite a stir by impugning the name of comparatively menial figures, but his next targets were far grander. Since the very beginning of the inquiry the name of the Marquis de Feuquières had featured on a number of occasions. He had been spoken of as a client of la Vigoreux, and Marie Bosse's son had said that Feuquières had expressed interest in 'talking with a spirit'. Under torture Marie Bosse herself had gone further, alleging that M. de Feuquières and his cousin, the Maréchal-Duc de Luxembourg had wanted to communicate with the devil.[36]

Following his arrest Lesage had intimated that he had recently been working on Luxembourg's behalf, though he stopped short of claiming to have been personally acquainted with him. Instead, he said merely that a servant of M. de Luxembourg had come to him in the hope that Lesage would aid him to recover some papers, which were of great importance to Luxembourg. Lesage had been pressed to say more about this, but as recently as 13 September he had declined to say anything to Luxembourg's detriment.[37]

At the end of the month, however, Lesage showed signs that he was prepared to abandon his earlier caution. He made a statement alluding to the fact that the Marquis de Feuquières had had an attachment with a married woman and, when news of this was relayed to Louvois, it threw him into a frenzy of excitement. Urgently he wrote to La Reynie that Lesage must be pressed to provide more information on this point as, not long ago, the husband of a woman whom Feuquières had often visited had died.[38] When called upon to elaborate, Lesage did so in spectacular fashion, casting aspersions not just on Feuquières but also on Luxembourg, by far the most distinguished person to have been embroiled in the inquiry.

Now aged fifty-one, the Maréchal-Duc de Luxembourg was one of France's foremost generals. Physically he was extremely unprepossessing, being cursed with what Saint-Simon described as 'an astonishingly repulsive exterior'. He was a diminutive hunchback whose body was so twisted and deformed that it was said of him that 'if he were to lose an arm or leg in the war one would hardly even notice'.[39] His face was dominated by a pair of bushy eyebrows, while his thin lips were renowned for sardonic comments, for Luxembourg possessed in full measure the malice and wit proverbially ascribed to hunchbacks. Though far from ideally formed for love, Luxembourg was a man of considerable sexual appetites. As well as pursuing court ladies with surprising success, he had a liking for prostitutes; in addition, there are hints that he was not averse to homosexual debauch.

At the outset of the King's personal rule Luxembourg had been out of favour, for he had sided with the rebels during the civil wars of the Fronde that had overshadowed Louis's minority and at one point had even fought with the Spanish army against France. When peace had come he had been given an amnesty but his earlier disloyalty was not easily forgotten. However, the King was aware that he had considerable military ability and during the Dutch War Luxembourg came to prominence. In 1672 he was made Governor of the occupied province of Utrecht and in this capacity he inflicted terrible cruelties on the civilian population who came under his control. The houses of all those who were deemed to have contributed insufficiently towards the upkeep of the army of occupation were ruthlessly burnt and later in the year Luxembourg devastated the surrounding countryside when his army had to retreat. Although his reluctance to restrain his men from pillage made him popular with the troops, the bestial treatment meted out to local inhabitants in these months was a permanent stain on France's reputation. The King, it is true, does not seem to have been concerned by this. On 11 February 1673 Luxembourg was appointed one of the four Captains of the Royal Bodyguard, a position described by the English ambassador as one of 'the chiefest places in trust about the King's person'.[40] Two and a half years later his services received still higher recognition when in July 1675 he was made a Marshal of France.

The following year Luxembourg had experienced a severe setback when he proved incapable of relieving the besieged city of Philippsburg, which fell in September 1676. Luxembourg seems to have felt that Louvois had let him down by failing to provide him with adequate reinforcements, but others blamed him for the reverse, and at court and in Paris he became the butt of much mockery. Although the

King insisted that he personally did not consider Luxembourg to have been at fault, the Duc felt his loss of reputation keenly. Despite the fact that he had since taken Valenciennes and played a prominent part in victories at Cambrai and Cassel, Luxembourg did not consider that he had managed to recover his lost esteem. The end of the Dutch War had deprived him of opportunities to redeem himself with further feats of valour for, as he himself remarked 'in peacetime men of war are well and truly despised'.[41]

Although the King respected Luxembourg's gifts as a soldier he had never had much personal affection for him. When the King had greeted him warmly after Luxembourg's return to court following the campaign of 1674, this cordial reception excited surprised comment from observers. At that stage of his career, however, the Maréchal was on good terms with Louvois. On many occasions they had enjoyed convivial dinners together and the letters Luxembourg sent the Minister from Utrecht testify to the good understanding that existed between them at that time. Admittedly, these missives scarcely redound to the credit of either man: in them Luxembourg merrily describes the ravages caused by troops under his command and how they incinerated the houses of recalcitrant Dutch peasants with women and children inside. In one he concludes teasingly, 'Knowing how compassionate you are I thought of not telling you this for fear of causing you distress, but I have not been able to withhold it, for one must tell things as they are.'[42]

Louvois's support of Luxembourg had been considered a crucial factor in Luxembourg's promotion to Maréchal in 1675. However, the fall of Philippsburg had caused tension between them, for Louvois declared that by this failure Luxembourg had 'made the finest French army which was ever in Germany entirely useless'. Luxembourg responded by drawing closer to Colbert. The German diplomat Ezechiel Spanheim noted that whereas initially Luxembourg and Louvois were so close that Luxembourg was regarded as being 'entirely of his dependence', this was no longer the case after the Treaty of Nymwegen.[43] Admittedly, he wrote this in 1690, with the benefit of hindsight, and in 1679 few people were aware that a rift had developed. Nevertheless, the eager way in which Louvois seized on the claims Lesage now made, and the manner in which the War Minister encouraged the magician to proceed further, make it clear that Louvois had become alienated from his former ally and was thrilled that an opportunity had presented itself to destroy him.

The Marquis de Feuquières was a staunch adherent of his cousin, the Duc de Luxembourg, whom he had served as an aide-de-camp during several campaigns. Arrogant and haughty even by the standards of the French aristocracy, he was disliked by many of his contemporaries. Saint-Simon wrote that he would have gone far 'if only his supreme spitefulness had allowed him to hide, at least a little, that he had neither heart nor soul'. The normally more charitable Primi Visconti was equally scathing: he described Feuquières as Luxembourg's 'damned soul' and noted he had the 'fatal physiognomy' of a man who deserved to be hanged.[44]

Both Luxembourg and Feuquières had superstitious leanings. An aristocratic acquaintance of Luxembourg's recorded that he had a 'childish weakness for fortune tellers'[45] and he employed a personal astrologer. How far his interest in such matters had extended now became the point at issue.

On 6 October[46] Lesage revealed that he had had at least one meeting with Luxembourg and Feuquières. He had been introduced to them on 31 January 1676* at the house of the Marquise de Fontet, a Parisian hostess in whose salon Luxembourg was always welcome. Having been informed that Lesage knew how to perform marvels, the Marquise had invited him to entertain her guests, and Feuquières and Luxembourg – who were both present on that day – had expressed a wish to see what he could do. After the two men had gone upstairs with Lesage he had asked them to write down a list of demands, which could be transmitted to the world of spirits. Lesage had then performed his favourite feat of prestidigitation, convincing the onlookers that what they had written had gone up in flames when in reality he had secreted the paper away for his own purposes. He then took it home with him so he could read it at his leisure.

It was the contents of this paper that now became a matter for dispute. When called upon to give an account of this incident, Luxembourg and Feuquières were both adamant that they had merely set down a few light-hearted questions as an amusing exercise. Lesage's recollection was very different, for he claimed that on inspecting the document, he had found that the pair had compiled a ruthless set of demands designed to secure their advancement and to ensure that anyone who might stand in their way should be obliterated.

Lesage contended that Feuquières had expressed a wish that an uncle of a woman he wished to marry should die. Luxembourg's desires had been more extensive, if no less chilling. Besides expressing a wish that he might win victories, which would efface the memory of his failure

---

* Ravaisson dates this encounter 31 January 1678. However, several witnesses state that the Marquis de La Vallière was present and since he died in October 1676, the meeting must have occurred prior to that.

at Philippsburg,* he had sought the elimination of one of his foremost military rivals, the Maréchal de Créqui. He had also written that he wanted to marry his eldest son to Louvois's daughter, and had followed this by a demand that his own wife should die and leave him a widower. Such a request on Luxembourg's part was not utterly incredible in view of the fact that the Duchesse de Luxembourg was described by Primi Visconti as 'the ugliest person of her day', while her appearance reminded Saint-Simon of 'a great vulgar fishwife in a herring barrel'.[47] She had been a great heiress and Luxembourg had derived his ducal title through her but he had never showed her much affection. For the most part he had left the Duchesse to live out a 'sad and twilight existence' at her chateau in the country, while he amused himself elsewhere. However, it had long been whispered that his sister-in-law, the Princesse de Tingry, was much more to his liking, even though many people considered her to be only marginally less hideous than her sister. There were persistent rumours that Luxembourg's relations with her had been indecently close and Lesage now encouraged this idea by claiming that Luxembourg had stipulated as one of his requirements that he wanted the Princesse to love him.

After Lesage had tricked Luxembourg and Feuquières into thinking that he had destroyed their list of demands, he took his leave of the two men, promising that the paper would soon be miraculously restored to them. As Lesage left, Luxembourg had given him two pistoles with which to drink his health but, according to Lesage, the Maréchal not only assured him of a larger reward if the paper was returned, but even undertook to pay him as much as 2000 livres once the wishes enumerated there had been fulfilled. Three days later Lesage had sent back the original document, untouched by flame. Luxembourg had supposedly been filled with wonder and perplexity, though Lesage had to admit that despite the fact he had assured the Maréchal that his wishes had been made known to the spirits, Luxembourg had refrained from giving him any more money.

In his statement of 6 October Lesage explained that it had since come to his knowledge that Luxembourg and Feuquières had then turned to other members of the Paris underworld in the hope of furthering their desires. Feuquières had asked la Bosse and la Vigoreux to contrive the death of the person who he feared would impede his marriage and if this man (whose name had unfortunately slipped Lesage's memory) was still alive it was only because la Bosse and la Vigoreux

---

* Lesage must have been lying about this because when this meeting happened the siege of Philippsburg had not yet taken place.

had failed to gain access to him. Luxembourg had also had recourse to la Bosse because he wished to recover some documents relating to a property transaction. The papers were in the possession of a business-man named Dupin, and Lesage said he had been told that Luxembourg 'had done several things' to bring about the death of this man and his partner. Agents acting on Luxembourg's behalf had arranged for spells to be performed, and had taken hearts transfixed with nails into churches. These agents had recently approached Lesage himself, asking him to aid them, but Luxembourg had not left matters entirely in their hands. Lesage had understood that the Maréchal had personally raised the subject with a Breton gentleman called Chambelan, who did distil-lations for la Voisin and who had fled Paris just before his 'good friend' Magdelaine de La Grange had been tried.

Much of Lesage's statement had been incoherent and rambling, as well as lacking in verifiable detail, but La Reynie regarded it as a vital breakthrough. He at once informed Louvois and suggested that matters would progress still further if the Minister of War assumed a direct role in the inquiry. Louvois responded promptly to his proposal. On 7 October he visited Lesage at Vincennes and there held out the hope to him that the King would show him mercy, provided he revealed all he knew of any matter relating to poison.[48] While surprised that his reve-lations about Luxembourg had been greeted with such enthusiasm, Lesage recognised that he had been cast a lifeline and eagerly grasped it.

On 8 October Louvois wrote to inform the King of recent develop-ments. Far from suggesting that Lesage's account deserved to be treated with caution, he placed the worst possible construction on his words. He brushed aside the fact that even if Lesage's allegations were accept-ed without reservation, it did not appear that Luxembourg and Feuquières had actually committed crimes, but only that they had had malign intentions. It may be that Louvois's horror at what he had learned was compounded by his own superstitious nature: the Duchesse d'Orléans would write that Louvois himself believed 'in sor-cerers, in fortune-tellers, the whole lot of them'.[49] The fact that Luxembourg had apparently been so intent on securing a union between his son and Louvois's daughter may also partly have account-ed for the virulence of the Minister of War's reaction for, while others might object that such a match would have constituted a *mésalliance* for one of Luxembourg's lineage, Louvois clearly had no difficulty believ-ing that the Maréchal had coveted it so ardently. Nevertheless, even if one grants this, the manner in which Louvois now set out to inflame the King does suggest that he also nourished a bitter animus against both Luxembourg and Feuquières.

In a state of excitement that came close to elation, Louvois informed the King,

All that your Majesty has seen against Monsieur de Luxembourg and Monsieur de Feuquières is nothing in comparison to the [enclosed] declaration [by Lesage]...in which Monsieur de Luxembourg is accused of having asked for the death of his wife, that of Monsieur the Maréchal de Créqui, the marriage of my daughter with his son...and to do enough fine things in war to make your Majesty forget the mistake he made at Philippsburg. Monsieur de Feuquières is depicted there as the wickedest man in the world who sought opportunities to give himself up to the devil, to make a fortune and to ask for poisons with which to poison the uncle or guardian of a girl he wished to marry.[50]

While the King was digesting all this, Mme Voisin came up with some startling revelations of her own for, like Lesage, she too had been subjected to relentless pressure to divulge more about the well-connected people who had come to her. Having delved into her memory, on 9 and 10 October[51] she obliged, excusing her earlier reticence on the grounds that she had hitherto thought it improper 'to reveal secrets which were confided to her by persons of quality'. Now, however, she felt it incumbent on her to tell everything she knew about some prominent court figures who had confided to her their 'evil thoughts'. La Voisin insisted that, far from encouraging these individuals, she had been horrified by their proposals, particularly when she had realised that their malevolence was directed against the King himself.

Casting back about thirteen years in time, la Voisin declared that the Comtesse du Roure had initially been a client of hers but had then been enticed away by Lesage. However, prior to losing her in this way, la Voisin had found out that the Comtesse was on poor terms with her husband, though she found her brother-in-law far more pleasing and was on a 'close footing' with him. She had aspired higher than that, however, for she had wanted to acquire 'influence over the mind of the King' and she had hoped Lesage could arrange this for her. Such was her determination that she had several times spoken of poisoning Louise de La Vallière.

According to la Voisin, the Comtesse was not unique in contemplating such a step, for the Vicomtesse de Polignac (who, like Mme du Roure, had started with la Voisin before defecting to Lesage) had held similar aims. Like so many others, the Vicomtesse had longed to be rid of her husband but besides this, she had wanted to be loved by the King. With this in mind she, too, had plotted to poison Mlle de La Vallière.

This was electrifying enough, but the shock was still greater when la Voisin named the Comtesse de Soissons as a former client of hers. For many years Madame la Comtesse (as she was known at court) had occupied the highest position in the Queen's household. She had also been a great favourite of the King, though once he had fallen in love with Louise de La Vallière his affection for her had cooled. La Voisin now recalled that many years earlier (she did not give a date but certainly no later than 1666) the Comtesse de Soissons had paid her a visit. She had been accompanied by the Maréchale de La Ferté and another friend, Mlle Bénigne de Fouilloux, who subsequently had married the Marquis d'Alluye.

La Voisin said that, without telling her who she was, the Comtesse de Soissons had ordered her to read her hand. On doing so, she had seen the Comtesse's palm was marked by a pronounced 'solar line' which, in view of the fact that the King's personal emblem was the sun, had an obvious significance. La Voisin told her client she could see that she had once been loved by a great prince, whereupon the Comtesse demanded sharply whether there was any chance that that love would reawaken. La Voisin had said that it was possible, but the Comtesse made it plain she would be satisfied with nothing short of a positive response. Fuming that she could not endure looking like a fool, she had declaimed angrily against Louise de La Vallière before demanding that la Voisin supply her with the means of eliminating her. When la Voisin had protested that this would be extremely difficult, the Comtesse had flown into a rage, shouting that it was absolutely imperative that la Voisin should help her. She had then uttered the most ominous words of all, declaring that if she could not obtain satisfaction against Louise, 'she would carry her vengeance further, and would stop at nothing'. This could be interpreted as a threat on the life of the King himself.

La Voisin said that after this occasion she had never seen the Comtesse de Soissons again. She would indeed have remained unaware of her visitor's identity had not Mlle de Fouilloux disclosed the Comtesse's name to her just before leaving. However, while la Voisin was adamant that she had done nothing to further the Comtesse's ambitions, she could not guarantee that the Comtesse had not persevered in her design with the aid of other less scrupulous persons.

Attention now switched back to Lesage, who may have hoped that his revelations about Luxembourg and Feuquières would prove sufficient to secure a pardon, but who soon discovered that far more was required of him. La Voisin's latest evidence suggested that Lesage was still withholding information, and it was made clear to him that this would not be tolerated. On 11 October Louvois instructed La Reynie to remind Lesage that the offer of clemency made to him had been conditional on his full co-operation and that, unless he did better, his trial would take place shortly.[52] Faced with this threat, Lesage abandoned his earlier inhibitions.

A month earlier la Voisin had suggested that Lesage had done business with the Duchesse de Vivonne, sister-in-law of Mme de Montespan, and on 14 October Lesage confirmed this. He explained that, having become a client of the divineress Françoise Filastre, Mme de Vivonne had put her name to a pact drawn up by la Filastre, which contained 'terrifying things' in some way relating to the King. (He alleged that the Duchesses de Vitry and d'Angoulême had signed the same pact, but since the last named lady was proverbially virtuous, it was deemed inconceivable that this could be so and this part of his evidence was ignored.) Lesage said this had come to his knowledge when the Duchesse de Vivonne had grown anxious that this compromising document had remained in la Filastre's possession. Desperate to recover it, the Duchesse had gone to Lesage and begged him with tears in her eyes to secure it for her. Lesage had promised he would regain it, though in fact he never managed to do so. Since he had not seen the document, he could not be specific as to its contents, but he said he understood that la Filastre had been promised a payment of 3000 livres if the wishes of those who had signed it were granted.[53]

A fortnight later Lesage named further members of the aristocracy who had been involved in questionable activities.[54] He disclosed that the Comtesse de Soissons's younger sister, the Duchesse de Bouillon, had come for a consultation with him when he was lodging at la Voisin's. Following his well-practised routine, Lesage had invited her to put down her desires on paper and had then pretended to destroy what she had written. As usual, however, he had abstracted the paper and, on inspecting it, had discovered that the Duchesse had requested that her husband should die, leaving her free to marry the Duc de Vendôme. Lesage said that since then the Duchesse had sent to him several times, wanting to know whether he could fulfil her desire. On one occasion she had even tempted him with a bagful of coins but Lesage maintained that he was unwilling to commit himself to so hazardous an undertaking and had rejected her offer.

Lesage next identified the Marquis de Cessac as another of his clients. Cessac had been expelled from court in 1671 for cheating during a game of cards, but had been permitted to return three years later. Lesage reported that some years prior to his disgrace, Cessac had asked him to provide him with a secret means of winning at cards, particularly when playing against the King. A little later Cessac had confided that he was in love with his sister-in-law and, since he wanted to marry her, he asked Lesage to devise a way of killing his brother, the Comte de Clermont. Lesage had promised to effect this through magic and to this end had performed a distasteful ritual in Cessac's presence. He had sent Cessac's servant to dig up a bone from a nearby cemetery and then uttered incantations while the servant sewed the relic into the sleeve of a shirt. Cessac had promised Lesage that he would pay him 1000 pistoles upon the death of his brother but since Clermont had remained in good health, Lesage had received no more than twenty écus.

Contrary to la Voisin's assertion, Lesage declared that the Comtesse du Roure had never been one of his customers, but he did not deny that, before going to the galleys, he had had extensive dealings with the Vicomtesse de Polignac. He recollected that when she had first come to him her demands had been quite modest, for she had merely wanted to be assured of the continuing affection of her current admirers, the Comte du Lude, the Vicomte de Larbouste and M. Doradour. In due course, however, she had grown more ambitious. Having learned that la Voisin had offered to procure the King's affection for the Comtesse du Roure, Mme de Polignac had asked Lesage to do the same for her and she had also wanted him to arrange for the permanent removal of Louise de La Vallière. For good measure she had requested Lesage to make her husband die, as she desired her freedom.

In order to achieve this Lesage had conducted various ceremonies with Mariette, the priest who at that time was his partner. First there had been a recitation of magic formulas from an ancient book of spells; then, at dead of night, Mme de Polignac had gone by coach with Mariette and Lesage to the Bois de Boulogne, so that two pigeons' hearts could be buried. The culminating desecration had come when Lesage had accompanied Mme de Polignac to Saint-Germain, so they could observe the King attend chapel. As mass was performed, Mme de Polignac had murmured incantations specially formulated by Lesage, designed to fill the King with slavish adoration for her.

Lesage contended that in doing all this he had performed a valuable service for, by preoccupying Mme de Polignac with these infantile distractions, he had prevented her from doing things that were truly wicked. He congratulated himself on having persuaded her 'to quit la Voisin and her wicked poisoning ways', for by this means he had ensured that no harm had come to Louise de La Vallière. It was understandable, however, that when Lesage's statement was relayed to the King, he took a less sanguine view of the matter.

Lesage's admissions had caused terrible consternation, but Mme Voisin's capacity to shock was still equal to his. In a fit of vindictiveness she now sought to damage France's leading writer who, many years before, had incurred her displeasure. On 21 November she made a solemn declaration to the effect that in December 1668 the playwright Jean Racine had poisoned an actress named Thérèse Du Parc, who at that time was his mistress.

In 1653 the twenty-year-old Thérèse Du Parc had come to Paris with Molière's troupe of actors, after being spotted performing acrobatics in the market square at Lyon. Later that year she had married a comedian in the company with the stage name of Gros René, but she had attracted many other admirers, including the ageing playwright Corneille, whose advances she had rejected. In 1664 she had danced before the King in a skirt split to the thigh, and the sight of her wonderful legs encased in silk stockings had excited much admiring comment. Following the death of her husband in 1667, she had joined Racine's theatre company at the Hôtel de Bourgogne. Despite the fact that some people considered her an indifferent actress she had become the company's leading lady, appearing in the title role for the first performance of *Andromaque*. At some point she had also become Racine's mistress, though he was not the only man to enjoy her favours. In the summer of 1668 there were even unfounded rumours that her aristocratic lover, the Chevalier de Rohan, was contemplating marriage with her. Despite this, when she had died on 11 December 1668, Racine had appeared prostrate with grief, presenting a heart-rending spectacle as he walked behind her coffin.

Before long Racine had found consolation with a new mistress. This was the actress Marie Champmesle, a married woman who, like her predecessor, took other lovers besides Racine. Perhaps he tolerated this because she was a brilliant interpreter of his work, who successively played the leading female roles in *Iphigenia*, *Britannicus*, *Bérénice*, *Mithridate* and *Phèdre*. However, in 1677 Racine had given up his career as a dramatist, and not merely out of pique at the mixed reception accorded to *Phèdre*. In moralists' eyes the whole world of the theatre was inherently sinful and Racine, whose values had been shaped by his strict education at the religious community of Port Royal, could never free himself from the sense that his occupation was unworthy and degrading. When he had become a playwright his revered aunt had written deploring his association with people 'whose name is abominable to all persons who have the slightest piety, and with reason'. Racine's conscience had also been troubled when the polemicist Desmarets de Saint-Sorlin denounced the authors of verse plays as poisoners of the soul rather than the body, who were guilty of innumerable 'spiritual homicides'.[55]

According to his son, Racine ultimately came to accept that playwrights were truly 'public poisoners' and that, in view of his exceptional talent, he was 'the most dangerous of all'. As a result, when the King offered him the well-paid post of Historiographer Royal in September 1677, Racine acclaimed this as a 'favour from God, who had procured him this important post to detach him entirely from poetry'.[56] It was, of course, ironic that Racine believed his new career would bring him spiritual redemption when others saw the court as an even more corrupt environment than the artistic circles in which he had formerly moved, but such was his perception.

Racine now repudiated his past completely. He became an accomplished courtier, adept at delivering polished compliments to the King and the nobles he encountered. Somewhat curiously, he saw nothing wrong with drawing royalties from revivals of his plays but his wife, whom he had married in the spring of 1677, was never permitted to see or even read any of his works. He never deviated from his view that his life at court was far more worthy than the profession he had previously followed and he earned the approval of the Duc de Saint-Simon for having 'nothing of the poet' about him.[57]

Racine had become a figure of the utmost respectability but la Voisin threatened all that when she maintained that the man who acknowledged that his work had poisoned minds was a poisoner in the literal sense. Admittedly, her justification for this was absurdly slight. Having proclaimed herself to have been a great friend of Thérèse Du Parc, la Voisin complained that during the actress's final illness, Racine had denied her access to the dying woman. La Voisin then alleged that at the time it had been rumoured that Racine had poisoned la Du Parc and that his behaviour had inclined her to believe this. It was her contention that Racine had secretly married la Du Parc, but he had remained 'jealous of everyone and particularly of her, Voisin', until this had finally driven him to murder. La Voisin described indignantly how, as Mlle Du Parc lay dying, Racine had hovered at the bedside, ignoring his mistress's pleas to be allowed to see la Voisin. In support of her claims la Voisin observed that Thérèse Du Parc's daughters by Gros René had stigmatised Racine as 'the cause of their misfortune', though as they had been aged nine and ten at the time of their mother's death this was not as significant as it might seem. She further alleged that once la Du Parc was dead, Racine stole her jewels.[58]

The fact that la Voisin stated that Thérèse Du Parc had also vainly begged Racine to summon to her sickbed her chambermaid Manon, who had been trained as a midwife, has given rise to another theory. After Racine's death his great friend Boileau told a biographer that Mlle Du Parc had died 'in childbirth', prompting speculation that, having become pregnant by Racine, she either did not survive labour or, alternatively, suffered fatal complications following an abortion. However, this does not seem very likely. It is, in fact, possible that in May 1668 Thérèse Du Parc had a child by Racine, who was brought up by foster-parents,[59] but since she lived for six months more this does not vindicate Boileau's assertion.

Furthermore, the fact that Mlle Du Parc was accorded a funeral service in the church of Saint-Roch, prior to being buried in the cemetery of a Carmelite convent, militates against the idea that the circumstances surrounding her death were in any way irregular. In seventeenth-century France all those who earned their living on the stage were under such a stigma that the Church refused to administer the last rites to actors unless they promised never to perform again even in the event of their recovery. Those who declined to do so died unshriven and could not be buried in hallowed ground. Years later Racine would be very censorious when he heard that his former leading lady Marie Champmesle was proving reluctant to renounce her stage career, despite being stricken by terminal illness. Sneering that apparently 'she found it very glorious to die an actress', he expressed the sanctimonious hope that she would repent once she realised that death was imminent, 'as most people usually do who put on proud airs when they are feeling well'.[60] Clearly Thérèse Du Parc had made a full confession on her deathbed and had been granted absolution, for otherwise no priest would have officiated at her funeral.

The evidence that Racine had been responsible for Thérèse Du Parc's death could hardly have been more risible. While proof of association with la Voisin might be considered legitimate grounds for suspicion, in Racine's case it was the fact that he had refused to have anything to do with her that was adduced against him. Nevertheless, la Voisin's testimony was treated seriously. On 11 January 1680 Louvois told Bezons that if he so desired a warrant for Racine's arrest would immediately be issued by the King.[61] In the event, however, good sense prevailed and Racine was never taken into custody.

Mme Voisin had excelled herself by alleging that France's greatest dramatist was a murderer, but Lesage now effectively trumped her by unveiling claims that were still more disturbing. The names of various priests had already featured peripherally in the inquiry. As more had become known about Mariette's past activities, orders had been given for the priest's arrest in September 1679, although he was not actually found until several months later. While the search was still in progress, there had been ominous signs that Mariette had not been alone in defiling his sacerdotal office. When questioned about some other priests, including a pair named Huet and Henault, Lesage had suggested that they too had been involved in dubious activities. However, he did not specify in what way they might have profaned their calling, confining himself to saying that he believed that they had worked with Mariette on 'matters of consequence'.[62] It was only in late November that Lesage became more explicit, providing the first real intimation that there were several priests in Paris who, far from striving to bring their flock nearer to God, preferred to act as instruments of the devil.

On 16 June la Voisin had mentioned that she had introduced Lesage to her husband's confessor, Gilles Davot, who was a priest at her local church. Lesage had asked him to bless the hazel wands he used when performing spells and also to supply him with wax from candles burnt on the altar while mass was celebrated. Davot had complied, saying he saw no harm in this, but his readiness to help Lesage had led to his arrest on 12 July.[63] On 28 November Lesage made a statement indicating that Davot had done much more for him than had earlier been alleged.

Lesage admitted he had suborned Davot to say masses for clients of his, some of whom wanted to conclude advantageous marriages, whereas others were hoping for the death of a designated person. To bring this about Davot would pass a note under the chalice as it was elevated during the consecration of the sacraments. Lesage did his best to underplay the significance of this. He stressed that doing such things had been 'in no way his idea' but were rather 'in the old style of la Voisin' who, together with Mariette, had first conceived of this procedure.

To try to distract attention from the services that Davot had rendered him, Lesage now alleged that the priest had engaged in far worse acts in conjunction with la Voisin. He said he had it on their authority that la Voisin had frequently prevailed on Davot to say mass in her lodgings 'for various affairs'. On one such occasion the ceremony had been performed in la Voisin's house 'on the stomach of a girl...and Davot also said that he had had carnal knowledge of her and that, while saying mass, he kissed her private parts'. Lesage said he believed there were witnesses to this incident (though for the time being he could not think of their names) and that Davot was not the only priest who had committed such outrages. In particular, he believed a priest named Gerard had done similar things.[64] As Lesage had calculated, these new allegations propelled the inquiry into a fresh dimension of horror.

At his own request the King had been kept fully informed of the progress of the inquiry. His initial shock on learning of the allegations against Luxembourg and Feuquières had only been compounded when he had been informed that several ladies with whom he was well acquainted had subsequently been implicated in the investigation. On 16 October, after Lesage had made his attack on the Duchesse de Vivonne, Louvois noted that the King had 'listened...with horror' when the latest reports sent by La Reynie had been read to him. Nevertheless, far from concluding that it would be best to draw a veil over such matters, the King had instructed that the inquiry must be pursued with the utmost vigour in order to obtain 'all possible proofs against those named' by Lesage and la Voisin.[65]

Nothing he had learned in the intervening weeks had shaken his resolve. Instead, each successive revelation had merely convinced him that the depths of iniquity had not yet been plumbed and that with further probing more evidence would emerge that people at his court had been involved in acts that were truly shameful. By 3 December some of the commissioners of the *Chambre Ardente* were anxious to proceed with la Voisin's trial on the assumption that she had now told them everything of importance and was therefore expendable. The King, however, still considered this premature. He denied permission for the trial to start, evidently believing that la Voisin would yet prove a valuable source of information.[66]

For the remainder of the month the King pondered what action to take against those high-ranking persons who had been implicated, and after Christmas he reached his decision. On 27 December he summoned La Reynie, Bezons and MM. Boucherat and Robert, who were respectively the President and Attorney-General of the Chamber, to an audience at Saint-Germain. La Reynie later recorded that at this meeting the King urged them 'in extremely strong and precise terms' to uphold the law and do their duty, for it was essential that they 'penetrate as far as possible into the wretched traffic of poison in order to cut it off at the root'. He assured them that nobody, no matter how grand, would be immune from prosecution, declaring solemnly that in the coming weeks he required them to exercise 'an exact justice, without any distinction of rank, sex or person'.[67]

# SEVEN

# A COURT IN CHAOS

There were many people who believed that in 1670 the King's English sister-in-law, Henriette-Anne, Duchesse d'Orléans, had been killed by poison. Her death had been officially ascribed to natural causes, but the distressing nature of her final hours, during which she herself declared she had been poisoned, ensured that this verdict had been received with widespread scepticism. It is impossible to know the King's views on the matter. He certainly professed to accept the doctors' findings but he may still have experienced occasional nagging doubts that poison had been involved. However much he tried to dismiss such fears, it would be understandable if the incident had made him more receptive to the idea that poison plots could pose a risk even to members of the royal family.

Henriette-Anne was aged only twenty-six at the time of her death. Married in 1661 to the King's younger brother 'Monsieur', she was on very bad terms with her homosexual husband, who blamed her for the banishment of his favourite, the Chevalier de Lorraine, and was jealous of the fact that the King was using her as an intermediary to forge closer links with England. She had been in ill health for some time (the Duchesse de Montpensier said that in the weeks before her death she looked like a corpse with rouged cheeks) but even so, the suddenness and speed of the attack which carried her off meant that her demise came as a terrible shock to the court.

Shortly after drinking a cup of chicory water on the evening of 29 June 1670 Henriette-Anne had suddenly clutched at her side and collapsed in agony.[1] Having been helped to her bed she lay there in terrible pain, repeatedly insisting that she had been poisoned. The devoted lady-in-waiting who had prepared the chicory water protested that she had drunk some herself without ill effect while Monsieur (who appeared as alarmed as everyone else and who betrayed no signs of guilt) demanded that some of the liquid should be tested on a dog to see if it was harmful. The physicians summoned to treat Madame stubbornly maintained that she was merely suffering from colic and gave her purgatives and emetics. They also administered oil to settle her stomach and various other dubious remedies such as powder of vipers. Despite their efforts Madame's pains did not lessen and as she grew steadily weaker it became apparent that she would not survive the night. Towards midnight the King had an emotional last meeting with her, bidding her farewell with tears in his eyes. Subsequently the English ambassador came to her bedside and asked her directly if she still thought she had been poisoned. At this the confessor who was in attendance sharply intervened, urging, 'Madame, accuse no person but make your death an offering of sacrifice to God.' Dutifully Madame 'made no other answer than by shrugging up her shoulders', but this hardly allayed the ambassador's suspicions.[2] Only with her death in the early hours of the morning of 30 June did Madame's torment finally cease.

The Savoyard ambassador, the Marquis de Saint-Maurice, claimed that after seeing Madame on her deathbed the King swore that, should it emerge that she was a victim of foul play, the crime would not go unpunished. 'He said out loud that if this princess was poisoned...all those who could have had any part in it would be put to death with the harshest tortures. It is even said that he mentioned the Chevalier de Lorraine and protested that if he had been involved in this death through poison he would perish and his family would feel the effects of it.'[3] However, no one else mentions such an outburst on the King's part and it would certainly have been out of character for him to utter something so inflammatory at this sensitive juncture.

Because of the suspicious nature of her death an autopsy was performed on Madame, attended by doctors nominated by the English ambassador. When the first cut was made such an 'insupportable smell' emanated from the body that for a time it was impossible to proceed, but on resuming their task the doctors found that Madame's liver and intestines were badly decayed, and that her lower belly, duodenum and gall bladder contained a great quantity of 'extremely offensive' bile. They found no evidence of poison: the King's physician Vallot observed that if Madame had been poisoned the lining of her stomach would have been livid, but this was not the case. Instead, the doctors pronounced that 'it was very boiling bile, very corrupt and malign and very impetuous which caused all the disorders in the aforesaid parts and gangrened them'.[4]

The English in theory accepted these findings but their ambassador still had reservations. He was not alone in this, for he noted that it was generally accepted at court that Madame had been poisoned and that the populace was also 'riveted in this opinion'. According to the

Marquis de Saint-Maurice, Queen Marie-Thérèse was among those who remained convinced that poison was responsible. Monsieur's second wife, the German princess Elizabeth Charlotte of the Palatinate, would also subscribe to this view. She later alleged that her husband's equerry, the Marquis d'Effiat, had poisoned the cup containing chicory water, though she believed he had done this without Monsieur's knowledge.[5]

Less than two years after Madame's death the King agreed that the Chevalier de Lorraine could come back to court. The English ambassador was furious, observing in a despatch, 'If Madame was poisoned, as is believed by most, all France look upon him as the person who did it.' However, the fact that the King permitted Lorraine's return indicates that he was satisfied the Chevalier had played no part in Madame's death. One can dismiss Saint-Simon's absurd claim that a senior member of the late Duchesse d'Orléans's household had already told the King that Lorraine had sent poison to France from his exile in Rome. Without consulting Monsieur, the Marquis d'Effiat had then enabled the Comte de Beuvron, Captain of Monsieur's guards, to poison the jug of chicory water. According to Saint-Simon the King was so relieved to learn that his brother had been ignorant of the plot against his wife that he decided to take no action against the culprits,[6] but it is surely beyond belief that this could be so.

Though many people at the time could not accept that Madame had died from natural causes it is no longer feasible to entertain doubts on the matter. While the exact cause of death cannot be established definitively, there is no shortage of explanations for her symptoms, but no evidence has ever emerged to support the idea that she was poisoned. It has been plausibly argued that she died of peritonitis caused either by a ruptured appendix or a burst stomach or duodenal ulcer. Peritonitis could equally have resulted from bile causing minute perforations in the pancreas and seeping through it; if so, the doctors who at the time attributed her death to excess bile were, in essence, correct. Alternatively, an ectopic pregnancy or intestinal blockage could have killed her. It has also been suggested that through her great-grandmother, Mary Queen of Scots, Madame had inherited porphyria, a genetic disease which often proves fatal when it manifests itself for the first time.[7]

The controversy surrounding Madame's death demonstrated the readiness of people at court to suspect poisoning even if firm proof was lacking. Hugues de Lionne, the King's Secretary of State for Foreign Affairs who died in 1671, was also thought by some people to have been a victim of poisoning, though it would seem that the belief only became current ten years after his death. At the time his demise was variously attributed to a poor diet, the ill effects of a fistula, or to his doctors prescribing him emetic wine, 'the passport of those who long to pass to the next world'.[8]

In 1678 the mysterious death of the Princesse de Monaco, who was believed to have had an affair with the King, prompted fresh rumours. She had been assailed by an undiagnosed disease, which left her formerly beautiful features blackened and shrivelled, and it was assumed she had been poisoned. Her husband was the obvious culprit but Mme de Scudéry reported that, despite the fact that he was Italian, he was not thought to be responsible as he had treated his wife with great kindness during her final illness. The Comte de Bussy, however, did not accept this reasoning, for in his view the husband's nationality settled the matter. He declared he had no doubt that Mme de Monaco had been poisoned simply because 'she deserved to be, and her husband is Italian'. He added that the Prince de Monaco's considerate behaviour towards the dying woman merely confirmed his suspicions, and had been nothing other than a deliberate ploy to conceal his crime.[9]

Despite the widespread belief that there had been instances of poisoning at court, at the beginning of 1680 people there were blissfully unaware that several of their number had been linked with the prisoners currently being held at Vincennes. The agitation caused by the arrest of Mmes de Dreux and Leféron (who were both still awaiting trial) had long since subsided and the courtiers were preoccupied by other matters. Interest centred on the King's infatuation with Mlle de Fontanges, which was currently at its height. In mid-January it became known that she had suffered a miscarriage but this was not deemed especially significant, for no one foresaw that it would irretrievably damage her health.

There was also great excitement about the marriage of the King's illegitimate daughter by Louise de La Vallière with the Prince de Conti. The wedding, which took place on 16 January, was a very splendid affair. The bride wore a white dress sprinkled with diamonds and pearls while the groom was dressed in straw-coloured satin, embroidered in black and enriched with jewels. After the ceremony in the chapel at Saint-Germain there was a ball at the palace, where four temporary staircases had been erected outside first-floor windows to ensure that the 600 guests could gain easy access to the festivities. A table fifty-four feet long had been set up in the gallery, supporting nineteen silver and gold baskets filled with anemones, hyacinths, jasmine and tulips. Such a profusion of out-of-season blooms – which some of the guests at first assumed were artificial – made it 'difficult to remember that it was the sixteenth of January'. After the dancing, a 'superb repast' of many dishes was served, including 16,000 livres' worth of ortolans, small birds regarded as an exquisite delicacy.[10]

Few present on this lavish occasion would have guessed that a sordid scandal would shortly tarnish the lustre of the court. Some of the guests would be directly affected: the Princesse de Tingry, for example, would soon have to defend herself against accusations of black magic and poison. The sister-in-law of the Cardinal de Bouillon, who had conducted the wedding ceremony, would likewise find herself the object of hostile scrutiny and others invited to the party would before long flee the country in disgrace. By another irony, Racine's *Iphigenia* was performed at the start of the evening; those who watched the play with enjoyment were ignorant of the fact that only five days earlier Louvois had told Bezons that if he thought it appropriate, arrangements could be made for the author's arrest.

Since their audience with the King in late December, La Reynie and Bezons had been diligently pursuing their enquiries. Mme Voisin had been relentlessly interrogated and fresh confrontations had been staged between her and Lesage. On each occasion Lesage had been indefatigable in heaping fresh accusations on her head, but though she had indignantly denied these, she had stood by her earlier claims regarding her aristocratic clients.

Lesage proved eager to supplement his evidence in other ways. In early January he asserted that President Lamoignon, who had died nearly eighteen months after he had presided over Mme de Brinvilliers's trial, had been poisoned. An autopsy had been carried out at the time, which had concluded that death had been caused by a stone blocking the ureter and preventing urination, but Lesage's alternative explanation was taken very seriously. Lamoignon's son was informed and busied himself questioning his late father's servants to see if he could find out if anyone had held a grudge against the dead man. To La Reynie he wrote earnestly, 'I do not doubt that if this terrible crime has been committed, God will provide enlightenment so it is not left unpunished.' By the end of the month he was making dark hints that perhaps the Comtesse de Soissons was behind the murder. He claimed that when the Brinvilliers case was being investigated, his father had 'found out something about Mme la Comtesse de Soissons', and that she had never forgiven the President.[11] Since he provided no further details it is impossible to judge whether his suspicions of the Comtesse had even the slightest justification.

Although on the whole Lesage was guaranteed an attentive hearing some of the claims he put forward at this time were so manifestly absurd that they were rejected out of hand. At one point he claimed that M. de Riantz, Attorney-General at the Châtelet, and M. d'Effita, the Criminal Lieutenant of Paris, had systematically protected Parisian poisoners and that this explained why crime had flourished in the capital in recent years. Carried away by his own eloquence, he urged that vigorous action be taken against the miscreants, fulminating, 'Nothing at all must be spared on the issue of poisons, as much with regard to those who have sold it as to those who have authorised the trade, as they have done with all the other detestable crimes of which they have been the accomplices and protectors.'[12] Lesage's aspersions against these two eminent lawyers were dismissed but this did not result in other parts of his testimony being treated with greater caution.

On 15 January Louvois wrote to M. Robert, who was acting as the *Chambre Ardente's* Attorney-General. Robert was evidently alarmed by the prospect of bringing people of the highest rank before the commission and Louvois hastened to reassure him that he need not worry about the consequences. Louvois noted,

> The problems ... which you are worried about, that some of these procedures will result in the discrediting of important persons, might well happen, but it would be worse if it was seen that his Majesty had given protection to people accused of crimes of the sort in question. It is this which has made him take the position of leaving everything to the conduct of the judges and in all these matters to use his authority only to support the execution of things which might be asked of him for the cause of justice.[13]

Louvois explained that the King's resolve to see things through was such that he had made only two provisos. Louis had asked that if, in future, further allegations were made against important court figures such as the Duchesse de Vivonne, he should be kept informed. Furthermore, although he had not seen fit to question the accusations against some of the grandest people in the realm, he had urged that caution should be exercised with regard to one individual. As Louvois explained, the King had been reluctant to accept that Mme de Montespan's former chambermaid – and his former lover – Mlle des Oeillets, could be mixed up in anything disreputable, considering it 'impossible that Lesage told the truth when he spoke of her'.[14] Accordingly, Louis had indicated that she should not be bothered by the Commission unless Lesage's testimony was verified by others. As yet there was no sign of this, for whenever Mme Voisin was questioned about Mlle des Oeillets she insisted she had never laid eyes on her. Accordingly, Mlle des Oeillets was left in peace but the lives of others named by la Voisin and Lesage were now disrupted in the most dramatic fashion.

On 23 January 1680 arrest warrants were issued for the Comtesse de Soissons, the Vicomtesse de Polignac, the Marquis de Cessac and the Maréchal-Duc de Luxembourg. Lesser forms of summons were served on the Duchesse de Bouillon, the Comtesse du Roure, the Princesse de Tingry, the Marquis d'Alluye and the Marquis de Feuquières, who were all subpoenaed to appear at the Arsenal to answer questions on specified days.

The news caused stupefaction in Paris society and at court. Mme de Sévigné informed her daughter that all was in chaos, saying that the only event she could recall having a comparable impact had occurred ten years earlier, when an engagement had been announced between the King's cousin, the Duchesse de Montpensier, and the Comte de Lauzun. As on that day, everyone became frantic with curiosity, rushing to friends' houses to exchange the latest gossip. Père du Rosel assured the Prince de Condé that the talk in Paris was of nothing else and Mme de Sévigné echoed this although, frustratingly, she added that it would be imprudent to set down in writing all that was being said.[15]

At the outset the general consensus was that those who were to be remanded in prison must have committed terrible crimes for, as the English ambassador pointed out, 'they are of a rank not to be treated severely without good evidence'. He added, 'There is great astonishment here as everyone is linked to those accused through affection or family ties.' The Venetian ambassador pitied the predicament of the King, whose repose had been shattered by the discovery that he was surrounded by untrustworthy persons. The ambassador did not doubt that the King was 'greatly upset to see the greatest lords in the realm defiled by such excesses' and that he felt 'insecure in the midst of so many criminals'. It was widely believed that the scandal was still in its infancy and more arrests would follow. The Maréchal d'Estrades expected that during the coming week eighty more prominent people would be taken into custody and M. Brayer, who was keeping an acquaintance in the *Parlement* of Provence abreast with developments in Paris, made similar predictions. In the event, these proved mistaken, but M. Brayer was well informed in other respects: by 26 January he had heard that Mme de Vivonne's name had featured in the inquiry.

In Paris a play entitled *The Divineress*, written by Thomas Corneille and Donneau de Visé, was just coming to the end of its run, but the sudden eruption of the scandal ensured that all fashionable Paris became desperate to see the topical piece. Up to 400 theatregoers had to be turned away each night and the play ended by taking more money than any production previously mounted in France.[16] It was even rumoured that M. de La Reynie had collaborated with the authors to ensure that the details were authentic. This cannot have been true, for it is inconceivable that that merciless scourge of fortune-tellers and conjurers could have had a hand in this light comedy, in which the eponymous divineress is depicted as an engaging rogue rather than a genuine menace.

It was the order for the arrest of the Comtesse de Soissons that perhaps occasioned the greatest shock in fashionable circles, despite the fact that she was never actually placed in custody. Since he had little desire to bring her to trial, the King instructed her brother-in-law, the Duc de Bouillon, to warn her that guards would shortly be coming for her, giving her time to escape. Towards midnight on 23 January Bouillon interrupted a gaming session over which the Comtesse de Soissons was presiding in her Paris house. Since the Duc had left the party not long before, the Comtesse was puzzled to see him, but when he explained the reason for his reappearance she wasted no time. After receiving the disastrous advice that she would be able to resolve matters from outside the country, she decided that she could not endure imprisonment and trial, and that her best recourse lay in flight. Having induced her best friend, the Marquise d'Alluye, to accompany her, she drove out of Paris at three in the morning of 24 January, taking with her an impressive quantity of jewels and cash.

The King was clearly much relieved that the Comtesse had elected to flee even though he implied that his conniving at her escape from justice had caused him some qualms of conscience. He told the Comtesse's mother-in-law, the Princesse de Carignan, that while he had wanted Mme de Soissons to seize the chance to save herself, 'Perhaps one day I shall answer for it before God and my people.'[17]

The King certainly had good reason to afford the Comtesse special treatment as for many years she had been on exceptionally close terms with him. The Comtesse (whose maiden name was Olympe Mancini) had been born in Rome in 1638 but before reaching her teens she had been summoned to France by her uncle, Cardinal Mazarin. In the next few years she had been much in the company of the adolescent King. Though endowed with no more than a 'mediocre beauty' she developed into a striking brunette with owl-like eyes and a long thin nose, which earned her the nickname of 'the snipe'. In 1657 she had married Prince Eugène Maurice de Carignan Savoie, a first cousin of the Duke of Savoy who was recognised as a 'foreign prince' at the French court and who soon took the title Comte de Soissons. In the years following her marriage the King remained strongly attached to her, so much so that many people believed they were lovers. They danced, gambled and laughed together and, far from objecting to her 'continual teasing' of him, the King granted her 'a certain liberty of talking to him more boldly than others'.[18]

When the King married Queen Marie-Thérèse, the Comtesse de Soissons became *Surintendante* of the Queen's household, the most important position a woman could hold at court. The King constantly visited her apartments, which became a social centre for all the court. The Queen was conscious of being outshone by her lady-in-waiting and was also jealous of her flirtatious manner with the King, which led her to believe that 'gallantry still found a place in their conversation'.[19]

The Comtesse de Soissons had been extremely displeased when the King had fallen in love with Louise de La Vallière. Fearing that her standing at court would decline now that the King was spending less time with her, the Comtesse decided she must find a way either of forcing the King to terminate his relationship with Louise or, if that could not be arranged, at least to use the Comtesse as an intermediary in his dealings with her. Accordingly the Comtesse and her lover, the Marquis de Vardes, had arranged for an anonymous letter to be sent to the Queen, informing her that Louise had become the King's mistress. The plan failed when the letter was intercepted but for the next three years the King never managed to discover who had sent it. However, in March 1665 the Comtesse had made the mistake of falling out with the King's sister-in-law, Henriette-Anne, after the latter had had the Marquis de Vardes sent away from court for insulting her. Having been turned out of Madame's box during a ballet performance, the Comtesse took revenge by telling the King that she could show him letters that both compromised Madame's honour and proved his sister-in-law had been disloyal to him. When the King confronted Madame about this, she retaliated by revealing to him the part played by the Comtesse and Vardes in the affair of the anonymous letter.

The King had reacted with cold fury. He considered that Vardes and the Comtesse de Soissons were guilty of a fundamental breach of trust, and the episode helped convince him that it was not possible for him to be on free and easy terms with members of his court. Vardes was imprisoned and the Comtesse was told that, though the King would continue to treat her as befitted her rank, henceforth she would never enjoy his confidence. By the end of the month she and her husband had been made to feel so unwelcome that they departed for Champagne, their prospects at court apparently irreparably blighted.[20]

People were surprised, therefore, when in October 1666 the King had invited the Comte and Comtesse de Soissons to return to court. The King seemed pleased to see her again, telling Monsieur that 'she was the best woman in the world' who was 'not at all mischievous' provided she was kept apart from people who had a bad influence on her. However, the Comtesse's addiction to intrigue remained as strong as ever. In 1670 the King was displeased by reports that she had arranged for her husband's serving men to seduce Louise de La Vallière's chambermaids to provide her with good sources of information on the state of the King's private life. Later that year she was barred from accompanying the court on its tour of northern France after the King heard she had made mocking remarks about Mme de Montespan. Within a few months she was on better terms with him, but her reluctance to cede her position as *Surintendante* of the Queen's household, which Mme de Montespan coveted, was a continued source of tension. Further damage was caused by rumours that she had defied the King's authority by having a secret meeting near Paris with the Marquis de Vardes, who had been ordered to stay away from the capital after his release from prison.[21]

These repeated provocations meant that the Comtesse was already on poor terms with the King when the news arrived that her husband had died on 7 June 1673 at Unna in Westphalia, having been struck down by illness as he was travelling through Germany to join Turenne's army. His symptoms had been 'fever and retention of urine' but he died proclaiming he had been poisoned. Because of this a post-mortem was carried out and, according to the Savoyard ambassador, the Marquis de Saint-Maurice, the doctors who performed it claimed to have discovered signs of poison in the body. Even so, the ambassador considered it very unlikely that the Comte de Soissons had been murdered.[22]

Saint-Maurice stressed at the time that the Comtesse de Soissons appeared very upset by the death of her husband but years later the Duc de Saint-Simon (who was less than six months old when Soissons died) would assert that people at court always suspected her of having killed him. Certainly, when the Comtesse fled France in January 1680 it was at once assumed that Mme Voisin had indicated she had poisoned her husband, though in fact la Voisin had not suggested anything of the sort. Yet even those who most readily entertained the possibility that Mme de Soissons could have done such a thing were mystified as to her motive, for the Comte de Soissons was known to have been the most accommodating of husbands. At one point during the Comtesse's affair with the Marquis de Vardes, Soissons had taken the trouble to reconcile the lovers after they had quarrelled, and after Vardes had been expelled from court Soissons had not objected when his wife had embarked on an affair with the Marquis de Villeroi. On hearing of the Comtesse's precipitate flight from France the Marquis de La Rivière commented that for her to have murdered her husband would have been 'a crime as unreasonable as it is great' for 'why kill a man who let her live in complete freedom with all others?'[23]

As the Marquis de Saint-Maurice had pointed out at the time, Soissons's death certainly had not benefited his wife in material terms. Though she herself was independently wealthy, during his lifetime she had become aware that Soissons had failed to make adequate provision for his children in the event of an early death. Had he lived longer he might have been able to rectify the position, but as it was he left his children severely straitened. Furthermore, without her husband's protection, the Comtesse's own status at court became more precarious. The fact that she so clearly resented the King's failure to confer the Comte de Soissons's military and administrative posts on her sons merely made Louis more ill disposed towards her, and his decision in 1679 to remove her from her post of *Surintendante* of the Queen's household emphasised how isolated she had become. The King may have been slightly nervous that her late husband's relatives in Savoy would protest at her treatment, but when informed the Duchess of Savoy made no objection. In 1680 he was therefore confident that he could take action against the Comtesse with impunity.

Some observers considered that Mme de Soissons had done the right thing by fleeing in order to avoid imprisonment and the 'shame of being confronted by hags and villains'. Having made enquiries, Mme de Sévigné had been amazed to learn that the things of which the Comtesse had been accused were 'mere fooleries, which she had told everyone about a thousand times'. In the circumstances she sympathised with the Comtesse's decision to absent herself, declaring, 'There is something quite noble and natural about this way of proceeding and for my part I approve of it.' Others, however, took the view that Mme de Soissons had left the country because she knew herself to be guilty of serious crimes. M. de La Rivière was sure that 'Mme de Soissons's aversion to being locked up in no way justifies her escape...I see clearly that she has not taken the part of an innocent.' M. Brayer was equally convinced that her flight could be taken as proof of her guilt.[24]

It certainly put her in a disastrous position from a legal point of view. The King was very pleased that she had spared him the embarrassment of bringing her to trial and although he went through the charade of sending soldiers to the border with orders to bring her back if they overtook her, it is clear that the last thing he wanted was for her to be captured. However, by removing herself from French jurisdiction she had indisputably committed a contempt, which constituted a capital offence in itself. The result was that on three successive days an announcement was read out in Paris to the sound of trumpets, formally branding her contumacious.

The irony is that all the evidence suggests that had she stayed in France she would in all probability have been vindicated. The Marquis de Sourches later acknowledged this, noting that La Reynie could never have found sufficient proofs to convict her, while the Marquis de La Fare expressed the view that even the order to arrest her was quite unjustifiable. Certainly, the allegations against her scarcely amounted to much, even though Mme Voisin had by now somewhat embellished her original account of the Comtesse de Soissons's visit to her. On 16 January la Voisin recalled that after the Comtesse had spoken angrily of the way the King had discarded her for Louise de La Vallière, she had said that, unless things changed, 'she would do away with one or the other'. Yet if Mme la Comtesse had said such a thing – and the evidence rests on la Voisin's word alone – there was no reason to think that she had ever taken steps to execute her threat. However, as Mme de Sévigné remarked, the matter related to the King and 'everything is significant on such a subject'.[25]

Louvois appears to have been conscious that the charges levelled against Mme de Soissons were embarrassingly meagre and he did his best to lengthen the indictment. On 3 February he excitedly informed La Reynie that he now understood that, with the aid of a woman called Rouvière, Mme de Soissons had killed two or three of her servants who had inconvenienced her in some way, but this does not seem to have proved a fruitful line of enquiry. Six weeks later Louvois asked La Reynie to pursue the matter on his behalf, for his own efforts 'would only serve to cause sensation and could prevent one from knowing the truth'.[26] Since nothing came of this, one must assume that La Reynie fared no better in his bid to accumulate more evidence implicating Mme de Soissons.

Louvois's attempts to compile a damaging dossier against Mme de Soissons goes some way to support Primi Visconti's contention that the Minister was motivated by an 'old rancour' against her and her late husband. Visconti believed that Louvois had conceived a lasting grudge after Soissons had mocked him when he fell off his horse out hunting, while Mme de Soissons had caused offence more recently when she had been contemptuous of the suggestion that Louvois's daughter might marry one of her sons. She was said to have scoffed, 'A fine thing it would be to see a bourgeoise the wife of a prince' and Louvois never forgave her for this. Several sources allege that Louvois vindictively pursued her in exile and it is certainly true that a spy kept him informed of the hostile reception she was given by the populace in Brussels when first she settled there. According to Abbé Choisy, she only experienced such difficulties because Louvois arranged for funds to be distributed among the local street urchins, in return for their shouting insults as she passed. Mme de Sévigné and Primi Visconti both heard that one of Louvois's agents surreptitiously released a horde of black cats into a church where Mme de Soissons was attending a service, provoking panic among the congregation that a witch was in their midst.[27]

Primi Visconti suggested that for his own part the King had been reluctant to take action against the Comtesse de Soissons. Visconti was sure that he had only done so because Louvois had misrepresented the evidence against her, making out that the Comtesse had been set on the King's destruction, despite the absence of proof for such a claim. The Marquis de La Fare was more inclined to blame La Reynie for the unfair way Mme de Soissons was treated and Primi Visconti did not dispute that La Reynie, too, was guilty of an abuse of power in her regard. He reported that when the other commissioners complained to the Police Chief that there was no justification for ordering her arrest and that she should instead have merely been called in for questioning, La Reynie arrogantly rejected their objections on the grounds that 'it was the King's will that she be imprisoned'.[28]

One should not, however, exclude the possibility that in saying this La Reynie was simply telling the truth and that the King played a far more active role in the persecution of Mme de Soissons than her sympathisers were prepared to concede. Though Louvois may have spurred him on, the King had inspected the written reports of at least some of la Voisin's and Lesage's interrogations before authorising the arrests of people of rank and he should therefore have been aware of the limited nature of the evidence against Mme de Soissons. Considering the insubstantial nature of the allegations, it is curious how intractable he showed himself towards her. There is more than one report suggesting that Mme de Soissons tried to negotiate terms for her return. She was said to have requested that she should be placed under house arrest rather than in Vincennes or the Bastille while awaiting trial or, more moderately still, that the King would guarantee her case would come to court within six months. Louis firmly refused to give any such undertakings.[29]

It is impossible to say whether the King genuinely suspected that the

Comtesse de Soissons had murdered her husband, or that she had contemplated killing him or Louise de La Vallière. What is clear is that over the years he had come to distrust and dislike her intensely and that, knowing her as he did, he found it easy to believe that she had uttered the menacing words la Voisin had attributed to her. He had therefore determined not to tolerate her presence and, by her precipitate flight, Mme de Soissons had freed him from the burden of proving she was guilty.

Ten years after Mme de Soissons had left the country, the King's sister-in-law, the Duchesse d'Orléans, expressed her view of the matter. Though her judgement tended to be wild and unmeasured, in this instance her analysis seems shrewd. When her aunt asked her for her opinion of the Comtesse, the Duchesse wrote, 'From what I know of her I should say she was quite innocent of causing her husband's death. I do not believe that she poisoned him and I don't think they really believe it of her either, but only pretend to do so in order to frighten her and drive her … to seek flight, for she is feared because she is very clever and supposed to be an intriguer.'[30]

The Marquise d'Alluye, who had loyally accompanied the Comtesse de Soissons into exile in Flanders, was subsequently permitted to return to Paris, but even so she paid a high price for her friendship with her. She had not even been present when the Comtesse had had her fateful encounter with Mme Voisin, all those years ago, for though they had gone to her house together, Mme d'Alluye (or Mlle de Fouilloux, as she then was) had waited in the garden while Mme de Soissons had gone into the consulting room. La Voisin had testified that after Mme de Soissons had left her, Mlle de Fouilloux had asked whether the Comtesse would succeed in destroying her rival and regain her former favour with the King. This had been enough to ensure that Mme d'Alluye had been summoned to appear before the Chamber. After her departure from Paris it was rumoured that she had poisoned her aged father-in-law, but the only reason for such conjecture was that it was assumed she would never have been called before the commission unless suspected of a major crime.[31]

Mme d'Alluye's husband had stayed behind in Paris when she absconded and in her absence he loyally defended her. He maintained that the Chamber had overreached itself and tried to incite others who had been called before it to assert their rights. He sought to persuade the Duc de Bouillon that he should not let his wife be questioned by the commissioners, reminding that none but the highest court of *Parlement* was entitled to try members of the nobility. Alluye only succeeded in incensing the King, who ordered him to withdraw to

Amboise. Though he was later allowed to come back to Paris, he remained barred from court until his death in 1690.[32]

As for the Marquise d'Alluye, she was permitted to return to Paris after Louvois's senior clerk was prevailed upon to intercede on her behalf, but she too never reappeared at court. She does not seem to have minded her exclusion very much, for Saint-Simon reported she led a delightful existence in the capital, free of 'care or constraint and entirely given up to pleasure'. Recording her death in 1720, Saint-Simon related that she had

> spent her entire life immersed in love affairs and, when age forbade them for herself, lived just as passionately those of other people...
> Until the moment of her death she was the receptacle for the secrets of all the gallants of Paris who came each morning to confide in her.
> She doted on society and gambling...and spent everything she possessed at cards...So she lived, plump and hearty, free from all infirmities until she died at eighty-five after a very short illness.[33]

The Comtesse de Soissons, who died in 1708, was prohibited from ever returning to France. When she first arrived in Brussels she had a disagreeable time, for the populace reviled her as a witch whenever she drove through the streets. Her notoriety soon faded, however, since the grander residents of the city were much more welcoming. The Duchess of Modena proclaimed her the victim of a serious injustice and before long the Comtesse settled down so well that she acquired a new lover. He was the Prince of Parma, a fat and gouty grandee who was perhaps not the most romantic of figures but who represented quite a conquest for a lone female fugitive in her late forties.[34]

In August 1682 there were reports in France that the Comtesse was poised to return, but if the King had ever contemplated sanctioning this he ultimately thought better of it. Accordingly, Mme de Soissons's exile continued. After travelling for a time in Germany, in 1686 she went to Madrid in hopes of arranging a prestigious match for one of her sons. There she struck up a friendship with the young Queen Marie Louise, a niece of Louis XIV's who had married Charles II of Spain in 1679. When news of this reached Louis, he was appalled at the prospect of his inexperienced niece falling under the influence of a woman whom he viewed with such aversion. He ordered his ambassador in Spain, the Comte de Rebenac, to stay 'well informed about [Mme de Soissons's] intrigues in order to give the Queen advice on the matter that best suits her interests'.[35]

In October 1688 the Comtesse de Soissons became caught up in a fresh controversy. It would seem that the King of Spain suffered from premature ejaculation (in the delicate words of the French ambassador, he 'had a natural debility, which was attributed to too much vivacity on the part of the King') and this had prevented him from consummating his marriage. In the autumn of 1688 he suddenly decided that his incapacity had been caused by the Comtesse de Soissons bewitching him and consequently he sent orders that she should leave Spain. The Comtesse appealed to the Queen but, to her annoyance, Marie Louise said she should do as the King desired. Undaunted, the Comtesse gained the support of the Imperial ambassador in Madrid, the Comte de Mansfeld, and he evidently prevailed on the King to permit her to remain a while longer, for she did not leave Spain till the following summer.[36]

On 12 February 1689 Queen Marie Louise of Spain died after enduring 'three days of continual vomiting and colic'. The circumstances were remarkably reminiscent of the agonising death of her mother, the Duchesse d'Orléans, nearly twenty years earlier, and though Marie Louise herself insisted that poison was not responsible it was inevitable that in France there were suspicions she had been murdered. In his memoirs Saint-Simon asserted that she was poisoned by the Comtesse de Soissons in league with the Comte de Mansfeld, who wanted to break the alliance between France and Spain. Saint-Simon stated that the Comtesse gave the Queen iced milk, which had been poisoned at the Imperial embassy, and then immediately left the country before the King could apprehend her.[37] However, since the Comtesse remained in Spain till July 1689, the story is patently inaccurate.

The Comte de Rebenac did have grave concerns about the manner of the Queen's death, but he believed the most likely culprits were the Spanish nobles the Count of Oropesa and Don Emmanuel de Lira, aided by the Queen's lady-in-waiting, the Duchess of Albuquerque. Had the Comtesse de Soissons enjoyed access to the Queen, it is inconceivable that he would have failed to name her as a prime suspect but, when the Queen died, the Comtesse had been excluded from court for several months.[38]

One certainly cannot rule out that the Queen of Spain was poisoned in 1689. The faction at the Spanish court that desired closer links with Vienna undoubtedly had strong motives for wishing to be rid of her, and Marie Louise herself had reportedly expressed fears for her safety when writing home. She had requested that antidotes to poison be sent to Spain for her own use and a consignment from her father was said to have arrived there the day after she died.[39] The available evidence is not sufficient to resolve the question once and for all (though, once again, porphyria has been posited as a possible cause of death) but one can at least be reasonably certain that Saint-Simon wronged the Comtesse de Soissons when he laid the blame at her door.

After leaving Spain the Comtesse de Soissons once again took up residence in Brussels. There are signs that she still pined for her former life in Paris and a letter she wrote in July 1692 also suggests that she recognised that her decision to leave France without facing trial had been a catastrophic error. By that time France was again at war and the Comtesse wrote to the Maréchal de Luxembourg (who was in charge of the army of Flanders) requesting that she should be permitted to travel unmolested about the environs of Brussels. 'Who would have said in days gone by that I should be reduced to such an extremity,' she lamented, 'I, who was accustomed to receiving the favours of the greatest King in the world.' Then, alluding to the fact that Luxembourg had been implicated in the Affair of the Poisons and had been vindicated at his trial, she noted that they had a mutual experience of misfortune, adding wistfully that her disgrace would doubtless have been as ephemeral as his if it had been fitting 'for a woman like me to adopt the course you followed'.[40]

But though it is clear that the Comtesse de Soissons was still bitter at the way she had been forced to forsake her adopted homeland, it is not true, as Saint-Simon claimed, that her final years in Brussels were spent in penury and loneliness. To the end of her days she occupied an eminent position in Brussels society and, far from being ostracised, she welcomed at her salon French acquaintances from former years who were passing through the town. She no doubt also derived consolation from the knowledge that her younger son, Prince Eugène, had exacted a satisfying revenge for the humiliations she had endured. Denied a position in the French army by Louis XIV, the Prince had volunteered his services to the Emperor and, as commander of the Imperial forces in the War of the Spanish Succession, he inflicted a sequence of crushing defeats on the French.

The Comtesse de Soissons was the grandest individual to be driven from France in January 1680, but she was not alone in thinking that exile was preferable to facing the justice of the *Chambre Ardente*. The Vicomtesse de Polignac was in the Auvergne when the warrant was issued for her arrest, but a detachment of guards was sent to escort her back to Paris. However, friends of hers sent an express courier to warn her that a prison cell awaited her there and she quit France before the officers of the law arrived. Unable to lay hands on her, the King had to content himself with seizing all the furniture in her Paris house, prompting furious if ineffectual protests from the Vicomte de Polignac, who had not accompanied his wife abroad.[41]

Despite the fact that on 18 July 1680 Mme de Polignac was officially declared contumacious, she seems to have taken the view that the fuss would die down in due course and that, after a discreet interval had elapsed, she would be able to slip back into the country. However, when in March 1686 she reappeared in Paris, intent on arranging a marriage between her eldest son and the Dauphine's maid of honour, Mlle de Rambures, she discovered that the King's indignation against her was undiminished. Louis sent word that he was astonished she dare show herself in Paris and he also did his best to dissuade Mlle de Rambures from proceeding with the marriage. When someone 'took the liberty of representing to him that he was causing severe mortification to a man of rank [the Vicomtesse de Polignac's son] who had never done anything to displease him', the King answered coldly that 'his aversion was directed not at Monsieur de Polignac, but rather at Madame his mother'. In the end Mlle de Rambures refused to abandon a match which, whatever its disadvantages, was undeniably prestigious and the King gave his consent. The Comte de Bussy commented that he was not surprised the King remained so hostile towards Mme de Polignac, for 'His Majesty has reason to fear the dealings of a woman who wanted to give him a philtre to make him fall in love'.[42] Because of his intransigence, the Vicomtesse could never return to Paris until after the King's death.

On learning of the warrant for his arrest the Marquis de Cessac had also opted to avoid imprisonment and trial by fleeing France. M. de La Rivière jeered, 'By adding to his bad reputation as a gamester that of a poisoner he has strongly indicated his contempt for worldly esteem.' However, Cessac's decision to abscond was not universally condemned, for an influential body of opinion considered it commendable that he had opted against being dragged to prison as a public spectacle. Cessac headed for England, where he had already lived for a time during his first disgrace. The English ambassador to France sent his superiors forewarning of his arrival, explaining that Cessac was supposed to have consulted a sorcerer in hopes of beating the Kings of France and England at cards. Clearly amused that such absurdities were taken seriously by the French, the ambassador commented jocularly, 'I am sure that our master will easily forgive him, for the devil has never been able to make him play for high sums either with [Cessac] or anyone else.'[43]

Cessac was based in England for some years. In 1685 it was rumoured at the French court that he was planning to marry Mlle de Gramont on the understanding that her family would effect his return. Unfortunately, when the possibility was mentioned to the King he growled that nobody had consulted him about it, and in the end the match did not go ahead. Inexplicably, however, Louis proved more accommodating six years later. Presumably, by that time the King had decided that the accusation that Cessac had tried to murder his brother using witchcraft had been baseless, for by April 1691 Cessac had been authorised to return to France and to rejoin the army. Later in the month he came to court and was permitted to make his bow to the King. The following September proceedings were inaugurated to purge him of the stain of contumacity that still attached to him in consequence of his earlier evasion of justice. Matters were not finally resolved until nearly a year later, but after Cessac had presented himself voluntarily at the Bastille on 28 July 1692 a special hearing discharged him of his contempt and a week later he was freed.[44]

Cessac, who 'accounted scorn and insults as nothing', imperturbably resumed his life in Paris. Despite being a known cheat, he had no trouble attracting dedicated gamblers to his house to play for high stakes. Cessac's willingness to hazard huge sums soon caught the attention of Monsieur, whose passion for gambling overrode all other considerations. Keen to try his luck against a man who would not place limits on his bets, Monsieur sought the King's permission to invite Cessac to his house at Saint-Cloud. Louis agreed and soon the Dauphin also asked his father to let him entertain Cessac at his country house. In this way gambling, which had earlier brought Cessac into such disrepute, served to procure his rehabilitation. In June 1696 the King himself asked Cessac to stay at Marly, the exquisite retreat he had built near Versailles. He invited him because Monsieur was coming to visit and Louis wanted keen card players to be on hand for his brother's amusement. Soon Cessac became a regular guest at the King's house parties, an honour to which all courtiers ardently aspired, but which was only extended to an envied few.[45]

Flight had been the course favoured by several prominent figures facing arrest by the *Chambre Ardente*, but the Maréchal de Luxembourg proved less pusillanimous. For some months prior to January 1680 it had been rumoured that Luxembourg had links with prisoners detained at Vincennes. Luxembourg was vulnerable not merely on account of his 1676 encounter with Lesage at the house of the Marquise de Fontet, but also because his man of business, Pierre Bonnard, had had extensive dealings with the magician. The reason for this was that some years before, Luxembourg had sold a sizeable area of woodland for an inflated sum to a consortium of businessmen. The deal had been brokered by a middleman named Dupin, but when the purchasers realised they had been overcharged they sought to renege on their agreement. Anxious to complete the transaction, Luxembourg needed to repossess documents currently held by Dupin, which established that the lands had been overvalued. Luxembourg's secretary Bonnard had undertaken to obtain the documents for him, but securing them proved more difficult than anticipated. Consequently, Bonnard had enlisted the help of Lesage, who promised that he would procure the documents by magical means.

With Bonnard's enthusiastic concurrence Lesage had performed spells designed to enable Bonnard to acquire the documents. Lesage had also commissioned the priest Davot to pass notes under the chalice during mass, requesting the return of the papers. Lesage then informed Bonnard that if he wished to succeed, he must obtain a signed paper from Luxembourg, giving him Power of Attorney to proceed on the Maréchal's behalf. Bonnard duly presented such a paper to his master and Luxembourg signed it, having first asked his legal adviser to verify that it contained nothing untoward. However, when Bonnard showed the deed to Lesage, the latter prevailed on him to add a clause empowering him to perform 'all necessary conjurations' to achieve the desired ends and mentioning a 'donation to the spirit'.[46] Lesage then took the paper to the lawyer acting for the businessmen who had purchased Luxembourg's woods, calculating that they would pay him well if he provided them with a document that compromised the Maréchal. However, before he could profit from his action, Lesage was arrested in March 1679.

Shortly after this the lawyer who had been given the paper bearing Luxembourg's signature contacted Luxembourg and suggested the Maréchal should sell his woodlands for a lesser sum than that originally agreed. As Luxembourg later recalled, the lawyer explained that in this way Luxembourg 'would hide ... a thing that would cause me harm in the world', namely 'that my man of business was making pacts with the devil in my name'. Fearful that he had been compromised by Bonnard's indiscreet behaviour, Luxembourg went to Louvois and suggested that Bonnard should be arrested and questioned by the commissioners of the *Chambre Ardente*. Louvois rejected the idea, saying that the Chamber was only concerned with cases of poisoning, 'and that if Bonnard had done something idiotic', Luxembourg had merely to dismiss him.[47] Accordingly, Luxembourg told Bonnard that he never wanted to see him again and he then met with Duparc, the lawyer who was acting for the purchasers of his land. An agreement was thrashed out between them regarding the sale of his woods but, foolishly, Luxembourg neglected to retrieve from the lawyer the signed paper that Bonnard had drawn up in his name. This later found its way into the hands of La Reynie and formed an important part of the evidence against Luxembourg.

As Luxembourg himself subsequently noted, 'For some months I remained calm about this business without worrying very much about the absurd rumours that were beginning to circulate.' However, at the beginning of January 1680 he was suddenly summoned by Louvois and told 'that I was being talked of at the Arsenal Chamber instituted against poisoners'. Luxembourg was not unduly shaken by the news. 'This surprised me without alarming me,' he recorded, for he was unaware, of course, that Louvois had been inciting Lesage to damage him as much as possible. Clearly irritated by this composure, Louvois did his best to convince Luxembourg that his position was untenable, maintaining that it looked to him as if Luxembourg would be wise to leave the country. Luxembourg sensibly declined to adopt a course that would have ruined him for ever, replying with dignity, 'Far from going away, if I was accused I would think myself obliged to come back from the ends of the earth to justify myself.'[48]

The next day Luxembourg obtained an audience with the King in hopes of clarifying the situation. The King explained that Lesage had been making serious accusations against him and that, among other things, he had claimed that Luxembourg had sought to use magic to murder his wife and kill the Maréchal de Créqui. Having protested that 'there was not a word of truth' in this, Luxembourg formed the impression that the King was satisfied by his assurances, for Louis declared that, provided Luxembourg had not put his signature to anything discreditable, there was nothing to worry about. By the time he took his leave, Luxembourg felt that he had cleared up all misunderstandings and he was still more reassured when the King followed up the interview by making him a surprise gift of a magnificent sword with a jewel-encrusted hilt.[49] He was not the first person to be given a false impression by the King adopting a misleadingly gracious demeanour.

It therefore came as a ghastly shock to Luxembourg when, early in the morning of 24 January, his friend the Duc de Noailles was sent to inform him that a warrant had been issued for his arrest. Noailles urged him to flee but Luxembourg would not hear of it, even though Noailles returned several times during the day to repeat his advice. All that Luxembourg asked was that he should be allowed to go to the Bastille on his own, instead of being escorted there under guard like a common criminal. This was granted to him and at five in the evening he set off on his melancholy journey through Paris. Though he had succeeded in preserving some shreds of dignity, it was clear that he was utterly crushed by the calamity that had befallen him. En route to the

Bastille he stopped off at the Jesuits' church to pray, but Mme de Sévigné heard that he was so unused to practising his devotions that he appeared uncertain as to which saint he should appeal in his hour of crisis. Sombrely he lamented that 'having abandoned God, God had abandoned him' and went on his way. When nearly at the Bastille he encountered Mme de Montespan coming from the other direction in her coach and Luxembourg wept openly when she alighted to commiserate with him on his ordeal.[50] She would no doubt have shed tears too, had she known that within a few months she herself would become the object of horrendous allegations.

The Governor of the Bastille, who had not been forewarned of the arrival of this illustrious prisoner, was amazed when Luxembourg presented himself before him. The startled official put the Maréchal in one of the most comfortable rooms he had at his disposal but the following day, on the orders of La Reynie, Luxembourg was moved to a cramped cell in one of the towers. No more than six and a half feet long, it overlooked the rubbish-filled moat and was consequently damp and smelly. Luxembourg would later claim that his health had been permanently undermined by being confined in these insalubrious conditions for more than three months.

On 26 January La Reynie and Bezons came to question the Maréchal, but for the moment their primary aim was to see whether Luxembourg would accept that the Arsenal Chamber had jurisdiction over him, rather than to subject him to a detailed interrogation. Having established that to their satisfaction, they left Luxembourg alone for some weeks while they concentrated on building up a case against him.

While Luxembourg festered in his malodorous cell, rumours swirled around Paris regarding his crimes. Fictitious versions of his supposed pact with the devil were widely circulated, some of which were more imaginative than others. One opened with the somewhat prosaic request that the devil should preserve Luxembourg from being robbed by his servants, as well as protecting him from cannon and musket fire, and providing him with a ring, which rendered its owner invisible. In addition, Luxembourg craved the ability to read and write all languages fluently, 'the appearance of a good Christian in order to avoid scandal' and the secret of universal medicine. In another purported pact Luxembourg voiced more sinister demands. As well as desiring to be as invulnerable as Achilles on the battlefield, to be wealthy and loved by the King, he asked for knowledge of 'the secrets of la Brinvilliers'. In return, Luxembourg promised to attend 'all the nocturnal assemblies of familiar spirits … in the realm, and to take orders there from the infernal powers'.[51]

Many people were sure it was Luxembourg who had secured Lesage's release from the galleys, and there was also talk that he had embezzled funds destined for the troops under his command and had then poisoned an official who had known of the fraud. Luxembourg's supporters were alarmed to learn that La Reynie was 'making an elephant out of a mouse' by seeking to establish that Luxembourg had been involved in a counterfeiting racket. Before long the most fantastic claims gained credence. His cousin heard to his dismay that people were saying that Luxembourg and twelve nude women had participated in a procession led by a priest who was naked save for his sacerdotal stole, and that this had been merely one of many 'orgies or sacrifices made to the devil'.[52]

The most outrageous stories were also spread about Luxembourg's sister-in-law, the Princesse de Tingry. She was a former nun who, years before, had 'exchanged her veil for a *tabouret*'. After learning that she had grown discontented with the religious life, Luxembourg had made her promise that she would not impede his marriage to her immensely wealthy sister and had then arranged for her to leave her convent to take up a prestigious position at court.[53] The Princesse was still in theory bound by her vows of chastity, but this had not prevented whispers that she had sexual relations with her brother-in-law. Lesage had also alleged that she had been a client of la Filastre and, since she stood to benefit from the projected sale of the woodlands, she was suspected of being involved in Luxembourg's criminal activities connected with that.

On 29 January 1680 the Princesse was questioned by La Reynie and Bezons at the Arsenal and her uncertain performance, coupled with the fact that she left the Chamber in tears, merely encouraged the most frightful smears against her. It was put about that Luxembourg had impregnated her three times and that on each occasion Mme Voisin had aborted the infant. Some held that the remains had been burnt in the stove in la Voisin's consulting room, while others maintained that the bodies had been dried and powdered for use in spells. Only the Marquis de La Rivière defended the Princesse on the grounds that she was so plain that she could not possibly have had a lover. 'I would never have suspected the Princesse de Tingry of gallantry,' he tittered. 'For me her face had guaranteed her reputation.' He added, 'If I had a mistress like her I would never have feared anyone other than blind men for my rivals.'[54]

As Luxembourg fretfully awaited trial in the Bastille, his wife and mother materialised in Paris. Intent on showing that, despite the fact that her husband was supposed to have contemplated murdering her, he had not forfeited her loyalty, the Duchesse de Luxembourg threw herself at the King's feet, imploring permission to visit her husband in prison. Whether Luxembourg would have derived much solace from her company is a debatable point, but the King declined to grant her wish, saying she must wait patiently for all to be resolved. As the weeks went by without any alleviation in Luxembourg's position, there were reports that he had become hopelessly demoralised and many people took the view that he would have been wiser to follow the Comtesse de Soissons's example by fleeing the country, rather than risk facing trial.[55]

Meanwhile, those court figures who had received summonses had presented themselves at the Arsenal to undergo questioning. The most prominent of these was the Comtesse de Soissons's sister, the Duchesse de Bouillon. Born in 1649, she was the youngest of Cardinal Mazarin's five nieces and the fact that she was of Italian origin made it easier for the French to suspect that she had been ready to use poison.

The Duchesse de Bouillon was described by one observer as 'not beautiful but singularly seductive'. Instead of sharing her sister's brunette colouring and elongated facial features, she had a retroussé nose and tiny hands and feet of which she was very proud. In April 1662 she had married the immensely wealthy Godefroy, Duc de Bouillon, 'at that time without question the best match in all France'. He was the nephew of the King's great general, Turenne, and though he had none of his uncle's distinction or talent, the King recognised that he was a loyal subject and an honourable man, and valued him accordingly. Since 1658 the Duke had held the court office of Great Chamberlain, the second most important position in the royal household. His status had recently been enhanced still further for, by the Treaty of Nymwegen, he had been recognised not merely as a prince, but as independent sovereign of the principality of Bouillon.[56]

The Duchesse had not been faithful to her dull husband, treating him, according to Saint-Simon, with something akin to contempt. She had had many lovers, though at least it was conceded that she only took one at a time. Some years earlier she had conducted such a blatant affair with the Comte de Louvigny that she became anxious that her husband's family would intervene to protect his honour. To calm things down she had retired voluntarily to a convent for a time, but her husband was most upset by her decision to absent herself. Primi Visconti noted, 'Without his wife the Duke was a body without a soul; he did not bother about the others provided he had his share.' Much to Bouillon's relief, she rejoined him after a brief separation.[57]

The Duchesse was believed to be particularly close to her nephews, the Vendôme brothers. If one may believe Saint-Simon, her youngest son, the Chevalier de Bouillon, once alluded to this in the crudest possible fashion. Saint-Simon related that when in 1690 the Duc de Bouillon upbraided the Chevalier for his debauched ways, the younger man responded coolly that he was surprised the Duc should presume to lecture him in this manner. When the Duc countered that he was exercising the natural authority of a father, the Chevalier guffawed, 'You my father! You know very well that you're not and that it's Monsieur *le Grand Prieur* [Philippe de Vendôme].'[58]

The Duchesse's reputation was so notorious that in 1677 the King was said to have remarked she would be the ideal woman to give his son his sexual initiation. The Comte de Bussy was inclined to dismiss the report, not because the observation was in any way unfair but because it would have been out of character for the King to be so coarse about a woman of her high social standing.[59]

It will be recalled that the Duchesse had been called before the commission because Lesage had alleged that, during her visit to him, she had set down a written request for the death of her husband. This would have freed her to marry the Duc de Vendôme (who had accompanied her on that occasion) and Lesage testified that the Duchesse was so eager about this that she subsequently pestered him relentlessly, sending a servant to summon him to her on several occasions. At one point she had offered him a sack of gold if he would help her but Lesage said, highly implausibly, that he had spurned this as he did not want to become entangled in her schemes. According to him, however, others had been less scrupulous. Some weeks after he had made his first allegations against the Duchesse, he stated that she had also been a client of la Bosse and la Vigoreux, and that those two women had been ready to poison the Duc de Bouillon.[60]

Once it became known that the Duchesse was to be questioned by the commissioners of the Arsenal Chamber there was lively speculation in Paris society as to the causes. An unfounded rumour gained currency that she was suspected of poisoning some servants who had become too knowledgeable about her infidelities. As ever, M. de La Rivière had a snide comment at the ready. 'I greatly pity Mme de Bouillon if she has poisoned a man to keep her love life secret,' he wrote waspishly. 'She has committed a great crime which has availed her nothing.'[61]

The Duchesse appeared before La Reynie and Bezons on 29 January. She arrived at the Arsenal flanked by her husband and the Duc de Vendôme, who in turn were followed by a cavalcade of more than twenty coaches, packed with friends and relatives. Her supporters had to wait outside while she faced the commissioners, but Mme de Bouillon was not in the least discomfited by the prospect of her solitary interrogation. Having entered the chamber 'like a little queen', she at once took off her gloves in order to display her fine hands to best advantage. She then insisted on formally recording that she had come there solely out of respect for the King, rather than in deference to the authority of the Chamber, whose jurisdiction she did not acknowledge extended to the higher ranks of the peerage. Only once she had registered these objections did she deign to answer questions in a 'laughing and disdainful' manner.[62]

The Duchesse was adamant that she had never had any contact with la Vigoreux, but she readily agreed that she had once seen Lesage in the presence of the Duc de Vendôme. She explained that the two of them had written a few frivolous questions on a piece of paper, which Lesage had appeared to burn but, to her amazement, two or three days later the magician had given her note back to her. She had been so intrigued by this that she had asked him to perform the trick a second time. She had then written another note, which Lesage had again reduced to ashes, but this time he never returned it to her, even though she had several times sent a servant to enquire what had become of it. She concluded, 'She had found the whole thing so ridiculous that she told several people about it and even wrote of it to Monsieur le Duc de Bouillon ... who was with the army.'[63]

When asked whether she had written a request that her husband should die prematurely she indignantly denied it. Mme de Sévigné heard that she expostulated, 'Me, get rid of him? You have only to ask him if he thinks so. He accompanied me right up to the door.' When the commissioners had finished their questions she demanded mockingly, 'Well, Messieurs, is that all you have to say to me?' On being told that she was free to leave she exclaimed, 'Truly, I would never have believed that clever men could ask me so many stupid things.'[64] She went out to receive a rapturous welcome from the crowd clustered about the door of the Arsenal, all of whom were delighted by her stylish refusal to be intimidated.

Elated by the reception accorded her by her admirers, the Duchesse delighted in recounting how she had routed La Reynie and Bezons. Doubtless she could not resist embroidering the way she had defied them, for the witticisms which were now attributed to her certainly do not feature in the written record of her interrogation. It was said, for example, that La Reynie had asked her if she had ever seen the devil, to which she supposedly fired back, 'Yes, I have seen him and he looked just like you.'[65]

The Duc de Bouillon was so proud of his wife that he even asked the King if he could print an account of the interview to be distributed throughout Europe, but the King curtly refused. He had been much displeased by the way the Duchesse had glorified her interview with the commissioners, which threatened to turn the Chamber into an object of ridicule. Furthermore, the King and La Reynie were evidently not convinced that the Duchesse's airy dismissal of Lesage's allegations against her meant they were baseless. Serious consideration was given to arranging a tripartite confrontation between her, Lesage and la Voisin, to see if they could make her change her story. In the end, however, the King decided simply to order the Duchesse to leave Paris for an indefinite period. Even this did not subdue her, for she contrived to turn her departure into a triumphal progress. As she set off for Nérac in the Pyrenees, a crowd of family members and well-wishers gathered in the street to give her a rousing send-off.[66]

The Duchesse was permitted to return to Paris and the court in March 1681. However, as she doubtless realised, the King still disliked her. He tolerated her presence only out of respect for her husband and was relieved that she came to court infrequently. In 1685 the Duchesse exasperated the King once more after she expressed herself indiscreetly when Louis disgraced her son and her brother-in-law, the Cardinal de Bouillon. Once again she was expelled from Paris and this time she was not able to return for five years. In 1690 she was finally allowed to resume her place as 'a sort of queen' in Paris society, and presided over a salon graced by numerous poets and artists. Until her sudden death in 1714 she was seen at Versailles only rarely, though she did not stay away out of shyness. Saint-Simon said that when she did visit the palace, one could hear her confident tones from two rooms away.[67]

Perhaps calculating that she would achieve celebrity by appearing before the commissioners, the Maréchale de la Ferté volunteered to be questioned by La Reynie and Bezons, even though they had not planned to interview her. There had been speculation in some quarters that la Voisin had performed abortions for the Maréchale, but this was never more than idle gossip.

Despite the fact that the Maréchale was giving evidence of her own volition, many of her aristocratic circle formed the impression that she was being harassed by the *Chambre Ardente*, and she was elevated to the status of heroine. In a show of solidarity, numerous friends accompanied her to the Arsenal, 'all murmuring against the commissioners'. Her husband, too, was at pains to defend her, saying that she had only visited Mme Voisin in hopes of acquiring a winning formula for gambling. Having answered a few inconsequential questions, the Maréchale emerged to great acclaim, 'delighted at being innocent for once in her life'.[68]

The Marquis de Feuquières was another of those required to submit himself for interrogation. To his father he drawled, 'This business would be terribly disagreeable if one were on one's own; but... the company I am in diminishes the unpleasantness.'[69] On 1 February he appeared before the tribunal and gave laconic answers to the questions put to him. He confirmed that some years earlier he had encountered Lesage at the Marquise de Fontet's house and that on that occasion he and Luxembourg had written down a few trivial queries. About a week later Lesage had visited Feuquières at his house but Feuquières said he had realised the magician was wasting his time and had sent him packing.

As for la Vigoreux, Feuquières deposed that he had only spoken to her on one occasion when she had come to his door with a young boy who she claimed was a godson of Feuquières's late mother. She had wanted Feuquières to give him a job but the Marquis had declined, saying the boy was too young. When asked whether he had known Marie Bosse, Feuquières returned an absolute denial. After the interview was over Feuquières professed himself disgusted with the inanity of the questions put to him. 'If I had said "yes" to every one, there still would not have been enough there to have a lackey whipped,' he shrugged.[70]

However, Feuquières was far from being in the clear. He was well aware that La Reynie – whom he referred to as a 'rabid lunatic' – was still doing everything possible to construct a case against him. He declared himself at a loss to know why the Police Chief was pursuing him so obsessively, unless it was simply that La Reynie had become 'enraged at not finding any criminals, for all the hubbub he has made'. On 19 April Feuquières reported that in recent days La Reynie had considered issuing an arrest warrant against him, but in the end he had not dared go through with it. The Marquis added nonchalantly that he did not mind having to wait for the matter to be settled, as Paris was so pleasant in the springtime.[71]

In the coming weeks Feuquières resisted all attempts to frighten him into fleeing the country, rightly judging this would be the surest way to ruination. His confidence proved justified, for in June he was formally discharged of all imputations. In no way embarrassed by his ordeal, Feuquières took formal leave of the King and Louvois before going to take the waters at Bareges.

Feuquières was incomparable at projecting an aura of injured inno-cence but it is possible that he had had more extensive dealings with la Vigoreux and Lesage than he admitted. The Marquise de Fontet, who had introduced him to Lesage, testified that Feuquières had once confided to her that he had buried twelve pistoles in a spot designated by Lesage. Lesage had told him that if he did so, the coins would be transformed into something much more valuable. However, when Feuquières had returned to the site, he had found nothing apart from a large hole, and all the money had disappeared.[72]

Given what we know of Feuquières's superstitious nature, it is also likely that la Vigoreux had been telling the truth when she claimed that Feuquières had approached her in hopes of acquiring a charm that would prevent him being wounded in battle. Besides this she said that he had wanted her to arrange for him to 'speak with the spirit' and this cannot be dismissed in the light of later evidence, which proves beyond doubt he was interested in such things.

In 1696 letters from Feuquières were found addressed to a sorceress who had recently been arrested. A few years later it emerged that he had consulted another divineress called Marie-Anne de la Ville, from whom he had purchased talismans designed to bring luck in gambling and love affairs. He had also been present when she had sought to conjure up 'Prince Babel', who Feuquières hoped would guide him to hidden treasures.[73] One should not necessarily deduce from this that in the past Feuquières had also tried to poison people, but he clearly had an obsession with the occult, which he sought to keep secret.

While under suspicion in 1680, Feuquières had conducted himself with a disdain and lack of humility that even his father feared was foolishly provocative. When criticised for this, Feuquières denied he had displayed 'harmful pride', insisting he had merely acted as a man who, 'knowing himself to be quite innocent, loftily receives all calumnies and forcefully responds to them'. Once Feuquières had been discharged his father wrote to the King expressing the hope that since it was acknowledged that the accusations levelled against his son had been false, the King would evince no less compassion for the sufferings Feuquières had undergone than if he had been wounded in battle. This was a deluded hope. Feuquières's aunt was more realistic: on learning that her nephew was in trouble she had commented, 'Whatever happens, I cannot but fear that this will always have an evil effect on him and his fortunes.'[74]

Admittedly, despite Saint-Simon's contention that Feuquières never really recovered from the Affair of the Poisons and that thereafter he 'remained in some way touched by it', his military career went quite well for some years after the scandal had died down. When he became an infantry brigadier in 1688 the Marquis de Sourches commented that he was the best choice the King could have made, though he added that Feuquières's bravery and past services should have carried him higher still.[75] The following year Feuquières became a Maréchal de Camp and in 1693 he was promoted to Lieutenant-General. However, despite his undoubted abilities, he never advanced further.

Saint-Simon claimed he was ruined by his overweening jealousy and infernal ambition, for his superiors could not trust a man who was always scheming to supersede them. Certainly by that time he had fallen out with his former protector, Luxembourg. In September 1692 he complained to the Minister for Foreign Affairs that on campaign Luxembourg surrounded himself with a homosexual coterie of 'little favourites' who were 'all in some ways amorous of him'. These men were singled out for praise in despatches, while the exploits of others outside the charmed circle were ignored. When it became clear that Feuquières resented this, Luxembourg had asked the King that he should never again serve with him.[76] In this instance it does seem that Feuquières had genuine cause for complaint, but in other ways he was responsible for his misfortunes, for the revelation that he still associated with conjurers and divineresses damaged him in the eyes of the King and contributed to the failure of his career.

Disenchanted by his lack of advancement, in 1701 Feuquières retired from active service. In 1711 (to use Saint-Simon's words) 'he ended his life abandoned, abhorred, poor and obscure'. From his deathbed he wrote to the King lamenting that he had obviously displeased him, 'and though I do not know precisely how, I do not think myself any the less culpable for that. I hope, Sire, that God will forgive me my sins for I sincerely repent them. You are the image of God and I dare implore that you at least forgive my son for those faults of mine which I would have wished to expiate with my blood.'[77] Perhaps touched by this plea, the King permitted Feuquières's son to retain the pensions formerly conferred on his father.

The Comtesse du Roure was another person whose life was permanently blighted by the Affair of the Poisons, despite the fact that in former years the King had been very fond of her. By 1680 she was a mature woman of thirty-five but she had come to court as a teenager to serve Monsieur's first wife as a maid of honour. Known at that time as Mlle d'Artigny, she had forged a firm friendship with Louise de La Vallière. When Louise had embarked on her affair with the King, Mlle d'Artigny had sometimes acted as an intermediary between the lovers. However when she had fallen out with another maid of honour called Mlle de Montalais, the latter had sought to bring about her dismissal after discovering that early in her career Mlle d'Artigny had become pregnant. At the time she had managed to conceal this by retiring from court on some pretext and returning after the birth, but when Mlle de Montalais revealed this to the Duchesse d'Orléans, the latter wanted to expel Mlle d'Artigny from her household. In desperation Mlle d'Artigny appealed to the King to save her. Having gone to him and told him all about her earlier lapse from virtue, she begged him not to let her be sent from court in disgrace. 'The King was touched by her frankness and ever since then he always treated her very kindly ... even though she was a person of very mediocre merit.' Not only did he prevent her dismissal but in January 1666 he gave her a sizeable dowry when she married the Comte du Roure, son of the King's Lieutenant-General in Languedoc. In this way, 'from being poor and crushed by ill fortune, she became a great lady'.[78]

After her marriage the Comtesse du Roure remained close to Louise de La Vallière. When Louise turned up unbidden at La Fère in July 1667, Mme du Roure accompanied her. The Comtesse du Roure also continued to enjoy cordial relations with the King. In January 1669 he gave her husband the right to succeed his father as Lieutenant-General of Languedoc and took the trouble to convey the good news in person to the Comtesse du Roure.[79] Yet none of this sufficed to protect her once la Voisin started making accusations against her.

What makes this more curious is that the allegations were so contradictory and feeble. La Voisin had said that, having discovered the Comtesse du Roure was her client, Lesage had succeeded in luring her away from her. However, before this happened the Comtesse had indicated to la Voisin that she wished to bring about the death of Louise de La Vallière, and she had also revealed that she was on very bad terms with her husband and having an affair with her brother-in-law.

But when Lesage had been questioned about this on 28 October 1679 he had flatly denied that the Comtesse du Roure had ever been a client of his. On that day he merely acknowledged that la Voisin had once told him that Mme du Roure had come to her in hopes that the King could be induced to admire her, though by 7 January 1680 Lesage could recall being told by la Voisin that Mme du Roure had wanted to poison Louise de La Vallière. A week later la Voisin modified her original story. She now agreed that the Comtesse du Roure had never been one of Lesage's clients. She also confessed she had been mistaken when she stated that the Comtesse had an adulterous relationship with her brother-in-law, having muddled her with the Vicomtesse de Polignac. She still maintained that Mme du Roure had wanted to poison Louise de La Vallière, though they had touched on this only briefly, whereas she had discussed the matter in much more detail with the Vicomtesse de Polignac.[80] La Voisin's evidence with regard to Mme du Roure could thus hardly have been more confused and unsatisfactory. When one further considers that the Comtesse du Roure had always been considered a close friend of Louise de La Vallière, it seems extraordinary that la Voisin's claims were treated seriously.

On 1 February Mme du Roure was interrogated by La Reynie and Bezons at the Arsenal. She was adamant that she had never had any dealings at all with la Voisin or anyone like her. Writing to Louvois to inform him of this, Bezons registered his amazement at her complete disavowal, for he claimed that la Voisin's testimony regarding Mme du Roure had contained 'so many particularities' that it carried great weight.[81] Bezons's comment was misleading, to say the least, for as we have seen, la Voisin's account was full of flaws. His reluctance to accept that the evidence against Mme du Roure was weak helps explain why some people formed the view that he and La Reynie were intent on obtaining convictions, whether merited or not.

On 16 February a confrontation was set up between the Comtesse du Roure and la Voisin. The result was startling, for la Voisin failed to recognise the woman she had spoken of as her client. When the news came out, there was general outrage in Paris society at the way the Comtesse du Roure had been harassed for no good reason.[82]

On 26 April 1680 the Comtesse du Roure was formally discharged from all accusations. Oddly, however, it appears that her vindication was not complete. According to Saint-Simon, because of her involvement in the Affair of the Poisons, she was exiled from Paris by the King. Some years before her death in 1720 she was permitted to visit the capital for a few months, but apart from that she spent the rest of her life in Languedoc, having come to an arrangement with her husband whereby she resided in one chateau and he occupied another. 'She was feared everywhere,' Saint-Simon declared with a melodramatic flourish, although unfortunately without specifying why she inspired this universal dread.[83]

As each distinguished person was hauled in front of the commission without anything emerging that could warrant this intrusion, the attitude of the aristocracy changed perceptibly. At the outset it had been assumed that the commission would not have inaugurated proceedings against such privileged individuals unless there was good reason to believe they had committed major crimes. The prospect that members of their circle might have engaged in repugnant activities provoked genuine shame and consternation among the nobility. Mme de Sévigné wrote sombrely, 'We breathe here nothing but poison, and are in the midst of sacrilege and abortion.' The Marquis de Trichâteau lamented, 'See how the French court is seriously discredited abroad thanks to the ladies and the courtiers,' while the Comte de Bussy expressed the view that in all of French history 'one has never seen such horrors amongst people of rank ... as are visible today'.[84]

However, as the days went by and nothing was established that could justify the Chamber's proceedings, observers became more critical. By 31 January Mme de Sévigné was writing, 'The trend today is to speak of the innocence of those named and of horror at the scandal.' There was widespread agreement that the prisoners in Vincennes were merely seeking to prolong their lives by casting suspicion on prominent figures and that it was a mistake to pay any attention to their slanders. Mme de Sévigné, in particular, was sure the commissioners had made grave errors of judgement. After the Duchesse de Bouillon and the Princesse de Tingry had been questioned at the Arsenal she had commented scathingly, 'They have been given this affront for very trifling matters.' Two days later she said that while both of them might have behaved stupidly, as far as she could gather 'there was nothing black about their follies'. She added, 'If nothing more is discovered, people of such high rank could have been spared a great scandal.'[85]

Admittedly, Mme de Sévigné appeared to think that even if the Duchesse de Bouillon had expressed interest in poisoning her husband, this was something it would have been more seemly to overlook. She explained to her daughter, 'The Duchesse de Bouillon went to la Voisin to ask for a little bit of poison to kill an old husband ... who was boring her to death ... When a Mancini commits a folly like that it's nothing. These witches treat this in all seriousness and are horrifying all Europe for a trifle.' On 2 February she reported that there was general indignation 'at the lack of wisdom of the judges who have made such a commotion ... by scandalously naming such grand people on such slight grounds'.[86]

While aristocratic arrogance undoubtedly played a part in this anger, it should not be dismissed merely as the petulant outpourings of a decadent and selfish minority. It was understandable that members of the court nobility felt there had been an abuse of power and that their privileges had been trampled on without good cause. None of them dared censure the King for authorising the campaign of persecution, but the part played by Louvois was recognised and deplored. Primi Visconti recalled that even though Louvois had no official responsibility for the establishment of the commission, 'the rumour spread that Louvois was insinuating himself as an adviser to the Chamber'.[87]

However, as the role played by La Reynie and Bezons was more visible, they attracted more resentment than Louvois. In the opinion of the Marquis de La Fare, La Reynie was 'the motor of the Affair of the Poisons' and it was widely believed that he and his colleague had forced the other commissioners to countenance excesses which ran contrary to their instincts. Mme de Sévigné heard that one commissioner protested to La Reynie that they seemed to be occupying themselves exclusively with accusations of witchcraft, which was a crime the *Parlement* of Paris no longer recognised. 'Our commission is for poisons, so why are we hearing about other things?' he demanded. La Reynie brusquely brushed aside these objections 'Monsieur, we have secret orders,' was all he would say.[88]

Yet despite the strong feeling in aristocratic circles that the Chamber was acting unreasonably, direct protest was muted. It was easier to turn the whole thing into an object of mockery. Primi Visconti noted, 'All Paris ... ridiculed the Chamber's proceedings which were compromising the existence and honour of the grandest people for mere trifles.' Conversations and letters abounded with jokes in poor taste, which subtly mocked the commission without explicitly questioning its authority. On 2 February, for example, Mme de Sévigné's son inserted a playful message to his sister in the letter his mother had written to her. 'It's not Monsieur Lesage who is taking up the pen,' he teased. 'Here I am ... at Paris ... by the side of dear little Mama ... whom nobody yet accused me of having wanted to poison, and I assure you that these days that's no mean achievement.' Later in the year a servant of a notably pious lady named Mme Grondeuse was taken into custody on suspicion of poison, causing speculation that this would be followed by Mme Grondeuse's own arrest. The Comte de Bussy was sure however that 'she has never poisoned anyone, unless it's with her breath'.[89]

Despite the ill feeling among his courtiers, the King was making it clear that the commission still had his full support. On 4 February Louvois wrote to M. Boucherat, President of the *Chambre Ardente*, assuring him that the King wished the commissioners to continue its proceedings against suspected poisoners and 'to act with complete liberty against all those ... convicted of a crime of such enormity'. Louvois continued that, having learned of the mutinous mutterings made in Paris when the arrest warrants had been issued, 'his Majesty ... has commanded me to let you know that he wishes you to assure the judges of his protection and that ... he expects that they will continue to render justice with the firmness with which they began, without letting themselves be diverted by any considerations whatever.'[90]

To counter the insinuations being spread in some parts of Paris that the commissioners were exceeding their instructions, the King issued new letters patent broadening the Chamber's remit. These stressed that the Chamber was required to deal 'not merely with poisonings and *malefices* [instances of harm brought about by witchcraft] but also... with sacrilege, impieties and profanations through words, invocations, notes or other criminal practices'. This amplification of the Chamber's powers prompted the despairing cry from the Marquis de Feuquières, 'That's all that's needed to perpetuate it!'[91]

Far from feeling that the investigation had been too wide-ranging, the King was actually contemplating extending it further. On 6 February he summoned M. de La Reynie to Saint-Germain. Having pointedly indicated his support for the police chief by addressing him graciously during his levee, Louis closeted himself with La Reynie for 'two whole hours' later in the day. In the course of this interview he growled that he now saw 'it was necessary to make war on another crime'.[92] At the time he did not specify what he meant, but it is a reasonable assumption that he was referring to homosexuality.

The King had been infuriated to learn of an outrage recently committed by some wild young gentlemen of the court and it was almost certainly this which had prompted his remark. A group including the Duc de La Ferté, the Marquis de Biron and the Chevalier Colbert (son of the Controller-General of Finance) had tried to force themselves on an attractive seller of confectionery. When he had resisted their advances, they had badly injured him with their swords. Rather curiously the culprits had merely been severely admonished, though the King had made it clear that any future misbehaviour would result in instant banishment. Doubtless he had been lenient out of gratitude to Colbert (though the Minister himself had chastised his son's transgression harshly, administering him a fearful thrashing) for the Comte de Bussy pointed out that 'better men than they have been sent away for much slighter reasons'. The Marquis de Trichâteau commented ruefully that all that was needful for France's reputation to sink still lower in the eyes of foreigners was for 'the violated confectioner to add his tale to that of Lesage and la Voisin'.[93] Nevertheless, nothing came of the King's cryptic comment to La Reynie and for years to come homosexuality continued to flourish.

As it was, the *Chambre Ardente* had quite enough to keep it busy. During the past few months the trial of la Voisin had been repeatedly postponed on the grounds that there was more information to be gleaned from her. To keep her co-operative it had been implied to her that it would be some time yet before a date was set for a hearing, which in her case would inevitably be followed by torture and execution. By mid-February, however, there was agreement that matters were now ready to be taken a stage further.

On 17 February Mme Voisin was interrogated on the *sellette* by the assembled commissioners.[94] After she had been led out they unanimously pronounced her guilty and on 19 February she was informed that she had been sentenced to being burnt alive. However, before going to the stake she was subjected to another intensive examination, which stretched over three days, the final stages of which were conducted under torture.

The outcome was not entirely satisfactory. La Reynie later claimed that this was because the torture had not been applied with the usual rigour and thus 'produced no result'. This is seemingly corroborated by the fact that Mme de Sévigné heard that even on the evening of 21 February la Voisin was in remarkably robust form, despite having emerged from the torture chamber only a few hours earlier. Having eaten a hearty supper and drunk a great deal of wine, she began singing rude songs, ignoring suggestions from her guards that since her execution was scheduled to take place the following day it would be more appropriate to immerse herself in prayer.[95] Against this it should be noted that the written record of her torture session, which is interspersed with her shrieks and pleas to her tormentors to have pity on her, hardly supports the contention that she was gently handled.

Under questioning la Voisin proved ready enough to make alarming statements about the prevalence of poison. She affirmed sorrowfully, 'Paris is full of this kind of thing and there is an infinite number of people engaged in this evil trade.' Pressed to give examples of those who, 'under pretext of divination or reading hands, or of seeking treasure and the Philosopher's Stone...engage in the sale of poisons, abortion and impieties', she named several individuals. These included Vautier, 'a very dangerous man', who knew a lot about poison and perfumes; la Bergerot, who was 'deep in intrigues' connected with poison and magic; and la Poulain, 'a very vicious woman'. La Voisin said la Pelletier had agreed to supply poison to kill a sister of Mme Brissart but had changed her mind on finding that the intended victim was pregnant. The herbalist Maître Pierre, who was exceptionally knowledgeable about both the curative and noxious properties of numerous plants, had planned to poison the husband of Mme Roussel, though for some reason he had not succeeded in doing so. All this did little more than confirm what la Voisin had said earlier and almost everyone she named was already in gaol.

Regarding her own clients la Voisin proffered the worrying information that 'a great number of persons of every sort of rank and condition addressed themselves to her to seek the death of or to find the means to kill many people'. However, when it came to specific details she had little new to say. She confirmed that Mme Lepère had been her partner in a thriving abortion business, estimating that between them Mme Lepère and her daughter had aborted about 10,000 infants. She confessed that she had been involved in the poisoning of M. Leféron, M. Brunet and M. de Canilhac. She repeated that Mme de Dreux had wanted to poison both her husband and another lady of whom she was jealous, while stressing that she herself had done nothing to effect these wishes. When she was questioned about the court ladies she had testified against, she maintained that everything she had said about the Comtesse de Soissons, the Duchesse de Bouillon, the Vicomtesse de Polignac and the Comtesse du Roure had been true, but she did not enlarge on her earlier allegations. To the end she categorically denied knowing Mlle des Oeillets and insisted she had never been aware of priests conducting black masses.[96]

On 22 February la Voisin was transferred from Vincennes to the Bastille, before being taken to the Place de Grève for execution. Special care had been used in selecting a suitable priest to hear her final confession, for there were fears that the priests who ministered to those arrested on suspicion of poisoning were discouraging their charges from being too frank about their crimes. It does seem that there was some cause for concern: Mme du Fontet, at whose house Luxembourg had met Lesage, said that her confessor had told her to reveal nothing about the divinations that had taken place under her roof, as it was best 'to forget about all that'.[97] It is not clear why the priests should have wished to suppress such revelations, unless the Church authorities feared they would lead to disclosures about renegade priests conducting black masses. Alternatively, the confessors may have wanted to protect grand members of Parisian society from being implicated in the scandal, but whether this was for corrupt reasons or simply because they did not want anyone to be wrongfully accused can only be conjectured.

Despite the trouble taken to pick a reliable confessor for la Voisin, things did not go as planned. After being closeted with the *Grand Pénitencier* of Paris, Mme Voisin summoned the registrar of the *Chambre Ardente* and said she wanted to retract an allegation she had formerly made against Mme Leféron. Hitherto la Voisin had maintained that she had supplied Mme Leféron with a phial of liquid, obtained from a woman named la Leroux, and that this had been given to M. Leféron shortly before he died. Now, however, la Voisin said that though Mme Leféron had once referred to a phial of liquid in her possession, neither she nor la Leroux had provided her with it. Irritated that doubt had thus been cast on a crucial piece of evidence, Louvois ordered that in future *M. le Grand Pénitencier* should not be employed to receive confession in such controversial cases.[98]

At five in the afternoon la Voisin was placed in the cart that was to transport her through the crowded streets to the execution site. Agog to see for herself the celebrated poisoner, Mme de Sévigné had stationed herself in the Rue Saint-Antoine. As a result she caught a brief glimpse of la Voisin as she passed, dressed in a white smock and looking startlingly red in the face.

In former days la Voisin had been glib in her use of Christian terminology, invoking the Good Lord while simultaneously engaging in impious practices. Now, however, as her horrific death loomed, she spurned the consolations of religion and when her confessor stretched out his crucifix towards her, she angrily pushed it away. On arriving at the Place de Grève she refused to disembark from the tumbril and had to be dragged out by force, swearing dreadful oaths. Even after she had been chained to the stake she continued to resist her fate, for when straw was heaped upon her to ensure that she was speedily incinerated she kicked it away in desperation. These last grim struggles impressed themselves on the memory of the watching crowd but 'at last the flames got up and she was lost from sight'. Sprightly as ever, Mme de Sévigné commented that la Voisin had now passed from the midst of one fire to another.[99]

Mme de Sévigné noted that it was widely expected that la Voisin's torture and execution would bring about significant developments 'which will surprise us' but, in fact, it was followed by a hiatus in the commission's proceedings. On the day of la Voisin's execution the King had departed to welcome the new Dauphine on her arrival in France and the *Chambre Ardente* held no further hearings until after he returned to Saint-Germain in March.

Once sittings had resumed, the trial of la Voisin's alleged accomplice, la Leroux, took place on 4 April. After being found guilty she was interrogated one last time the following day and then tortured. At the outset she declared that she would shortly be facing the last judgement and was therefore ready to reveal all. In accordance with this she agreed that she had supplied la Voisin with a water which she knew to be poison and which was subsequently handed on to Mme Leféron. She also discredited Mme de Dreux, saying that Magdelaine de La Grange had told her that Mme de Dreux had approached her and Marie Bosse in hopes of obtaining poison. Mme de Dreux had planned to use it to kill her husband, though she had baulked at the sum of 2000 écus which Mme de La Grange and Mme Bosse had named as their price.[100] Having unburdened herself of these secrets, la Leroux was executed at four in the afternoon of the same day.

On 7 April the trial was held of Mme Leféron, a much more important defendant. She had been incriminated by numerous witnesses and the case against her was strong, not least because her husband was actually dead, whereas other putative victims of poisoners remained very much alive. La Voisin had more than once given a detailed account of how she had supplied Mme Leféron with poison and though she had subsequently withdrawn this, the fact that la Leroux had corroborated the original story had undermined la Voisin's attempt to exculpate her former client. Nevertheless, when questioned on the *sellette*, Mme Leféron still maintained her innocence. She did concede that at one of their consultations la Voisin had suggested that M. Leféron's death could be hastened, but Mme Leféron insisted she had rejected the idea. At the time M. Leféron was already suffering from 'an illness which would not permit him to make old bones' and therefore 'she did not want to listen to anything, given that her husband was incurable and could not go on much longer'.[101]

The commissioners apparently accepted that M. Leféron had not been murdered: at the end of the trial his widow was merely fined 1500 livres and banished from Paris and its surroundings for nine years. The sentence, which fell short of completely exonerating Mme Leféron, pleased nobody. Mme de Sévigné observed sarcastically, 'That was really worth the trouble of dishonouring her,' while the Comte de Bussy reported that people were saying that Mme Leféron deserved either to be punished more severely or not at all.[102] Certainly, the sentence reinforced the damaging perception that although the commissioners of the Arsenal Chamber could be merciless when it suited them, considerations of class and professional solidarity were apt to sway their judgement.

A day later the flautist Philbert, who had been in prison for months and whose wife had been executed the previous June, came up for trial. No evidence had emerged to suggest that he had aided his wife to poison her first husband, M. Brunet, or even that he had been aware that his predecessor had been murdered. He was therefore acquitted and freed without any stain on his character. Once restored to liberty, he attained a certain celebrity as a result of his narrow escape and was fêted by hostesses all over Paris.

On 27 April it was Mme de Dreux's turn to come before the Chamber. Her case was aided by the fact that though it was alleged that she had wanted to poison her husband and a rival mistress of her lover M. de Menars (who had preceded the Duc de Richelieu in her affections), neither of her alleged victims had come to any harm. Her husband had been highly supportive of her while she was in prison, for despite the fact that for many years they had been on distant terms (la Voisin had said they neither shared a bed nor took their meals together) he either could not believe she was capable of murder or considered that it would be a stain on his honour if she were convicted of such a crime.

Since her arrest Mme de Dreux had at all times insisted she was innocent. In a petition submitted to the commissioners she deplored the fact that she had been incarcerated, lamenting that while in Vincennes 'she had not even heard mass, nor had any counsel or consolation apart from her innocence, which enabled her to bear with patience and tranquillity the pain' of being falsely accused. On a more practical note, she submitted that Marie Bosse's evidence against her was inadmissible as la Bosse had a conviction for coining.[103]

Having considered her case, the commissioners confined themselves to admonishing Mme de Dreux and fining her 500 livres. Mme de Sévigné heard that several of them were reluctant even to inflict this modest sanction, while the Comte de Bussy believed that although 'this woman was innocent...the judges imposed this little penalty on her to save their honour'. M. Brayer took a different view, for he concluded that she had been let off so lightly 'more out of consideration for some members of her family than on account of her innocence'.[104]

On emerging from the Arsenal after her trial, Mme de Dreux was 'received with open arms by her husband and all her family', but her mother could not be there to meet her. She had died while Mme de Dreux was in prison, her end hastened, so Mme de Sévigné believed, by 'grief at seeing her daughter in this condition'. M. de Dreux did not dare tell his wife of her loss until they reached home, whereupon she fainted, and on reviving proved inconsolable. Mme de Sévigné confided to her daughter, 'Today she is still shedding tears which M. de Richelieu cannot wipe away; he has performed marvels throughout this whole business.'[105] Mme de Sévigné admitted that she had nearly wept herself on hearing this affecting tale but evidence yet to be uncovered would show that her sympathy was misplaced.

Meanwhile La Reynie and Bezons had been working to accumulate evidence for the prosecution of the Maréchal de Luxembourg. Although this was taking a surprisingly long time, Bezons would by no means admit it was proving difficult to assemble a case. On 9 February he confidently informed Louvois that Lesage had just given them new information which, though in some respects contradictory, clarified many matters that had hitherto been obscure. Yet the written record of

Lesage's interrogation on that date[106] hardly warrants Bezons's enthusiastic interpretation and suggests that if he was ready to attach such importance to an inconsequential interview of this sort, he and La Reynie were struggling more than they cared to admit to bring the investigation to a successful conclusion.

The case that was being so laboriously constructed depended heavily on Lesage's account of his encounter with the Maréchal at the Marquise de Fontet's house. However, since describing that, Lesage had made much more serious allegations against Luxembourg. He had claimed that Luxembourg had attended sacrilegious ceremonies conducted by the priest, Gilles Davot, who had passed notes under the chalice to gratify Luxembourg's desires. According to Lesage, Luxembourg had not only encouraged his secretary Bonnard to join with Marie Bosse and Mme Vigoreux in order to poison the businessman who was causing him problems, but the Maréchal himself had dealt directly with that disreputable pair. Furthermore, Luxembourg had commissioned Mme Vigoreux and her husband to arrange the murder of his wife. They had actually placed an assassin in the Duchesse de Luxembourg's household, who had been waiting for an opportunity to poison her.

Since it was obviously unsatisfactory to rely solely on Lesage's testimony, every effort was made to persuade Bonnard to divulge information damaging to Luxembourg. A combination of threats and inducements seem to have been used, for Luxembourg heard that Bonnard was told that if he did what was required of him he would be treated leniently. However, all this took time. Some of the other commissioners became disturbed that the case was taking so long to come to court, but when one of them expressed concern at the way Luxembourg was being kept in prison without trial, La Reynie peremptorily silenced him. He declared he possessed written proof in Luxembourg's own hand, which established beyond doubt that the Maréchal had done wicked things and that, this being so, the King had authorised him to proceed as he saw fit.[107]

Luxembourg himself had been intermittently questioned, but long intervals elapsed without him seeing La Reynie or Bezons. It was not until 5 May that mention was made of the signed paper Luxembourg had given to Bonnard. Then, at an interrogation session at the Bastille, the registrar of the *Chambre Ardente* held up a document and Luxembourg was asked if he recognised this as the Power of Attorney he had signed. Luxembourg replied that as far as he could see, it was, but when denied permission to inspect it closely he grew suspicious. Stepping forward briskly, he snatched the document and, having perused it carefully, saw that several lines of writing had been squeezed between the original text and his signature. Luxembourg pointed out that the insertion had been written in a different hand and a different coloured ink, and that the space was so tight that the final line almost overlapped his signature. He suggested that a handwriting expert should be called in who could independently verify this and, although La Reynie declined to do this, it became obvious that this document, to which the Police Chief had attached so much importance, would never on its own secure Luxembourg's conviction.[108]

Undaunted, La Reynie next brought in Bonnard for a confrontation with Luxembourg, but this too did not go as he had hoped. Bonnard began by denying that Luxembourg had supplied him with two bottles of poisoned wine to be given to a key figure in the forestry sale. He was then asked if Luxembourg had been aware that Bonnard had purloined material which could be used to fabricate counterfeit money, but Bonnard insisted that Luxembourg had not been privy to what he was doing. At this point M. Bezons intervened. He reminded Bonnard sharply that in an earlier interview he had said the opposite and that, if he contradicted depositions he had made under oath, he laid himself open to severe penalties. When Luxembourg indignantly demanded of Bonnard whether he had really uttered such false things, Bezons imperiously silenced the Maréchal, warning that if Luxembourg interrupted again he would be removed from the room. In answer Luxembourg growled that he was not accustomed to hearing lies told to his face and that, 'in prison, as elsewhere, I could not permit it'.[109] During the remainder of the confrontation La Reynie and Bezons tried to persuade Bonnard to incriminate Luxembourg in a number of other ways and they could barely hide their fury when their efforts failed.

Bonnard was tried on 8 May but at his trial nothing further emerged that could be used against Luxembourg. Bonnard himself was found guilty of *malefice* and impiety and sentenced to the galleys in perpetuity. Mme de Sévigné could not decide whether the poor man should be praised for his loyalty to his master or reviled for having caused such trouble, musing that he was either 'a very good or a very bad servant'.[110]

Despite Bonnard's failure to provide him with the evidence he wanted, La Reynie remained determined to prove his case. On 12 May an unnamed priest was brought into Luxembourg's cell. In an account he wrote shortly afterwards Luxembourg noted that he had never seen this man before, but he later discovered that he was Gilles Davot, who was supposed to have regularly performed conjurations for him. La Reynie asked the priest if he recognised the prisoner before him; when he answered that he did not, La Reynie menacingly cautioned him, 'Be very careful, for you do know Monsieur.' When this still failed to elicit the desired response La Reynie made an even more blatant attempt to jog the priest's memory, demanding, 'Are you not well acquainted with Monsieur le Duc de Luxembourg?' All proved in vain, for Davot replied that he knew Luxembourg only by reputation.[111]

Still La Reynie would not admit defeat. The next person brought in to confront the Maréchal was the husband of the late Mme Vigoreux, and he too was asked to identify Luxembourg. At first Vigoreux said that he did recognise him, but almost immediately he changed his mind and said that he had mistaken him for the Comte de Gassilly. Luxembourg noticed that La Reynie showed no interest in questioning Vigoreux about his dealings with Gassilly, which led him to 'conjecture that because M. de Gassilly... was allied with a minister [Louvois]', La Reynie did not want him to be implicated in the affair.[112] Luxembourg's comment indicates that he believed La Reynie was working to uphold the factional interests of Louvois and that this had a tremendous bearing on the way the inquiry was conducted.

Apparently unperturbed by these successive failures, La Reynie still had a final card to play, for Lesage was now taken before Luxembourg in hopes that he could force the Maréchal to change his story. Fortified with several glasses of wine, which La Reynie had given him to prevent his nerve failing, Lesage reiterated his story of his encounter with Luxembourg at the Marquise de Fontet's house. Once again he rehearsed how Luxembourg had not only expressed a wish that both his wife and the governor of a certain province should die, but had also sought the love of the Princesse de Tingry and entreated that a marriage might be arranged between his son and Louvois's daughter.

Luxembourg gave a dignified response to every one of these points. He said that while Lesage alleged he had wanted to eliminate the provincial governor so that he could succeed to his position, 'I had not thought it necessary to give myself up to the devil for that.' Regarding a marriage between his son and Louvois's daughter he remarked that he came from a dynasty 'where we do not purchase alliances through crime; that it had been a great honour for me had my son married Mlle de Louvois, but I would never have done anything for that about which I could reproach myself'. He continued that he was proud to have the friendship of the Princesse de Tingry (at this point Lesage interrupted with a snigger that what the Maréchal wanted was her love) but that it was quite untrue that he had ever wished ill to his wife, who had given him no cause for complaint.[113]

Lesage then changed tack and accused Luxembourg of having obtained poison from la Vigoreux to poison the businessman Dupin. Luxembourg countered this by informing him that la Vigoreux's husband had failed to identify him during their confrontation. Lesage's next ploy was to claim that he had regularly brought the priest Davot to see Luxembourg, and that he had performed ceremonies designed to bring about the death of Luxembourg's enemies. It was at this point, however, that La Reynie was obliged to admit that it was Davot whom Luxembourg had seen earlier and who had been at a loss when asked to name him.[114]

On 14 May Luxembourg was finally brought to trial but because of the setbacks experienced by La Reynie the result was a foregone conclusion. After inspecting the evidence, the Attorney-General of the *Chambre Ardente* recommended that the Maréchal should be discharged and this further predisposed the commissioners in Luxembourg's favour. When Luxembourg came before them to answer questions, he ended by expressing the hope that he had exonerated himself from the 'false, horrible and absurd accusations' that had been brought against him, and the commissioners did not disappoint him. After Luxembourg had been taken back to the Bastille they deliberated only briefly before acquitting him.

It appeared that he had been completely vindicated. Loyal supporters of the Maréchal, such as his cousin the Prince de Condé (who had stationed himself outside the Arsenal during Luxembourg's trial), were jubilant, though it is true that several of Luxembourg's fellow dukes criticised him for having allowed the *Chambre Ardente* to sit in judgement on him contrary to the privileges of the peerage. As far as Mme de Sévigné was concerned, however, Luxembourg had emerged from his ordeal 'whiter than a swan', while the Comte de Bussy observed that the commissioners ought to be ashamed of themselves for having issued an arrest warrant against an officer of the crown on such frivolous grounds.[115]

However, an unpleasant shock awaited Luxembourg. It had been assumed that he would be welcomed back at court to resume his position as Captain of the Guard, but as it turned out, 'everyone had been mistaken about this, and he himself more than the others'.[116] The day after the trial the King agreed that Luxembourg should be freed from the Bastille but he appended an order that the Maréchal should at once leave Paris and sequestrate himself in one of his properties in the country. Clearly, the verdict of innocent had left Louis dissatisfied.

Luxembourg accordingly retired to his country estate at Piney, his reputation and career apparently in tatters. The Princesse de Tingry, who had been formally absolved the day after his acquittal, understood herself to be comprehended in his disgrace and retreated to one of her chateaux in another part of France. It looked as if the matter had been closed and that Luxembourg would never be given a chance to redeem himself.

It therefore caused stupefaction when in June 1681 the King not only summoned Luxembourg back to court but reinstated him as Captain of the Guard. Mme de Sévigné exclaimed in wonder, 'How could the King make a more striking reparation than to give [Luxembourg] the care of his sacred person?' The Comte de Bussy was so amazed by the transformation in Luxembourg's fortunes that he declared there was nothing like it in the whole of French history, though he added that if he had treated a man as the King had treated Luxembourg he would take care never to employ him in a close capacity about his person. On his return to court Luxembourg found himself fêted by an eager throng of admirers and Mme de Sévigné told her daughter it would make her laugh if she could see how all those who had been the loudest to condemn the Maréchal were now full of praise for him.[117] In November 1681 the seal was set on Luxembourg's rehabilitation when the Princesse de Tingry, who had been contemplating renewing her vows as a nun, was invited to come back to court and resume her place as a lady-in-waiting to the Queen.

The Comte de Bussy attributed the King's change of heart as proceeding from the workings of a 'delicate conscience' and it is difficult to put forward a more precise explanation than this. After Luxembourg had been sent away, Colbert had written in protest to the King, reminding Louis of all the services Luxembourg had rendered him, and perhaps this had had a belated effect. Some people at court thought that the King's confessor, Père de La Chaise, had taken up Luxembourg's cause, while others actually believed Louvois was responsible for the turnaround.[118] There can be no doubt, however, that they were wrong in thinking this.

When Luxembourg had been exiled from Paris the President of the *Chambre Ardente* had remarked, 'We only pass judgement on proofs, but the King needs nothing more than indications.'[119] At the time the King had evidently decided that though it was not possible to convict Luxembourg, there was good reason to believe he had been involved in shameful activities. Now he apparently thought otherwise, having perhaps concluded that nothing Lesage said could be relied upon. However, this did not save others who remained in gaol as a result of being denounced by the magician.

Although the King never regarded Luxembourg with real warmth, he always treated him graciously after his restoration to court. In 1688 Luxembourg was appointed Governor of Champagne and in March 1690 he received a still greater mark of royal esteem when he was put in command of the army of Flanders. Aware of the continuing rift between Luxembourg and Louvois, the King informed the Maréchal that when on campaign he could bypass the Minister of War and communicate directly with him. In the next few years Luxembourg justified the King's faith in him by winning a string of victories, although some of his opponents alleged that this owed nothing to his military skills. Instead, they preferred to believe that his successes were due to his having leagued himself with his old ally the devil.[120]

Though Luxembourg never tried to revenge himself on Louvois for his conduct during the Affair of the Poisons, his resentment towards La Reynie never abated. In 1691 he asked the King for permission to bring a legal action against La Reynie 'for prevarications in the exercise of his charge' eleven years earlier. The King flatly forbade it, insisting that he did not want to revive matters which were 'finished and fallen into oblivion'.[121]

In 1695 Luxembourg – who 'at the age of seventy-seven had been living the life of a twenty-five-year-old' – fell mortally ill of double pneumonia. He made a pious end, attended by the great preacher Père Bourdaloue, who remarked that whereas he would not have liked to live as Luxembourg had done, he would be proud to die like him. However, despite his edifying end and the military honours he had won for France, Luxembourg never quite shook off the sinister reputation that had attached itself to him as a result of the Affair of the Poisons. His death was greeted by a rash of illegally printed pamphlets, suggesting that the devil had finally come to claim him as one of his own.

In May 1680 all this lay far in the future. Following the humiliating collapse of the case against Luxembourg it was widely assumed that the *Chambre Ardente* was completely discredited and that there was no likelihood of further prosecutions being brought. M. Brayer prophesied that the Chamber would soon be dissolved and that the cases of any prisoners remaining at Vincennes (whom he described as mere 'rabble') would be dealt with at the Châtelet in the normal way. In a fit of rancour Mme de Sévigné reported that La Reynie was now abominated by all right-thinking persons and snorted that the fact that he was still alive 'proves there are no poisoners in France'. Utterly exasperated, she demanded whether anyone had ever heard of a story which began and ended in such an extraordinary manner,[122] but, contrary to her belief, the Affair of the Poisons was by no means over. The King had issued instructions that enquiries should be continued and in weeks to come the prisoners still detained at Vincennes would manage to cast aspersions on yet more eminent people.

# EIGHT

# ACCUSATIONS AGAINST
# MME DE MONTESPAN

Contrary to general expectation, the *Chambre Ardente* was not on the point of being disbanded, for M. de La Reynie was sure that it still had important work to do. In particular, there were outstanding questions about the conduct of the Duchesse de Vivonne, Mme de Montespan's sister-in-law, and he considered it essential that these should be resolved.

The Duchesse de Vivonne had married Mme de Montespan's only brother in 1655. She had been endowed with a sizeable fortune, but she and her husband lived so extravagantly that the money was all dissipated by the time Vivonne died in 1688. In one respect they had been an ideally matched pair: the Duchesse had 'a wit of such high quality that it well befitted her to marry into the Mortemarts'. Unfortunately, they proved incompatible in other ways. Saint-Simon heard that 'they did not often meet and cared little for one another', and he understood that Mme de Vivonne had not remained faithful to her husband. Saint-Simon implied that M. de Vivonne accepted the situation without protest, though there was an awkward moment when his putative eldest son lay dying. Coming to the bedside, M. de Vivonne gazed at the young man and then remarked thoughtfully, 'Poor fellow! He will not recover. I remember seeing his father die in just the same way.' According to Saint-Simon, Vivonne believed that the boy's real father had been one of his grooms.[1]

Saint-Simon claimed that Mme de Montespan and her sister Mme de Thianges both did their best to remain on good terms with Mme de Vivonne, but the latter was apt to be impatient with them, resulting in 'disputes and excellent scenes'. In 1675 the Savoyard ambassador reported that Mme de Montespan was trying to persuade her sister-in-law to spend more time with her, partly because she hoped in this way to repair relations with her brother, who had previously made clear his disapproval of her relationship with the King. Until that point the King had not known Mme de Vivonne well, but he found he enjoyed her company enormously. However, Mme de Vivonne proved unwilling to come to court too often, 'for she was haughty, independent and capricious, caring very little for favours and privileges, and seeking only her own amusement'.[2]

In October 1679 Lesage had claimed that some years before the Duchesse de Vivonne had come to him in a state of panic. She had pleaded with him to recover a pact which she and the Duchesses de Vitry and d'Angoulême had all signed, and which had been drawn up for them by a divineress named Françoise Filastre. Lesage said that although he could not discover the exact text of the pact, it was clear that it contained 'terrifying things', which in some way related to the King.[3]

Confirmation of a sort was provided by the testimony of another divineress named Martine Bergerot, whom la Voisin had described as one of the most famous palmists in Paris. In November 1679 la Bergerot declared that about five years before Françoise Filastre had read her the text of a pact in which she gave herself, body and soul, to the devil. In return la Filastre hoped that the devil would empower her to grant the wishes articulated by high-ranking clients. La Bergerot claimed she had been startled to hear Mme de Vivonne mentioned by name in the pact for, some years before, Mme de Vivonne had been a client of hers. Around 1667 Mme de Vivonne had consulted her about 'divers curiosities' and she had once come to see her after quarrelling with Mme de Montespan. La Bergerot had sent Mme de Vivonne to see the man who had taught her to read palms and Mme de Vivonne had written down a list of demands for him. However, the Duchesse had subsequently become concerned that this document would compromise her if it fell into the wrong hands and she had been much relieved when she managed to regain possession of it.

On learning in 1675 that Mme de Vivonne was in contact with la Filastre, la Bergerot had thought it proper to caution the Duchesse against becoming more closely involved. She went to see Mme de Vivonne and warned her that la Filastre was making free with her name. The Duchesse, however, had appeared displeased to receive this unsolicited advice and since that time la Bergerot had not seen her.[4]

La Reynie had naturally been anxious to question la Filastre herself about all this but for some months she remained at liberty, having left Paris in September 1679 to travel to the Auvergne. In December she was located in Cusset and, having been taken into custody there, she was brought back to Paris and confined in Vincennes. Various associates of hers were also arrested. These included Mme Magdelaine Chapelain, who at one time had employed la Filastre as her maid and who had paid for her journey to the Auvergne. A peasant named Philippe Galet was also detained after it was discovered that on several occasions in the past la Filastre had travelled to see him in Normandy and that she had purchased powders from him. When first questioned about this Galet had explained that the powders were meant to bring success in love and at the gaming table, and they contained breadcrumbs, iron filings and 'a little pinch of powdered cantharides'.[5]

At her first interrogation la Filastre disclosed that she had taken steps to secure herself employment in the household of the King's mistress, Mlle de Fontanges. To bring this about she had enlisted the aid of a young soldier named Lafrasse who boasted of having good contacts at court. Lafrasse was immediately arrested, even though at this stage it was not considered particularly worrying that la Filastre had cherished this ambition. Six months later, however, concerns mounted on this score after la Filastre mentioned she had been so determined to obtain a job with Mlle de Fontanges that she had been ready to poison an acquaintance who was seeking similar employment. La Filastre had feared that unless she took such action, this woman might jeopardise her own chances of advancement. The fact that la Filastre had been prepared to be so ruthless was undeniably alarming, and her interrogators began to wonder whether her eagerness to attach herself to Mlle de Fontanges was motivated by a deeper purpose than a mere desire to further her career.

Such facts did not emerge until la Filastre had been imprisoned for some time. For the first few months of 1680 the energies of La Reynie and Bezons were concentrated on preparing for the trials of la Voisin and the Maréchal de Luxembourg. It was only once these cases had been concluded that the commissioners turned their full attention to la Filastre. Then – as Lesage had predicted when he had urged that la Filastre should be arrested – it was not long before they began to learn 'strange things'.

When la Filastre was interviewed on 26 May 1680 she admitted with remarkable frankness that she had been involved in sinister practices. In particular, she recalled the part she had played in a black magic ceremony, which had been performed six or seven years earlier when she had given birth to her lover's child. At the behest of another divineress, la Simon (who had taught la Filastre much of what she knew about occult lore), parturition had taken place in a circle of burning candles while la Filastre recited incantations renouncing the holy sacrament, mass and her baptism. The fate of the child remains unclear. La Filastre said la Simon had taken it away and she feared that it had been killed and offered up to the devil. However, when la Simon herself was questioned she said that, fearing that la Filastre intended to harm the baby, she had taken it to a foundling hospital for its own protection.[6] Others were prepared to testify that la Filastre had sacrificed the child herself, though proof was never forthcoming.

La Filastre also admitted that she had attended several black masses. At one that had taken place about five or six years earlier the officiating priest had been named Jacques Cotton and la Filastre explained that during the service he had invoked 'three demon princes' who could aid her to conclude a pact with the devil in order to enhance her magical powers. Another similar ceremony had been performed at dead of night in a cellar at Melun while a thunderstorm raged outside.[7]

Cotton was promptly arrested and, when interrogated, made no attempt to deny all this. He agreed that as well as celebrating these two masses he had conducted other services at the request of la Filastre. Sometimes wax figurines had been placed on the altar as he celebrated mass and, though la Filastre later maintained that the purpose was merely to aid clients in the conduct of love affairs, Cotton confessed that on at least one occasion he had understood that it was intended to bring about a death.[8] Besides this, la Filastre had arranged for Cotton to say masses on the powders which she had obtained from the Norman peasant, Philippe Galet, for it was thought that this process rendered them more potent. La Filastre kept some for her own use but passed others on to her former employer, Mme Magdelaine Chapelain. Since the latter was herself a successful divineress she in turn sold the powders to her own clients.

Magdelaine Chapelain, who like la Filastre was arrested in December 1679, remains a somewhat mysterious figure, for the records of many of the interrogations and confrontations she underwent are missing. La Reynie would later declare that as well as being 'suspected of several poisonings', she had engaged in 'a continual practice of impieties, sacrilege and *malefice*', but precise details are hard to establish. Though aged only twenty-eight she had accumulated a respectable fortune from her activities, enabling her to purchase a bureaucratic post for her husband, a former coachman. She was also a woman of property and at one time had let one of her houses to Louis Vanens, whose arrest in 1677 had precipitated the Affair of the Poisons. Vanens's servant La Chaboissière claimed that she was more than just a landlady, for she and Vanens had done distillations together.[9]

Mme Chapelain had earned her money by offering a wide range of services. As she herself admitted, when a man named Courville came to her because his wife was sick, she had looked into a glass to predict whether the woman would recover. In May 1680 tests were done on powders found at her home and, though Mme Chapelain initially tried to pretend they were medications for asthma, she later acknowledged they were aphrodisiacs, which the priest Cotton had blessed for her.[10]

It would seem, too, that Mme Chapelain had tried to harness the powers of darkness to her own advantage. Believing that the inhabitants of the spirit world could guide her to hoards of buried treasure, she had contemplated sending a woman named la Bellière to the Caribbean, after hearing that the people there 'talked very frequently to the devil'. Mme Chapelain had also conceived a desire to forge her own pact with the devil. La Filastre deposed that when in 1676 her employer had sent her to Normandy on her first visit to Philippe Galet, she was supposed not only to buy powders from him, but also to ask him for advice about how to enter into a satanic pact.[11]

If la Filastre was to be believed, Mme Chapelain had been involved in worse things than this. She claimed that Mme Chapelain had once asked her to use magic to kill a miller named Leroy, whose wife wanted to marry her lover. La Filastre said that when she had refused, Mme Chapelain had performed a spell herself, using human bones and excrement. La Filastre suggested that Mme Chapelain had also poisoned her former lover, Abbé Charpy, and that she had had at least one abortion. Mme Chapelain was also somewhat loosely linked to other mysterious deaths, which had recently come under scrutiny. At one point it was alleged she had poisoned Racine's late mistress, the actress Mlle Du Parc. How she did this was never specified, though one witness claimed that she had quarrelled with the actress and had killed her 'either out of resentment or to get her money'. There were even vaguer claims that Mme Chapelain had been in some way responsible for the death of the last President of the Paris *Parlement*, M. de Lamoignon, though the grounds for this are too hazy to warrant serious consideration.[12]

On 5 June la Filastre mentioned another priest who had aided her experiments in black magic. She said that, having heard this man was knowledgeable about such matters, she had gone to him seven or eight years earlier to ask for guidance about the best way of drawing up a pact with the devil. He had obligingly shown her one that he had composed for his own use, and had then told her that he had performed black masses in a cellar in the presence of two men and a woman.[13]

Orders were at once issued for the arrest of this priest, whose name was Étienne Guibourg. Now aged seventy, he was a hideous figure, with a pronounced squint and a dark red complexion. For the past twenty years he had shared his bed with a concubine but neither his flagrant disregard of his vows of celibacy nor his violation of every other priestly tenet had prevented him from finding employment as a sacristan or curate in numerous parishes in Paris and its outskirts.

M. de La Reynie would later remark that at times Guibourg appeared 'touched', and certainly some of his evidence is so rambling and incoherent that it suggests he was suffering from the onset of senility. At times he would deny knowing people with whom he was incontestably well acquainted and his sense of time was also hopelessly defective. When describing events he proved incapable of fixing them in specific years and instead shifted his chronology in the most disconcerting fashion. Yet in other respects his memory appeared remarkably vivid, for the accounts he supplied of the crimes he acknowledged committing (including poisoning, sacrilege and child sacrifice) were chillingly detailed. Whether he told the truth in doing so or whether he exaggerated in the belief that he would not be brought to trial for such horrific offences is not easy to evaluate.

When interrogated on 26 June[14] Guibourg at once disclosed that, after la Filastre had given birth to her child, he had celebrated mass on the afterbirth. He was then asked if he had ever performed mass on women's stomachs, a crime to which none of the priests arrested in the course of the inquiry had yet admitted. With a dreadful show of humility Guibourg referred himself to God's mercy before whining that others 'had taken advantage of his weakness' and prevailed upon him to commit such obscenities.

Guibourg then declared that he had first used the stomach of an unknown woman as an altar when he had celebrated a black mass at a Chateau near Montléry. He had done this at the request of a former official in the royal stables called Leroy. (This man was never arrested; if he had indeed existed, he may have since died, or Leroy may have been a pseudonym.) Four years ago the divineress la Pelletier (already in custody after la Voisin had named her as a seller of poisons) had arranged for him to enact a similar mass in a hovel in Saint-Denis. It was attended by a man who had hoped to summon up the devil in order to conclude a pact with him. Guibourg said he did not know the identity of the woman whose body had served as an altar, but he had understood she was a prostitute enticed off the streets by la Pelletier.

La Reynie now turned for further information to Lesage who, oddly enough, was still considered an authoritative witness, despite the manner in which his testimony had been rejected by the Maréchal de Luxembourg's judges. Lesage had never mentioned Guibourg in his earlier depositions, but he now claimed to know all about him. He said he had heard of other occasions when Guibourg had performed black masses and, for the first time, he linked Guibourg with la Voisin, claiming that some of these masses had taken place at her house. More controversially still, he claimed that the woman whose body had been profaned during the black mass in Saint-Denis was no common streetwalker but a lady of rank who was a client of la Voisin's.[15]

Lesage now also elaborated on his earlier claims about the Duchesse de Vivonne, insisting she was guilty of the foulest abominations. He not only stated that Mme de Vivonne had told him she had witnessed the sacrifice of la Filastre's child but he went further, declaring that the Duchesse had subsequently persuaded la Filastre to terminate an unwanted pregnancy of her own. La Filastre had agreed to help her on condition that she was permitted to say a black mass on Mme de Vivonne's body while the abortion was carried out and then to offer up the foetus to the devil.[16]

When these claims were put to la Filastre, she insisted there was no truth in them. She did, however, agree that the Duchesse de Vivonne had been a client of hers. She even said she had visited her at home and that on one occasion she had been invited into the Duchesse's bedroom. Having copied out a paper Mme de Vivonne had written containing a list of demands, la Filastre had taken this to Cotton, the priest who had helped her on other occasions. Once he in turn had transcribed the document, Cotton was required to perform spells in the hope of prompting some malign spirit to grant Mme de Vivonne's wishes.[17]

In due course Cotton was interrogated about this and he admitted having copied out the paper. When asked what it contained, he became vague and then said that, as far as he could remember, Mme de Vivonne had offered to give her soul to the devil in return for receiving a monthly sum from him. She had also wanted a certain person sent away from court and to be rid of her husband, whom she disliked.[18]

To add to the confusion, on 30 August Magdelaine Chapelain made a new accusation against the Duchesse de Vivonne.[19] She alleged that in 1676 it was Mme de Vivonne who had sent la Filastre to see Galet in Normandy. Mme de Vivonne had commissioned la Filastre to buy love powders and aphrodisiacs, which were to be given to the King to make him fall in love with her. Furthermore, the Duchesse had ordered la Filastre to obtain poison, which she could administer to Mme de Montespan so as to eliminate her as a rival for the King's affections.

By putting forward this explanation Mme Chapelain presumably hoped to dissociate herself from la Filastre's visits to Galet, despite the fact that la Filastre herself had claimed that she had gone to see him on the orders of Mme Chapelain. In a bid to establish the truth, on 5 September a confrontation was arranged between la Filastre and Mme Chapelain. At this la Filastre vehemently denied that she had been acting on Mme de Vivonne's behalf when she had gone to Normandy, but Mme Chapelain stuck to her story and La Reynie was inclined to believe it.[20]

By this time a new set of horrors was under investigation. On 29 July la Filastre had alleged that Guibourg had sacrificed several of the children he had had by Jeanne Chanfrain, a forty-eight-year-old woman who had been his mistress for the past twenty years. Jeanne Chanfrain was accordingly taken to Vincennes and when questioned on 9 August her answers suggested that there might be some truth in this. Of the seven children she had borne Guibourg, four could be accounted for, but the whereabouts of three were a mystery. Jeanne Chanfrain admitted that soon after she had given birth to her third child fathered by Guibourg, the priest had taken it away and she suspected he had murdered it. She claimed that at the time she had been so upset that she had attacked her lover, screaming, 'You wicked man, you've killed my child.' Guibourg had merely retorted that 'it was no business of hers and she would not be burdened with the sin of it.' Despite this callous rejoinder, Jeanne had not broken off her relationship with Guibourg. The twins she bore him next had also disappeared after being entrusted to his care.[21]

M. de La Reynie found it all too easy to believe that the missing infants had been sacrificed to the devil. He noted solemnly that such practices had been known since biblical times, while the researches of Jean Bodin, the great sixteenth-century French expert on witchcraft, had established that witches believed it would enhance their evil powers if they offered up children to their master.[22]

La Reynie also recalled a curious episode that had taken place in Paris in 1675.* That summer the stability of the city had been threatened after the populace became gripped by panic that children were being abducted and murdered on the orders of an ailing noblewoman. At the time, an English observer had reported, 'They speak here of some great princess who...is sick of leprosy and employs...armed men to steal away and catch off the streets little children not exceeding two years of age to make a bath of their blood, it being, they say, the best remedy against that disease.' There had been riots and assaults on suspected kidnappers, and order had only been restored when a woman who had

* La Reynie mistakenly thought it had happened in 1676.

played a leading role in the tumult had been sentenced to death, though she had later been reprieved on account of being pregnant. At the time La Reynie had regarded the incident as an outbreak of hysteria, but he was gradually coming to think that 'this extravagance could have been founded on fact'.[23]

La Reynie's readiness to contemplate the possibility that some noble-woman might have orchestrated a wave of infanticide owed much to the fact that the name of a court lady who occupied a far more prominent position than the Duchesse de Vivonne had now started to feature in the inquiry. By the end of the summer of 1680 La Reynie had grounds for believing that the King's mistress, Mme de Montespan, had had dealings with both Abbé Guibourg and Françoise Filastre. Worse still, there was a possibility that her activities had jeopardised the safety of the King himself.

The first indication of this had come on 10 August, when la Filastre had caused consternation by suggesting that Mme de Montespan had had links with Guibourg, which went back a long way. La Filastre had already testified that when she had first met Guibourg, seven or eight years before, he had shown her a pact with the devil that he had devised himself. Now she added the important detail that Guibourg had told her he wanted to conclude this pact so as to be better equipped to gratify the wishes of his influential clients. He had gone on to say that these clients included not only a man who wished to kill the Controller-General of Finance, Colbert, but also Mme de Montespan herself. Guibourg had further confided that when he had conducted a black mass on a prostitute in a humble dwelling in Saint-Denis, he had been acting for the benefit of Mme de Montespan.[24]

Informing Louvois of this development, La Reynie sounded a note of caution. He conceded that even if la Filastre's account was truthful, Guibourg might simply have been bragging in hopes of duping her into believing that his services were sought by the cream of Paris society. Yet although this was a possibility, La Reynie did not consider dismissing the story on that account. On the contrary, indeed, it filled the Police Chief with considerable unease.

While la Filastre was doing her best to convince her interrogators that Guibourg was acquainted with Mme de Montespan, others were suggesting that la Filastre herself had done business with the royal mistress. On 12 August a divineress called la Bellière alleged that before leaving Paris in September 1679, la Filastre had said something curious to her. She had told la Bellière that when she returned from her travels she wanted la Bellière to take some sort of love aid to Mme de

Montespan, promising that in return she would pay her 10,000 écus. Quite why la Filastre should have been prepared to pay this vast sum to an intermediary was never established, but La Reynie could only think it ominous. He grew more worried when la Bellière said that despite the cash incentive she had been reluctant to undertake an errand she feared would bring her to the gallows. La Reynie's concern deepened when la Bellière added that la Filastre had said she wanted to enter Mlle de Fontanges's service in order 'to restore Mme de Montespan to the good graces of the King'.[25]

That same day la Filastre was interrogated again and, in a desperate bid to force admissions from her, trickery was employed. She was told that in earlier interviews she had confessed that her former employer Mme Chapelain had worked for Mme de Montespan, although in reality la Filastre had never said anything of the kind. Understandably bewildered, la Filastre responded that she must have been confused at the time, for she and Mme Chapelain had never talked of Mme de Montespan.[26]

A few weeks later la Bellière repeated her claims during a confrontation with la Filastre. La Filastre repudiated her description of their exchange, conceding only that she had once remarked she wished she knew Mme de Montespan, as she would have been able to exploit the connection by earning herself 10,000 livres. She also denied she had ever discussed her plan to enter Mlle de Fontanges's household with la Bellière.[27]

Nevertheless, suspicions that Mme de Montespan had been a client of la Filastre's were strengthened when Galet, the Norman peasant who had supplied la Filastre with powders, was questioned on 1 September. He stated that when la Filastre had first come to him in 1676 she had asked him to sell her a poison that was undetectable. Galet said he had pretended to oblige, though in fact none of the powders he had handed over had been harmful. In addition la Filastre had asked him for love powders for a lady at court. According to Galet, this person was none other than Mme de Montespan who, la Filastre had said, was upset because the King no longer treated her as well as she desired. Galet had accordingly given her some powdered aphrodisiac containing cantharides.[28] Hearing this, M. de La Reynie began to wonder whether the headaches and 'vapours' that had bothered the King at the time had been caused by his having unwittingly ingested this alarming concoction.

It might be considered bizarre that La Reynie could attach such significance to this miscellany of uncorroborated and often contradictory assertions, but there was a reason why he dared not reject them out of hand. However unlikely it might seem that Mme de Montespan had maintained her position as royal mistress by recourse to black magic, poison and sexual stimulants, such claims tallied alarmingly with the evidence of another suspect detained at Vincennes who had recently become a key figure in the inquiry.

The name of this informant was Marie Marguerite Montvoisin, and she was the twenty-one-year-old daughter of the late Mme Voisin. She was now an orphan: by an irony her father, who had survived la Voisin's numerous attempts to poison him, had died of natural causes in May 1679. It is not quite clear why Marie had been arrested in the first place. Perhaps it was simply thought that since she had lived with her mother and had been constantly in her company, she must inevitably know a great deal about her activities. At any rate, by 16 January 1680 it had been decided that it would be worthwhile to take her and two of her brothers into custody, and formal warrants were issued for their arrest ten days later.[29]

The Controller-General of Finance, Colbert, would later seek to discredit Marie's testimony by arguing that, having realised she would inevitably face execution if brought to trial, she had sought to avert this fate by adopting a desperate stratagem. 'In this position, she felt all the terrors of torture and death. One is naturally ingenious in these extremities,' he observed. Yet, in fact, until she herself suggested otherwise, there was little reason to think that Marie had been more than peripherally involved in her mother's activities. At one point she herself pleaded she had never been anything other than a helpless bystander and that, though it had not escaped her that women were asking la Voisin to rid them of their husbands, 'as an unmarried girl devoid of wealth and without any means of subsisting away from her mother', she could do nothing to prevent this.[30] However, this attempt to portray herself as a passive observer conflicted with other accounts she gave suggesting she had been at the centre of a treasonous conspiracy masterminded by her mother.

One of the few compelling reasons to accept Marie's evidence as truthful is that her revelations damaged her own prospects. Had she been more circumspect there is a good chance that she would ultimately have been discharged, but once she had spoken out that became unthinkable. Perhaps she simply failed to assess the situation correctly and assumed she was in worse trouble than was, in fact, the case. It is unlikely, however, that fear provided the sole motive for her startling declarations. Reading her evidence, it is hard to escape the suspicion that she relished being the centre of attention and enjoyed depicting herself as a person of consequence whom her mother had entrusted with fearful secrets.

It was not, perhaps, surprising that Marie was a far from stable character. La Reynie described her as impulsive and fiery, 'with a strange cast of mind', and when first imprisoned she had tried to commit suicide by self-strangulation. Her background could hardly have been more unsettling, for even as a child she had been aware that 'strange things' went on in her mother's house.

At the time, care had been taken to conceal their exact nature, but the sense that things were being kept from her had merely stimulated her inquisitive nature and encouraged her tendency to fantasise. She possessed a vivid imagination as well as being an accomplished liar and by the time she reached adulthood she was – as Colbert put it – 'cunning and ingenious to an extent that is inconceivable in one of her age and condition'.[31]

Marie's mental equilibrium cannot have been aided by the emotional turmoil she had experienced within the past two years. Prior to her mother's arrest she had become pregnant by a lover who had seduced her on promise of marriage and then abandoned her. Fearful of what her mother might do, Marie had turned for help to the midwife Mme Lepère. The latter had either carried out an abortion or delivered Marie of a child that had failed to survive. In the spring of 1679 the shocking arrest of Marie's mother (towards whom Marie's feelings are hard to define) was followed in quick succession by the death of her father and this can hardly have failed to have affected her. It is true that Lesage once indicated that Marie had been aware of her mother's attempts to poison Montvoisin and he implied she had not minded in the least. On the other hand Marie herself gave the impression she had been fond of her father. According to her, far from conniving at her mother's attempts to murder him, she had only narrowly avoided dying alongside him. She claimed that she had been poisoned on at least two occasions, once accidentally, when she drank some soup prepared for her father and once after she had displeased her mother by talking too freely.[32] It is difficult to assess the truth of all this but at the very least it would be fair to say that Marie's family life had been unusually disturbed. It was particularly unfortunate that La Reynie's investigation would come to hinge so much on this highly strung and manipulative young woman.

La Reynie hoped that Marie would be able to clarify various matters which had remained unresolved at the time of la Voisin's execution. It particularly worried him that la Voisin had admitted that at the time of her arrest she had been planning to present a petition to the King. The petition had related to a lover of la Voisin's named Denis Poculot, Sieur de Blessis. This man, who at one time owned a business that manufactured artificial marble, had met la Voisin in 1676 when she had drawn up his horoscope. After that they had continued to meet secretly at the house of the divineress la Delaporte.[33]

La Reynie believed there was ample evidence that Blessis was an extremely dangerous man. Prior to her execution Marie Bosse had said that he knew how to poison gloves, while Lesage had related that la Voisin's husband had once burst out that it was 'that bugger of an apothecary' Blessis who had taught her to poison shirts and handkerchiefs. La Voisin herself never confirmed that he had such expertise, though under torture she conceded he knew how to make some kinds of poison. She acknowledged, too, that Blessis had once offered to arrange for her husband to be poisoned and recalled that he had once referred to orpiment as 'the father of poisons'.[34]

It is clear, however, that Blessis's abiding interest was alchemy. He had persuaded la Voisin and others that a dying Italian in Perpignan had given him the formula for a 'projection powder', which would enable him to convert base metal into gold. La Voisin became convinced that Blessis would make her fortune after he pulled off the remarkable feat of making silver using goat's fat, though he was never able to repeat the procedure.[35]

Unfortunately, word of Blessis's prowess soon reached others, with the result that he became a victim of his own propaganda. Hearing that he could convert copper into silver, a cousin of M. de Montespan's named Roger, Marquis de Termes decided he would exploit Blessis's knowledge for his own enrichment. In late 1678 Blessis was abducted and detained in Termes's chateau. Two furnaces had been installed in one of the towers and it was made clear to Blessis that he would not be permitted to leave until he had performed the miracle required of him.

La Voisin had been dismayed to be deprived of her lover, who she had hoped would bring her fabulous riches. After she had consulted with various friends of Blessis, it was agreed she should submit a petition to the King, requesting that he order the Marquis de Termes to release Blessis. Despite the difficulties of gaining access to the King, la Voisin had been determined to present this document personally to Louis.

When people wished to petition the King, the normal procedure was for them to place their written request on a table set up every Monday in the guardroom of whichever palace the King currently occupied. At the beginning of the reign the King himself had sat behind the table as the petitions were laid there, but in recent years he had delegated this task to Louvois. The petitions submitted in this way were generally returned about a week later, marked to indicate whether they would be granted, rejected or given further consideration.[36]

On occasion individuals were still able to hand petitions personally to the King, though to do so they had to gain the assistance of someone who could facilitate an approach to him. In 1678 an English visitor to Versailles saw a poor woman present a petition to the King as he sat at dinner and was impressed by the graceful manner in which Louis received it, 'with abundance of sweetness mixed with majesty'. Two years earlier the Comte d'Armagnac had introduced François Grandet to the King as the latter made his way to mass and Grandet had seized the opportunity to present Louis with a petition from the townspeople of Angers. Their request was subsequently granted though, in fact, this was an unusual outcome. Grandet was later told that petitions presented in this way were generally left in the King's pocket when he changed his coat and Louis tended to forget all about them.[37]

Mme Voisin had never managed to present her petition. Being admitted to the palace had not posed a problem, for anyone suitably attired was permitted to come to court, but gaining access to the King had proved another matter entirely. Realising that she would need the aid of an insider at court to stand any chance of a personal encounter, la Voisin had applied to the Duc de Montausier's valet. After she had asked him to arrange for her to be advantageously placed, the serving man had done his best to be helpful, but his influence had been too limited to achieve anything. In early March 1679 la Voisin had gone to Saint-Germain on three consecutive days in hopes of presenting her petition, but she never came anywhere near the King. She had intended to try again, but before she could do so she had been arrested.

La Reynie was worried that there had been any prospect of la Voisin having even the briefest contact with the King. He had become still more concerned when la Voisin had mentioned during one interview that Lesage had offered to 'fit up' the petition in a manner that would guarantee a successful outcome. La Voisin said melodramatically that she had not known what Lesage had meant by this and had not wanted to find out more.[38] If Lesage had made such an offer (which he denied) in all probability he had merely intended to say an incantation intended to improve the chances of the petition being granted. Unfortunately, a much more frightening explanation took seed in the mind of La Reynie.

Besides his anxiety on this score La Reynie was disturbed by some other things he had learned about la Voisin. Ever since Lesage had declared that he had heard la Voisin boasting she was on the brink of earning 100,000 écus, La Reynie had pondered anxiously what sort of feat could ever have netted the divineress the vast payment. When pressed to offer an explanation, Lesage had answered vaguely that he believed the sum was in some way connected with visits la Voisin had made to Saint-Germain about five years earlier. He alleged that she had gone there to deliver powders but, to the end of her life, la Voisin insisted she had never been to Saint-Germain on such a mission. However, after la Voisin had been executed, La Reynie became convinced she had been lying, for some women who had shared a cell with her testified that she had evinced a terrible dread of being questioned more closely about her visits to Saint-Germain.[39]

La Reynie noted that la Voisin had not denied telling people she had golden prospects and that she would soon be in possession of 100,000 écus. When La Reynie had questioned her as to the source, she answered that she had hoped Blessis's projects would bring her huge profits or, alternatively, that another of her associates, Latour, would show her how to stabilise the 'spirit of mercury', which would unlock the secret of the Philosopher's Stone. During her final interrogation she had declared that the 100,000 écus had been an insubstantial vision, 'a thing up in the air', but La Reynie remained convinced there had been more to it than that.[40]

If La Reynie had hoped that Marie Montvoisin would cast light on these matters, his initial interviews with her proved disappointing. At the end of March 1680 Marie was questioned about her mother's activities and she replied that though she had realised that odd things took place in her home, she had not witnessed them. 'Being young, she was always made to retire' when her mother saw clients, although the smell of sulphur and incense, which often emanated from la Voisin's cabinet, had left Marie in no doubt that bizarre rituals were being performed within. She recalled that on one occasion Lesage and her mother had despatched her to buy a live white pigeon. When she had brought it back, they had cut its throat and collected its blood in a goblet. However, they had then sent her away, so she did not know what they had done with it.

Marie was then asked what she knew about the petition her mother had tried to present to the King just before her arrest. Marie said the petition had been drawn up by one of Blessis's friends named Romani and it had been he who had been adamant that la Voisin must hand it

to the King in person. Marie remembered that Romani had commented, 'Provided that the King opened the petition himself it would be
enough.'

Marie added that she had heard Romani talk of another scheme. His
brother was a priest and he acted as confessor to Mme de Montespan's
former personal maid, Mlle des Oeillets. Romani had wanted to meet
Mlle des Oeillets and had announced he would gain access to her by
pretending to be a silk merchant with wares to sell. Having secured an
introduction in this way, he was confident she would prove a valuable
contact.[41] While there was nothing inherently sinister in this, La
Reynie was interested by the possibility that Mlle des Oeillets – who
Lesage had claimed was a client of la Voisin's – had been associated
with another member of la Voisin's circle.

More than three months elapsed before Marie Montvoisin was interviewed again but when she was next questioned on 5 July 1680,[42] she
began to hint that there had been some deeper purpose behind la
Voisin's attempts to present the King with a petition. She said la
Voisin's colleague and fellow divineress, Catherine Trianon, had
known of la Voisin's plans and had been fearful of the consequences.
On being informed by Marie that la Voisin had been arrested, la
Trianon had not appeared surprised. Instead, she had merely commented that she had predicted la Voisin's visit to Saint-Germain would
bring misfortune on her and that she had been engaged in a dangerous
business.

Marie also revealed that though her mother had failed to present her
petition during her abortive visit to Saint-Germain, she had intended
to try again. When la Voisin's husband had asked her why she was so
obsessed about handing over the petition, she had answered excitably
that she must achieve her objective or perish in the attempt. 'What,
perish?' the startled Montvoisin had exclaimed. 'It's a bit much for a
piece of paper.'

During this interrogation Marie was asked if she had ever met the
priest Étienne Guibourg. Later she would declare that she had watched
Guibourg perform the most atrocious acts imaginable but for the
moment she maintained that she barely knew him. She said she had
glimpsed Guibourg on two or three occasions at her mother's house
but had never really become acquainted with him.

Marie seemed taken aback by another question that was put to her
in the course of the interview. She was asked whether she had been
aware if the petition that had so exercised her mother had been treated
in some unspecified fashion. From this Marie deduced there were

suspicions that the document had been impregnated with poison. Startled, she blurted out that she did not think one could do something like that to a piece of paper and that, if the petition had really posed a danger, she would not have failed to warn the authorities.

Once back in her cell, Marie reflected on all this at her leisure. Having pondered her situation for a week, on 12 July she called La Reynie and Bezons to her, saying that she had important things to tell them.[43]

Marie proceeded to make a series of horrifying allegations.[44] She began by stating she had only just learned her mother had been executed and that this had spurred her into making a declaration. Hitherto she had been afraid that if she revealed all she knew, she would harm her mother, but now there was no point in trying to protect her. Marie then confirmed that the petition which was to have been presented to the King had been poisoned. The intention was to kill the King and the plot had been formulated with the connivance of la Trianon.

She went on to say that la Voisin had conceived another wicked plan with Romani, the friend of Blessis whom Marie had already mentioned. She had a good reason to hold a grudge against this man. In the months prior to her arrest, la Voisin had tried to persuade him to marry her daughter but, having discovered that Marie had already given birth to another man's child, Romani had shown little interest in the idea. Marie was now able to take a spectacular revenge for the manner he had spurned her.

She explained that Romani had intended to pose as a silk merchant while pretending that a friend of his named Bertrand was his servant. Thus disguised, he had hoped to approach the King's mistress, Mlle de Fontanges. Once admitted to her presence, he was going to offer her a piece of gorgeous cloth, which had previously been treated with poison and which would kill her if she wore it. In case Mlle de Fontanges showed no interest in purchasing the cloth, Romani was also going to bring with him a pair of exquisite gloves, which she would be unable to resist. They, too, were to have been coated with poison and, like the cloth, would prove fatal to their wearer.

It was envisaged that by the time the poison took its effect on Mlle de Fontanges, the King would already be dead, having succumbed to the fumes emanating from la Voisin's petition. Marie said she had heard her mother and Romani say that when Mlle de Fontanges died it would be assumed that grief had killed her. What was more, Romani had hoped to despatch another victim using similar methods. According to Marie, he was intending to murder the Marquis de Termes, Blessis's captor, by making him a gift of a poisoned dressing gown.

It was now incumbent on Marie to put forward a reason why her mother should have become involved in this assassination plot. She suggested that money was behind it, for she knew her mother was expecting a payment of 100,000 écus. She had also heard la Voisin talk of escaping to England, the implication being that after she had killed the King, France would no longer be safe for her. What was more, Marie had an idea as to the identity of the person who had commissioned her mother to carry out this deed. She recalled that la Trianon had once asked la Voisin how she could be sure they would be well rewarded for their efforts, to which la Voisin had answered she was confident Mme de Montespan would not betray them.

Marie turned out to have a great deal more to say on the subject of Mme de Montespan. She now saw fit to reveal that Mme de Montespan had been a client of her mother's for five or six years. Her mother and others had performed spells designed to strengthen the King's love for her, and on numerous occasions la Voisin had also delivered love powders to Mme de Montespan at Saint-Germain and Clagny. Sometimes la Voisin had taken priests with her and Étienne Guibourg had been one of those who had regularly accompanied her. However, it had recently become apparent that all these measures had proved ineffective. Realising that the King's love for her was inexorably declining, Mme de Montespan had determined to punish him for his rejection of her.

Marie concluded with some new information about another person whose name had already featured in the inquiry. She declared that not only had Mlle des Oeillets known all about her employer's dealings with la Voisin, but the maid herself had regularly come to la Voisin for consultations. She had tried to preserve her anonymity by asking la Voisin never to address her by name but one day Marie had discovered who the mystery client was when la Voisin had thoughtlessly called out to Mlle des Oeillets as she was leaving.

It all added up to an extraordinary story and if even only part of it was true the implications were terrifying. In a bid to assess the truth of it La Reynie next interrogated Romani, who had been arrested in consequence of Marie's claims that he had planned to poison Mlle de Fontanges. Romani struck La Reynie as a person ideally fitted to lead an audacious secret conspiracy. He was a highly personable man of thirty-five who had 'had all sorts of professions', though at the time of his arrest this former soldier, servant and postal clerk was unemployed. He had a natural wit and frank air that was very appealing but, according to Marie Montvoisin, he was also such a master of disguise that he had sometimes been quite unrecognisable when he visited her mother. La Reynie found this easy to believe, for even though Romani's answers under interrogation do not convey an impression of enormous cunning, the Police Chief summed him up as 'the most crafty and subtle man one could possibly imagine'.[45]

La Reynie's apprehension became still more acute when Romani corroborated some aspects of Marie's story. He agreed that he had encouraged la Voisin to present her petition in person, for he had thought this the best way of securing the release of his friend Blessis. He also confirmed that he had hoped to devise a way of selling gloves or rich materials to Mlle de Fontanges, although he insisted he had simply desired to make some money and that his intentions had been in no way malign. When asked how he intended to finance the enterprise, or from where he would obtain his wares, he became vague, saying he had not thought as far ahead as that. La Reynie was no less disturbed when Romani acknowledged that he had been introduced to Mlle des Oeillets by his brother. Though he claimed to have spoken to her no more than two or three times, he said he had thought she might use her influence to procure him a job in a noblewoman's household.[46]

On 26 July Marie Montvoisin was questioned again. The written record of the interview is missing but it may have been now that she put forward a slight refinement of her earlier tale. Certainly, about this time she explained how it had been agreed that if la Voisin did not manage to present her petition to the King la Trianon would murder him instead. She had planned to do this by going to court and throwing herself before him as he passed. Then, while she clasped his knees in seeming supplication, she would deftly slip some poisonous powder into his pocket. The next time the King used his handkerchief he would die.

As the Controller-General of Finance, Colbert, later pointed out, carrying out this plan would have been 'an absolutely impossible thing'.[47] It was preposterous to think that la Trianon would have been permitted to accost the King in this fashion, let alone that she could then have accomplished the feat of filling his pocket with poison unobserved. Nevertheless, despite its obvious flaws, Marie's story was taken seriously.

On 13 August Marie went through her story one more time and provided a few more embellishments.[48] She stated that whenever Mme de Montespan had feared the King's love for her was wavering she had contacted la Voisin. The latter would then arrange for masses to be said so that the King's desire would reawaken and la Voisin would also provide Mme de Montespan with love powders she could give to Louis. Some of these powders had been made stronger by being passed under Guibourg's chalice while he was saying mass. Mme de Montespan's maid, Mlle des Oeillets, would sometimes come to collect these powders for her mistress. Marie had seen her do this on numerous occasions and she was confident that if Mlle des Oeillets were brought before her she would recognise her. On the other hand, she had never laid eyes on Mme de Montespan.

Marie then sorrowfully related how Mme de Montespan's fury had mounted as, despite la Voisin's best efforts, the King's love for her had steadily receded. Athénaïs had therefore decided to adopt more extreme measures, which la Voisin had viewed with repugnance, but with which she reluctantly collaborated. La Trianon was also in on the murder plot, though she had not been directly employed by Mme de Montespan. Instead, she had been retained by another mystery individual, whom she had referred to as 'Monsieur le Marquis'.

On 17 August some attempt was made to verify Marie's claims when a confrontation was arranged between her and la Trianon. Clearly aghast at being accused of such things, la Trianon frantically denied that she had been trying to kill the King, but Marie was merely spurred on by these rebuttals. Quite undaunted, on 20 August she made a new statement[49] saying that, since la Trianon would not tell the truth, she had no alternative but to disclose fresh facts.

Marie's new revelations were shocking in the extreme. She declared that Guibourg had carried out black masses on the stomachs of naked women at her mother's house and that Mme de Montespan had been one of those who had permitted her body to be thus defiled. Marie then went into abundant detail about what took place during these ceremonies, recalling how each lady had lain stretched out on a mattress, supported by two chairs placed fairly close together. The head protruded backwards over one side, but was cushioned by a pillow placed on another slightly lower chair, while at the other end the legs were left dangling. Guibourg would then place the cross and the chalice on the naked woman's stomach.

Marie said that to the best of her knowledge the first time such a mass had taken place at her mother's had been six years ago. At that time la Voisin had considered Marie too young to watch the proceedings, but Marie had been permitted to help with the preparations by arranging the mattress on the chairs and lighting candles. Once Marie was a bit older, her mother had allowed her to be present when black masses were celebrated.

It was Marie's recollection that Mme de Montespan had first had a black mass celebrated on her about three years earlier. Once the ceremony was over, la Voisin had told Mme de Montespan that if she wanted her wishes to be hearkened to, it was necessary to repeat the procedure on two separate occasions. At this the lady had protested that she really could not find the time, whereupon la Voisin had offered to spare her the inconvenience by acting as her proxy at the two remaining masses. The lady had assented to this proposal and Marie had been present when Guibourg had once again performed his ungodly ritual, with la Voisin in Mme de Montespan's place.

Marie's testimony is so ambivalent that it is unclear whether or not she wished it to be thought she had been present when Mme de Montespan had had mass celebrated on her. Certainly, however, she now contradicted her earlier assertion that she had never met Mme de Montespan. She said that her mother had first begun delivering powders to Mme de Montespan about two and a half years ago and that since then she had several times used Marie as a courier. One day when Mme de Montespan had been visiting la Voisin the latter had brought Marie before her and asked if Mme de Montespan would be able to recognise her. It was then arranged that in a few days' time Mme de Montespan was to go to a Paris church, where Marie would be waiting outside. When Marie saw the lady she was to signal her readiness by pretending to spit; then, as the two women walked past each other, she would slip Mme de Montespan a packet of powder. This worked so well that Marie was subsequently employed again on similar errands. On one occasion she was instructed to wait on the road between Ville Avray and Clagny, and when Mme de Montespan drove by she briefly halted the coach so that Marie could hand her more powders.

La Voisin had been planning to make further use of Marie. Shortly before her arrest she had told her daughter that she intended to send her to Clagny to ask Mme de Montespan for a down payment of 2000 écus. This sum could be used by Romani to purchase the rich cloth and gloves that would be used to kill Mlle de Fontanges.

As Marie's tale had unfolded, the King had been kept fully informed, but we do not know what he thought of it. Louis had spent the summer of 1680 touring northern France and the border regions of Flanders. Mme de Montespan had followed with the rest of the court but it is clear that throughout the voyage she saw very little of him. This was interpreted merely as being a sign of her continuing decline, but the King's aloofness was doubtless also attributable to the reports concerning her that were being sent from Paris.

Louis now had to contemplate the possibility that the woman with whom he had had the most prolonged and passionate love affair of his life, and who had borne him seven children, had sustained their relationship by participating in repellent practices, and recourse to witchcraft and drugs. When these methods had failed her, she had allegedly turned to poison to satisfy her twisted desires.

It is not clear whether the King believed any of this, but one thing is noteworthy. When he had been told in January 1680 that Mlle des Oeillets had been accused of dealings with la Voisin he had protested that this must be a monstrous slur, for it was unthinkable that she could be involved in anything disreputable. Now that Mme de Montespan had come under suspicion the King, so far as we know, did not raise similar objections.

Following Marie Montvoisin's disclosures on 12 July, La Reynie had at once written to Louvois to tell him what she had said. On 21 July Louvois wrote back from Calais saying he had informed the King of all this. Without mentioning Mme de Montespan, Louvois stated that the King desired La Reynie to do everything he could to establish the truth about the petition to which so many prisoners had alluded.[50]

On 2 August the King followed this up with a letter of his own. He did not suggest that the accusations against Mme de Montespan were unfounded, though he was anxious to prevent the news that she had been implicated from seeping out. Having instructed La Reynie that any depositions relating to her must be taken down on separate sheets of paper, which should for the moment be withheld from the other commissioners, he stressed that he wanted La Reynie to pursue the inquiry with all diligence.[51]

Meanwhile, Marie's revelations had left La Reynie in a state of acute anxiety. As yet, he was not convinced she had been telling the truth. In a memorandum he drew up on 2 September he noted that without being quite sure why, he thought there was more reason 'to presume these horrible things to be false' than to believe them. A little later he likewise observed that Marie's claims about the poisoned petition were 'extremely doubtful'[52] but, even so, he was disinclined to dismiss everything she had said.

One reason for this was that La Reynie had found Marie a convincing witness, who had about her 'a certain air of ingenuousness'. She had shown particular conviction when she had given her deposition of 20 August and she had been so persuasive that La Reynie thought it unlikely it had all been lies. He considered it significant that prior to her execution la Voisin had reportedly told her cell mates that she feared being questioned about her visits to Saint-Germain, nor could he forget that Romani had acknowledged that he hoped to peddle merchandise to Mlle de Fontanges. The result was that even though La Reynie did not delude himself that he had uncovered the whole truth, he felt sure that 'somehow or other there is certainly something in all this which is not right'.[53]

He also believed that the role played by Mlle des Oeillets needed to be examined carefully. He considered it suspicious that to the end of her life la Voisin had denied being acquainted with Mlle des Oeillets, for it had been established to his own satisfaction that they had, in fact, known each other. Quite why he was so positive on this point is strange, for his belief rested on the unproven statements of Lesage and Marie Montvoisin. However, since he was sure of this, he commented that if Mlle des Oeillets now tried to maintain that la Voisin had been a stranger to her, this could only augment suspicions that she had something to hide.[54]

As the lines of enquiry converged upon Mme de Montespan, La Reynie decided that his best chance of disentangling fact from fiction lay in pursuing the case against Françoise Filastre. Throughout September confrontations were therefore organised between la Filastre and the other prisoners who had given evidence against her. At some of these, further efforts were made to establish the truth about la Filastre's dealings with the Duchesse de Vivonne. La Filastre herself still maintained she had visited the Duchesse at home and had copied out a pact that Mme de Vivonne had written out earlier. When the priest Cotton was brought in for a confrontation, he agreed that la Filastre had shown him this document, but his recollection of its contents differed from that which he had previously put forward. He now said the pact had requested the restoration to power of the disgraced Minister, M. Fouquet, and the death of M. Colbert.[55] This was particularly surprising in view of the fact that Mme de Vivonne was not known to be at all antagonistic towards Colbert. On the contrary, indeed, a marriage had only recently taken place between her eldest son and M. Colbert's daughter.

On 25 September a confrontation took place between la Filastre and Lesage. At this Lesage repeated his claim that la Filastre had coerced Mme de Vivonne into offering her aborted infant as a sacrifice to the devil. La Filastre categorically denied this and she was equally dismissive of Lesage's claim that the Duchesses d'Angoulême and de Vitry had been co-signatories of a satanic pact drawn up by Mme de Vivonne, insisting she had never heard of either lady.[56]

However, it was la Filastre's links with Mme de Montespan that were most deeply probed during these encounters. Some of the confrontations ended in stalemate and took the inquiry little further. For example, when brought face to face with Galet on 6 September la Filastre denied telling him that she was buying powders for Mme de Montespan, but he stuck to his former story. However, a confrontation between la Filastre and Guibourg, which took place four days later, proved more productive: at this Guibourg was positively eager to acknowledge that he had worked on behalf of Mme de Montespan. He launched into a rambling narrative, relating how, some years earlier, a man had brought him powders and asked him to re-establish Mme de Montespan in the King's favour by passing these under the chalice. Shortly afterwards the same person, acting on the instructions of a widowed man of rank who lived near Notre-Dame with his two children, had taken Guibourg to a hovel in Saint-Denis. There Guibourg had sought to enlist the devil's support for Mme de Montespan by performing a black mass on the stomach of an unknown woman.[57]

These new disclosures prompted la Filastre to enlarge on her earlier statements. She now alleged that Guibourg had told her the woman on whom he had performed the black mass had been Mme de Montespan herself, who had been brought to Saint-Denis in disguise. As yet, however, Guibourg could not bring himself to admit this and he declared it to be false.[58]

Even without la Filastre's contribution, Guibourg's story was full of oddities. It was strange, for example, that he had discovered so much about the personal circumstances of the man who had recruited him to aid Mme de Montespan without ever managing to learn his name. But rather than focus on such anomalies, La Reynie was more concerned by the affinities between Guibourg's statement and Marie Montvoisin's testimony.

By early September the King had returned from his travels and on 10 September Louvois ordered La Reynie to report to the monarch at Versailles in two days' time. There is no record of what was said at this meeting. However, it is clear that the King shared La Reynie's concern about recent developments. For the rest of the month the King was kept informed about everything that happened at the confrontations held between la Filastre and other prisoners. On 25 September Louvois wrote a letter to M. Robert, Attorney-General of the *Chambre Ardente*. Although there is no mention of Mme de Montespan, it gives some indication of what the King was thinking and shows that, far from being dismissive of the latest allegations, he was on the brink of sanctioning further arrests of highly placed people.

Louvois wrote that having read La Reynie's reports, 'His Majesty has seen with displeasure...that it appears that Mme de Vivonne has had a criminal commerce with la Filastre and other prisoners at Vincennes.' As this had not yet been fully proven, though, the King had decided to defer taking the controversial step of arresting Mme de Vivonne. Instead, he thought it safer first to bring la Filastre to trial, believing that once he had had a chance to study what she said under torture he would be better placed to make up his mind about how to proceed.[59]

On 30 September the trials took place of la Filastre and Jacques Joseph Cotton, the priest who had performed conjurations for her and officiated at black masses. When questioned on the *sellette*, la Filastre had little new to say. On being asked why she had wanted to secure a job with Mlle de Fontanges, she said she had acted out of a simple desire to advance her family. When taxed with Galet's claim that she had said she was buying powders for Mme de Montespan, she said the very reverse was true, for it was Galet who had boasted to her that Mme de Montespan had obtained powders from him for the King's consumption. La Filastre still maintained that Guibourg had told her he had said a black mass in a cellar on Mme de Montespan's behalf, although she did not repeat her earlier claim that Mme de Montespan herself had participated. The judges found her guilty of sacrilege and selling poison, and decreed that she should be burnt alive after torture. Cotton was given the same sentence after being convicted of 'treason against the divine order, sacrilege, profanations, impieties and conjurations'.[60]

The next day the wretched pair were tortured. The King's expectation that this would yield more precise information about Mme de Vivonne did not prove justified. La Filastre repeated that she had drawn up a pact for her, but Cotton's evidence on the subject was very vague. He agreed that la Filastre had shown him a pact, which she said was for the Duchesse de Vivonne, but though the Duchesse's initials featured in the text, her name nowhere featured.[61]

From this point in the affair there were no further allegations against Mme de Vivonne. It cannot be ruled out that at some point she had been a client of la Filastre but if so, the nature of their transactions was never defined. Presumably, on reflection the King concluded that Mme de Vivonne had done nothing truly reprehensible, for he took no action against her. In later years he gave every appearance of being very fond of her. When she was widowed in 1688, the King ensured she was adequately provided for financially and Saint-Simon reported that he always made her welcome when she came to court and would have liked to see more of her.

It was against Mme de Montespan that la Filastre made the most devastating allegations under torture. During the initial phases of the interrogation she merely reiterated what she had said at her trial about Galet and Guibourg, but as her agony intensified more damaging confessions were wrenched from her. For as long as she could, she resisted the pressure to add to her earlier statements. One person who saw the full written record of her interrogation was struck by the manner in which 'in the midst of the torments...she cries out loudly that she is going before God, and that she does not want to burden her conscience with lies and calumny...She expresses herself in terms which are truly affecting.'[62] However, as more wedges were driven into the *brodequins*, crushing her legs unbearably, she could not sustain this resolve. Desperate to end her suffering, she gave her interrogators the information they wanted.

She began by admitting that her child had been sacrificed to the devil and then moved on to what she had done for Mme de Montespan. La Reynie would later observe that she did this without any prompting but this was disingenuous, for la Filastre knew that those questioning her were particularly interested in that subject. La Filastre now stated that when her employer Mme Chapelain had sent her to see Galet in 1676, she had ordered her to buy powders for Mme de Montespan. More recently her journey to the Auvergne had also been undertaken for Mme de Montespan, and la Filastre said that as well as buying love powders there she had been looking for poison, which was to be given to Mlle de Fontanges. It was Mme Chapelain, at the instigation of Mme de Montespan, who had instructed her to seek a position with Mlle de Fontanges, the plan being that once la Filastre was ensconced in the young woman's household it would be easy to poison her.[63]

Having been released from the *brodequins*, la Filastre was given only a brief respite before being confronted with several of the prisoners she had just incriminated. When Mme Chapelain was brought before her she said that la Filastre's allegations about her were untrue. She pleaded with her former employee to retract them, but la Filastre could not be moved.[64]

That same day la Filastre was taken from Vincennes to the Bastille, in readiness for her execution. She spent her last hours with the curé of Saint-Laurent, even though Louvois had once expressed misgivings as to his reliability as a confessor. After she had been closeted with him for some time, she sent an urgent summons to La Reynie and Bezons, stating she had something important to say. When they came to her she announced that everything she had told them about la Chapelain and Mme de Montespan had been false, and that she had only said these things 'to free herself from the affliction and pain of the torments, and out of fear of the torture being reapplied'. Although she had stood by her words at the confrontation with Mme Chapelain, this too had been motivated by 'fear and respect' for the commissioners. Now, however, she did not want to go to her death oppressed by the knowledge that she had wrongfully accused anyone. She did admit that she had once asked Galet for poison, but said she had intended to use it to kill the wife of her own lover, rather than to harm Mlle de Fontanges. She also now denied that her child had been sacrificed to the devil.[65]

Having unburdened herself in this way, la Filastre could go to her execution with one less sin on her conscience. By decree of the Chamber, she and Cotton were then taken to the Place de Grève and burnt. As the flames engulfed her, la Filastre perhaps derived some consolation from the belief that she died without having accused anyone unjustly. However, events would show that the damage she had wrought in her last hours could not be so easily rectified.

# NINE

# THE CHAMBER IS SUSPENDED

Details of la Filastre's last statements were promptly relayed to the King. He had hoped that they would enable him to resolve upon an appropriate course of action but, in fact, he found himself in an alarming quandary. If the correct procedure was followed, the written record of la Filastre's declarations under torture ought to be shown without delay to the *Chambre Ardente*'s assembled commissioners. Yet the King was sure that once this was done, it would not be long before all Paris was buzzing with reports of what la Filastre had said. As yet he had no idea whether Mme de Montespan was innocent or guilty, but for the moment he did not want anyone to learn of the suspicions that had been voiced against her. Instead, he wanted La Reynie to pursue his enquiries undisturbed, doubtless hoping that in due course these would exonerate her. However, if the public learned of the accusations against her, her reputation would be irreparably smeared, and the taint of diabolism and poison would cling to her for ever. It would also not have escaped the King that he, too, would become an object of mockery if word spread that his mistress had used aphrodisiacs and love potions to enslave him sexually.

When the King's wishes were made known to La Reynie, he was not unduly disturbed, for at first he did not think it would be too difficult to preserve secrecy while he investigated further. On 6 October he expressed the view that it would not, in fact, have mattered much if la Filastre's confessions had been read to the commissioners, for when her final retraction was taken into account, any sensible person would realise that this nullified everything she had said before. However, he conceded that there was a chance that irresponsible individuals 'would draw on these facts ... to make up stories and perhaps to sow malicious rumours', and it was obviously desirable to avoid this. For the time being, therefore, he recommended that when the transcript of la Filastre's torture was read to the commissioners, all mention of the attempt on Mlle de Fontanges's life – as well as la Filastre's subsequent retraction – should be excised.[1] It was only after he had thought rather longer about this that it dawned on him that this course was more problematical than he had realised.

As the King desired, La Reynie continued to interrogate the leading figures in the affair, but this merely caused the inquiry to descend ever further into the realms of horror. On 3 October Guibourg called to mind several other instances when he had celebrated black masses. While he was sure that none of these had taken place at la Voisin's house, he could provide no enlightenment as to the precise locations. This was because he himself had often been uncertain as to his whereabouts and on at least one occasion a stranger had conducted him blindfold in a coach to the place where the mass was held.[2]

Guibourg's efforts to convince La Reynie that he and la Voisin had seen very little of each other were undermined by the fact that Marie Montvoisin was able to conjure up the most lurid memories of things that he and her mother had done together. On 9 October she made her most sickening declaration to date.[3] She said she had been present when Guibourg had performed a black mass on Mme de Montespan and that, during this ceremony, her mother had instructed her to hand Guibourg a newly born baby. Guibourg had cut the child's throat and collected its blood in a chalice. At the appropriate point in the ceremony he elevated this vessel and the blood took the place of the sacramental wine. When the mass was over, Guibourg had torn out the butchered infant's entrails and given them to la Voisin so she could have them distilled. The blood had been poured into a phial and carried away by Mme de Montespan.

It was at this point that Marie also began to make startling new claims about Mlle des Oeillets. Unfortunately, the written record of her interrogation only summarises what she said and her exact words remain unclear. Nevertheless, the record indicates that whereas before she had merely testified that Mlle des Oeillets had frequently visited her mother and that she had delivered powders to Mme de Montespan, Marie now suggested she had done far more terrible things. She recalled that on her visits to la Voisin, Mlle des Oeillets had often been accompanied by a mysterious 'English milord' and this shadowy individual had apparently been co-ordinating a terrible conspiracy against the King. Guibourg had at one point conducted obscene ceremonies for the pair, and Marie believed that the stranger intended to transport Guibourg and la Voisin to England once his objective had been accomplished. After the arrest of her mother she herself had received a letter offering to smuggle her out of the country, but being reluctant to leave France she had declined.

The following day Guibourg was invited to comment on all this[4] and he at once acknowledged that much of it was true. He stated that over the years he had performed four black masses on the same naked woman and that on each occasion a child had been sacrificed. The first of these masses had been arranged by a M. Leroy and had taken place in Menil. As he had performed the evil rite, he had uttered a supplication to 'Astaroth and Amodeus' on behalf of the lady who lay exposed before him. Speaking for her, he had begged these demonic beings 'to accept the sacrifice which I offer in return for the things which I ask of you, which are: the affection of the King and Monseigneur the Dauphin; to be honoured by the princes and princesses of the court, and that nothing which I ask of the King is denied me, or my relatives and servants'.[5] Having previously purchased a child for an écu, he had then slaughtered it and drained its blood. Its heart and entrails had been used to make powders for Mme de Montespan to give to the King.

The second of the four masses had been celebrated in a hovel in Saint-Denis, where the 'same ceremonies' had been enacted. After that, however, la Voisin had provided him with more convenient facilities for, though only the week before Guibourg had been adamant that he had never performed a black mass at her house, he now remembered that this was where the third and fourth human sacrifices had, in fact, taken place.

Having initially stated that the third mass had occurred eight or nine years earlier, Guibourg suddenly changed his mind, placing it instead at some time in 1666–7. The last of the four masses had been celebrated only five years ago, once again at la Voisin's. Guibourg related that afterwards he had been just about to leave when he had caught sight of a piece of paper that had been left on a chair. Written on it were a series of requests couched in the form of a satanic pact, which had so impressed itself on Guibourg's mind that he was able to recite it verbatim. The pact ran:

> I ask that the affection of the King and Monseigneur the Dauphin be continued towards me; that the Queen be sterile, that the King leave her bed and table for me; that I obtain from him all that I will ask of him for myself and my family; that my manservants and maids are agreeable to [the King]; [that I be] well treated and respected by the high nobility; that I can be called to the King's councils and know what happens there; and that this affection redoubling…the King abandon and not consider la Vallière and that, the Queen being repudiated, I can marry the King.

Naturally Guibourg was asked to identify the woman on whose body these hideous acts had been perpetrated, but though he had encountered her four times in such unforgettable circumstances his answer was strangely hesitant. He explained that on each occasion the lady had kept her face hidden behind a veil, so he had no idea what she looked like. However, he had been led to believe that she was Mme de Montespan.

Guibourg also confirmed that it was at la Voisin's that he had ministered to the depraved requirements of Mlle des Oeillets and the titled Englishman, and he recalled an instance when he had performed a particularly distasteful spell for them. After Mlle des Oeillets had provided Guibourg with a sample of her menstrual blood, the Englishman masturbated into a chalice, then bats' blood and flour were added to the semen collected there. Once Guibourg had uttered an incantation on this mixture, Mlle des Oeillets and her male companion took it away.

At some point La Reynie was given more details about this incident, although it is not clear whether Guibourg or Marie Montvoisin provided the information. At any rate, La Reynie somehow learned that the object of the exercise had been to kill the King. Mlle des Oeillets had manifested great bitterness towards him, at one point growing so angry during her consultation with Guibourg that the Englishman had had some difficulty calming her. It was the prospect of revenge that had finally quietened her, for Guibourg's revolting confection (La Reynie later received the impression that the blood of a murdered child had been mixed in with the other ingredients) was thought to have fatal properties. Mlle des Oeillets intended to smear it on the King's clothes, or even to strew it in his path, and she and the English milord were confident that Louis would die shortly afterwards.[6]

Guibourg's story contained some obvious discrepancies. He claimed that around 1666–7 he had been instructed to utter a conjuration imploring that his client should gain the affection of the Dauphin, but at that time the heir to the throne was a child of five or six, whose personal inclinations were not of much significance. Conversely, Guibourg suggested that the last time he had performed a mass for the lady he had caught sight of a written pact requesting that the King should cast off Louise de La Vallière. However, this was supposedly in 1675, by which time Louise was already in her convent. It was odd, too, that the pact betrayed such an urgent desire that the King should find the lady's servants congenial. The King had, in fact, already impregnated Mlle des Oeillets, so one would have thought Mme de Montespan had little cause to worry that her female staff were displeasing to him. Quite apart from this, it seems odd that this was an issue of such importance to her that she was ready to sell her soul for it.

M. de La Reynie took a different view. The fact that Guibourg had been able to recite the text of the pact with such fluency convinced the Police Chief that the priest had really seen the document. To La Reynie the pact had seemed full of detailed information and he questioned whether an outsider from the court like Guibourg could have picked up such 'things of consequence' about Mme de Montespan. It is difficult to understand why La Reynie thought this, for the pact hardly indicated a highly specialised and accurate knowledge of court gossip. Indeed, the fact that it made no mention of matters that would logically have featured among Mme de Montespan's most pressing concerns, such as her troublesome husband or the future of her children by the King, was decidedly curious. La Reynie, however, thought it 'morally impossible' that Guibourg could have made all this up[7] for, as a man who himself was endowed with only a limited imagination, he was apt to underestimate the powers of invention possessed by others.

Other concerns were now troubling La Reynie. Whereas in his memorandum of 6 October he had suggested to the King that, before she died, la Filastre had withdrawn all the allegations she had made against Mme de Montespan, he now realised this was not strictly accurate. For a start he questioned whether la Filastre's final retraction should be regarded as legitimate. He believed that confessors tended to encourage condemned prisoners to issue such disclaimers, and for this and other reasons 'there are many judges who take no regard whatever of this kind of contrary declaration'.[8] However, even if her retraction was allowable, it had to be borne in mind that it had not been absolute. La Filastre had never repudiated her claim that Guibourg had told her he had carried out a black mass on behalf of Mme de Montespan and her allegation that Galet had bragged of supplying powders to Mme de Montespan likewise remained extant. It could, of course, be argued that neither of these points was very significant. If Galet and Guibourg *had* made these remarks, there was a good chance they had simply been trying to impress la Filastre with idle boasts. Furthermore, in theory hearsay evidence was not legally admissible, though La Reynie does not seem to have recognised the force of this objection. As far as he was concerned, when Guibourg's and Galet's statements during their confrontations with la Filastre were taken into account, this amounted in judicial terms to 'absolute proof' that la Filastre's testimony on these points had been correct.[9]

It had taken a little time for the full implications of the course of action he had earlier recommended to the King to become apparent to La Reynie. He had suggested that the written record of la Filastre's examination under torture could be amended, so that the judges were not shown the passages relating to the supposed conspiracy to poison Mlle de Fontanges. Now, however, La Reynie had grasped that if this was done, his ability to bring the cases of other prisoners awaiting trial to a successful conclusion would be gravely compromised.

Unless la Filastre's final confessions were shown in their entirety to the commissioners, none of the evidence that had emerged during the investigation into her crimes could be used to prosecute other defendants. Juridical practice laid down that if this evidence was to feature in other trials, it must be relayed in full to the judges, rather than being presented to them selectively. This meant nothing that la Filastre had said could be used to secure the convictions of individuals such as Guibourg, Galet or Mme Chapelain. Furthermore, this did not represent the full extent of the problem. It was unlawful to bring a defendant to trial if any part of the evidence relating to the case had been withheld from the court. Since this would apply to every prisoner whom la Filastre had mentioned at any point in her testimony, the consequences would be considerable.

Nor was this all. It had gradually dawned on La Reynie that if the King considered it desirable to suppress la Filastre's final testimony he might also be reluctant to proceed with the trial of any other prisoner who was likely to produce embarrassing statements against Mme de Montespan. If so, even if the other legal difficulties were overcome, there were many wicked individuals who would not be brought to judgement.

Profoundly disturbed by such a possibility, on 11 October La Reynie prepared another memorandum for Louvois outlining his difficulties.[10] Lamenting the 'impenetrable darkness' that surrounded him, he admitted there was no obvious solution to his predicament, for there were indisputable drawbacks to permitting such sensitive material to enter the public domain. On the other hand he passionately believed it would be wrong to prevent 'so many evils' from coming to light.

Since the dilemma was so intractable, La Reynie considered it best to delay making a decision. He advocated that for the moment, no measures should be taken that might prejudice the outcome of the inquiry. This would give him some breathing space during which he would seek to establish whether the suspicions against Mme de Montespan could be substantiated.

La Reynie's advice was followed. He was authorised to pursue his investigation and in the meantime the *Chambre Ardente* was suspended. This was envisaged as a purely temporary measure, for it was agreed that its sessions would resume as soon as La Reynie had brought some

clarity to the situation. However, this proved much harder than anticipated. In the event the commission did not sit again until 11 May 1681,
a gap of more than seven months in its proceedings.

Doggedly La Reynie applied himself to the task that had been set him.
On 23 October a confrontation was arranged between Marie
Montvoisin and Guibourg.[11] Though they differed on some minor
details, in essentials their testimony accorded. Both described how a
baby had been eviscerated during a black mass at la Voisin's and
Guibourg spoke too of the bizarre proceedings he had undertaken for
Mlle des Oeillets. But although their accounts were graphic in their
details, they did not provide La Reynie with fresh insights. To achieve
a breakthrough, he concluded, it would be necessary to approach the
subject from a different angle.

La Reynie believed he could do this by reopening an inquiry that
had been closed years before. It will be recalled that in 1668 Lesage and
a priest called Mariette had been tried for having committed impieties.
At his trial Mariette had named Mme de Montespan as one of their
clients and this had been noted in the court record without further
comment. Lesage had been sent to the galleys, but Mariette had been
treated more leniently. He had merely been sent to Saint-Lazare, a dis-
ciplinary establishment for delinquent priests. After a short time he had
absconded and, with the aid of la Voisin, had escaped to the provinces.
However, following la Voisin's arrest in 1679, determined efforts had
been made to locate him and in February 1680 he had been arrested in
Toulouse. La Reynie now determined to find out more about what
Mariette and Lesage had done for Mme de Montespan all those years
before, hoping this would provide some enlightenment as to whether
Athénaïs was capable of the sort of acts described by Marie Montvoisin
and Guibourg.

Between 5 and 8 November La Reynie separately questioned
Mariette and Lesage.[12] It proved a fruitful exercise: Lesage appeared
eager to revisit those distant events and Mariette at least partially corroborated his account. Both men agreed that by 1667 Mme de
Montespan had become a client of la Voisin's. At first Mme Voisin had
arranged for Mariette to say conjurations for Athénaïs on his own, but
then Lesage had been enlisted to act as his assistant. Soon afterwards,
the pair had deserted la Voisin to set up business independently, taking
with them Mme de Montespan's custom. In early 1668 they had performed ceremonies for her in the apartment of her sister, Mme de
Thianges, at Saint-Germain. These had consisted of Mariette intoning
the gospels over her while Lesage burnt incense and Mme de

Montespan read out a specially formulated incantation. In this Mme de Montespan had expressed her desire to secure the King's good graces and Lesage testified that she had also sought the death of Louise de La Vallière. Mariette demurred at this, saying that Mme de Montespan had merely wished her rival to be sent away from court.

The two men concurred that Mme de Montespan had subsequently been present when Mariette had performed a mass on her behalf in a chapel at Saint-Séverin. As instructed, she had previously supplied the priest with two pigeons' hearts, which he passed under the chalice during the service. Lesage claimed that a consecrated wafer had also featured in the ritual, but Mariette would not admit to having committed this much more serious act of sacrilege. They both agreed that two or three similar ceremonies had later been enacted in the same place. Lesage said that at one of these Mariette had performed a spell using dead men's bones, the object being to bring about the death of Louise de La Vallière. Mariette denied this, reiterating that Mme de Montespan had never tried to harm Louise.

In La Reynie's eyes, this constituted a powerful proof against Mme de Montespan. He considered that these latest disclosures tended to validate the other allegations against her which, for the sake of discretion, were now always referred to as 'the particular facts'. Noting that it seemed extremely likely that Mme de Montespan had had several encounters with Mariette and Lesage, he argued that this in itself could be regarded as 'one of the strongest conjectures and greatest presumptions of the truth ... of the other particular facts'.[13]

It is reasonable to query this conclusion. For a start, caution is in order as to whether Mariette and Lesage were being truthful. The apparent conformity in their accounts is somewhat deceptive, for Mariette's statement was far from independent. Instead, he was told what Lesage had said and then, 'forced to declare it by the thing itself', he gave his own version.[14] On the other hand the fact that he contradicted Lesage on a number of key points does indicate that he was not merely endorsing things he knew to be untrue.

La Reynie considered it significant that Mariette seemed to know a great deal about the steps taken by Mme de Montespan to secure her father the Governorship of Paris. Mariette described how anxious she had become when it appeared that the King was going to award the place to another candidate and her delight when the appointment was finally made. La Reynie noted that she had evidently kept nothing back from Mariette about this, confiding to him all her hopes and fears.[15] Yet La Reynie should have spotted that there was something wrong here, for the Duc de Mortemart was not appointed Governor of

Paris till January 1669, nine months after Mariette's arrest. It was therefore impossible for Mariette to have witnessed Athénaïs's joy at her father's triumph.

Despite this discrepancy one cannot rule out the possibility that in 1667–8 Mme de Montespan was availing herself of the services offered by la Voisin, Lesage and Mariette. Even if one discounts Lesage's more serious allegations and instead relies solely on Mariette's testimony, this would mean that Athénaïs had participated in ceremonies verging on the sacrilegious and which probably contravened the law. Her actions would not have been so very different from those allegedly committed by the Vicomtesse de Polignac, and when those had come to light orders had at once been given for Mme de Polignac's arrest. Nevertheless, to deduce from this that Athénaïs subsequently progressed to much worse crimes was surely tendentious.

La Reynie seemed to think that, having acquired a taste for dubious practices, Mme de Montespan would not have been able to renounce them, and that once Mariette and Lesage were no longer active in Paris she had reverted to being a client of Guibourg and la Voisin. There was, however, a good reason why this was unlikely. By the summer of 1668 Mme de Montespan's freedom of movement had become greatly circumscribed, for fears that her husband might abduct her had led the King to provide her with an armed guard who usually accompanied her when she rode in her coach. Although it does seem there were occasions when she travelled more discreetly,[16] she was not truly independent during these years. The idea that she could have visited la Voisin regularly without anyone having the least notion of her whereabouts verges on the absurd.

In one respect, at least, the evidence of Mariette and Lesage can be used in defence of Mme de Montespan. They both agreed that in the ceremonies performed in 1668, pigeons' hearts had figured prominently. Yet Guibourg had testified that prior to this she had participated in black masses where babies had been slaughtered. If she had already offered live human sacrifices to the devil, it would surely have been eccentric of her to think that on subsequent occasions he could be propitiated by an oblation comprised of the vital organs of small birds.

Having once again secured La Reynie's attention, Lesage did not confine himself to the subject of Mme de Montespan. He now offered an astonishing explanation as to why la Voisin had believed herself to be on the verge of acquiring 100,000 écus. It turned out, amazingly, that Mlle des Oeillets had promised to pay her this huge sum if la Voisin aided her to kill the King. Initially it had been hoped that this could be effected by magical means and some years before, Lesage had been brought in to perform spells which supposedly would send the King into a fatal decline. However, when this had had no effect, la Voisin had turned to two other male associates, Vautier and Latour, in the belief that they would achieve the desired results. This pair of ruffians had prepared deadly powders, which were handed over to Mlle des Oeillets. She had then devised an ingenious way of administering these to the King without being directly involved. When Mme de Montespan purchased love powders from la Voisin, it was Mlle des Oeillets who usually collected them for her. The next time Mlle des Oeillets was asked to do this, she substituted the aphrodisiacs with poison and gave it to Mme de Montespan. Mlle des Oeillets then waited for Mme de Montespan to give this to the King and thus unintentionally kill him.[17]

If Lesage could be believed, Mme de Montespan was not herself an assassin, but rather the unwitting dupe of her employee Mlle des Oeillets. To La Reynie this story seemed eminently plausible. He mused that there was at least one historical precedent, for Charles II of Navarre had poisoned his brother-in-law using a similar stratagem.[18] It also tallied with the Delphic warnings issued as far back as 1677 by Magdelaine de La Grange, who had intimated that the King was in danger of being poisoned by powders.

La Reynie was sure that the mysterious 'foreigner mixed up in all this' with Mlle des Oeillets was the key to the conspiracy,[19] for the assumption was that it was he who had provided her with the lavish funding that had enabled her to promise la Voisin such generous payment. It was true that La Reynie had not a clue as to this man's identity, still less did he have any idea about where his money came from or what his motive was for seeking to murder the King. Nevertheless, La Reynie saw no reason to doubt his existence on that account.

The story about the obscene ceremonies devised by Guibourg using semen and menstrual blood also appeared horribly convincing to La Reynie. He noted that when Guibourg and Marie Montvoisin had described this incident, 'they accorded with each other on circumstances which were so specific and so horrible that it is difficult to conceive that two people could have imagined and fabricated things so exactly alike without each other knowing'.[20]

It was obviously essential to find out more about all this and accordingly it was agreed that Louvois should question Mlle des Oeillets. La Reynie cautioned him that this must be done with the utmost sensitivity. He did not consider it imprudent to try to frighten her into volunteering information by hinting that prisoners in Vincennes had incriminated her. Alluding to love powders in the hope that this would evoke an unguarded response was also an acceptable risk. However, La Reynie advised Louvois that it would be dangerous to touch on subjects such as black masses and child sacrifice. Since Mlle des Oeillets remained at liberty, mentioning such things to her would fatally compromise secrecy and might alert others involved in similar activities.[21]

On 18 November Louvois interviewed Mlle des Oeillets. He was very impressed by the way she conducted herself, for she displayed 'inconceivable steadfastness' when questioned. She did not deny all knowledge of la Voisin, but was adamant that she had only ever visited her on a single occasion. That had been more than ten years earlier when she had gone to la Voisin's house accompanied by several female friends who had thought it would be fun to consult the celebrated fortune-teller. When Louvois informed her that several prisoners in Vincennes knew things to her discredit, she declared robustly that that was quite impossible. She added that, if brought before her, they would not even recognise her.[22]

Louvois passed all this on to La Reynie, who grudgingly admitted that Mlle des Oeillets's confident demeanour could be interpreted as 'a very favourable presumption' of her innocence. However, he did not fail to add that perhaps she was only calm because, knowing that la Voisin had died without incriminating her, she believed herself untouchable.[23]

Since Mlle des Oeillets had said she was willing to exhibit herself to the prisoners, she was taken at her word. On 22 November she was taken by Louvois to Vincennes, and there Guibourg, Lesage and Marie Montvoisin were separately led in to see her. Disconcertingly for Mlle des Oeillets, Guibourg and Lesage both identified her correctly. On the other hand Marie Montvoisin, who had said she would recognise Mlle des Oeillets with ease, initially failed to do so. A little later, however, she rectified this, saying she had been well aware who she was and had only pretended not to know her to spare her embarrassment. Since Marie had been under oath when she had initially said that Mlle des Oeillets was unknown to her, this in itself proved her readiness to perjure herself when it suited her.[24]

There can be no doubt that these three encounters had been a severe setback for Mlle des Oeillets. Nevertheless, the fact that Guibourg and Lesage had named her correctly should not be regarded as conclusive, for the identity parade had not been properly conducted. The way in which she had been shown to the prisoners on her own meant that the procedure was fatally flawed, for it would have been preferable if her accusers had been required to pick her out from among a group of women. As it was, it would not have been difficult for them to guess that this was Mlle des Oeillets who stood before them. All of them had been questioned extensively about her, and Marie Montvoisin had even been asked outright whether she would be able to recognise her.[25]

Understandably, however, Mlle des Oeillets was extremely shaken by what had happened. She told Louvois in desperation that she must have been mistaken for one of her relations, for she knew that a cousin of hers regularly frequented fortune-tellers. Louvois received these protestations coldly. Having lost all faith in her, he told La Reynie that no reliance could be placed on her assurances.[26]

As La Reynie tried to sift dispassionately through the evidence, he found himself plunged into 'a strange agitation'. He noted plaintively, 'I have done what I could to assure myself and to remain convinced that these facts are true and I have not been able to achieve this. Conversely I have looked for anything which could persuade me that they were false, and that has been equally impossible.'[27]

La Reynie admitted that his zeal to protect the King may at times have clouded his judgement. Perhaps, too, he had been prejudiced by cases such as that of Mme de Brinvilliers, for being exposed to such evil may have predisposed him to see it where none, in fact, existed. However, while he knew he must guard against excessive credulity, he considered that it would be criminally irresponsible to be too dismissive of these terrible allegations.

La Reynie spent December 1680 and January 1681 reassessing the facts. In one memorandum he penned around this time[28] he noted that it was almost incredible that an attempt could have been mounted on the King's life with a poisoned petition but, on the other hand, he found it hard to accept that an ill-educated girl of mediocre intelligence such as Marie Montvoisin could have invented such a story. It was true that no other witness had corroborated her tale, but this could be explained by the fact that the protagonists would have known that if it was established they had been seeking to kill the King the penalties they faced were far more terrible than those inflicted for other capital crimes. In 1610 Henri IV's murderer, François Ravaillac, had been tortured with red-hot pincers, then molten lead, boiling oil, resinous pitch and sulphur had been poured into his wounds. Once these preliminary agonies had been completed, he was pulled apart by wild horses, a process that lasted more than an hour.[29] Even an unsuccessful attempt on Louis XIV's life would have been punished with equal ferocity.

Other aspects of Marie's story seemed fairly plausible to La Reynie.

While it might strain the limits of credibility that Mme de Montespan could ever have contemplated murdering the King, she did at least have an obvious motive to try to eliminate Mlle de Fontanges. Taking this into account, La Reynie could accept that there might genuinely have been a scheme to poison the young woman using specially prepared material or gloves. While some might argue that this was not scientifically possible, La Reynie believed it had been independently established that Romani's friend Blessis had mastered the technique. Above all, Romani's admission that he had hoped to sell silks and gloves to Mlle de Fontanges was, in La Reynie's view, immensely significant. He noted, 'From that it follows that la Voisin's daughter did not invent what she said about that' and this led him to propound the dangerous syllogism that, if so, 'everything she said on that matter can reasonably be presumed to be true'. Once this premise was accepted, other conclusions could follow for 'if the plan of the stuffs and gloves is true, it is not impossible that that of the petition is true'.[30]

On the other hand, this went some way towards discrediting a claim made by la Filastre under torture. She had said that it was on the orders of Mme de Montespan that Mme Chapelain had instructed her to obtain a place in Mlle de Fontanges's household in order to murder her. La Reynie noted that this would have meant that, following the arrest of la Voisin and the consequent collapse of the plan to kill Mlle de Fontanges with poisoned gloves, Mme de Montespan had sought out Mme Chapelain and coolly devised a new way to rid herself of her rival. It was difficult to believe she would have had the gall to do this at a time when la Voisin was in gaol and might at any time reveal the murderous plot concocted by the two of them.[31]

While admitting to doubts on this score, La Reynie was far from exonerating Mme de Montespan and it was at this point that he introduced another argument, which he had so far kept to himself. He noted that Marie Bosse, the first person to be convicted by the *Chambre Ardente*, had mentioned Mme de Montespan under torture but that, at the time, it had not been considered appropriate to take note of this.[32] Unfortunately, this means that no record exists of her comments and, since La Reynie failed to specify the sort of accusations she made, it is impossible to assess their significance.

La Reynie believed there could be no question that at various times Guibourg had conducted black masses on naked women, which may have involved child sacrifice. 'These scoundrels have given so many details ... about them that it is very difficult to doubt it,' he remarked. It did not automatically follow, of course, that Mme de Montespan had played any part in this and there were considerations that militated against the idea. It was difficult, for example, to believe that an upper-class woman would have been willing to visit so poor an area of Paris as Saint-Denis, where one of the masses had allegedly taken place.

Of one thing, however, La Reynie did feel reasonably confident, for he detected 'a great appearance of truth' in Guibourg's claim that at la Voisin's he had seen a pact drawn up in the name of Mme de Montespan.[33] Once one accepted the existence of that, much else that Guibourg had said was arguably validated.

On reading through these arguments it is hard to avoid the conclusion that by early 1681 La Reynie thought that, on balance, there was more reason to believe than disbelieve that Mme de Montespan had been engaged in a wicked criminal conspiracy. However, he shrank from recommending a definite course of action, for he remained painfully conscious that proceeding further would stir up a destructive controversy. On 26 January he wrote a memorandum for Louvois in which, having surveyed the evidence, he summarised his dilemma. He pointed out that accusations had been made relating to '*lèse-majesté* against the divine and human order. There is nothing greater, and nothing is more important than the complete and perfect elucidation of these crimes.' However, while it was obviously desirable that such offences should not go unpunished, it was debatable whether it was conducive 'to the glory of God, in the interests of the King – and consequently that of the state – or for the good of justice to apprise the public of facts of this kind'. On the other hand, inaction was fraught with peril, for 'if these crimes are hidden, what other strange and unknown things will befall, if one does not dare to penalise crimes on account of their enormity?'

It might be that the allegations against Mme de Montespan were baseless and her reputation would be damaged unfairly if they were made known to the commission. On the other hand, refraining from bringing these cases to court on that account raised the appalling prospect that 'villains and monsters' would escape justice by virtue of having 'taken it into their heads... to accuse persons of high rank, to speak of the King, and to invent all these abominations'. Yet while it was clear that progress of any kind was impossible without resuming the judicial process, La Reynie recognised that this course was not without serious drawbacks.[34]

In this memorandum La Reynie raised another point to which he wished to draw attention. He said he found it curious that the eminent people named in the more recent phase of the enquiry had made no attempt to defend themselves from the aspersions that had been cast on them. He noted darkly, 'This silence surprises me; it even makes me suspicious.'[35]

In fact, there is no reason to think that either Mme de Montespan or Mme de Vivonne had any idea of the sort of things that had been alleged against them. La Reynie himself noted in the same memorandum that although la Filastre had alluded to both ladies at her trial, not a whisper of this had reached the public. Counting La Reynie and Bezons, ten people had been present when la Filastre had been tortured, but they had preserved absolute silence as to what they had heard on that occasion.[36] Unless, therefore, the King himself had informed Mme de Montespan, there is no way she could have learned of the extraordinary attacks on her character. Everything indicates that he had not chosen to enlighten her about this.

When the King had returned from his travels in September 1680, Mme de Montespan had also gone back to her apartment at Versailles. By now it was assumed that Louis no longer had a sexual relationship with her, but neither had he completely abandoned her. With his usual unfailing courtesy, the King continued to pay her afternoon visits although, to avoid awkwardness, he was usually accompanied by someone else such as his brother, who could act as a buffer between them.

By now the poor Duchesse de Fontanges had also lost her attraction for the King. Her health was in terminal decline and, though the King had the good manners to spend an hour a day with her, her sickliness had killed his passion. He still derived his greatest pleasure from his meetings with Mme de Maintenon, whose favour was undiminished. In the autumn of 1680 it was noted that the King appeared to be in an introspective mood,[37] and this may have owed something to Mme de Maintenon's influence. The strain of wondering whether Athénaïs was guilty of unspeakably foul practices doubtless also contributed to his pensive frame of mind.

While there can be no question that this was a difficult period for Mme de Montespan, she was clearly unaware of the horrors that were threatening to engulf her. Indeed, what is positively chilling is that throughout these months the King gave not the slightest indication that her conduct was under scrutiny, while all the time encouraging La Reynie to pursue enquiries against her. Far from betraying that he had any cause for disquiet, in November 1680 the King bestowed on Mme de Montespan a gift of 50,000 livres, 'as a gratification in consideration of her services'.[38]

Reassured by such gestures, by late 1680 Mme de Montespan was adapting fairly well to her changed circumstances. Her ambitions were now focused on securing the future of her children and throughout these months she devoted considerable effort to persuading the unmarried Duchesse de Montpensier to confer her vast inheritance on the Duc du Maine, Athénaïs's eldest son by Louis. In her memoirs the Duchesse recalled that whenever Mme de Montespan came to call on her at this time, she was as amusing and entrancing as ever; it is inconceivable that Athénaïs could have conducted herself in this fashion had she realised the vile suspicions that were currently entertained of her. In February 1681 she appeared as oblivious as ever to the threat that was hanging over her: an observer reported that she was busy setting up a lottery in which, at a price, everyone at court could participate.[39]

No one else at court had any conception that Mme de Montespan had been implicated in the Affair of the Poisons. Since the acquittal of the Maréchal de Luxembourg, interest in the proceedings of the *Chambre Ardente* had subsided. There was an awareness that the enquiry was still in progress, but now that no cases were pending against court notables the subject no longer dominated the consciousness of Paris society.

It is difficult to credit the claim by M. Sagot, Recorder of the *Chambre Ardente*, that following the suspension of the Chamber, several courtiers urged the King to dissolve it altogether. Sagot noted sourly that they put forward various 'different pretexts, of which the most specious was that a longer research into the question of poisons would discredit the nation in foreign countries'.[40] However, Sagot was correct in saying that another important person made pleas to this effect, for it was at this point that the Controller-General of Finance, M. Colbert, became involved in the affair.

Back in the spring of 1679 it had been Colbert who had signed the letters patent establishing the special tribunal, but despite the fact that he was the Minister with responsibility for Paris he had since then kept himself aloof from the *Chambre Ardente*'s proceedings. Now, however, his advice was sought because, with the inquiry at stalemate, it was felt that wider consultation was desirable. Instead of leaving everything in the hands of Louvois and La Reynie, the King decided to obtain the opinion of Louvois's father, M. Le Tellier (who was Chancellor of France) and Colbert. Accordingly, a full dossier on 'the particular facts' relating to Mme de Montespan was compiled. In early February 1681 one set of these documents was sent to Louvois on the understanding that, once he had read them to the King, he and Louis would examine them in detail. Copies of the papers (which filled three caskets in all) were also sent to Colbert and Le Tellier.[41]

Colbert had had misgivings about the *Chambre Ardente* for some time. According to Primi Visconti, 'Colbert looked unfavourably on this tribunal for, besides the fact that it was costing the King a great deal, he recognised that it was defaming the nation.'[42] The fact that most of the eminent people who had been summoned before the commission were affiliated to Colbert in some way, whereas no one close to Louvois had been affected, can only have intensified Colbert's disenchantment.

By this time he had come to question not merely the wisdom but even the legality of establishing such a commission. He now wondered 'if this affair had been entrusted in its entirety to the criminal lieutenants [at the Châtelet] ... it would have been more promptly concluded and more effectively punished, without falling into all these difficulties'. Furthermore, since the inquiry had been so protracted, he queried whether this had compromised its legitimacy, for the law stated that justice must be administered swiftly to all suspects. His principal legal adviser subsequently informed him that this would have been the case were it not for the fact that the inquiry was now dealing with matters that had a direct bearing on the King's safety, which meant that the normal rules did not apply.[43]

Already distinctly unenthusiastic about the *Chambre Ardente*, Colbert was absolutely appalled when he discovered that Mme de Montespan and Mme de Vivonne had fallen under suspicion. Colbert was now related by marriage to both ladies for in February 1679 his third daughter had married the eldest son of the Duc and Duchesse de Vivonne. Even before this, Colbert had always enjoyed cordial relations with Mme de Montespan, whereas she and Louvois had recently become estranged. Relations between them had been soured by Louvois's failure in 1676 to support Mme de Montespan's brother, the Duc de Vivonne, when the latter had been sent to assist the Sicilians in the struggle against their Spanish overlords. Vivonne had complained to his sister about Louvois's reluctance to provide him with reinforcements, but none had been forthcoming and in January 1678 the Duc had been ignominiously recalled from the island. Further bitterness had been caused because Louvois had showed warm approval when the King embarked on his affair with Mlle de Fontanges, whereas Colbert had done his best to prevent Mme de Montespan from suffering too humiliating a decline in status.[44]

All this had not prevented Mme de Montespan from suggesting to Louvois that his daughter should marry her nephew but 'he gave a deaf ear' to the proposal, 'which brought about a rupture between them'. According to one source, he had not wanted to conclude a marriage alliance with a young man whose parents were so heavily indebted and he was said to have told Mme de Montespan 'that his daughter did not have sufficient wealth to restore the affairs of that family'.[45] To compound the insult, Louvois had subsequently bestowed his daughter on the son of the Prince de Marcillac, who had acted as the King's pander when Louis had fallen in love with Mlle de Fontanges.

Having received this rebuff, Mme de Montespan had next turned to Colbert and he, in contrast, had been delighted to wed his daughter to the Vivonnes' heir. Having taken pride in allying himself with the family, he was naturally aghast to learn that his daughter's aunt and mother-in-law faced possible ruin. He at once took steps to avert this, fearing that an attack on them would not only be a grave miscarriage of justice, but would also damage his own prestige.

Determined to defend Mme de Montespan against 'this execrable calumny', Colbert enlisted the services of Claude Duplessis, a skilled advocate who often provided him with legal advice. He also examined the case himself with his customary thoroughness. He drew up a searching critique of it and this, coupled with Duplessis's analysis, exposes the many weaknesses which surround 'the particular facts'.[46]

Colbert had no doubt that the aim of Marie Montvoisin and the other prisoners who had defamed Mme de Montespan was to prolong the inquiry and thus delay their own trials. He drew attention to the contradictions and inconsistencies in Marie's evidence, and the way in which her claims had escalated with each successive interview. He observed that no one else had supported her allegation that the King was to be killed with a petition, or that there had been a conspiracy to murder Mlle de Fontanges with poisoned textiles. With regard to the petition, he pointed out that if there had been any truth in what Marie had said it was extraordinary that la Voisin had found it impossible to approach the King. Had she truly been in league with Mme de Montespan, the latter would have had no difficulty procuring her access to the King; failing that, Mlle des Oeillets could have arranged for la Voisin to be presented to him. As it was, however, la Voisin had sought the help of the Duc de Montausier's valet, a lowly individual who proved incapable of aiding her.

Like Duplessis, Colbert was sure that the prisoners at Vincennes would have had no difficulty communicating with one another for, as Duplessis noted, this was something 'the whole of human prudence cannot prevent'.[47] This, of course, was immensely significant, for it explained how Guibourg, Lesage and Marie Montvoisin had been able to co-ordinate their accounts.

The prisoners at Vincennes were not kept in solitary confinement but were housed at least three to a cell and this in itself would have increased opportunities for exchanging information and ideas. At several points in 1680 Louvois expressed concern that lax security at Vincennes was enabling prisoners to receive messages from outside the prison.[48] Repeated attempts were made to prevent such breaches, but even in September some doubts remained as to whether all the problems had been overcome. La Reynie also believed that some prisoners had maintained contacts with the outside world. When one female prisoner would not give him the answers he wanted, he was sure this was because she had been told not to break her silence by people still at liberty.[49] If it was theoretically possible to smuggle messages into Vincennes, it would surely have posed less of a problem to establish a surreptitious system of internal communications?

Colbert also pointed out that if Mme de Montespan had wanted to kill the King, it would not have been difficult for her to have poisoned him. She did, after all, frequently eat with him, but instead of availing herself of the opportunities this afforded she had adopted the difficult and circuitous route of employing la Voisin to present him with a petition.

It was also pertinent to query why Mme de Montespan might wish to kill the King. Colbert contended that for most of the time she had been royal mistress she had never had the least grounds for doubting the King's devotion to her and it was only in 1678 (presumably Colbert believed that the affair with Mlle de Fontanges had started then) that she had experienced 'some trifling jealous anxieties'.[50] Here Colbert was on weak ground, for before that point Athénaïs had often had occasion to feel disquiet about the strength of the King's attachment to her. When they had started their affair she had had to compete with the King's residual fondness for Louise de La Vallière. Later she had to cope with other rivals for, besides his flirtations with Mme de Soubise and Mme de Ludres, Louis was suspected of brief liaisons with many women. Athénaïs was also threatened by the King's conscience, which might prompt him to abandon her to save his soul. Certainly, when he attempted to terminate their relationship at Easter 1675 she would have had a motive to turn to la Voisin in hopes of retrieving the situation. Yet, as Colbert commented, resolving to punish the King by assassinating him would certainly not have done her any good. Her position at court was entirely dependent on Louis and if he died she would lose everything.

Then Colbert advanced his most telling argument, for he simply refused to accept that Mme de Montespan could have been capable of the unspeakably wicked deeds described by Guibourg and Marie Montvoisin. As he remarked, the King had lived in close proximity to

Athénaïs for many years and during all that time he had never seen anything that could justify these terrible suspicions. If Mme de Montespan had been involved in something so loathsome, it was beyond belief that she could have continued to stay by the King's side, apparently completely at her ease and displaying a perfect tranquillity of soul. 'These are things which cannot be conceived of,' Colbert urged. 'His Majesty, who knows Mme de Montespan to the very bottom of her soul, will never persuade himself that she had been capable of these abominations.'[51]

Without question these were powerful words but it is strange that they were uttered by Colbert, rather than the King. Colbert was by nature so glacial that Mme de Sévigné nicknamed him 'the North', while Abbé Choisy described him as being 'devoid of passion after giving up wine'.[52] On this occasion, however, his instincts proved more generous than his master's. For many years the King had had a loving relationship with Mme de Montespan but, so far as we know, he never voiced similar sentiments in her defence.

Colbert now applied his formidable mind to devising some way of bringing matters to a satisfactory close. He noted that there were several options to choose from, none of which was perfect. The *Chambre Ardente* could simply be dissolved forthwith, but if this happened it would inevitably excite unwelcome comment. People would wonder why the commission had been prevented from completing its task and, as Duplessis put it, 'the Chamber would cease [to exist] but the affair would not be over'. Alternatively, it might be advisable to allow the commission to try offenders such as la Trianon who, while guilty of sacrilege and other capital offences, had always denied having anything to do with Mme de Montespan. Once that had been done, it should be possible to prosecute Marie Montvoisin, Guibourg and Lesage for slander, thus ensuring they did not escape punishment. If that was deemed too risky, it would be preferable to transport all prisoners who might dishonour Mme de Montespan in a court of law to some of France's remoter colonies.[53]

Colbert's legal adviser Duplessis favoured another course. He believed it would be possible for the commission to proceed with all the cases that were still awaiting judgement provided that, after convictions had been obtained, torture was not applied. He believed it was the use of torture that had caused the inquiry to spiral out of control and, if it continued to be inflicted, this would provide an almost certain means 'by which the Chamber would be perpetuated and the affair immortalised'.[54] Yet while the avoidance of torture might have brought some benefits, it could not resolve all difficulties. After all,

Guibourg, Lesage and Marie Montvoisin had managed to create all this trouble without being subjected to physical torments.

In the early spring of 1681 the King summoned those conversant with 'the particular facts' to advise him what to do. In all, the King held four meetings on the subject, attended by Louvois, Le Tellier, La Reynie and Colbert. It is not known what was said at these meetings but clearly there was a great deal of argument, for each one lasted four hours.[55] One may conjecture that La Reynie would have been in favour of the Chamber reconvening, while Colbert would certainly have argued that at all costs Mme de Montespan's reputation must be preserved. The views expressed by Louvois and Le Tellier cannot be discerned.

Having listened to all this, the King made his wishes known. He decreed that although he had decided against disbanding the Chamber he did not wish it to hear any evidence which discredited Mme de Montespan. This meant that certain malefactors could not be brought to justice but he intended 'to provide for them ... by other means'.[56]

We have no clue as to the King's reasoning at this point. There is nothing to indicate whether he believed the terrible allegations against Mme de Montespan were baseless or if, on the contrary, he thought they were true. Many historians have concluded that he did indeed believe in her guilt but that he did not want her misdeeds exposed. According to this interpretation, the King decided to protect her in recognition of his past love for her, and because he considered it too embarrassing to inflict the appropriate punishment on the mother of his children.★

On 17 April 1681 La Reynie drew up a memorandum[57] for Louvois outlining how the King's orders could be executed. He proposed that when they next assembled, the commissioners of the *Chambre Ardente* should be shown a heavily edited transcript of what la Filastre had said under torture, omitting all mention of Mme de Montespan. They should be told that 'for good and just considerations important to his service', the King had decided to withhold from them certain facts which had no bearing on the case of any person who would be brought before them.

La Reynie reminded Louvois that this would have far-reaching consequences. It was obvious that if Mme de Montespan's name was to be

---

★ Both Ravaisson and Funck-Brentano believed that Mme de Montespan was guilty. Of more recent authors, Georges Couton thinks it 'probable' that she was present during black masses when babies were sacrificed.

kept unsullied, individuals like Marie Montvoisin, Lesage and Guibourg could never be brought before the tribunal. Moreover, since the records of la Filastre's trial and conviction were incomplete, any person she had mentioned in her testimony would also escape justice, for they could not be judged until all the evidence relevant to their case had been considered. As a result, it would be impossible to try a large number of people suspected of heinous crimes.

La Reynie acknowledged that the decision to censor la Filastre's final confessions might arouse curiosity, but though people might indulge in 'doubtful and uncertain conjectures', no one would know the real reason. Furthermore, while it was regrettable that so many miscreants would now be ineligible for trial, there were numerous other offenders on whom the commission could pronounce judgement. Once the *Chambre Ardente* reassembled, it would by no means remain idle. In fact, after the Chamber reconvened, on 18 May 1681, more death sentences were passed in the remaining months of its existence than during all its previous sittings.

# TEN

# THE END OF THE AFFAIR

In late March 1681 the poor young Duchesse de Fontanges retired to Port Royal convent in Paris. This was no mere Easter retreat, for she went there 'to prepare herself for the voyage to eternity'. Having been ailing ever since her miscarriage fifteen months earlier, her health had now deteriorated to a point where she was obviously 'in an irrecoverable condition'. Since death was so clearly imminent, her confessor had persuaded her to remove herself to a more fitting environment, for 'the court was not a proper place for that last act'. The English ambassador heard that her inexorable decline had 'cost many royal tears',[1] but though the King undoubtedly was saddened by her plight, his love for her had already so much diminished that the prospect of losing her did not leave him utterly desolate.

Her physicians had predicted she would not survive till Easter, but in the event she lingered a little longer and it was 28 June before she finally succumbed to the congestion clogging up her lungs. On being informed, the King initially indicated that he considered it undesirable for an autopsy to be performed,[2] presumably because he feared that this would encourage rumours that she had been poisoned. Despite this, a post-mortem was, in fact, carried out, perhaps at the insistence of her family.

The doctors found that her lungs were in an appalling condition (with the right one in particular being full of 'purulent matter') while her chest was flooded with fluid. This led an early twentieth-century doctor who took an interest in the case to conclude that she had died from pleuro-pneumonia induced by tuberculosis. However, in view of the fact that she is known to have suffered from a persistent loss of blood after her miscarriage, a more recent authority suggested that when she lost her baby, a fragment of the placenta lodged in her uterus. This would have been a source of infection, which ultimately brought about an abscess on the lungs. An alternative suggestion is that she was killed by a rare form of cancer, which occasionally develops after a cyst on the placenta is expelled during pregnancy. The fact that Mlle de Fontanges's heart and liver were described in the autopsy as somewhat 'blighted' and 'corrupted' did lead one person to argue that this could have been caused by the slow action of arsenic, but this has remained an isolated opinion.[3] On the whole the overwhelming probability is that she died from complications arising from her earlier miscarriage.

Among her contemporaries, that astute observer Primi Visconti was one of those who attributed Mlle de Fontanges's terminal illness to her pregnancy, for he observed wryly that she died 'a martyr to the King's pleasures'. Mindful that Louise de La Vallière and Mme de Ludres had also withdrawn to convents, the Comte de Bussy joked that sharing the King's bed appeared a sure route to salvation,[4] but the doleful spectacle prompted more sombre reflections in others. For them, the passing of the exquisite creature who had revelled in her conquest of the King, and whose extravagance and love of luxury had been so marked, appeared a grim illustration of the fleeting nature of worldly triumphs.

Inevitably, many people at court elected to think that Mlle de Fontanges had been poisoned. Although no reports of la Filastre's final confessions or Marie Montvoisin's allegations had reached the public, the fact that the young woman herself had blamed poison for her illness, coupled with the fact that poison was very much on people's minds, ensured that it was whispered that she had been a victim of foul play. It was equally predictable that Mme de Montespan should be named as the person responsible. Years later the Duchesse d'Orléans recalled how, at the time, there was talk that Mme de Montespan had given her rival poisoned milk, though the Duchesse conceded that she had no idea whether there was any truth in this. In her memoirs Mme de Maintenon's niece, Mme de Caylus, recorded, 'Many rumours circulated about this death to Mme de Montespan's detriment.' Even the cautious German diplomat Ezechiel Spanheim alluded to these suspicions when in 1690 he wrote a description of the French court, noting that Mlle de Fontanges had been carried off by 'a vexatious malady which stayed with her from her first childbed and which a fairly common report, perhaps without any foundation, attributed to a beverage given to her on Mme de Montespan's secret orders'.[5]

After a hiatus of nearly nine months the *Chambre Ardente* resumed its sittings on 19 May 1681. The King had seen to it that the commissioners should not hear the cases of those individuals who Marie Montvoisin and la Filastre claimed had conspired with Mme de Montespan, but there were plenty of other matters to which they could address themselves. The suggestion by Colbert's legal adviser,

Duplessis, that torture should no longer be used to elicit confessions was ignored. If anything, indeed, its use was intensified.

Several cases of sacrilege were now dealt with by the commissioners. In July Étienne Desnoyers, Jean Huet and François Lalande were executed. All had been present when Cotton – the priest who had been burnt alongside la Filastre – had performed black masses. On 9 July the priest Gilles Davot, who had performed masses for Lesage, was hanged and his body burnt. The public executioner declined to do the hanging because Davot had been his confessor. The task had to be carried out by his assistant, though he, too, may have suffered qualms, as Davot had once been his schoolmaster.[6]

The commission next meted out justice for a murder that had taken place almost fifteen years earlier. Before her execution, Mme Voisin had recalled being told by one of her clients that a woman called Mme Lescalopier had poisoned her husband. The allegation was treated seriously as M. Lescalopier's death had been considered suspicious at the time. Upon his death there had been talk of arranging an autopsy to discover whether he had been poisoned, but his widow had had him buried before one could be carried out.[7]

As a result of la Voisin's declaration, fresh enquiries were made and this led to the arrest of Anne Poligny and Denise Sandosme, who confessed to having supplied Mme Lescalopier with poison. On 16 July the pair were hanged. Mme Lescalopier herself could not be brought to justice as she had fled the country on hearing that her accomplices had been arrested. In her absence she was tried and sentenced to death. Although it had not been possible to lay hands on her person, symbolic justice was enacted when an effigy representing her was decapitated in the Place de Grève.[8]

Jeanne Chanfrain, concubine of the ghastly Guibourg, was also tried for murder. Several of her associates had declared that she had aided Guibourg to kill some of the children they had produced together. According to one account she had walled up one and thrown another into a river. It is not clear whether she had, in fact, done this, for she never confessed it even under torture. At one point she did imply that she had seen Guibourg murder one of her children but she subsequently retracted even this. Anyway, as she herself pointed out, before being placed in the brodequins, anything she said under torture should be discounted, as she knew that pain could drive her to admit crimes she had never committed.[9]

Another 'extremely dangerous' woman, who supposedly was as inveterate a poisoner as Mme Voisin, was brought to trial in late 1681. She was a forty-four-year-old widow named Marguerite Joly, who had been arrested the previous March after Guibourg had denounced her. Under interrogation she had admitted arranging abortions and had hinted that she knew of instances when children had been offered up to the devil. No less shocking was the discovery that for a long while la Joly's most devoted client had been Mme de Dreux who, only in April 1680, had been freed by the *Chambre Ardente* after being admonished and fined. At the time several of her acquaintances had been indignant that she had been given even this mild reprimand, but evidence now emerged that she was not as blameless as they had imagined. Indeed, la Joly herself would later claim that Mme de Dreux was 'worse than the Brinvilliers lady'.[10]

This was not entirely fair, as it seems unlikely that Mme de Dreux had ever succeeded in murdering anybody. According to Mme Joly, she boasted that she had poisoned two former lovers, a M. Pajot and M. de Varennes, but this was never proved. It does seem, however, that for years she had harboured murderous intentions. La Joly would later claim that if any woman so much as looked at Mme de Dreux's lover, the Duc de Richelieu, Mme de Dreux would want her out of the way. Furthermore, seven or eight years earlier Mme de Dreux had been intent on killing the Duchesse de Richelieu. La Joly had supplied her with a powder to do the job, but Mme de Dreux had been nervous of using it. She had thought it too risky to suborn one of Mme de Richelieu's servants to give it to her, fearing that either she would be caught or that the suspicions of M. de Richelieu (who had no conception of what she was planning) would be aroused. In the end she had decided it would be preferable to do away with the Duchesse by using magic. Accordingly, a wax figurine of the Duchesse had been fashioned. Mme de Dreux had planned to melt this in the belief that the Duchesse would go into a physical decline as the effigy representing her diminished.[11] Mme Joly added that Mme de Dreux had also wanted to kill her brother, M. Saintot, and his wife, though with an equal lack of success.

Far from being discouraged by these failures, Mme de Dreux had remained incorrigible. Not even her formal rebuke from the commissioners had deterred her from seeking to eliminate her enemies with la Joly's aid. La Joly claimed that shortly after her release from prison Mme de Dreux had contacted her again in hopes of liquidating a lady who was showing an unwelcome interest in the Duc de Richelieu.

On 16 July 1681 a fresh arrest warrant was issued against Mme de Dreux but she had fled the country on learning that la Joly was in custody. Even so, the case against her was presented to the commission early the following year and on 22 January 1682 judgement was passed on the fugitive. Although her husband and the faithful Duc de Richelieu had been soliciting the court to show her mercy, she was banished from France in perpetuity. Nevertheless, after a time Mme de Dreux felt able to flout the terms of her sentence. In March 1690 Louvois wrote a stern letter to M. de Dreux saying that the King had 'learned with surprise' that Mme de Dreux was currently in Paris. He warned that unless she left the kingdom within a week she would be sent to prison. However, within two years the King had modified the original sentence by acceding to a request that she could settle at her husband's country residence near Chinon.[12]

Mme Joly was not so fortunate. Her trial took place at the end of 1681 and resulted in her being sentenced to be burnt alive. On 19 December she was subjected to the water torture prior to execution. During this ordeal she not only repeated her claims about Mme de Dreux but admitted her own involvement in other hideous crimes. She said she had been present when the baby nephew of a friend of hers called la Poignard had been sacrificed. Twenty-two years ago, another child had been offered up to the devil in order to bring about a marriage desired by her client Mlle de Saint-Laurens. She stated that her associate Anne Meline had poisoned numerous people, including la Joly's own husband. She herself had despatched a number of victims using arsenic, which she obtained from a female apothecary. This woman was familiar with her needs and was well aware that when la Joly asked her for cosmetic lotion, what she really wanted was 'poison to send people to the next world'.[13]

After la Joly had endured an hour and a quarter of torture, the doctors present indicated that she would not survive if her agony went on any longer. Having been laid on a mattress to recuperate, she immediately retracted much of what she had just said. Although she still maintained that long ago a child had been sacrificed at the behest of Mlle de Saint-Laurens, she now denied that la Poignard's nephew had been slaughtered; she also changed her story about the apothecary, who she said had never sold her poison. In fact, she protested that she had never poisoned anybody, but whatever the truth of the matter her punishment had been fixed. That evening la Joly was burnt alive. A few days later her associates, la Meline, the abortionist, Marie Bouffet, and Louison Desloges (who had acted as an intermediary between la Joly and Mme de Dreux) were hanged.

Not all of those who came before the *Chambre Ardente* were dealt with so harshly. Mme Brissart, who had used spells to attract her lover, M. Rubantel, and who la Voisin had claimed had sought to poison her sister (though it seems the latter had died of natural causes) was banished from Paris for three years and fined 1000 livres. Mme Cottar was merely admonished and fined 100 livres for having employed magic and charms to win the heart of her admirer, M. Forne. On 14 July 1681 the Marquise de Fontet was given an absolute discharge by the Chamber, but since she had already spent eighteen months in prison she could be said to have paid a heavy penalty for having introduced the Maréchal de Luxembourg to Lesage.[14]

Although it had been agreed that persons alleged to have conspired with Mme de Montespan could not be brought to trial, when another plot on the King's life was uncovered, those implicated were treated with the full rigour of the law. The details came to light fortuitously, after La Reynie had begun investigating a reported attempt to kill Colbert. In the process, he had stumbled on the trail of a still more serious crime.

It was in December 1680 that Guibourg had set things in motion by telling La Reynie that, five years earlier, a man called M. D'Amy had come to see him. This had been at the suggestion of Jacques Deschault, an unsavoury character who was said to be willing to carry out contract killings for the tiny sum of thirty sols. D'Amy was an officer in the Chamber of Accounts in Provence and he had conceived a grudge against Colbert after losing money on a sale of timber to the navy. After he had told Guibourg that he wanted to poison Colbert, Guibourg had sent D'Amy to purchase drugs and had then arranged for these to be distilled to make them stronger. At the outset D'Amy had given Guibourg a promissory note for 1000 livres and, on receiving the drugs, he had made a cash down payment of 200 livres.[15]

Hearing this, La Reynie sent an agent to the notary's office where Guibourg had lodged the promissory note. He found that, just as Guibourg had said, the advance of 200 livres was recorded there, with the balance of 800 livres still outstanding. In La Reynie's opinion this showed incontrovertibly that Guibourg was telling the truth. 'It is a silent witness, an irreproachable written proof,' he enthused, although it is, in fact, possible that D'Amy had approached Guibourg not because he wished to kill Colbert, but because he hoped the priest would help him win at gambling.[16] The truth was difficult to establish, for D'Amy himself had since died.

However, Deschault was still alive and was arrested with a confederate of his named Debray, who Guibourg claimed had supplied people with cantharides. When they were questioned, nothing further emerged about the plot against Colbert, but evidence did accumulate suggesting that they were purveyors of poison. Their services had been enlisted by a widow named Anne Carada, who was passionately in love with a married man. Hoping that their union could be legalised, she had asked Deschault to engineer the removal of her lover's wife. Incantations were said to effect her wishes and Deschault had performed spells with wax figurines designed to bring about the death of the inconvenient spouse. The woman had subsequently died and, though Mme Carada herself maintained when questioned that she had only sought to hasten her end by using magic and had never had recourse to poison, it was regarded as a case of murder. Having been tried and found guilty, Mme Carada was beheaded for this on 25 June 1681.[17]

Debray and Deschault should in theory have preceded her to the scaffold, but there had been a new development on 19 June, the day scheduled for their execution. When both men had been tortured, nothing of interest had been gleaned from Deschault, who insisted he knew nothing whatever of poison. Debray, however, volunteered some startling information, which sparked fresh concerns for the King's safety.

Debray revealed he had sometimes worked in partnership with a shepherd named Christophe Moreau who operated a profitable sideline to his pastoral duties. Despite the ample choice of practitioners offering similar services in the capital, people from Paris would come to see this man for help with love affairs and marriages or, more sinisterly, when they wanted to procure the death of some person. Some years earlier Moreau had been consulted by a man who said he was a relation of M. Fouquet, the former *Surintendant* of Finance whom the King had imprisoned for life. The mysterious client had said he was determined to bring about Fouquet's restoration to power and that, to achieve this end, he would not scruple to kill the King.[18]

Debray's revelations engendered a flurry of arrests. Moreau was seized, along with Jean Perceval and Mathurin Barenton, whom Debray had named as Moreau's accomplices. Debray was kept alive to see if he could remember more about the conspiracy, while his former companion Deschault, who clearly knew nothing of all this, went to the gallows as planned.

When questioned, Moreau agreed that he had had a client who was a relation of Fouquet's and who had styled himself the Chevalier de La Brosse. He had been accompanied by his valet, who had been introduced as Dubois, though it seemed likely that these were assumed names. Moreau protested that the Chevalier had never expressed any interest in killing the King and had merely wanted to improve his standing at court, but his account was not believed. Such scepticism seemed justified by a statement from Barenton that when Moreau had brought the Chevalier de La Brosse to see him, the Chevalier had not sought to disguise his hostility to the King.[19]

The search was now on for the mysterious Chevalier and events took a new turn when evidence given by another suspect, Mathurin Chapon, led La Reynie and Louvois to believe that they had unmasked his true identity. They concluded that the Chevalier de La Brosse was the name adopted by Roger de Pardaillan de Gondrin, Marquis de Termes, a cousin by marriage of Mme de Montespan, who had already featured in the inquiry in a peripheral way.

Exactly what led Louvois and La Reynie to Termes is unclear, though he was known to have lost a fortune as a result of Fouquet's fall. Termes was a somewhat eccentric figure with a strange appearance and a pronounced speech impediment caused by a cleft palate though, oddly enough, he could enunciate perfectly when singing. Around the time of Fouquet's fall he had been briefly imprisoned in the Bastille and since then had led 'a highly licentious life'.[20] He had also devoted great efforts to restoring his lost wealth and had hoped to enrich himself by attaining the Philosopher's Stone. Using compulsion, he had set to work in his chateau a crew of alchemists including la Voisin's lover Blessis. Their resentment at having been pressed into servitude in this way had reportedly led some of them to consider poisoning Termes. Now, however, there were suspicions that Termes was more than just a potential victim and that his bitterness at being deprived of his fortune had led him to plot the King's death. Accordingly, he was arrested and a former employee of his named Antoine Monteran was also taken into custody.

Confusion mounted, however, when Moreau was interviewed again and pointed the manhunt in an entirely different direction. While ignorant of the true name of the Chevalier de La Brosse, he recalled that during one visit the Chevalier had been accompanied by M. Jean Maillard, a *Conseiller* in the Paris *Parlement*. Maillard was promptly arrested and agreed that he had once been to see Moreau with the late M. Jacques Pinon du Martroy, a former *Conseiller* in the Court of Inquests. Pinon du Martroy had once been immensely wealthy but had been ruined when his assets had been seized following the arrest of Fouquet. Since then he had become so heavily indebted that when he had taken Maillard to see Moreau, he had adopted the pseudonym of the Chevalier de La Brosse in hopes of avoiding being harassed by his creditors.[21]

Information provided by Guibourg added to the case against Pinon du Martroy, for when questioned about him the priest disclosed that

Pinon had been a client of his for many years. At first Guibourg merely had a vague memory that the *Conseiller* had asked for his assistance in wreaking revenge on his enemies. Having thought about it a bit longer, it suddenly came back to him that Pinon had confided he wanted to poison the King.[22]

The luckless M. Maillard insisted that his own and Pinon du Martroy's encounter with Moreau had been completely innocent, but he failed to disassociate himself from the conspiracy supposedly master-minded by his dead friend. It was true that no firm evidence ever emerged to link Maillard with the recently identified threat to the King, but on the other hand there were aspects of his past history that were disturbing. Some years before, Maillard had rented his country house to Sainte-Croix, the lover of Mme de Brinvilliers who had sup-plied her with poisons. Maillard protested that he had known Sainte-Croix merely 'on the footing of a man of pleasure',[23] but this failed to explain why he had bound himself to pay the sum of 4000 livres on the presentation of a bill of exchange he had lodged with Sainte-Croix. When the debt had been called in after Sainte-Croix's death, Maillard had paid the full amount to Belleguise, a crony of Sainte-Croix's who was also clerk to the financier Pennautier.

A possible reason why Maillard had owed money to Sainte-Croix was soon uncovered. Years before, Maillard had had an affair with the wife of M. Violet, an attorney in *Parlement* who had died suddenly in 1665. At the time Violet had employed a woman named Mme Guesdon who subsequently went on to work for both Mme de Brinvilliers and Sainte-Croix. Bearing this in mind, it appeared a plau-sible hypothesis that Mme Guesdon had been commissioned to poison Violet and that Maillard had promised to pay Sainte-Croix a substantial sum for arranging this. Violet's widow had since remarried, but when questioned about all this, she hinted that Maillard had been responsible for Violet's death. On the other hand her second husband had recently conceived suspicions that she had been trying to poison him, so it is not impossible that she had murdered Violet without any assistance from Maillard.[24]

The fact that Sainte-Croix's name was once again featuring in the inquiry prompted a revival of interest in his activities. Links had already been established between Sainte-Croix and M. Fouquet, for it was Sainte-Croix who had told Mme de Brinvilliers that Fouquet had sent the chemist Christophe Glaser to find out more about poison in Florence. This led La Reynie to speculate whether Maillard and Sainte-Croix might have jointly conspired to kill the King so that Fouquet might be freed.

Convinced that the two men had been bound together in some sinister way, La Reynie suggested that the widow of Christophe Glaser should be lured back from her retirement in Switzerland to see if she could shed any light on the matter. Understandably, however, on being asked to return to France to assist the inquiry, she turned down the invitation.[25]

Though nothing came of that approach, La Reynie was confident he could establish the truth about the Chevalier de La Brosse's plans to murder the King. He was spurred on by the King himself, who evinced a keen interest in the progress of the inquiry. The diligent way the matter was pursued was not motivated solely by concern for the King's safety, for if it could be established that poisoners posed a risk to the monarch himself, there could be no better justification for the existence of the *Chambre Ardente*. Previously Colbert had questioned the decision to establish a special commission to try offences which could have been adequately dealt with by the criminal courts. His legal adviser Duplessis had agreed that setting up the commission had been unwarranted unless it could be shown that *lèse-majesté* had been committed, for the dreadful threat posed by that crime justified the most extreme measures. Earlier it had, of course, been indicated to La Reynie that poison might be used against the King, but he had been prevented from laying the evidence before the commissioners. There was no problem, however, about bringing this case to trial and once it became known that the Chamber was adjudicating on a matter relating to the King's personal safety no loyal subject could dispute that it was fulfilling a vital function.

This consideration rendered it all the more imperative that those suspected of conspiring against the King should be compelled to admit their guilt. Louvois stressed the importance of this to the officer appointed to supervise their torture after conviction. Emphasising that 'this affair is of very great consequence', he gave orders that the torture of the guilty parties should be carried out with the utmost severity.[26] His admonitions were heeded all too slavishly, for there can be no doubt that the sufferings inflicted on these wretched men were particularly frightful.

Barenton was the first to be brought before the commission. On 5 September he was found guilty of 'treason in the highest degree for having known of the design against the King without revealing it; also of having ... traded in poisons'. At dawn on 6 September he was taken to the torture chamber where initially he insisted he had been wrongly convicted. He agreed that he had once met with the Chevalier de La Brosse but said that all he had ever given him was a water to bathe sore eyes. As the torture intensified, however, Barenton changed his story.

'Must I damn myself?' he wailed as it became clear to him that his resistance was crumbling. Having reached the limits of his endurance he then agreed that he had supplied poison intended to kill the King. He explained that the Chevalier de La Brosse had told him that Moreau had already sold him poison, which had proved ineffective, so he wanted Barenton to find him something stronger and more subtle, preferably made of toad venom. Barenton was left so weakened by his ordeal that when he was taken to his death later that afternoon he proved unable to perform the prescribed penance outside Notre-Dame, and there was a real fear he might die before reaching the Place de Grève.[27]

Three days later Debray, who had given the first warnings that the King had been targeted, was executed. He was not tortured again, but that morning he went into further details about the alleged plot, saying that he now remembered things which might be of importance. Piously thanking the Almighty for having deferred his execution so he could die with a clear conscience, he stated that he had seen both Moreau and Barenton hand poison to the Chevalier de La Brosse. Perhaps he hoped he would be kept alive for a bit longer to answer more questions, but now that he had served his purpose he was expendable. Some consideration was shown him, for when he pleaded for wine on his way to execution his wish was granted. Thus fortified, he died with dignity, telling the crowd he had been justly convicted and asking them to pray for him.[28]

The other members of the cabal exposed by Debray proved less willing to acknowledge their crimes. When Moreau came before them, the commissioners of the *Chambre Ardente* had no hesitation in finding him guilty. The statements he made under torture on 13 September apparently vindicated their verdict, for he admitted discussing poison with M. Maillard and agreed that he had supplied it to the Chevalier de La Brosse. However, after he had been taken to the Place de Grève to be broken on the wheel, he retracted all this. As he lay spreadeagled on the wheel with his limbs smashed by hammer blows, he called over the officer supervising the execution to say that he had not told the truth and his confessor had urged him to make amends for having accused others unjustly. By the terms of his sentence, Moreau was condemned to die slowly of his injuries, but the officer promptly ordered the executioner to put him out of his misery by strangling him. Whether this was done for humanitarian reasons or simply to prevent him repeating his denials is a matter for conjecture.[29]

Perceval proved equally reluctant to abide by the avowals wrung from him in the torture chamber. On 18 September he was tortured so severely that the doctors present feared he might die. Tormented beyond endurance, his agonised shrieks for mercy were interspersed with admissions that he, Barenton and Moreau had conceived a 'detestable design' against the King. At the instigation of the Chevalier de La Brosse they had 'sought to kill the King with poison and by magic, out of vengeance on account of M. Fouquet'. Nevertheless, before being taken to his execution that afternoon he withdrew everything, saying it had been 'the force of the torments' that had prompted his words and he was entirely ignorant of any design against the King.[30]

Though in his final moments Moreau had done his best to exculpate M. Maillard, this could not save the *Conseiller*. He was not brought to trial for some months but this was because it was hoped that more could be found out about his crimes, rather than because his guilt was considered doubtful. Although the investigation was shrouded in the utmost secrecy, the public gained some idea of the serious nature of the accusations against him. Having heard that Maillard and Pinon du Martroy had performed spells directed 'against the King's sacred person', one concerned citizen expressed the hope that Maillard would be punished by being torn limb from limb.[31]

In fact, when Maillard was found guilty of treason on 20 February 1682, the Chamber decreed he should be beheaded for, as a member of a sovereign court, he was entitled to an honourable form of execution. However, his privileged status did not mean he was spared torture. Far from it, indeed, for Louvois had urged Bezons 'to do everything humanly possible to draw the truth' from the convicted man. These grim instructions ensured that the prisoner was handled with a terrible ferocity, but through it all he remained steadfast, defiantly declaring they could torture him for eight hours and he still would tell them nothing. To the end he denied all knowledge of a plot against the King and held firm that he had never discussed poisons with Sainte-Croix. By the time his tormentors had finished with him he was in such a poor condition that he could not even hold a pen in order to sign the written record of his interrogation. Even so, no admissions had been extorted from him.[32]

Before being put to death, Maillard was permitted to spend some time with his confessor. There was great excitement when he unexpectedly summoned the Recorder of the *Chambre Ardente* to see him, but he merely asked him to arrange the return of modest sums of money to gambling companions he had cheated. Even when Maillard was on the scaffold, a final attempt was made to persuade him to divulge details of his misdeeds, but he remained as laconic as ever, On being asked why he had become indebted to Sainte-Croix, he answered shortly, 'Enough! Don't let's talk of that.' He then indicated to the executioner that he should proceed with the beheading.[33]

The next to suffer was the Marquis de Termes's servitor, Monteran. Since his arrest he had consistently denied having plotted against the King, but his attempts to clear himself had been undermined when he had been confronted with Debray, Moreau and Perceval. Despite Monteran's protests that he had never laid eyes on any of them, all three identified him as the man who had masqueraded as the Chevalier de La Brosse. There was no other evidence against him but in March 1682 it was decided that there were sufficient 'presumptions and half-proofs' against him to warrant him being tortured before trial. Accordingly, on 12 March 1682 he was subjected to the water torture, but the strain proved too much for his constitution. One person at court heard that he bore the pain for a considerable period without admitting anything but at length he was driven to say that if permitted a respite he would reveal all he knew. Monteran's offer was eagerly taken up, but once he had been laid upon the mattress his fortitude returned. Defiantly he declared that though desperation had forced him to bargain with them, now that he was no longer racked with pain he was not prepared to incriminate himself falsely. He was shown no mercy for having practised this deception, but his interrogators were left frustrated when, shortly after the torture was resumed, he died without having broken his silence.[34]

The Marquis de Termes still awaited trial. He had been imprisoned at Vincennes since his arrest the previous August, even though it was soon apparent that he was unlikely to have posed as the Chevalier de La Brosse. No one who had had any dealings with the elusive Chevalier had given a description that fitted Termes or made any mention of a speech defect. Yet he was still treated with suspicion, particularly when it was shown that years before, Termes had been in the Bastille at the same time as Egidio Exili. It turned out that Exili, who was credited with having provided Sainte-Croix with his knowledge of poisons, had cast Termes's horoscope while they were in prison, a coincidence which some considered sinister.[35]

Despite this, when Termes was brought before the *Chambre Ardente* on 18 March he was acquitted. It is not clear what evidence was presented against him. Although the public had become vaguely aware that he was suspected of 'magic and poison', the grounds for this had remained unclear. Termes himself was happy to consider the matter closed and, within days of his release, he reappeared at court.[36]

It seems that the King now decided that Termes had been unfairly victimised, for not long after Termes's release he put the Marquis's finances on a less precarious footing by taking him on as a Valet of the Bedchamber. The post was considered somewhat demeaning for a man of Termes's rank, but he appeared to relish his new status. Unfortunately, he soon made himself unpopular with his fellow courtiers. They disliked the way Termes spied on them and reported his findings to the King, and on at least one occasion Termes earned himself a beating. His reputation as a troublemaker was such that people took to fleeing at his approach, with the result that he lived 'in complete solitude in the midst of the greatest crowd'.[37]

Having dealt out harsh punishment to all those convicted of endangering the King, the commissioners of the *Chambre Ardente* next addressed some long neglected business. Months before the Chamber had come into being, the enigmatic Louis Vanens had been arrested. Ever since, he had remained at the Bastille, where he had been joined by several former associates, including the banker Cadelan and M. and Mme de Bachimont. The probe into their activities had given rise to fears that Vanens had been at the centre of an international consortium, which distributed poison all over Europe, but for the past three years the investigation had lapsed. In the interval, further information about Vanens had come to light, for he was an acquaintance of several of those taken to Vincennes on suspicion of poisoning, but nothing really justified the extravagant suspicions that had been entertained of him.

In the spring of 1682 Vanens and others connected with him were transferred to Vincennes. For the past few months he had been behaving so eccentrically that his sanity was doubted. When his cell mate had erected a crucifix in their chamber, Vanens had smeared it with excrement, and he had taken to worshipping the pet dog that had been his companion during his imprisonment.[38] Nevertheless, in April 1682 it was decided he was fit to stand trial.

The evidence that was put before the commission was remarkably feeble. It amounted to little more than allegations that Vanens, like hundreds like him in the Paris underworld, had preyed on others' credulity by offering to unearth treasures, or to supply powders which supposedly could effect marriages or prolong love affairs.[39] He had also produced quantities of a mysterious liquid, which had probably been put on sale after being decanted into bottles. However, there was no proof whatever that this had been poison and it could not be established that Vanens was responsible for the death of a single person. As for the suggestion that he had assassinated eminent figures such as the Duke of Savoy, this was deemed too controversial to be placed before the Chamber.

Vanens was sentenced to serve in the galleys for the rest of his life. Louvois was dissatisfied by this, for though it had proved impossible to convict Vanens of capital crimes, he remained convinced that he was an exceptionally dangerous man. Even in the galleys he might pose an unacceptable security risk and it was also important to prevent word from leaking out that a French national might have been responsible for assassinating a neighbouring head of state. Louvois therefore gave orders that Vanens should be imprisoned for life in a remote fortress in Franche-Comté. When making the arrangements, Louvois cautioned the official in charge that it was 'very important for the public good to prevent Vanens from communicating with anyone at all'. None of his guards must be permitted to exchange a word with him, for he was 'one of those skilled in making poison' who would try to win them over by offering to teach them the secret of the Philosopher's Stone.[40]

Since the outcome of Vanens's trial had been so unsatisfactory, it was decided that it would be preferable to deal with most other members of his gang through the exercise of arbitrary power. The exception was Vanens's valet, La Chaboissière, whose alleged offences were not of the same magnitude as his master's. Evidence had been amassed suggesting that La Chaboissière had habitually used poison to settle disagreements or to rid himself of inconvenient neighbours and it was easier to obtain a conviction for these straightforward acts of malice than to permit the commission to deliberate on the role played by Vanens in the death of the Duke of Savoy.

After being found guilty, La Chaboissière was tortured on 16 July 1682. Following his detention he had made the mistake of hinting that he was in possession of secret information which, if revealed, would save fifty lives a year. This merely ensured that under torture he was pressed more severely than would otherwise have been the case. Vainly he protested that he knew nothing of interest and implored that he should be put to death rather than having his sufferings prolonged. When he was finally taken to the Place de Grève to be hanged, it came as a relief. On the scaffold he asked the crowd to pardon him for all the scandal he had caused.[41]

La Chaboissière was the last person to be judged by the *Chambre Ardente*. On 21 July 1682 the King sealed letters patent formally disbanding the commission; its closing session took place two days later. The decision to terminate the Chamber 'gave great joy' to all the commissioners, 'who were very weary of hearing those abominable matters spoken of every day'.[42]

The *Chambre Ardente* had certainly not been idle during its brief existence. In all it had held 210 sittings. It had issued 319 arrest warrants
and, though a significant number of those named in these had evaded
capture by fleeing Paris, 194 persons had been taken into custody. A
total of 104 people had been tried by the commission for a wide range
of offences. The commission had passed thirty-six death sentences and
thirty-four executions had been carried out, with offenders being variously burnt alive, decapitated, hanged, strangled or broken on the
wheel. Besides this, two people had died under torture. In a time when
prison mortality was exceptionally high it was inevitable that there had
also been deaths in custody. In the early months of 1682, for example,
the priest François Mariette and the divineress Catherine Trianon, both
key figures in the case against Mme de Montespan, had died.

The Chamber had given absolute discharges to sixteen individuals
who had come before it. Seventeen offenders had been banished and a
further insignificant number fined or admonished. Yet despite all this
activity, by no means all those arrested had been brought to trial.[43]

Having reviewed every case, La Reynie drew up a list of forty
persons who could safely be released without further action being
taken. Even after this, however, numerous prisoners remained at
Vincennes. Twenty of these had in fact been judged by the Chamber
and had only been given mild sentences. La Poignard, who la Joly
claimed had sacrificed her nephew, came into this category, as did the
herbalist Maître Pierre. He had been sentenced to a mere six months in
prison, but because he was considered a menace to society he was kept
in confinement for the rest of his life.[44]

The giddy Mme Vertemart was placed in permanent detention for
slightly different reasons. She had been taken into custody for having
gone to la Voisin in hopes of being freed from her husband. Subsequently it had been claimed that Mme Voisin had sought to place her
in Mme de Montespan's household and after la Vertemart had been
questioned about this she had deduced that grave suspicions were being
entertained about Mme de Montespan. At one point she claimed Lesage
had once told her that Mme de Montespan was in league with la Voisin
and he feared for the consequences.[45] It was considered essential that she
was given no chance to repeat such statements.

On 24 July 1681 Mme Vertemart's case had been heard by the commission. Her official punishment for having asked la Voisin to say
prayers for the death of her husband had been banishment from the
realm. However, the King feared that while abroad she might spread
gossip about Mme de Montespan. It was therefore agreed that she
should spend the rest of her life in a convent for fallen women.[46]

At one time it was thought that Mlle des Oeillets had been confined for life in a similar institution. In his great work the *Archives de la Bastille* (where the vast majority of documents relating to the Affair of the Poisons are printed) François Ravaisson published a letter sent from Louvois to La Reynie in September 1686, informing the Police Chief that 'la des Oeillets, who was shut up by order of the King in the Tours workhouse, died there on the eighth of this month'. However, when Jean Lemoine researched the life of Mlle des Oeillets he found it was not true that she had died in captivity. It has since been proved that Ravaisson had wrongly transcribed the name and that Louvois had in fact been referring to Aymée Drodelot, sister of Anne Poligny, who had been incarcerated in the Tours workhouse in December 1682.[47]

Things had certainly looked bad for Mlle des Oeillets following her confrontation with the prisoners at Vincennes, but she had managed to retrieve the situation. In February 1682 she had written to Louvois once again protesting her innocence and suggesting that perhaps one of the Comtesse de Soissons's maids had impersonated her when visiting la Voisin. Louvois had been impressed by her arguments[48] and she had not been troubled again in connection with this matter.*

In 1681 Mlle des Oeillets had rented a Paris house in the Rue Montmartre and three years later she purchased a country property, the Château de Suisnes. Thenceforth she divided her time between the two houses, living in some degree of comfort, for her will makes it plain that she employed three servants and owned two coaches. She died on 18 May 1687, leaving money to pay for prayers to be said daily for the King's health and prosperity.[49]

The decision had been reached that all those alleged by Marie Montvoisin or la Filastre to have been in league with Mme de Montespan would be imprisoned for life without trial. Now that la Trianon and Mariette were dead, they comprised fourteen individuals. Besides Marie herself, Lesage and Guibourg, they were Romani and Bertrand, Vautier and his wife, Mme Chapelain, Galet, Latour, la Pelletier and la Delaporte (both of whom were alleged by Marie to have attended black masses celebrated by Guibourg for Mme de Montespan) Lafrasse (who had sought to obtain la Filastre employment with Mme de Fontanges) and la Bellière.

There were some other unfortunates who were recognised to be personally blameless but who had had the ill luck to be told more than

---

* In *L'Affaire des Poisons* Petitfils nevertheless argues that the accusations against Mlle des Oeillets were well-founded.

was good for them about Mme de Montespan. Mme Vertemart's brother, Lemaire, was one such person. Having been arrested with scant justification, he had been placed in a cell at Vincennes with Guibourg and it was feared the latter had relayed to him all the scurrilous things he had said about Mme de Montespan. To prevent this gaining a wider circulation it was agreed that Lemaire should be conducted to the border, where he was to be given a comfortable travel allowance. He was told he would receive a comparable sum every year, provided he behaved discreetly, but he could never return to France without the King's express authority. For the same reason it was considered too hazardous to let Marie Montvoisin's cell mates regain their freedom. Instead, they were placed in convents, at the King's expense.[50]

There were other individuals who had never been formally tried by the commission but who were nevertheless deemed sufficiently dangerous to warrant their being locked up for ever. There was obviously an element of injustice in this, but in some cases there were at least reasonable grounds for considering it would be unsafe to give these persons their liberty. For instance, one can understand the logic behind the decision to imprison Mme Guesdon, who was suspected of being responsible for the death of M Violet, even if the matter had not been considered in court. Similarly, there were grave suspicions against a woman called la Salomond, whom Debray and Deschault had accused of being a poisoner.

There were, however, others who now disappeared for ever into dungeons who could, surely, have been released without risk. For example, the Maréchal de Luxembourg's personal astrologer, the self-styled Vicomte de Montemayor (in reality a former apothecary from Lyon called François Bouchard) had been arrested at the same time as his master. This engaging rogue, who cheerfully admitted that his powers of prediction were flawed and who never seems to have done anyone any harm, was to spend the rest of his life in prison. La Voisin's servant Margot, who denied all knowledge of her employer's crimes, was likewise incarcerated for ever in Fort des Bains.[51]

Another woman, the Demoiselle Robert, was deemed guilty by association, for La Reynie considered that the mere fact that she had been a great friend of Magdelaine de La Grange justified her being shut up for life in a particularly unpleasant workhouse. Ten years after she had been placed there, her relations (one of whom, piquantly, had been Attorney-General of the *Chambre Ardente*) sought to have her freed, pleading that at worst she had been guilty of 'foolish things rather than crimes'. La Reynie passionately resisted the move, saying that in his view her closeness to such an 'abominable woman' meant that her confinement was 'just and necessary'. It is pleasing to relate that la Robert's family persevered with their efforts to free her, with the result that one year later she was transferred to a more agreeable convent.[52]

The permanent imprisonment of the various individuals whose dealings with Louis Vanens had led to their arrest was also considered a vital precautionary measure. Among them were M. and Mme de Bachimont, who were probably guilty of nothing worse than a misguided enthusiasm for alchemy. The banker Cadelan was another who was considered ineligible for release despite never having been tried. In April 1682 it was noted that he had not even been questioned during the past three years and languishing all that time in gaol had left him mentally unhinged. When La Reynie and Bezons had tried to interview him after this long interval, they found him to be suffering from a 'troubled mind' and he answered all their questions 'in an extravagant manner'. By the summer he was 'in a mania approaching frenzy', but there was no question of his being freed on compassionate grounds. When taking steps to have him removed to the citadel of Besançon, Louvois commented it was vital that his confinement was especially rigorous, for he was 'extremely wicked and capable of attempting anything'.[53]

La Reynie found it frustrating that individuals who had owned up to ghastly crimes should escape the horrible punishment they merited. He also regretted that the decision to close down the *Chambre Ardente* had necessitated the abandonment of proceedings against others who could have been prosecuted without embarrassment. It may be that Louvois had exerted pressure on him to bring matters to a conclusion; certainly in the latter phases of the Chamber's existence, Louvois's letters to La Reynie, formerly so encouraging, betray a certain impatience.[54]

La Reynie had been apprehensive that if the Chamber ended precipitately, it would send out the wrong signals. In April 1682 he wrote that while he recognised it would be undesirable to keep the commission in being for much longer, it would be unfortunate to give the impression that it was being ended out of 'lassitude', or because the judges had become disheartened. If that happened the fortune-tellers and treasure seekers of Paris would look on it as a victory and would resume their activities with renewed vigour. While the Chamber had been in session they had ceased operations, but La Reynie believed they were merely biding their time in the expectation of 'more freedom once this investigation is over'.[55]

One thing consoled La Reynie. He was aware that despite the grisly punishments inflicted on those convicted of capital crimes by the Chamber, the memory of these executions would fade astonishingly quickly. However, the knowledge that some of those arrested had been locked away with no prospect of release would act as a permanent deterrent, for the members of Paris's criminal underworld had a peculiar dread of perpetual confinement. La Reynie noted with satisfaction that the thought of former acquaintances mouldering in grim chateaux far from Paris would form 'a living example' to others who otherwise might consider it an acceptable risk to emulate their crimes. He explained that 'in the eyes of those ... who are in the same business ... prison, abstinence from wine ... [and] a life of constraint are ... more difficult to support than death, which they hardly fear at all'.[56]

Initially La Reynie had proposed that no fewer than eighty-five prisoners should be sent to heavily guarded fortresses outside Paris, but the King had baulked at the expense and insisted that the figure be reduced. Having reviewed the list, La Reynie agreed that some of those selected could be sent to less high-security establishments. For example, Dalmas, the blind crony of Vanens's valet La Chaboissière, could be sent to a workhouse. Yet despite a bit of pruning the list remained long and La Reynie acknowledged that the King was performing 'a great charity to the public' by paying for the upkeep of persons who, when at liberty, had committed detestable crimes.[57]

In the end at least sixty-five prisoners were allocated places in royal fortresses in different parts of France. In December 1682 eighteen male prisoners were sent to Salces, including Bertrand, Latour and Montemayor. Twelve women were sent to Bellisle, including Marie Montvoisin and Mme Chapelain. In Franche-Comté two strongholds received a consignment of prisoners. Among the ten men sent to Besançon were Lesage, Guibourg, Galet and Romani, while fourteen women were confined in St André de Salins. Five more women were shut up in Fort des Bains in Cerdagne and another six were despatched to the Château de Villefranche, near Perpignan.[58]

La Reynie derived comfort from the thought that the fate of these people could be considered 'a hundred times worse than death'. This was hardly an exaggeration, for the prisoners were held in conditions of extreme physical discomfort. It was specified that throughout their captivity they must be shackled to the wall of their cell by the ankle or wrist. Although their chains were long enough to permit them to lie down on the palliasse provided for them, all other movements were restricted. Louvois explained to the Intendant of Franche-Comté, who bore overall responsibility for the fortresses of Besançon and St André de Salins, that 'as these people are scoundrels who deserve the most extreme torments, the King intends them to be attached in this way for fear that they will insult the people appointed to guard them and who go in and out of their chamber to bring them food or remove their bodily waste'.[59]

Shortly after their arrival at St André de Salins it was agreed that the women prisoners could be left unchained provided they behaved well and the governor guaranteed there was no danger of their escaping. However, as soon as they caused trouble they must immediately be put back in shackles. The male prisoners in other fortresses were not even allowed this latitude. Louvois gave orders that Romani must be kept under particularly strict surveillance, for he was 'more vigorous and artful' than his fellows. Although Marie Montvoisin's claims about him had never been corroborated by a single person, he was kept in fetters for thirty-four years. In 1714 another prisoner was sufficiently moved by his plight to unchain him, but this man was punished for his insubordination by being placed in irons himself.[60]

The prisoners' confinement was hard in other ways. They were provided with sheets and blankets but there were no fireplaces in their cells. It was only in January 1687, when they had been incarcerated for more than four years, that the women at Bellisle were permitted braziers in midwinter. An allowance of only ten sols a day was allocated for each prisoner, out of which not just their food but also the wages of their guards had to be paid. Even when expenses had been pared to a minimum at Vincennes, daily costs per prisoner had amounted to twice that sum. However, the governor of Besançon managed very well on these modest resources, for he spent so little on food that he was said to pocket a sizeable profit.[61]

Perhaps the most terrible aspect of the prisoners' existence was the way they were utterly cut off from human intercourse. All the castles in which they were imprisoned were geographically remote, but other precautions were taken to ensure the prisoners were completely isolated. Prior to entrusting any of them to his care, Louvois outlined the reasons for this to the *Intendant* of Franche-Comté. He cautioned, 'As these are all highly enterprising people they must be guarded with great care and treated very severely if they give the least reason for it, so that if anything whatever escapes from them, the chastisement they receive for it obliges them to restrain themselves.' Explaining that, above all, they must be prevented from indiscreet utterances, he warned of the possibility that the prisoners might start to shout things about Mme de Montespan, for in the past they had made claims about her 'without any foundation'. If there was any sign of this, the guards must threaten 'to discipline them so cruelly for the slightest noise...that not one of them will dare to breathe'.[62]

To guard against fraternisation, none of the guards garrisoning the citadels were permitted to know the prisoners' names. Louvois added it hardly needed to be said that all the women prisoners should be guarded by custodians of the same sex, to ensure they could not use feminine charms to effect an escape. Even visits from priests were severely restricted, for the prisoners were permitted only to receive Easter communion or final unction.[63]

There was at least one prisoner who could not accept that the situation was irretrievable. In April 1683 Lesage indicated to the governor of Besançon that he was ready to disclose some secret information relating to the King's safety. He soon discovered that the days had passed when such contrivances could secure him more favourable treatment. On being informed, Louvois thanked the governor for bringing the matter to his attention, but remarked that this was a typical ploy from Lesage, who had 'long plied a rogue's trade'. Since the matter concerned the King, it could not be ignored altogether, but Louvois had no doubt that rough handling of Lesage would provide the best means of establishing the truth. If Lesage proved reluctant to elaborate, he should be put on bread and water and beaten morning and night. Louvois concluded, 'You cannot be too harsh towards that rascal who, all the time he was at Vincennes, could never say a truthful word.'[64]

A few months later M. and Mme de Bachimont tried a similar ruse. They were imprisoned in St André de Salins, where they were permitted to share a cell, and in December 1683 they approached the Governor to say that they knew of a secret conspiracy against the King. The Governor sent word of this to Versailles, but the King was deeply sceptical. He commented that this was probably just 'a device they have conceived to bring them back to Paris'. Despite this, it was deemed prudent to look into their claim. The Bachimonts were told that if they revealed all, they could rely on the King's protection, but when the Governor interviewed them it became apparent that the whole thing had been a deception. Louvois told the Governor that the Bachimonts must 'do penance for their imposture', ordering him to punish them by putting them in separate cells.[65]

By 1688 the Bachimonts were once again sharing living quarters but they were still not reconciled to their confinement. In a vain attempt to attract sympathy, they kept shouting from the window of their cell and dropping messages scrawled on scraps of cloth. Louvois ordered the prison Governor to put an end to this insubordination by giving them nothing but bread and water for a month'.[66]

As the years went by, the number of prisoners dwindled. From time to time Louvois was notified that one of them was no more. Cadelan died in September 1684. Guibourg's passing was noted in January 1686 and Bertrand followed him to the grave fifteen months later. Vanens died in December 1691 at St André de Salins.[67] There is no record of the dates when some of the other prisoners died. We do not know, for example, how long Lesage survived, or if Marie Montvoisin reached old age.

A handful of prisoners outlived the King. Mme Guesdon did not die till August 1717, when she was aged seventy-seven. Out of her tiny allowance for food, she had somehow amassed savings of forty-five livres, which she left to her cell mate with a request that she prayed for her soul. 'That's one pensioner less for the King,' commented the official who relayed the news to Paris. The last relic of the Affair of the Poisons was Mme Chapelain, who died in June 1724, aged sixty-eight. So much time had elapsed since her arrest that the man who notified the Minister of War of her demise was unsure of the exact reasons for her detention, though he had a vague idea that she had once been an accomplice of Mme de Brinvilliers.[68]

# ELEVEN

# CONCLUSION

Contrary to what has sometimes been asserted, it is impossible that Louis XIV could have allowed Mme de Montespan to remain at court despite having come to believe that she was a poisoner and Satanist. The King was a ruthless man. When he had deemed it necessary he had never hesitated to deal harshly with individuals who were thought to be close to him. In November 1671, for example, he had had no qualms about arresting his supposed 'favourite', the Comte de Lauzun, for an offence whose exact nature remains unclear. Lauzun was incarcerated in the distant fortress of Pignerol, where he remained in solitary confinement for nine years. If the King was capable of that, it is beyond belief that he would have taken no action whatever against a woman he suspected had not only plotted to kill him and Mlle de Fontanges but had also committed foul acts of sacrilege and participated in human sacrifice.

If the King had harboured such thoughts, ridding himself of Athénaïs's presence would have presented little difficulty. Since she was the mother of six of his surviving children, imprisoning her would have been embarrassing, but she could easily have been forced to enter a convent. It could have been given out that she had done so of her own volition and, after a brief flurry of interest, this would have excited little comment. It is inconceivable that Louis would have baulked at adopting such a course had he believed her guilty of unspeakable crimes.

The King may have accepted that in 1667 Mme de Montespan had briefly been a client of la Voisin's and that the latter had introduced her to Mariette and Lesage. If so, this was something he decided to overlook, having presumably satisfied himself that after the arrest of Mariette and Lesage in 1668 she had had no further dealings with people of that kind. On the other hand Louis may have concluded that everything Mariette and Lesage had said about her had been untrue and that he need have no worries on that score.

Exactly when the King resolved this matter to his satisfaction is hard to say. It would seem that in late February 1681, when Colbert and Duplessis wrote their memoranda in defence of Mme de Montespan, the King still needed to be convinced that Athénaïs could not have done these dreadful things. While it is unclear at what point Colbert's arguments prevailed, it is noteworthy that on 28 March the King and Colbert both signed a document approving the foundation of a convent of Ursuline nuns, which Athénaïs had set up at her own expense. Since the document states that the King was 'desirous to treat the said lady favourably', this perhaps indicates that he was now persuaded of her innocence. Certainly by 17 April, when La Reynie wrote a memorandum noting that the King had decided what action to take against prisoners like Guibourg, Galet and Mme Chapelain,[1] it can be assumed that Louis had also made up his mind about Mme de Montespan.

Mme de Montespan therefore continued at court, almost certainly unaware of the manner in which she had been traduced. However, her life there was no longer enviable. It was true that Mlle de Fontanges no longer posed any kind of threat to her, but even after that poor young woman retired from court, the King showed no desire to resume a sexual relationship with Athénaïs. This was doubtless partly attributable to the fact that she was now fatter than ever: in July 1681 Mme de Maintenon informed a correspondent that Athénaïs was now an 'astonishing' size, 'having grown a foot stouter since you saw her'.[2]

To the amazement of the court, the King did not seek a replacement for Mlle de Fontanges. He never took another mistress, 'in spite of the advances that did not fail to be made him'. At first people remained on the lookout for the advent of a new favourite, but none appeared on the scene. In August 1681 Mme de Maintenon quashed rumours that the King had embarked on a flirtation with a young woman who had recently come to court, telling a cousin he could deny such reports 'without fear of appearing ill-informed'.[3]

Mme de Montespan was still *Surintendante* of the Queen's household, so the King's abandonment of her did not result in a complete loss of status. She took her duties seriously and liked to think she was indispensable, boasting to her sister in 1683 that she had had the greatest difficulty persuading the King to grant her leave of absence.[4] Athénaïs's position as mother of the King's children also earned her a measure of respect. In November 1681 her two youngest children by Louis were legitimised and brought to court, and this official recognition enhanced her own prestige.

Athénaïs still participated with apparent enjoyment in all court festivities and although she and the King were no longer lovers Louis did
not ostracise her. She was invariably included in the house parties that
the King gave in his newly built retreat, Marly, and, once back at
court, he paid her daily visits. He went to see her immediately after
attending mass and called on her again when he had finished supper.
However, these visits were always brief and more than one source
states that the King took care to be accompanied by courtiers so he
would not have to be alone with her.[5]

What was most galling for Athénaïs, however, was that while the
King still treated her with courtesy and consideration, it was obvious to
all that he much preferred to spend time with Mme de Maintenon.
Things were slightly eased by the fact that Athénaïs now saw relatively
little of the former governess. In September 1681 Mme de Maintenon
reported that in the last month they had encountered each other only
once and on such occasions they usually managed to keep up an
appearance of civility. At one point in the summer of 1681 they went
for a stroll together, arm in arm and roaring with laughter. However, as
Mme de Maintenon sourly commented later, this did not diminish
their underlying enmity.[6]

In late July 1683 the Queen developed a boil in her armpit and by
bleeding her repeatedly 'the doctors...killed her as surely as if they had
thrust a dagger into her heart'. Though briefly upset, the King was more
shocked than truly afflicted by this unexpected event; the ironic thing
was that it was Mme de Montespan who probably felt the bereavement
more keenly. She had taken good care of the Queen in her final hours
and though her tears when Marie-Thérèse died were presumed insin-
cere, she had suffered a severe loss with the Queen's passing.[7] Now that
she had no office in Marie-Thérèse's household, Mme de Montespan's
presence at court was redundant and her future looked more uncertain.

Mme de Maintenon was concerned that now he could no longer
sleep with the Queen, the King would be tempted to look elsewhere
for sexual satisfaction. Twelve days after Marie-Thérèse's death she
urged a friend to devote all her energies 'to praying for the King: he
has more need of divine grace than ever to sustain a way of life contrary to his inclinations and habits'.[8] In the event the King endured no
more than a brief period of celibacy. Although the exact date is
unknown (the night of 9 October 1683 has been suggested or, alternatively, some time in January 1684, when mourning for the Queen officially ended), within a few months of his wife's death the King secretly
married Mme de Maintenon.

The marriage was never officially acknowledged, but gradually rumours began circulating that the King had taken her as his wife. Many people were initially inclined to dismiss the reports as ridiculous, but in time even the most sceptical observers accepted them. The German diplomat Ezechiel Spanheim professed himself mystified as to why the King had yoked himself to this forbidding woman who was some years his senior. In the end he suggested that he had done so in order 'to mortify his senses out of penitence for his unlawful love affairs' but, in fact, as Mme de Maintenon herself acknowledged, Louis 'loved her as much as he was capable of loving'. The marriage did not provide her with the same degree of emotional fulfilment, but she believed she had been called upon by God to perform the valuable task of securing Louis's salvation. While applying herself conscientiously to carrying out what she saw as her primary duty, she lamented that her destiny had prevented her from leaving a court she despised. As she herself reflected many years later, 'God did me the favour of making me insensible to the honours which surrounded me and only feeling the subjection and constraint.'[9]

The extraordinary elevation of her former employee constituted a severe trial for Athénaïs. If she desired a favour from the King she now had to humble herself and approach him through Mme de Maintenon. In December 1685, for example, she wanted her son by M. de Montespan to be given a position in the Dauphin's entourage and this was only granted after Mme de Maintenon informed the King of her wishes. Such enforced obsequiousness did not accord well with Athénaïs's natural temperament and even when she strove to be friend-ly towards the former governess, people felt sure that before long she would find it impossible to keep up the effort. In 1685 Mme de Maintenon told a friend that Mme de Montespan had recently invited her to Clagny, but one of Mme de Maintenon's servants had declared that she 'did not think I was safe there'. This has been taken as an allu-sion to Mme de Montespan's reputation as a poisoner, though it may simply have referred to the possibility that she would be seized by a fit of rage and become abusive. By this stage she was 'so mad ... when she was in a temper' that she might even resort to violence.[10]

As was only to be expected, there were all too many occasions when Athénaïs's self-control proved unable to withstand the strain and she permitted her sarcastic tongue an over-free rein. As Ezechiel Spanheim put it, 'The jealousy of the aforesaid lady towards a person who was in every way inferior to her ... and whose fortune, so to speak, she had made, could not but break out on several occasions.' With regrettable regularity she gave vent to her mortification by letting fly with 'pungent barbs and bitter jokes' that subtly denigrated Mme de Maintenon and made everyone present uncomfortable.[11] Mme de Maintenon seemingly shrugged off these incidents and would even repeat Mme de Montespan's comments to amuse her friends, but despite her outward composure Athénaïs's repeated needling left her seething. Far worse, by indulging her ill humour at Mme de Maintenon's expense, Mme de Montespan succeeded in antagonising the King.

In December 1684 Athénaïs experienced what Saint-Simon described as 'the first major step of her disgrace' when the King moved her out of the lodgings adjoining his own apartment at Versailles and relocated her in a suite of rooms on the ground floor. Mme de Montespan did not take kindly to being relegated to the sidelines and in 1686 there was an unpleasant incident after she received what she considered to be an intolerable affront. That year, unbeknown to most of the court (including Athénaïs) the King had been afflicted by an anal fistula. On 21 May it was announced that for the good of his health he would leave for the spa town of Barèges in three weeks' time, but Mme de Montespan was not among those who were selected to accompany him. Incensed at her exclusion, on 25 May Athénaïs had a showdown with the King. She became 'so carried away that she openly complained' and was reported to have shouted 'several things which would not have been prudent to say'. She then stormed from court, announcing she would seek refuge with her sister at Fontrevault Abbey. She wanted her two youngest children to join her there but next day, as they were climbing into their coach, the King sent word that he would not permit his son the Comte de Toulouse to leave.[12]

In the end all was smoothed over. On 27 May the King decided that after all, he would not go to Barèges. He ordered the Duc du Maine to inform his mother of the change of plan and she at once returned to court. The next day the King visited her as normal without making any reference to the contretemps that had occurred.[13] But though the incident appeared forgotten, it had weakened Athénaïs still further by underlining that the King's tolerance was not inexhaustible and that she remained at court on sufferance.

After this Mme de Montespan took to spending long periods away from court. In the spring of 1687 she absented herself to take the waters at Bourbon and then went to stay for several weeks with her sister at Fontrevault. She did not return to Versailles until September and in subsequent years she repeated this pattern. However, as one courtier remarked, these 'long absences...merely ruined her little remaining credit; it was furthermore thought [she took them] more to ease her peevish temper than for health reasons'. During the months she did attend court, the King no longer unfailingly visited her in the evenings and she was also not automatically included on excursions to Marly.[14]

Despite the fact that she was being gradually shut out from the King's inner circle, Athénaïs was unable to summon up the will to leave the court. Although in former days her pride had been legendary, she could not bring herself to forsake this demeaning existence and instead endured a succession of slights in order to cling on to a life which had become utterly pointless. When at last she did the right thing, it was almost by accident.

Having hitherto been responsible for arranging her children's education, Mme de Montespan was understandably furious when, without prior consultation, her youngest daughter, Mlle de Blois, was entrusted in March 1691 to the care of Mme de Montchevreuil, a hideous, humourless prude who was the best friend of Mme de Maintenon. The provocation made Mme de Montespan 'forget all her wise resolutions... not to give the King any pretext to get rid of her'. She angrily sent word to Louis that since she was being deprived of her children, she would like him to authorise her retirement from court. It was a fatal blunder, for the King had been longing for her departure for some time. He 'joyfully responded' that she had his permission to withdraw and then, to guard against her changing her mind, he allocated her apartment at Versailles to the Duc du Maine.[15]

Before long Mme de Montespan came to regret her precipitate action. The following month she told friends 'that she had not absolutely abandoned the court; that she would still see the King sometimes and that in truth they had been a bit hasty to remove the furniture from her apartment'.[16] It turned out, however, that she had taken an irrevocable step: she would never see the King again.

Occasionally, when the King was absent, she crept back to Versailles, paying brief visits when he was away during the summer of 1691, and again in April 1694. Such appearances only made people compare her with those 'unfortunate souls who return to the places they inhabited to expiate their faults'.[17] Despite her evident yearning to be readmitted, her exclusion from the royal presence remained absolute. She was not even invited to the wedding of her daughter, Mlle de Blois, to the Duc de Chartres in February 1692, or that of the Duc du Maine a month later.

Mme de Montespan lived for sixteen years after her withdrawal from court and, much as she had dreaded leaving, there is reason to believe she found happiness elsewhere. When in Paris she lived at the Filles de

Saint-Joseph, a convent of which she had been a munificent patron for some years and which recently had been enlarged at her expense. Her life there was far from reclusive: although she had become estranged from the Duc du Maine, she kept in touch with her other children, including her son by the Marquis de Montespan. Besides this, aristocratic ladies and old friends from court made a point of visiting her. After a time she bought properties at Petit Bourg and Oiron in Poitou, and she also paid regular visits to the spa town of Bourbon. In addition she spent several months each year with her favourite sister at Fontrevault Abbey.

Merely because she passed so much time in religious institutions, it should not be thought that her life was devoid of fun. She once described Fontrevault as 'a convent which nobody can resist...and where all the nuns are a thousand times happier than anyone who lives in the world'. She succeeded in communicating her enjoyment of what it had to offer to those around her, for she still possessed the quality of infectious gaiety that had been so marked in her youth. Once, when she was at Fontrevault, a niece of hers wrote that Mme de Montespan had the talent of making every day seem like a fête day. Even hearing a sermon with her could be fun. In 1696 Mme de Coulanges informed a friend that Athénaïs was taking her to listen to a celebrated preacher who bore a striking resemblance to Mme de Montespan's late brother the Duc de Vivonne. Vivonne had died 'rotten in body and soul' a few years before and Mme de Coulanges admitted that she and Athénaïs were never able to repress their laughter when they heard pious exhortations and holy sentiments issue from the mouth of one who reminded them so strongly of that renowned debauchee.[18]

Gradually, however, pleasure ceased to be of such importance to Athénaïs. She had always given generously to charity, but in later years she devoted most of her annual income to deserving causes. Apart from her endowment of the Filles de Saint-Joseph, where she set up an embroidery workshop for poor girls, she established orphanages at Fontainebleau and Oiron, and also alleviated the lot of numerous needy individuals. Even after her departure from court she had continued to receive an allowance from the King of 12,000 gold louis a year, much of which she gave away. In January 1707 the King informed her that his wars were costing him so much that this year he could only give her 8000, to which she replied that while she did not mind for herself, she felt sad on behalf of the poor, who would suffer in consequence.[19]

As well as giving away her money, she immersed herself in good works, sewing shirts for paupers. All her life she had been renowned for keeping a good table, but now she ate more simply and fasted frequently. Long periods were set aside for prayer and she not only wore a hairshirt at all times but mortified her body in other ways. In 1707 she even asked her old friend the Duchesse de Noailles not to write to her with news from court as, though she had not yet reached the stage where such matters were of no interest to her, she did not want to distract her mind from higher things.[20]

A letter she wrote in 1704 to a female friend demonstrates the depth of her piety. She confided that she longed for God 'to create a solitude in the bottom of my heart' so she could meditate on her salvation at her leisure and then urged, 'Let us go to him, my dear...Let us weep for our sins now in order not to shed one day...tears of despair'. She reminded her unnamed correspondent that they must guard against dying steeped in sin for, after death, those who had lived 'in forgetfulness of God and the Church will regret in vain their waste of time'.[21] The use of devotional language was, of course, more commonplace at the time and some might be inclined to dismiss these sentiments as worthless on the grounds that even Mme Voisin could feign piety when it suited her. It would be harsh, however, to doubt that Athénaïs's convictions were deeply held and her evident belief that salvation was attainable provides another argument against believing that in earlier years she had dedicated herself to the devil. While she demonstrated an awareness of her sins of the flesh, these were hardly the words of a woman who had committed actions that would have put her beyond hope of redemption.

Saint-Simon claimed that, though even in old age Mme de Montespan enjoyed excellent health, she was plagued by a fear of death. Much has been made of the fact that she was also afraid of the dark. She never went to sleep without candles burning in her bedroom and to ensure that she was never left alone, she employed old ladies to sit with her and watch her as she slept. This has been attributed to her terror that Satan would come to claim the soul that had been pledged him, but this is fanciful, for she had been nervous of the dark all her life. In 1675 she mentioned in a letter that she 'cannot sleep without light' and it is clear that this had been the case for some time.[22]

In the end she met her death in exemplary style. In May 1707 she had just arrived at Bourbon to take the waters when she was suddenly taken ill. Her condition worsened after the Maréchale de Clairambault gave her an overdose of emetic and it became apparent she would not survive. Saint-Simon recorded that 'nothing could have been more edifying than her final hours'. She called her servants to her and proclaimed her regret for her sins, apologising for her bouts of ill temper and the scandal she had caused. Betraying no sign of the dread of death from which she had suffered in the past, she received the final sacraments evincing a serene confidence in the mercy of God.[23]

The news was at once sent to the King at Marly. Saint-Simon maintained that the King appeared callously indifferent to her death and that when the Duchesse de Bourgogne expressed surprise at this, he told her that Mme de Montespan had been dead to him ever since her departure from court. It seems, however, that the news did not fail to move him, for the diarist Dangeau recorded that on that day the King broke his usual routine by walking in his gardens till nightfall. As for Mme de Maintenon, much as she had detested Mme de Montespan, the news of her death left her strangely shaken. Ever since Athénaïs had left court, Mme de Maintenon had resolutely severed all contact with her, making it clear she did not want to receive even an occasional letter. Yet, on learning of her death, she secluded herself on her *chaise percée* to have a good weep and she told her confidante the Princesse d'Ursins that she had inevitably been affected by the loss of a person who had always excited strong emotions in her.[24]

Two years later, on 14 June 1709, the former Lieutenant-General of the Paris Police, Nicolas de La Reynie, died at the great age of eighty-four. Civic-minded to the last, he left instructions that his body should not be interred in a vault within a church, as he did not want 'the rotting of my body to contribute to the corruption and infection of the air in the place where the holy mysteries are celebrated'.[25]

In 1686 the King had demonstrated his continuing high regard for La Reynie by making him a Councillor of State, a post to which he had long aspired. For some years, however, he had also remained in charge of the Paris police, only relinquishing the position in 1697. By then he was 'worn out by age and work' but even so, Saint-Simon had so high an opinion of his abilities that he was sad the King did not appoint La Reynie to succeed M. Boucherat as Chancellor when the latter died in 1699.[26]

During La Reynie's lifetime the King had relied on his fidelity and discretion to prevent the public from discovering that Mme de Montespan had been linked with the Affair of the Poisons, even though others had thought that more stringent precautions were necessary. In 1681 Colbert's legal adviser, Duplessis, had recommended that the records of the *Chambre Ardente*'s proceedings should be burnt as they were filled with 'execrable impieties and abominable filth whose memory . . . should not be conserved'.[27] At the time this course had not been followed, perhaps because the King thought La Reynie would have interpreted such action as an implicit criticism of his conduct of the case. However, now that La Reynie could raise no objection, the King sought to obliterate all the evidence implicating Mme de Montespan.

In 1681 the documents relating to 'the particular facts' about Mme de Montespan had been entrusted to Sagot, Recorder of the *Chambre Ardente*. Then, nine years later, they were transferred into the custody of the King's secretary, Gaudion. On 13 July 1709, a month after the death of La Reynie, the King sent Chancellor Pontchartrain to retrieve the coffer containing the documents from Gaudion. When it was brought to him in the council chamber, Louis unlocked the coffer with a key which had belonged to La Reynie. Having perused the documents it contained, he methodically burnt them.[28]

Presumably the King believed that by doing this he would protect Mme de Montespan's reputation for ever and, for a remarkably long time, he succeeded. None of Mme de Montespan's contemporaries were aware of the accusations that had been levelled against her and for 150 years after her death the same secrecy was preserved. However, it turned out that La Reynie had kept other copies of the documents Louis XIV had burnt in 1709 and in the second half of the nineteenth century these came to light. François Ravaisson devoted four volumes of his work *Les Archives de la Bastille* to reproducing the records of the *Chambre Ardente* and when these were published in 1870–4 the black legend that Mme de Montespan was a murderer and worshipper of the devil at once came into existence.

Those who did not find the available evidence absolutely convincing still hesitated to exonerate Mme de Montespan, for it was assumed that some of the documents destroyed by the King might have contained irrevocable proof of her guilt. However, this is most unlikely. Colbert had access to all the documents detailing the accusations against her and in his searching analysis of them he never refers to any evidence that cannot be found either in Ravaisson's work or in various Paris archives. Although there are areas of the Affair of the Poisons which are not fully documented (for example, the records relating to the trial of the Maréchal de Luxembourg are incomplete), we can feel reasonably confident that nothing damaging to Mme de Montespan has been hidden from us.

In late June 1681, when the *Chambre Ardente* was at its most active, one of its commissioners boasted to an acquaintance, 'You cannot imagine the good this Chamber has done.' It is questionable, however, whether his pride in the Chamber's achievements was justified. The commissioners would no doubt have argued that their greatest service lay in having safeguarded the life of the King, which had been shown to be menaced by poisoners. Yet from what we know of the plots against Louis XIV uncovered by the Chamber, it is hard to believe that his life had ever been in any danger. There is, of course, no disputing that, as the Marquis de Sourches approvingly noted, during its three years of existence the Chamber 'purged France of several monsters'.[29] Marie Bosse and Mme Voisin, for example, were each responsible for more than one murder and merited severe punishment. On the other hand there was no need to set up a special commission to bring them to justice, for they could have been satisfactorily dealt with by the normal course of law.

It is worth querying exactly how much poisoning was going on in France prior to the establishment of the Chamber, even though it is difficult to give a precise answer. La Reynie, for one, had no doubt at all as to the scale of the problem. In a memorandum penned in early 1682 he asserted, 'Human life is publicly up for sale; [poisoning] is practically the only remedy used in all family troubles; sacrilege, impieties and abominations are commonly practised in Paris, the provinces and the countryside.' This was certainly an exaggeration but others who were not altogether uncritical of the *Chambre Ardente* did believe that poisoning was becoming more widespread and that firm action was needed to suppress it. The Marquis de La Fare, for example, recorded in his memoirs that it was right to have set up a commission 'to punish culprits and to halt the progress of this crime which increased every day'.[30]

However, if one tries to give figures for cases of poisoning which occurred in the fifteen years before the Chamber was set up, the numbers do not appear very significant. Besides the three victims of Mme de Brinvilliers, one can put forward the names of M. Faurye (who was probably poisoned by Magdelaine de La Grange), M. Brunet, M. Leféron, the Marquis de Canilhac, M. Lescalopier and M. Ferry. It is possible, too, that Mme Anne Carada poisoned the wife of her lover. There were others who could be said to have been fortunate to have escaped with their lives. If Mme de Dreux had been left at liberty she might have progressed to poisoning her husband or the Duchesse de Richelieu; Mme Poulaillon might have succeeded in harming her husband. Had Mme Voisin continued to operate, the toll of victims would doubtless have continued to mount and may indeed have been higher than can be proved. Both Marie Montvoisin and Lesage named numerous other clients of la Voisin who allegedly sought her help in murdering individuals, but it is impossible to ascertain whether this was so.

In the absence of efficient forensic techniques, establishing that a long dead person was a victim of poisoning was highly problematic. As Colbert's legal adviser, Duplessis, noted at one point, it was difficult to attain the truth in an instance where 'for example, a man has died several years ago in the arms of his family; poison has not been suspected; he has been buried and his body has not been inspected; later on, an accusation of poison occurs. In this case, how can one convict the author of the crime, when one cannot really prove that a crime has been committed?'[31] It is improbable, however, that large numbers of poisonings went undetected. On the contrary, indeed, the problem tended to be overstated for in the absence of scientific proof, all too often deaths that did not deserve to be considered suspicious were wrongly attributed to poison. During the Affair of the Poisons it was alleged that Chancellor d'Aligre, M. Lionne, the former Minister for Foreign Affairs, and the late President of the Paris *Parlement*, Guillaume Lamoignon, had all been poisoned, but there is no evidence to suggest their deaths were anything other than natural.

Disproportionate fears as to the prevalence of poisoning excited irrational panic. One source claimed that following the revelations of the Brinvilliers case, 'Every father suspects his son and closely watches his movements...Children take precautions against their parents; a brother or sister does not dare eat anything brought by another brother or sister.' Primi Visconti recorded that at the time of the Affair of the Poisons, 'Almost no one trusted his friends any more...As soon as someone felt ill from having eaten too much, he believed he had been poisoned.' Commonplace cases of gastroenteritis and stomach upset resulted in chefs and servants being arrested, prompting one wag to remark that if all the bad cooks in Paris were seized, the prisons would soon be overflowing.[32]

Nerves were overstretched at court as elsewhere and in the autumn of 1680 the tendency to leap to unfortunate conclusions was illustrated when a servant of the new Dauphine's named Bessola fell ill and poison was assumed to be the cause. Two scullery boys were immediately taken into custody, even though there was no proof they had committed any crime, and they were only released when Bessola recovered. It was then grudgingly acknowledged that her illness had not been caused by anything untoward but, as the Comte de Bussy commented, 'In the era of the *Chambre Ardente*, anything a bit out of the ordinary passes for poison.'[33]

Fears of this kind were naturally exacerbated by the fact that when unexpected deaths occurred, medical science was often not sufficiently far advanced to establish the true cause. Few people displayed the caution of the Marquis de Sourches who in 1689, when others at court were confidently asserting that the Queen of Spain had been poisoned, noted soberly, 'It would be dangerous to reason in this way about all sudden deaths ... as young people die just as often as old ones.'[34] When the Affair of the Poisons was at its height those capable of bringing such a measured judgement to bear were scarcer still.

If it is difficult to estimate whether poisoning was on the increase at this period, it is impossible to know whether children had really been sacrificed in black magic ceremonies in Paris. Obviously, at a time when poverty and lack of contraception ensured that there were many unwanted babies, finding infant victims would not have presented an insuperable problem and, given the strength of people's belief in the devil, one cannot rule out that such horrors took place. One must, however, be wary of being too credulous. La Reynie took the view that the descriptions of child sacrifice supplied by Marie Montvoisin and Étienne Guibourg were so detailed and vivid that they must have been present at these events, but his reasoning was flawed. History abounds with cases where 'witches' have confessed to participating in atrocities and abominations, which we know to be fictitious.[35]

A recent authority has suggested that under relentless interrogation witches 'engaged in a peculiar kind of dialogue with their interlocutors, adapting their responses to meet expectations' and it is now recognised that under extreme stress individuals will 'mingle themes from their cultural milieu with elements derived from dream and fantasy to generate self-incriminating narratives which have their own psychological significance'. Even in Britain today, allegations that children are being ritually murdered by Satanists are regularly made, but when such claims have been investigated by the police, horrific eyewitness accounts of cannibalism and infanticide have invariably been shown to be imaginary. On the other hand the recent discovery in the River Thames of the body of a male child who is thought to have been murdered so that his body parts could be used to make black magic medicines does make one cautious about asserting that similar things could not have happened in France more than 300 years ago.[36]

Fears that children were being kidnapped and murdered for such purposes provoked bouts of hysteria in Paris long after the *Chambre Ardente* had been disbanded. In 1701 the Royal Attorney at the Châtelet reported that fresh rumours that a high-ranking person was having children butchered in order to bathe in their blood had led to widespread disorder. The Attorney remarked wearily that this was an all too familiar phenomenon. 'These fancies and movements of popular fury are not new; I have seen some happen which were carried to such excess that in various quarters of Paris there were women who were almost beaten to death ... because they were accused of being abductors of children'.[37]

In the wake of the Affair of the Poisons, practical measures were instituted to reduce the incidence of poisoning. On 31 July 1682 a royal edict was registered in the Paris *Parlement* tightening up that area of the law.[38] Having noted that poisoning was 'not only the most dangerous and detestable [crime] of all but also the most difficult to discover', it decreed that henceforth anyone convicted of supplying poison for murderous purposes, whether or not it resulted in fatalities, would be liable to the death penalty.

Because poison could be fabricated in laboratories supposedly devoted to the quest for the Philosopher's Stone, alchemy was now placed under scrutiny. The edict prohibited the private 'preparation of drugs or distillations under pretext of [finding] chemical remedies or [doing] experiments ... or searching for the Philosopher's Stone' unless those engaged in such research obtained an official permit to set up a workshop.

Furthermore, since in the past it had been too easy to obtain all forms of arsenic and mercury sublimate, restrictions were now placed on their sale. In future these substances could only be sold to professional men who were authorised to use them in the course of their work, such as doctors, apothecaries, surgeons, goldsmiths, dyers and blacksmiths. Whenever a purchase of poison was made by a legitimate person, the shopkeeper was required to inscribe the transaction in an official register kept for the purpose.

This was a sensible measure, which was later emulated by other countries. Bizarrely, however, it does not seem to have greatly diminished the fear of poison within France, for people there continued to display what Voltaire called their 'unhappy propensity to suspect natural death of being occasioned by violent means'. In 1689 there were even renewed fears that the King himself was being targeted by poisoners after an anonymous letter was found referring to 'a certain great tree, which must be felled'. To deal with the threat a new *Chambre Ardente* was set up in the Arsenal and La Reynie once again served as its *rapporteur*. On 27 June the Marquis de Sourches noted that there was a lot of talk in Paris about the executions ordered by this body. A carpenter who had posed as a physician had recently been put to death 'for having poisoned several persons and carried out abortions for a large number of women.' It was surmised that he had had some design against the King's person and had been in secret communication with some exiled Huguenots, but this was not really proven.[39]

There was an irony in the fact that two years later Louvois, who had formerly been so active in persecuting poisoners, was himself believed to have fallen victim to poisoning. On 16 July 1691 he was in conference with the King when he suddenly felt unwell. Realising he was ill, Louis suggested that he withdraw, but soon after reaching his own apartments, the Minister collapsed and died in the arms of his doctor.[40]

An autopsy was carried out, which makes it plain he had suffered a pulmonary embolism that had impeded the flow of blood to the heart. Nevertheless, the fact that Louvois was known recently to have drunk from a pitcher of water that was kept constantly replenished in his study led to suspicions that he had been poisoned; these were much exacerbated when the King's physician, D'Aquin, said he had been killed by 'that sort of poison which blights the heart and suddenly blocks the circulation of the blood'. A floor polisher who had had access to the Minister's study and who came from Savoy (with whom France was currently at war) was immediately arrested, though he was freed not long afterwards.[41]

Despite the lack of supporting evidence, people at court continued to believe Louvois had been poisoned. The Duchesse d'Orléans held typically robust views on the subject. Having toyed with the possibility that the Minister had been killed by his own sons, she next propounded the theory that he had been poisoned by her *bête noire*, Mme de Maintenon, who she claimed had long ago mastered 'the art of Mme de Brinvilliers'.[42] Within a few years, however, it would be brought home to Madame how horrible it was to cast such aspersions.

In April 1711 the King's only legitimate son, the Grand Dauphin, died of smallpox. As usual the Duchesse d'Orléans believed he had been killed by 'a terrible poison'. 'I was told yesterday that after his death a black vapour was seen to rise from his mouth and his face turned as black as pitch and remained that colour,' she breathlessly informed a correspondent.[43]

A year later death made far more terrible incursions into the royal family. In February 1712 the enchanting young Duchesse de Bourgogne, who was married to the King's eldest grandson and heir apparent, contracted a highly infectious disease whose symptoms included a rash and high fever, and which has been tentatively identified as measles, scarlet fever or a form of typhus. Within days of her death on 12 February her husband, the Duc de Bourgogne, also fell dangerously ill and he followed her to the grave on 18 February. The tragedy was compounded when the young couple's elder son, a child of five, was struck down with the same disease and died on 7 March.

Predictably, the grim succession of fatalities was widely ascribed to poison and, to the horror of Madame, the finger was pointed at her son, who had succeeded his father as Duc d'Orléans in 1701. Not only had Orléans's own chance of succeeding to the throne been much improved by the snuffing out of so many of his male relations, but he was known to be interested in chemistry, which still had sinister connotations. Madame claimed that the fact that her late husband had also been associated in the public mind with the death of his first wife in 1670 meant that people were more ready to think evil of his son. 'Whoever dies at court, my son is blamed,' she wailed in March 1712,[44] but though the King heartily disliked his nephew, he did not believe these slanders. When Louis died in 1715, to be succeeded by his five-year-old great-grandson, Louis XV, the Duc d'Orléans was appointed regent.

The edict of July 1682 had not been concerned solely with poisons, for it was also directed against superstitious abuses. In one respect it represented an advance, because it marked an important stage in the process whereby witchcraft was no longer recognised as an offence. The very existence of witchcraft was implicitly questioned, for penalties were set out only for those who, by pretending they were 'diviners, magicians or sorcerers', corrupted the gullible. The edict ordained that all those who fell into this category should leave the realm forthwith on pain of corporal punishment, while anyone convicted of the more serious offence of sacrilege would be sentenced to death.[45]

Colbert's adviser Duplessis had stressed the importance of mounting a purge against fortune-tellers and practitioners of magic, stressing that unless all those involved in this 'detestable commerce' were driven out of business, the public would assume that such activities were acceptable.[46] La Reynie, too, believed it was essential to halt their operations on the grounds that they seduced their clients into crime. Yet though it is clear that the highest priority was attached to cleansing Paris of these parasites, the attempt to eliminate them was an utter failure.

Even at the end of the seventeenth century, successors to Mme Voisin were still at work in Paris and they continued to number people of high rank among their clients. In 1696 a woman of this kind was arrested 'for the greatest infamies in the world' and, when her premises were searched, letters were found written to her by the Marquis de Feuquières. More shocking still, the letters made clear that the King's nephew, the Duc de Chartres (the future Duc d'Orléans), had had deal-ings with her.[47] The King suppressed the evidence and the woman was never brought to trial, but the episode showed that the divineresses were far from eradicated.

In October 1702 La Reynie's successor as Lieutenant-General of the Paris Police, René Voyer, Comte d'Argenson, reported that the capital was plagued by 'a great disorder which is growing from day to day and which is not confined to the corruption of morals but tends to the destruction of every principle of religion'. This alarming situation was caused by a proliferation of 'false diviners, would-be sorcerers, [indi-viduals] who promise to discover treasure or communicate with spirits', as well as numerous persons 'who distribute powders, talismans and pentacles'. There was a huge number of these charlatans and their clients were multiplying all the time.[48]

The details supplied by d'Argenson make familiar reading to anyone acquainted with the Affair of the Poisons. Those rounded up by his officers at the time included one Jemme, who specialised in drawing up pacts with the devil, and another man, Bendrode, who claimed to have the secret of the Philosopher's Stone. A priest named Père Robert was said to have performed 'sacrifices' in order to consummate diabolic pacts and to have supplied clients with pieces of rope retrieved from the neck of a hanged man, which he had blessed with a consecrated wafer. He claimed that whoever possessed a section of this rope 'would make himself loved by all women, would win at gambling... and would succeed in all affairs'. The Baron de Saugeon and his wife sold 'a water to re-establish virginity', while a pregnant woman named Lebrun who had volunteered to surrender her infant to the devil had 'given birth within a magic circle to a child who was carried off that very instant'.[49]

What was more, these people catered to prestigious clients. The divineress Marie-Anne de La Ville, who was arrested at this time, num-bered among her customers not just the incorrigible Marquis de Feuquières but also Mme de Grancey, an intimate of the late Duc d'Orléans. Another man named Boyer who performed conjurations and told fortunes claimed to have accurately predicted the future to unnamed 'duchesses'.[50]

D'Argenson regarded all this as a serious problem, but he did not want the offenders tried in any form of court, not even a secret tribu-nal. He noted that not only might it prove problematic to obtain con-victions when all the witnesses for the prosecution were associates of the accused and themselves of bad character, but also that 'the impact made on the public by investigating cases of this kind creates the sort of scandal which dishonours religion and makes the Protestants more unruly'.

His preferred solution was that the culprits should be imprisoned in distant chateaux or confined to workhouses by order of the King. He was confident that such measures, 'executed by means of the highest authority will make more impression on the public and instil more fear into the inquisitive than a long series of investigations and sixty sentences [passed] by an extraordinary commission'.[51] Clearly d'Argenson was aware of the difficulties that had beset the *Chambre Ardente* and had no wish to be sucked into a similar quagmire.

D'Argenson's reluctance to emulate La Reynie is the more understandable in view of the fact that, while it was in being, the *Chambre Ardente* was considered to have caused great damage to France's international reputation. When the scandal first broke, it was assumed there must be real substance in the allegations against eminent figures, and at court there was widespread shame at the prospect that people of high rank had committed foul crimes. Mme de Sévigné commented that the accusations of poison, sacrilege and abortion were 'filling all Europe with horror' and lamented that henceforth 'a Frenchman will be synonymous with a poisoner in foreign lands'.[52] However, as it became apparent that grand individuals were being called before the commission for 'mere trifles', there was a change of emphasis. Not only was it considered deplorable that the superstition and credulity of members of the French élite should be paraded before foreigners, but there was a feeling that by taking such absurdities so seriously the authorities had unnecessarily exposed the kingdom to the mockery of outsiders.

Colbert's objections to the activities of the *Chambre Ardente* stemmed partly from his belief that they were damaging to national prestige, and certainly the affair aroused a great deal of interest outside France. Foreign ambassadors stationed there were careful to include details in despatches, and printed accounts of episodes such as the Duchesse de Bouillon's appearance before the commissioners were also circulated in some countries. The father of M. de Feuquières was serving as French ambassador to Sweden when his son was summoned before the commission, so he was well placed to observe the impact that the affair created overseas. In July 1680 he wrote to inform the King that 'for the past six months, the affairs of the Arsenal Chamber have caused a sensation in Sweden'. He explained that for fear of being thought partial, he had refrained from drawing attention to this until his son had been discharged by the commissioners. Nevertheless, the experience had showed him 'how disheartening it is, Sire, when one is concerned for the glory of the fatherland, to see it discredited by a low affair'.[53] Certainly, it was ironic that Louis XIV, who was so passionate about upholding the glory of France, should have done so much to compromise it by setting up the *Chambre Ardente.*

By the later years of the reign the perception had developed that the Affair of the Poisons was a painful episode to which it was wiser not to draw attention. In her memoirs, written towards the end of her life, the Duchesse de Montpensier mentioned that the Comtesse de Soissons left the country because 'she was mixed up in the business of the *Chambre Ardente*', but added cautiously, 'I will not attempt to talk of that; the matter is too delicate and [to do so] one must be better informed about it than I am.' Mme de Sévigné also gives the impression that the subject was best avoided: in 1689 she wrote that at court 'one does not talk of poison; that word is forbidden at Versailles and throughout all France'.[54]

Shortly before her execution Mme Voisin declared, 'Debauchery is the primary incentive of all these disorders' and this pronouncement was thought to contain much truth. Prior to the trial of Mme de Brinvilliers, a lawyer who wrote a tract protesting her innocence had urged his readers not to be prejudiced against her on account of her sexual misconduct, for it was essential to bear in mind 'the distance which separates dissolute morals from the infamy of crime'.[55] However, her conviction and subsequent admission of guilt suggested that, on the contrary, the two were often closely interlinked. The fact that all those at court who were called before the *Chambre Ardente* were known to have irregular private lives reinforced the idea that there was a connection.

When the Affair of the Poisons was at its height the celebrated preacher Père Bourdaloue gave a sermon at court on 2 February 1680 in which he explicitly linked immorality with far worse offences. He began by praising the King for having taken firm action against those who were currently menacing French society, declaring that 'there were monsters hidden within France, and your Majesty is the hero whom God has raised up to crush and stifle them'. He then thundered that 'the sacrilege, impiety and homicide which have spread throughout France' were the 'fatal but infallible consequence of debauchery and licentious morals', before once again encouraging the King to seek out the culprits. 'It is to you, Sire, to whom the public will be indebted for being purged of them,' he intoned.[56]

Bourdaloue's strictures inevitably made the King reflect and it is notable that from this point Louis made a sustained effort to improve the morals of the court. He now led by example and, though the onset of his forties and the influence of Mme de Maintenon partly accounted for the alterations in his own way of life, the things he had learned during the Affair of the Poisons also played a part. The revelations that emerged in the course of it, and the fact that he had had to contemplate the possibility that his former mistress had committed the most frightful abominations, not only aided his resolve to live a purer life himself but convinced him of the importance of discouraging immorality in others.

The King did what he could to inaugurate a religious revival. Always a sincere believer, his piety became still more pronounced and he evinced what one German diplomat described as 'a great inclination for devotion'. Though he failed to fill the exacting standards of Mme de Maintenon, who complained he still attached too much importance to outward observance rather than developing an inner spirituality, he strove to be more godly. He also tried to make his courtiers more religious. During a visit to France in 1679 the English philosopher John Locke had noted that traditional fasts enjoined by the Church were now widely ignored. He reported, 'The observation of Lent at Paris is come almost to nothing. Meat is openly to be had... and dispensation commonly to be had from the curate without any more ado and people of sense laugh at it.' The King set out to change such disrespectful attitudes. In April 1684 the Marquis de Dangeau recorded in his diary, 'The King at his levee spoke strongly about courtiers who do not perform their Easter duties, [saying that] he greatly esteemed those who performed them properly, and that he urged them all to think about this very seriously.'[57]

The King's desire for reformation soon made a difference. In September 1683, shortly after the death of Queen Marie-Thérèse, Mme de Maintenon wrote exultantly to her brother, 'I think the Queen asked God for the conversion of the whole court; that of the King is wonderful, and the ladies who seemed farthest from it are never out of churches.' Noting that Mme de Montespan, her sister Mme de Thianges, the Comtesse de Gramont and the Princesse de Soubise were among the most assiduous, she crowed, 'Normal Sundays are like Easter days in former times.'[58]

A few years later Mme de Maintenon again expressed delight that 'piety is becoming very much in fashion', but she did worry that not all those who professed devotion were sincere. This was a valid fear. In 1688 the Duchesse d'Orléans observed, 'It is true that people are wearing diamond crosses, but they are purely for ornament and have no religious significance.' Eleven years later she went further, declaring, 'Faith is extinguished in this country to the point where not a single young man is to be found who does not choose to be an atheist.

But the most amusing thing is that the same young man who plays the atheist in Paris acts pious at court.'[59]

Saint-Simon relates a story which suggests that much of the religious enthusiasm at court was indeed feigned. The Marquis de Brissac, Adjutant of the Royal Bodyguard, was sure that many of the ladies who came to the late service, which the King attended twice a week in the chapel at Versailles, only did so because they wanted to be noticed by Louis. Determined to catch them out, one evening the Adjutant dismissed the royal bodyguard before the King appeared. When asked the reason, Brissac said that the King was going to miss evensong on this occasion, whereupon most of the female worshippers filed out of the chapel. Brissac then recalled the bodyguard in time for the King's arrival and when Louis entered he was mystified to find the chapel virtually empty. The mischievous Brissac then explained how he had tricked 'the pseudo-saints'.[60]

Some old reprobates simply proved incapable of reformation. The famously promiscuous Maréchale de la Ferté, who had featured peripherally in the Affair of the Poisons, did not die till 1714, when she was aged over eighty. Towards the end of her life she attended a Lenten service in the company of her equally notorious sister, the Comtesse d'Olonne. The priest preached a sermon on hellfire and the need for fasting and repentance, thoroughly alarming the elderly pair. The Maréchale quavered, 'Sister, this is becoming serious; it is no laughing matter; if we do not do our penance we shall be damned. Sister, what must we do?' There was a long pause. 'My dear,' replied Mme d'Olonne, 'this is what we must do: we must let the servants fast.'[61]

Now that the King was doing his best to suppress all forms of licentious behaviour, the excesses of his youth were succeeded by what Saint-Simon called 'the long years of gravity'. Looking back on what France had been like when he arrived there seven years earlier, Primi Visconti remarked that by 1680, it seemed like 'a different country'. The balls, banquets and concerts, which had enlivened the court in the past, were now a rarity, and life there was much quieter. 'Few people have fun and...circumspection is necessary, particularly at court,' Visconti lamented. 'Debauchery, [frequenting] places of ill repute, drunkenness, indecent clothing...and even obscene speech ruins a man with the King.'[62]

The King's sister-in-law, the Duchesse d'Orléans, was one of those who had difficulty adapting. In 1685 the King ordered her confessor to reprimand her for being too free in her speech (she herself admitted that she often talked 'about crapping and pissing') and for permitting her maids of honour to have lovers. The King said he had been so annoyed about this that were it not for the fact that she was his sister-in-law he would have banished her from court. Despite her anger at being treated 'like a chambermaid', Madame wrote to apologise for her coarse language, saying she had not realised the King was offended by it. With regard to her maids, she said that it was hard for her to control their behaviour and – doubtless remembering a time when her household had been dubbed 'the nursery garden for mistresses of the King' – added slyly that she 'knew such conduct to be not without precedent and quite usual at any court'. Finding the new strait-laced atmosphere of the court uncongenial she grumbled, 'The King thinks he is being pious when he arranges for everyone to be eternally bothered and pestered.'[63]

In 1690 another observer commented on the great change that had taken place at court, which now bore little resemblance to its former incarnation. Ezechiel Spanheim noted, 'Debauchery, dissoluteness, blasphemy and other scandalous vices [which were] formerly fairly commonplace at court are no longer tolerated nor unpunished.' Gallantry was neither 'in vogue nor in credit, which can be attributed to the King having immersed himself in piety'. Spanheim added that while he made no claim 'to guarantee the virtue of all the ladies at the French court or to make of them so many vestals', the fact remained that flighty ladies were now frowned upon rather than being welcomed as in the past.[64]

In one area the King's will could not prevail for, despite his strong convictions, he never managed to curb homosexuality at court. This was not for want of trying, but the fact that so many men in the highest echelons of the nobility had homosexual predilections ultimately frustrated him. In June 1682 there was a major scandal when 'a large number of important persons' were sent away from court, which was now said to resemble 'a little Sodom'. Devastatingly for the King, they included not only one of the Princes of the Blood, the Prince de la Roche-sur-Yon (whose exile was only brief) but also Louis's son by Louise de La Vallière, the Comte de Vermandois, who died not long afterwards, still in disgrace. Three years later there was another wave of expulsions after intercepted letters were found to contain shocking details of 'ultramontane debauch'. Even so, what the Duchesse d'Orléans called 'that horrible sodomy' showed no signs of declining. In 1699 Madame lamented that it was now 'so much the fashion here that no one attempts to conceal it any longer'; two years later she declared that that species of vice was now more common in France than in Italy.[65]

According to one authority, Jean Lemoine,[66] the inquiry into the Affair of the Poisons was dominated by Louvois, who directed it for his own ends. As Lemoine saw it, the inquiry coincided with a time when Louvois felt that Colbert was edging ahead of him in the factional rivalry in which they were permanently engaged, for in November 1679 Colbert's brother had replaced the disgraced Minister for Foreign Affairs, Pomponne. Louvois therefore sought to use the Arsenal Chamber to redress the balance of power by summoning before it individuals who were themselves, or came from families, antagonistic to him. The Bouillons, for example, were closely related to the great general, Turenne, who prior to his death in 1675 had repeatedly clashed with Louvois over the conduct of the Dutch War. The Comtesse de Soissons, Luxembourg, Feuquières and Mme de Montespan were likewise known to be on poor terms with him.

Louvois's involvement in the affairs of the *Chambre Ardente* was unofficial, but his interest in it was widely recognised. Primi Visconti stated that the setting up of the Chamber 'was his work' and added that many people believed that the tribunal had been brought into being with the express object of 'satisfying the vengeful desires of two or three individuals'. The father of the Marquis de Feuquières likewise hinted that the Chamber was being used as an instrument of faction when he informed the King that in Sweden it was assumed that it provided 'a means to satisfy private passions and to sow divisions'. Feuquières himself was sure the inquiry was conducted in a highly partisan manner and that hostile testimony was solicited by Louvois's stooge, La Reynie, against those whom he wished to bring low.[67] Unfortunately, it is difficult to assess the truth of this as the written records of the interrogations often do not include the questions which were put to suspects, but only their answers, with the result that one cannot judge the extent to which they were prodded into incriminating specific individuals.

Others at the time were equally sure that Louvois manipulated events to suit himself. The Marquis de La Fare commented in his memoirs that the Affair of the Poisons provided Louvois, 'a malignant and hate-filled man, with a fine opportunity to ruin whomsoever he wished'. Before fleeing the country the Comtesse de Soissons reportedly said she dared not stay to defend herself as she knew that her 'mortal enemy' Louvois would have no compunction about falsifying evidence against her to secure a conviction. In 1680 the Marquis de Saint-Maurice, who by that time had returned to his native Savoy, was told by an informant in France that Louvois completely controlled the *Chambre Ardente*, acting 'to suppress proceedings against some persons and to pursue others to extremity'.[68] Certainly it is mysterious that even though serious accusations were made against certain individuals such as the Marquise de Vassé or the Comte de Gassilly, they were never called before the commission. Perhaps the reason why they were left alone was that they enjoyed Louvois's protection.

However, there is a danger that by placing too much stress on the part of Louvois in these events one overlooks the contribution of the King, which was of key significance. Primi Visconti indeed asserted that one reason why Louvois interfered so energetically in the proceedings of the *Chambre Ardente* was that he saw it as a way of commending himself to his master, 'having noticed that he was fearful of poison and that he was intent on extirpating it by the root'.[69] Admittedly, it is problematic to gauge the extent of Louis's involvement. It is not clear, for example, how many of the documents detailing the accusations against eminent people were read by him, or whether he usually relied on Louvois and La Reynie to keep him informed. If he followed the latter course it would, of course, have been easier for them to distort facts and inflame him against selected individuals. Yet the King was not by nature a passive ruler who permitted his ministers to impose on him and it is likely that he monitored this affair with his customary vigilance. When the scandal was at its height it is significant that whenever the King went far away from Paris (as in early 1680, when he went to meet the Dauphine, or that summer, when he went on a northern tour) the *Chambre Ardente* did not hold hearings in his absence. Clearly, the King did not want to permit it too great autonomy and was determined to remain in control of developments.

The King had no doubt that poison posed a genuine danger to his subjects and was ready to accept that he personally could be at risk from it. The Affair of the Poisons revealed how extraordinarily mistrustful he could be, even towards intimates, and exposed his chilling capacity to believe evil of others. Yet despite its searching nature, the inquiry failed to show that anyone at court had used poison and still less that a single person there had contemplated poisoning Louis. As Primi Visconti put it, 'Not so much as a bad thought against the King was found.' Obviously it was disquieting that the Vicomtesse de Polignac had allegedly resorted to conjurations and impious ceremonies to make the King enamoured of her, but even she could be said to have acted from a perverted form of devotion. It merely went some way to proving Primi Visconti's contention that 'all at court, particularly the ladies, would have given themselves to the devil for love of the King'.[70]

There is no doubt that the King was convinced that he was acting in the best interests of the public by setting up the *Chambre Ardente* and he would have considered it a dereliction of duty if he had intervened to protect eminent people who were suspected of involvement with poisoners. It is conceivable, however, that in encouraging the Chamber to pursue enquiries against such persons the King had an additional agenda, though he may not have acknowledged it, even to himself. The *Chambre Ardente* provided the King with a means of reminding his courtiers of his authority and checking indiscipline. For a King who prided himself on being well informed about his courtiers, it had been alarming to discover how many were engaged in unauthorised activities and the inquiry afforded him an opportunity to reassert control over them.

It was no accident that the *Chambre Ardente* contravened the privileges of the nobility, which entitled them to be tried by the highest chamber of *Parlement*. By insisting that they were subject to the jurisdiction of his special commission, the King had found a new way of subjugating them to his will and anyone who protested at this infringement of his or her rights was penalised. The King ensured that those who felt they had been wrongly treated by the *Chambre Ardente* could never obtain redress, as when he prevented the Maréchal de Luxembourg from bringing proceedings against La Reynie after his restoration to court. Those summoned before the Chamber were expected to suffer the indignity in silence, for criticism was not tolerated. After being discharged the Marquis de Feuquières wrote an account of his experiences (sadly lost) to his father, but prudence dictated that he sent it to him in cipher. He urged him not to show it to a soul, 'for I would be a ruined man if certain people came to know of it'.[71]

In his memoirs the Marquis de La Fare wrote that he was amazed at the meekness with which those affected accepted their treatment by the *Chambre Ardente*. 'I do not know whether it must be attributed to the King's authority or to the servility of the high nobility, which was excessive in this reign,' he mused. While he did not specify how the individuals concerned could have shown more defiance without disgracing themselves irredeemably, he believed the episode illustrated 'the contempt which King and ministers had for the grandest people in the country'. Primi Visconti wrote that Louvois considered the *Chambre Ardente* to be 'a fine invention to keep subjects on the alert'[72] and one may surmise that the King regarded this as an equally desirable outcome. The findings of the commission encouraged people to be more watchful of his safety while reminding the court nobility that their conduct was subject to his scrutiny.

In the view of Primi Visconti the proceedings of the *Chambre Ardente* amounted to nothing less than 'a state inquisition of conscience', before which 'all France trembled'. Mme de Sévigné believed there had never been 'a comparable scandal at a Christian court' and was sure that people who studied it a hundred years later would 'pity those who witnessed these indictments'.[73] Certainly, it is an extraordinary story, though sympathy for Mme de Sévigné's aristocratic acquaintances is not perhaps the dominant emotion it excites.

For three years the realm was convulsed while La Reynie 'turned upside down the best families in Paris',[74] but the benefits arising from this upheaval were modest. The streets were rid of some undesirable characters and a few cases of murder were resolved, but these could have been settled in the regular courts without undue trouble. By failing to deal harshly with exceptional cases such as Mme Leféron, who may well have killed her husband, the Chamber undermined one of the main reasons for its existence, which was to administer justice impartially even to the rich and well-connected.

The real problem, however, was that the commission had been set up as a result of a fundamental misconception. From the start the obsessive belief that poisoning had reached epidemic proportions and that many important people were involved in it distorted the investigation and prevented those in charge from assessing the evidence dispassionately. As suspects and false leads proliferated, so confusion mounted, until it became difficult to differentiate between the genuinely wicked and those who had merely been misguided. The inquiry showed that the superstitions and delusions which still dominated popular culture retained a following even in the rarefied world of Versailles, but it failed to prove that a significant number of the courtly élite were guilty of anything more serious. Although many people at court were – in the words of Louise de La Vallière – 'poisoned by the infectious air one incessantly breathes there',[75] this resulted in moral corruption rather than undermining their physical well-being.

The King had sought to cleanse the realm of poisoners, but in reality it was his mind that had been poisoned. In 1670 the Chancellor of the University of Paris had observed that since witches abounded only in areas where people believed in witchcraft this led him to conclude that 'there are maladies of the imagination which are contagious'.[76] In France, during the Affair of the Poisons, when lies, intrigues and exaggerated fears conspired to triumph over reason, a similar affliction can be said to have taken hold.

# NOTES

## Abbreviations Used

| | |
|---|---|
| AN | Library of the Assemblée Nationale, Paris |
| BA | Bibliothèque de l'Arsenal, Paris |
| BN | Bibliothèque Nationale, Paris |
| Norton *SSV* | Lucy Norton, *Saint-Simon at Versailles* |
| PRO | Public Record Office, Kew |
| Rav. | François Ravaission, *Archives de la Bastille* |
| Sév. | *Lettres de Madame de Sévigné*, ed. M. Monmerque |
| SS (Norton) | *Historical Memoirs of the Duc de Saint-Simon*, ed. and trans. Lucy Norton |
| SS (Truc) | Saint-Simon, Duc de, *Mémoires*, ed. Gonzague Truc |

Details of books and authors cited are in the Bibliography that follows the Notes.

### Foreword [pp. 1–5]

1 Trevor-Roper, p. 119.
2 Lewis, pp. 9–10.

### 1: Mme de Brinvilliers [pp. 6–40]

1 Clement, *Police*, p. 119; Pirot I, p. 93.
2 Ibid., pp. 77, 2; Sévigné IV, p. 423.
3 La Rynie believed this story. See Rav. VI, p. 396; see also Primi Visconti, p. 279, La Fare, p. 209.
4 Sév. IV, p. 504.
5 Danjou, p. 120; Pirot I, p. 112; ibid., II, p. 36.
6 *Factum pour... Marquise de Brinvilliers*, Danjou, p. 6.
7 Berryer, pp. 175–6.
8 BN 4-FM-15043, *Factum pour... veuve... de Saint-Laurens*, fo. 7.
9 BN 4-FM-15043, fo. 6; Danjou, p. 83.
10 *Procès contre... Mme de Brinvilliers*, Danjou, p. 83.
11 Saint-Germain, *Mme de Brinvilliers*, pp. 123, 76.
12 Rav. IV, pp. 199, 185, 199.
13 BN 4-FM-15043, fos. 7–8.
14 Rav. IV, p. 196; BN 4-FM-15043 fo. 7; Danjou, pp. 83–4.
15 Rav. IV, p. 293; Saint-Germain, *Mme de Brinvilliers*, pp. 56–7; Rav. IV, p. 293.
16 Glaser, pp. 271, 274–5, 277.
17 Ibid., p. 199.
18 Pirot I, p. 105; *Procès contre la dame de Brinvilliers*, Danjou, p. 104.
19 Rav. IV, p. 244; Fouquier, *Brinvilliers*, p. 35.
20 Latruffe-Colomb, p. 641.
21 *Factum for Pennautier*, BN 4-FM-27378, fo. 24; Rav. IV, p. 195; Saint-Germain, *Mme de Brinvilliers*, pp. 75–6.
22 BN 4-FM-15043, fo. 7; Rav. IV, p. 200; BN 4-FM 15043, fo. 12; Saint-Germain, *Mme de Brinvilliers*, p. 131; *Procès contre la dame de Brinvilliers*, Danjou, p. 82.
23 Rav. IV, p. 243; *Procès contre la dame de Brinvilliers*, Danjou, p. 84.
24 *Factum pour... Mme de Brinvilliers*, Danjou, pp. 69–70; Ormesson II, p. 472.
25 *Procès contre la dame de Brinvilliers*, Danjou, p. 85.
26 Ibid., Danjou, p. 86.
27 Rav. IV, pp. 198, 68; Danjou, p. 86; Rav. IV, p. 98.

28  Ibid., p. 195.
29  Ibid., p. 228; *Factum pour Pennautier*, BN 4-FM 27378, fo. 68.
30  *Procès contre la dame de Brinvilliers*, Danjou, p. 87.
31  La Reynie believed this story, see Rav. VI, p. 396; *Factum pour … veuve … de Saint-Laurens*, BN 4-FM-15043, fo. 24.
32  Rav. IV, p. 300; *Procès contre la dame de Brinvilliers*, Danjou, p. 89.
33  *Procès contre La Chausée*, Danjou, p. 116; Rav. IV, p. 67; *Factum pour Mme de Brinvilliers*, Danjou, p. 12 says 11 June.
34  *Procès contre la dame de Brinvilliers*, Danjou, pp. 89–90.
35  BN FP-2662, fo. 5; Pirot I, pp. 12–14.
36  *Factum du Procès … fait à La Chausée*, Danjou, p. 112.
37  Ibid., p. 118.
38  Lebigre, *Justice du roi*, pp. 208–9, 277n.
39  Rav. VI, p. 396.
40  Esmein, pp. 239–40.
41  Lough, *France Observed … by British travellers*, p. 109.
42  Rav. IV, pp. 168–9.
43  Her confession is printed in Saint-Germain, *Mme de Brinvilliers*, pp. 131–2.
44  Sévigné letters, ed. Duchêne, II, p. 279; Rav. IV, p. 227n.
45  *Factum pour Marquise de Brinvilliers*, Danjou, p. 28; *Procès contre Mme de Brinvilliers*, Danjou, p. 96.
46  Rav. IV, p. 177; *Factum pour Mme de Brinvilliers*, Danjou, p. 65.
47  Ibid., p. 72; Rav. IV, pp. 192–3; Robert, p. 42; Fouquier, *Mme de Brinvilliers*, p. 21.
48  Rav. IV, pp. 203–4.
49  Pirot I, p. 45.
50  Ibid.
51  Ibid., pp. 89–90.
52  Ibid., p. 160.
53  Sourches I, p. 81n.
54  Saint-Germain, *Mme de Brinvilliers*, pp. 199–200; Pirot I, p. 177; Soman (i), p. 804.
55  Le François II, pp. 104–7.

56  Rav. VI, p. 117; Pirot II, p. 2.
57  *Arrest contre … dame … de Brinvilliers*, Danjou, p. 77.
58  Pirot II, pp. 171–2.
59  Sév. IV, pp. 528–9.
60  Rav. IV, pp. 184, 186.
61  Fouquier, *Mme de Brinvilliers*, p. 12.
62  Rav. IV, pp. 178, 188–9.
63  Le François II, p. 229.
64  Pirot I, p. 199; ibid. II, p. 101.
65  Sév. IV, pp. 534, 541–2; BN 4-FM-15043, fo. 14.
66  BN FP 2662, fos. 24–25.
67  Saint-German, *Mme de Brinvilliers*, p. 199.
68  Pirot I, p. 203.
69  Sév. IV, pp. 506–7; Clement, *Police*, p. 123.
70  Colbert VI, p. 45; Primi Visconti, pp. 281, 280.
71  Sév. IV, p. 552.
72  BN 4-FM-27378; BN FP 2662.
73  Rav. VI, p. 18.
74  Sévigné letters, ed. Duchêne, II, p. 1247; Sév. IV, pp. 541–2; Sévigné letters, ed. Duchêne, III, p. 1148; Primi Visconti, p. 281.
75  BN 4-FM-27378, fo. 19; Clement, *Police*, p. 122.
76  *Factum pour … Marquise de Brinvilliers*, Danjou, p. 5.
77  Rav. VI, p. 397; Pirot II, p. 105; Fouquier, *Brinvilliers*, p. 16.
78  Rav. IV, p. 68; Saint-Germain, *Mme de Brinvilliers*, p. 222.

## 2: Louis XIV and his Court
[pp. 41–79]

1  Sévigné, ed. Duchêne II, pp. 350–3.
2  Choisy I, p. 169; La Fare, pp. 175–6, 180; Voltaire I, p. 160.
3  Ibid., p. 424; Gould, p. 123; Lough, *Locke's Travels*, p. 150.
4  King, pp. 290, 293, 299–300; Dunlop, *Versailles*, p. 28.
5  Voltaire I, pp. 12–13; Bluche, *Louis XIV*, p. 121, Sonnino, p. 30.
6  Ibid., pp. 42, 37, 242; Spanheim, pp. 74, 93.
7  Wolf, p. 230.

8 Sév. III, pp. 415–16; Voltaire I, p. 161.

9 Clement, *Mme de Montespan*, p. 383; Norton, *SSV*, p. 262.

10 Sévigné, ed. Duchêne II, p. 353; Felibien, *Versailles*, pp. 31, 33.

11 Lafayette, *Memoirs of the Court*, p. 191.

12 Lough, *op. cit.*, p. 172; Mongredien, *Vie Quotidienne*, p. 38; Norton, *SSV*, p. 264.

13 Kroll, p. 110; Dangeau VII, p. 36n; Bussy III, p. 456.

14 Lough, *op. cit.*, p. 268.

15 Sonnino, p. 176.

16 Voltaire I, p. 335.

17 Maintenon, *Conseils* I, p. 118.

18 Primi Visconti, p. 252; Mossiker, *Madame de Sévigné*, pp. 300–1.

19 Patin III, p. 496; d'Antin, p. 77.

20 Sourches I, p. 138n; Vallot, p. 108, Patin III, p. 784; Magne, pp. 2–3; SS (Norton) I, p. 82.

21 Couton, p. 45; Kroll, p. 37.

22 Elias, p. 94.

23 Sonnino, p. 144.

24 Magne, pp. 122–3, 292.

25 Saint-Maurice I, pp. 374–5.

26 Sourches V, pp. 248–9; SS (Truc) I, p. 390.

27 La Bruyère, p. 222; Couton, p. 45; d'Antin, pp. 77–9.

28 Magne, p. 327; Mossiker, *op. cit.*, pp. 301–2.

29 Moine, pp. 136, 133.

30 For a description see Felibien, *Les divertissements de Versailles … en l'année 1674, passim*.

31 Quoted Moine, p. 215.

32 Norton, *SSV*, p. 261; d'Antin, p. 28.

33 Clement, *Police*, p. 407; Sév. IV, p. 168.

34 Ibid., V, p. 507; ibid., IV, p. 247.

35 Primi Visconti, p. 132.

36 Sév. II, pp. 113–14; Saint-Maurice II, p. 35.

37 Scott-Stevenson I, p. 255; Choisy I, pp. 222–3; Scott-Stevenson I, p. 254.

38 Voltaire I, p. 345; Couton, p. 74.

39 Scott-Stevenson II, p. 176;

Drevillon, *Lire et écrire l'avenir*, pp. 238, 236, 238.

40 Primi Visconti, p. 60.

41 Ibid., p. 63; Ravaisson V, pp. 342, 345–6, ibid., VI, p. 286; ibid., VII, pp. 8–10.

42 Primi Visconti, p. 124.

43 Ibid., p. 20.

44 Montpensier III, p. 570; Voltaire I, p. 13; Bluche, *Vie Quotidienne*, p. 68.

45 Voltaire I, p. 310; Bluche, *op. cit.*, p. 46; SS (Truc) I, p. 42.

46 Levron in Hatton, *Louis XIV and Absolutism*, p. 134.

47 Sourches II, p. 30; La Bruyère, pp. 222, 221.

48 Ibid., p. 222; quoted Maintenon, *Lettres* III, p. 253; Primi Visconti, p. 251.

49 Amiel, p. 44; Voltaire I, p. 337; Saint-Maurice I, p. 169.

50 Sév. II, p. 331.

51 Bussy II, pp. 12, 16.

52 SS (Truc) II, p. 499; Duchêne, p. 112; Saint-Maurice I, p. 131; Mossiker, *op. cit.*, p. 307.

53 SS Norton II, p. 320; Boiteau II, pp. 421, 416; Bussy V, p. 51.

54 La Fare, p. 166; Voltaire I, pp. 336–7.

55 Sourches I, p. 206; Bussy V, p. 52; Boiteau III, p. 345.

56 Saint-Maurice I, p. 389; Primi Visconti, p. 131.

57 Ibid., p. 302.

58 Louis XIV, *Oeuvres* II, p. 457; Sonnino, p. 29.

59 Norton, *SSV*, p. 247; Colbert I, p. 468; Louis XIV, *Oeuvres* II, p. 457; Primi Visconti, p. 109; Lavallée II, p. 163.

60 Vallot, pp. 115–16; Primi Visconti, p. 113, SS (Norton) I, p. 307n; Vallot, pp. 130, 125–7.

61 Ibid., pp. 130, 125.

62 Ibid., pp. 110, 118.

63 SS (Norton) I, p. 69.

64 Sonnino, p. 30; Primi Visconti, p. 33; Choisy I, p. 25; Norton, *SSV*, p. 247.

65 Ibid., p. 259; Berwick II, p. 216; Mossiker, *Mme de Sévigné*, p. 345.

66 Spanheim, p. 68; Caylus, pp. 90–1; Kroll, p. 237, Norton, *SSV*, p. 247.

67 Sonnino, pp. 200–1.

68 Labatut, p. 112; Sonnino, p. 45; Louis XIV, *Oeuvres* II, p. 460.

69 Dunlop, *Louis XIV*, p. 266.

70 Primi Visconti, p. 114; Mongredien, *Vie Privée*, p. 176; Sourches II, p. 25.

71 Levron in Hatton, p. 151; Sourches I, p. 199; ibid. IV, p. 283; SS (Norton) I, p. 33.

72 Colbert VI, p. 468; Primi Visconti, p. 31.

73 SS (Norton) I, p. 277.

74 Sonnino, p. 30.

75 SS (Norton) I, p. 283; Levron, *Daily Life at Versailles*, p. 77; Levron in Hatton, *Louis XIV and Absolutism*, p. 148.

76 Louis XIV, *Oeuvres* II, pp. 460–1; Sonnino, p. 36; Primi Visconti, pp. 58–9.

77 Voltaire I, p. 378.

78 Primi Visconti, p. 260; Spanheim, p. 290.

79 Patin III, p. 619; Sourches I, p. 56; Saint-Maurice I, pp. 506–7; Sourches II, p. 45.

80 Sonnino, p. 208.

81 Saint-Maurice I, p. 212; Saint-Germain, *Louis XIV Secret*, pp. 54–5.

82 Ibid., pp. 149–50; Sourches III, p. 85; Primi Visconti, pp. 164–5.

83 Ormesson II, p. 566.

84 Saint-Maurice II, pp. 525, 505.

85 Rav. IV, p. 7; Saint-Maurice II, pp. 420–1.

86 Ormesson II, p. 552.

87 Amiel, p. 274; Locatelli, p. 177; see also Maintenon, *Lettres* II, p. 432.

88 Montpensier IV, p. 455; Saint-Maurice II, p. 5.

89 Caylus, p. 138; Saint-Maurice I, p. 254; Caylus, pp. 135–6; Norton, *SSV*, p. 247; Primi Visconti, p. 57.

90 Magne, p. 330.

91 Primi Visconti, p. 57.

92 Lemoine & Lichtenberger, p. 61.

93 Sév. II, p. 439.

94 Rav. VI, p. 33.

95 Brunet I, p. 286; ibid. II, p. 25; Saint-Maurice I, p. 255.

96 Caylus, pp. 135–6; Bussy II, p. 352.

97 Primi Visconti, p. 214; Saint-Maurice II, p. 5.

98 Magne, p. 319; Ormesson II, pp. 274–5; Primi Visconti, pp. 73–4.

99 Couton, pp. 214–15; Saint-Maurice I, p. 212; ibid. II, p. 111.

100 Sonnino, pp. 246–7.

101 Scott-Stevenson I, p. 135; Fénelon, p. 153; Spanheim, p. 88.

102 Primi Visconti, p. 273.

103 Krailsheimer, pp. 95, 100.

104 SS (Norton) II, p. 33.

105 Ormesson II, pp. 147–8.

106 Motteville III, pp. 301–2.

107 Couton, pp. 34, 40.

108 Guitton I, pp. 75–6; SS (Truc) III, p. 20; Guitton I, p. 81; Bussy IV, pp. 84–5, 82.

109 Decker, p. 129.

110 Saint-Maurice I, p. 389.

## 3: Sex and the Sun King [pp. 80–123]

1 Lafayette, *Histoire de Madame*, pp. 89–90; Primi Visconti, p. 39; Scott-Stevenson II, pp. 208–9; Ormesson II, p. 442; Locatelli, p. 177; Magne, p. 209; Montpensier IV, pp. 394–5.

2 La Vallière I, pp. 70–1; Magne, p. 266; Lafayette, p. 120.

3 Ibid., pp. 101, 111.

4 Motteville III, p. 294.

5 Ormesson II, p. 69; Colbert VI, p. 463; Ormesson II, p. 463.

6 Magne, pp. 2–3; Caylus, pp. 39, 41; Lemoine & Lichtenberger, p. 165.

7 Caylus, p. 51.

8 Norton, *SSV*, p. 131.

9 Primi Visconti, pp. 9–10; Montpensier IV, pp. 32–3; Choisy II, p. 34.

10 Magne, p. 309.

11 Primi Visconti, p. 10.

12 Brunet I, p. 267; Caylus, p. 51; Voltaire I, p. 340; Clement, *Mme de Montespan*, p. 163; SS (Norton) I, p. 414; Norton, *SSV*, p. 134.

13 Clement, *Mme de Montespan*, pp. 272–3; Petitfils, *Mme de Montespan*, p. 67; Primi Visconti, p. 246; Montpensier IV, p. 54.

14 Ibid., pp. 31–2; Saint-Maurice II, pp. 412–13.

15 Montpensier IV, p. 46.

16 Scott-Stevenson II, p. 103; Clement, *Mme de Montespan*, pp. 272–3.

17 Caylus, pp. 86–7; Lavallée I, pp. 361–2; Rouben, pp. 163–4.

18 Bussy III, p. 213, ibid., IV, p. 358; Saint-Maurice II, pp. 221–2; Couton, p. 38.

19 Caylus, pp. 85–6; La Fare, p. 152.

20 Spanheim, p. 80; Norton, *SSV*, pp. 131–2; Scott-Stevenson II, p. 158; Montpensier IV, p. 506.

21 Rav. VI, p.435.

22 Montpensier IV, p. 48.

23 Ibid., p. 52.

24 Saint-Maurice I, pp. 407, 426.

25 Norton, *SSV*, pp. 275, 283–4.

26 Bussy II, p. 362; Scott-Stevenson I, pp. 208–9.

27 Lemoine & Lichtenberger, pp. 231, 237, 248.

28 Scott-Stevenson II, p. 257, Saint-Maurice I, pp. 231–2; Caylus, p. 140.

29 Clement, *Mme de Montespan*, p. 266.

30 Lemoine & Lichtenberger, pp. 265–6; Primi Visconti, p. 10; Lemoine & Lichtenberger, p. 269.

31 Saint-Maurice I, pp. 231–2.

32 Saint-Maurice I, p. 300.

33 Lemoine & Lichtenberger, p. 278.

34 Patin III, p. 751; Saint-Maurice II, p. 206.

35 Lavallée II, p. 460; Maintenon, *Conseils et Instructions*, pp. 43–4.

36 Lavallée II, p. 73.

37 Caylus, p. 18; Norton, *SSV*, p. 272; Aumale I, p. 51; Sév. II, pp. 514, 464.

38 Maintenon, *op. cit.*, pp. 43–4.

39 Saint-Maurice I, p. 226.

40 Ormesson II, p. 562; Bussy I, p. 343; Sév. II, p. 24.

41 La Vallière I, pp. 25, 102.

42 Bussy I, p. 379; Sév. II, pp. 62, 70.

43 Bussy I, p. 382; Sév. II, p. 62; Bussy I, pp. 386, 382.

44 Sév. II, p. 84, Saint-Maurice II, p. 32; Montpensier IV, p. 261.

45 Scott-Stevenson II, p. 211; La Vallière I, p. 52.

46 Bossuet, *Oeuvres* XVII, p. 29.

47 Bussy II, pp. 344–5.

48 Montpensier IV, p. 337.

49 Sév. V, pp. 106–7.

50 La Vallière I, p. 155.

51 Clement, *Mme de Montespan*, pp. 365–74.

52 Ibid., pp. 248–9.

53 Scott-Stevenson II, p. 257.

54 Marie I, pp. 4–6.

55 Ibid., p. 17; Primi Visconti, p. 110; Marie I, p. 24.

56 Maintenon, *Lettres* II, pp. 128–9.

57 Montpensier IV, p. 406.

58 Bussy III, p. 34; Sév. III, p. 521; Clement, *Mme de Montespan*, p. 225.

59 Bossuet XVII, p. 46.

60 Ibid., p. 45.

61 Sévigné, ed. Duchêne II, p. 21; Montpensier IV, pp. 439, 455; Maintenon, *Lettres* II, p. 142n.

62 Primi Visconti, pp. 112–13.

63 Sév. III, p. 534.

64 Ibid., IV, p. 527.

65 Saint-Maurice I, pp. 256, 342; SS (Norton) I, p. 412; Primi Visconti, pp. 305–6.

66 Spanheim, pp. 75–6; SS (Truc) I, p. 525.

67 SS (Norton) II, p. 264.

68 Sév. V, pp. 56, 82, 49, 82.

69 Sév. III, p. 295; Primi Visconti, p. 42.

70 Bussy III, pp. 213, 226; Primi Visconti, pp. 186–7.

71 Bussy III, pp. 223–4; ibid., IV, p. 32; ibid., III, p. 269.

72 Sév. V, pp. 170, 175.

73 Bussy III, p. 283.

74 Ibid., IV, pp. 21, 43; Sév. VII, p. 96.

75 Bussy III, pp. 354, 381.

76 Ibid., IV, p. 45; Clement, *Mme de Montespan*, p. 97.

77 Bussy IV, pp. 106–7.

78 Primi Visconti, pp. 206–7.

79 Scott-Stevenson II, p. 105; Choisy II, p. 35.
80 Bussy IV, p. 258; Primi Visconti, p. 208.
81 Bussy IV, p. 320.
82 Primi Visconti, p. 208.
83 Bussy IV, pp. 319, 340.
84 Ibid., pp. 344–5.
85 Clement, *Mme de Montespan*, pp. 250–1.
86 Bussy IV, pp. 386, 428; Clement, *Mme de Montespan*, p. 133.
87 Bussy IV, pp. 344–5; Primi Visconti, p. 241.
88 Bussy IV, p. 386.
89 Sophia, pp. 212–13; Bussy IV, p. 469.
90 Ibid., V, pp. 8, 4, 469, 461.
91 Ibid., p. 38.
92 Sév. VI, p. 283.
93 Ibid., pp. 316–17.
94 Ibid., p. 347.
95 Bussy IV, p. 461; Caylus, p. 33; Bussy V, p. 117; Sév. V, pp. 361–2, 365–6.
96 Bussy V, pp. 107–8.
97 Ibid., pp. 110–11.
98 Sév. VI, pp. 510, 534.
99 Ibid., VII, p. 50.
100 Bussy V, pp. 110, 116.
101 Sév. VI, p. 419.
102 Ibid., p. 445.
103 Maintenon, *Lettres* II, p. 207.
104 Ibid., p. 88.
105 Ibid., p. 331.
106 Ibid., pp. 189, 107.
107 Caylus, pp. 45, 49; Clement, *Mme de Montespan*, pp. 225–6.
108 Maintenon, *Lettres* II, pp. 401–2.
109 Caylus, p. 45; Maintenon, *Lettres* II, pp. 401–2; Montpensier IV, p. 451; Clement, *Mme de Montespan*, pp. 257–9.
110 Ibid., p. 271; SS (Norton) I, p. 19; Clement, *Mme de Montespan*, pp. 241–2, 245; Scott-Stevenson I, p. 103.
111 Maintenon, *Lettres* II, pp. 91, 180, 270, 87; Sév. IV, pp. 22–3.
112 Lavallée II, pp. 454–5, 458; Maintenon, *Lettres* II, p. 93.
113 Ibid., pp. 109–10, 92; Dangeau III, p. 301n.
114 Maintenon, *Lettres* II, pp. 119, 133; Sév. IV, pp. 22–3, 434–5, 534.
115 Maintenon, *Lettres* II, p. 180; Sév. V, p. 49; Bussy III, p. 269; ibid., IV, p. 109.
116 Sév. VI, p. 142.
117 Ibid., pp. 316–17.
118 Ibid., pp. 322, 348; Bussy V, p. 94; Sév. VI, pp. 348, 438, 475.
119 Ibid., pp. 475, 511.
120 Ibid., p. 534.
121 Choisy I, p. 205; Spanheim, pp. 86–7.
122 Primi Visconti, p. 268.
123 Ibid.
124 Maintenon, *Lettres* II, pp. 26–7.
125 Caylus, pp. 135–6; Sév. VII, p. 43; Bussy V, p. 195.
126 Sév. VII, pp. 77–8.
127 Lavallée II, p. 458.
128 Ibid., p. 457; Aumale, pp. 67–8.
129 Lavallée II, pp. 73–4.
130 Maintenon, *Lettres* II, p. 302; Lavallée II, pp. 74–5.
131 Maintenon, *Lettres* II, p. 350; Clement, *Mme de Montespan*, pp. 100, 254–5.

**4: The First Arrests** [pp. 124–147]

1 Rav. VII, p. 150; BA 10359, fo. 98.
2 Saint-Maurice I, p. 66; Dangeau VII, p. 66; Scott-Stevenson II, p. 48; Rav. VII, p. 143.
3 Saint-Maurice II, p. 32; La Fare, p. 209.
4 Rav. IV, p. 285.
5 Stead, p. 16.
6 Ibid., p. 15.
7 Bernard, p. 41.
8 Ibid., p. 162; Primi Visconti, p. 154.
9 Clement, *Trois Drames*, pp. 264–5.
10 SS (Truc) I, p. 364.
11 Saint-Simon, ed. A. de Boislisle (1884) IV, p. 12; Saint-Germain, *La Reynie*, p. 21; Sourches I, p. 343; Saint-Germain, *La Reynie*, p. 21.
12 Rav. IV, p. 287.
13 Ibid., V, pp. 180–1n.
14 Ibid., IV, p. 325.

15  Ibid., p. 406.
16  Ibid., p. 431.
17  Ibid., p. 432.
18  Ibid., p. 451.
19  Ibid., pp. 464–5.
20  Ibid., V, p. 37.
21  Ibid., pp. 8–9.
22  Ricotti VI, p. 234.
23  Rav. V, p. 129.
24  Ibid., pp. 107, 109, 485.
25  Thomas, p. 271; Marshall, pp. 304–5; Nicholl, pp. 3–4.
26  Thomas, p. 270; Segur, *Tapissier*, p. 11; King, p. 27; Levron in Hatton, p. 151; SS (Norton) II, p. 114; Amiel, p. 283.
27  Rav. V, pp. 157–8; Primi Visconti, p. 298.
28  Rav. V, p. 252.
29  Ibid., pp. 170, 399, 440; AN 1127, fo. 85; Rav. VI, p. 184.
30  Ibid., V, p. 412.
31  Ibid., VI, p. 340; ibid., VII, p. 153.
32  Ibid., V, p. 241.
33  Ibid., p. 220.
34  Ibid., VI, pp. 59, 388.
35  Ibid., V, pp. 270, 280, 443.
36  Ibid., p. 312.
37  Ibid., pp. 373, 443, 445; Nass, pp. 154–5; AN 1127, fo. 85.
38  Colbert VI, p. 407.
39  BN Mss Français 7608, fos. 321–3.
40  Drevillon, *Lire et écrire l'avenir*, pp. 62, 66.
41  Ibid., pp. 23–4, 34.
42  Ibid., p. 44.
43  Ibid., pp. 94–5.
44  Soman III, p. 404.
45  Mandrou, *Magistrats et Sorciers*, p. 452.
46  Kroll, p. 197; Mandrou, *op. cit.*, p. 361.
47  Bussy V, p. 65.
48  Bossuet V, pp. 444, 452.
49  See Norton *SSV*, p. 252, Primi Visconti, p. 241.
50  Sév. V, p. 226; Forster, p. 174.
51  Briggs, *Communities of Belief*, pp. 34–6; Pirot I, p. 113.
52  Amiel, p. 381.
53  Rav. V, pp. 169, 178.
54  Ibid., VII, p. 152; ibid., V, p. 182; Colbert VI, p. 423.
55  Ibid., p. 55.
56  Rav. V, p. 179.
57  Ibid., pp. 178–93.
58  Ibid., pp. 193, 197–200.

**5: La Voisin** [pp. 148–166]

1   Rav. V, p. 205.
2   Ibid., pp. 229–32.
3   Ibid., pp. 299, 293.
4   La Fare, p. 150; Primi Visconti, p. 283.
5   Rav. V, p. 348.
6   Bussy IV, p. 335; Rav. V, pp. 339–40.
7   *Catalogue Général des Manuscrits des Bibliothèques Publiques de France*, IX, p. 47.
8   Rav. V, pp. 235, 248, 250, 248.
9   Ibid., pp. 258, 278.
10  Ibid., pp. 407–9, 380.
11  Ibid., p. 502; Primi Visconti, p. 285; Rav. V, pp. 319, 299; ibid., VI, p. 39.
12  For her drunken indiscretions see Rav. VI, p. 79; Primi Visconti, p. 290.
13  Rav. V, p. 381.
14  Ibid., VI, p. 26.
15  Ibid., pp. 31, 37.
16  Ibid., V, p. 489; ibid., VI, pp. 12, 28.
17  Ibid., V, pp. 257–67.
18  Ibid., pp. 267–74.
19  Ibid., pp. 276–82.
20  Ibid., p. 318.
21  Ibid., pp. 295, 360–1.
22  Ibid., pp. 470, 336, 305.
23  Ibid., pp. 314, 316.
24  Ibid., VI, p. 2; ibid., V, pp. 308, 336.
25  Ibid., p. 278.
26  Ibid., p. 338.
27  Ibid., pp. 284–5.
28  Ibid., p. 335; Bussy IV, p. 353.
29  Ibid., pp. 358–9.
30  Ibid., pp. 348, 354.
31  Rav. V, pp. 360–1.
32  Patin III, pp. 225–6; Maintenon, *Conseils et Instructions* I, p. 113.
33  Patin III, pp. 225–6; Primi Visconti, p. 298.

34 Rav. V, pp. 327–8, 354.
35 Ibid., p. 379.
36 Primi Visconti, p. 298; Rav. V, pp. 444, 331–3, 379, 324, 426.
37 Ibid., pp. 246, 403, 472, 433.
38 Ibid., pp. 348, 297–8, 414, 411, 291.
39 Nass, pp. 154–5; Rav. V, pp. 425, 443–4.
40 Ibid., pp. 425, 440, 474, 448.
41 Ibid., pp. 443–4.
42 Ibid., pp. 413, 407.
43 AN Mss 1127, fo. 75; Rav. V, p. 387.
44 Ibid., VII, p. 176.
45 Ibid., V, p. 386.
46 Ibid., pp. 393, 411.
47 BN Collection Clairambault 986, fo. 209.

## 6: The Magician Lesage [pp. 167–195]

1 Rav. V, pp. 468–74.
2 Ibid., pp. 479–81.
3 Ibid., p. 477.
4 Ibid., p. 242.
5 Ibid., p. 219.
6 Ibid., IV, pp. 11–13, 32.
7 Ibid., p. 15.
8 Clement, Police, p. 234; Mettam, Government and Society, p. 154.
9 Petitfils, L'Affaire des Poisons, p. 60.
10 Rav. VI, p. 84; ibid., V, pp. 373, 315.
11 Ibid., pp. 373, 437, 386, 378, 293.
12 Ibid., VI, pp. 57, 21–2; ibid., V, pp. 496–7; ibid., VI, p. 59.
13 Ibid., V, pp. 455–6, 407–9.
14 Ibid., pp. 377–8.
15 Ibid., VI, p. 172.
16 Ibid., pp. 21–2, 76.
17 Ibid., pp. 21–2, 84, 33.
18 Ibid., V, pp. 462–3, 367, 462–3.
19 Ibid., pp. 369, 287; ibid., VI, p. 91.
20 Ibid., V, pp. 448–9.
21 Ibid., VI, pp. 17, 12, 15.
22 Ibid., p. 17.
23 Ibid., pp. 88, 44–5.
24 Ibid., V, pp. 287, 448, 474–5, 291, 379, 448; ibid., VI, pp. 79–80, 84.
25 Ibid., V, pp. 421–3, 425.
26 Colbert VI, p. 413; Rav. V, p. 502; Beurain, p. 46.
27 Rav. V, p. 478.

28 See Lemoine, Les des Oeillets, passim.
29 Primi Visconti, pp. 108–9.
30 Colbert VI, p. 420.
31 Lemoine, op. cit., p. 49.
32 Rav. V, p. 483.
33 Ibid., pp. 483–5.
34 Ibid., p. 490.
35 Ibid., pp. 490–1.
36 Ibid., pp. 176, 360–1.
37 Ibid., pp. 286, 293; AN 1127, fo. 111.
38 Rav. V, p. 493.
39 SS (Norton) I, pp. 43-4; Segur, Tapissier, p. 15.
40 PRO SP 78/141/fo. 136.
41 Segur, Luxembourg … et … Orange, p. 536.
42 Ibid., pp. 287, 212.
43 Rowlands, p. 55; Spanheim, pp. 334–5.
44 SS (Truc) III, pp. 753–4; Primi Visconti, p. 145.
45 BN Mss Clairambault 1192, fo. 22.
46 Rav. V, pp. 495–501.
47 Primi Visconti, p. 144; SS (Norton) I, pp. 43–4.
48 Rav. V, pp. 501–2.
49 Scott-Stevenson I, p. 255.
50 Rav. V, pp. 501–2.
51 Ibid., VI, pp. 3–7.
52 Ibid., pp. 18–19.
53 Ibid., pp. 19–20.
54 Ibid., pp. 31–6.
55 L. Racine, p. 42.
56 Ibid., p. 69.
57 Ibid., p. 70; Lacretelle, p. 80.
58 Rav. VI, pp. 50–3.
59 Lacretelle, p. 97.
60 Ibid., p. 221.
61 Rav. VI, p. 95.
62 Ibid., p. 25.
63 Ibid., V, pp. 407–9, 426.
64 Ibid., VI, pp. 55–7.
65 Ibid., p. 25.
66 Ibid., p. 58.
67 Ibid., p. 67.

## 7: A Court in Chaos [pp. 196–241]

1 For a description of her death see Lafayette, Histoire de Madame, pp. 190–208.

2 Shelmerdine, p. 120.
3 Saint-Maurice I, p. 455.
4 Ibid., p. 453; Fabre, pp. 133, 198–9.
5 Shelmerdine, p. 114; Saint-Maurice I, p. 485; Scott-Stevenson II, p. 124.
6 Shelmerdine, p. 123; SS (Truc) I, pp. 923–5.
7 Marchesseau, pp. 64–8; Fabre, p. 164; John Rohl, Martin Warren & David Hunt, *Purple Secret* (1998), p. 193.
8 Sourches I, p. 16; Saint-Maurice I, p. 88; Patin III, p. 787.
9 Bussy IV, pp. 124, 137.
10 *Mercure Galant*, January 1680.
11 Rouben, pp. 163–4; Rav. VI, pp. 115, 117.
12 Ibid., pp. 120–3.
13 Ibid., pp. 96–7.
14 Ibid.
15 Sév. VI, pp. 213, 217–18.
16 Segur, *Tapissier*, p. 76.
17 Sév. VI, p. 214.
18 Motteville III, p. 116; Lafayette, *op. cit.*, p. 55.
19 Ibid.
20 Magne, pp. 157, 162.
21 Ibid., p. 311; Saint-Maurice I, pp. 405, 426; ibid., II, pp. 471–2, 573.
22 Saint-Maurice II, pp. 554, 581.
23 Lafayette, *op. cit.*, p. 136; Bussy V, pp. 50–1.
24 Sév. VI, p. 226; Bussy V, pp. 50–1; Rav. VI, p. 131.
25 Sourches I, pp. 134–5n; La Fare, p. 213; Rav. VI, p. 103; Sév. VI, p. 231.
26 Rav. VI, pp. 132, 193.
27 Primi Visconti, p. 289; Rav. VI, p. 147; Choisy I, p. 224; Sév. VI, p. 282; Primi Visconti, p. 291.
28 La Fare, p. 213; Primi Visconti, pp. 288–9.
29 Bussy V, p. 59; Rav. VI, p. 138.
30 Scott-Stevenson I, p. 98.
31 Bussy V, p. 45.
32 Primi Visconti, p. 287; Dangeau III, p. 49.
33 SS (Norton) III, p. 281.
34 Courtois, p. 159.
35 Sourches I, p. 125; René, p. 230.
36 Ibid., pp. 500–1.
37 SS (Truc) II, pp. 1200–2.
38 René, p. 243.
39 Sourches III, pp. 39–40. Lafayette, *Memoirs of the Court*, p. 205.
40 Segur, *Tapissier*, pp. 82, 82n.
41 BA Mss 10347, fos. 372–5; ibid., fos. 535–6.
42 Sourches I, p. 368; Bussy V, p. 528.
43 Ibid., p. 52; Rav. VI, p. 124.
44 Ibid., VII, pp. 145–6, 167.
45 SS (Truc) I, p. 488; Dangeau V, p. 427; SS (Truc) I, p. 488.
46 BN Mss Clairambault 1192, fo. 19.
47 Beurain, pp. 42–3.
48 Ibid., pp. 46–7.
49 Ibid., p. 47; Sév. VI, p. 218.
50 Rav. VI, p. 130; Sév. VI, p. 225.
51 BN Mss Clairambault 1192, fos. 24–24v; ibid. fo. 27.
52 Segur, *Tapissier*, pp. 104, 79.
53 SS (Truc) II, p. 627; SS (Norton) I, pp. 43–4.
54 BN Mss Clairambault 986, fo. 294; Sév. VI, p. 232; Segur, *Tapissier*, pp. 79, 94; Bussy V, pp. 50–1.
55 Segur, *Tapissier*, pp. 103, 89.
56 SS (Truc) IV, p. 322; Primi Visconti, p. 115; Choisy I, p. 78; Spanheim, p. 247.
57 SS (Truc) IV, p. 327; Primi Visconti, p. 115.
58 Dangeau III, p. 264.
59 Bussy III, pp. 374, 377.
60 Rav. VI, pp. 34, 142, 140.
61 Bussy V, pp. 45-6, 50–1.
62 Sév. VI, pp. 233–5.
63 Rav. VI, p. 119.
64 Sév. VI, pp. 233–5.
65 Primi Visconti, p. 288; see also Voltaire I, p. 345.
66 Sév. V, pp. 266–7.
67 PRO SP 78/143/fo. 88v; Spanheim, p. 248; SS (Truc) III, pp. 322–6.
68 Segur, *Tapissier*, p. 96; Sév. VI, p. 245.
69 Feuquières, *Lettres* V, p. 75.
70 Rav. VI, pp. 124–8; Feuquières, *Lettres* V, p. 76.
71 Ibid., pp. 169, 131.
72 Rav. VI, p. 190.

73 Scott-Stevenson I, pp. 136–7; Van der Cruysse, *Lettres Françaises*, pp. 132–4; Coynart, pp. 155–6.

74 Feuquières, *Lettres* V, pp. 165–6, 177, 77.

75 SS (Truc) III, pp. 753–4; Sourches II, p. 211.

76 SS (Truc) II, p. 42, ibid. III, pp. 753–4; paper given by Guy Rowlands to Society for Court Studies 17.06.02 on *The Court and Political Culture of the French Army under Louis XIV*.

77 Feuquières, *Lettres* V, pp. xxvii–viii.

78 Lafayette, *Histoire de Madame*, pp. 139–40; Motteville III, p. 344.

79 Saint-Maurice I, p. 278.

80 Rav. VI, pp. 31–2, 93, 102, 98.

81 Ibid., pp. 128–9.

82 BN Mss Clairambault 986, fo. 301; Bussy V, pp. 70–1.

83 BN Mss Clairambault 986, fo. 301; SS (Truc) VI, p. 578.

84 Sév. VI, p. 225; Bussy V, pp. 49, 48.

85 Sév. VI, pp. 231–2, 227, 229.

86 Ibid., pp. 229–30, 244–5.

87 Primi Visconti, p. 282.

88 La Fare, p. 213; Sév. VI, pp. 259–60.

89 Primi Visconti, p. 287; Sév. VI, p. 242; Bussy V, pp. 184, 187.

90 Rav. VI, p. 137.

91 Nass, p. 127; Feuquières, *Lettres*, V, p. 101.

92 Rav. VI, pp. 137–8.

93 Bussy V, pp. 46–7, 49.

94 BA Mss 10347, fos. 263ff.

95 Rav. VI, p. 423; Sév. VI, p. 278.

96 Rav. VI, pp. 150–81.

97 Ibid., p. 189.

98 Ibid., pp. 180, 183.

99 Sév. VI, pp. 278–9.

100 Rav. VI, pp. 199–201.

101 Ibid., V, pp. 479–81, ibid., VI, p. 203.

102 Sév. VI, pp. 357–8; Bussy V, p. 103.

103 BA Mss 10347, fo. 610.

104 Sév. VI, p. 368; Bussy V, pp. 107–8; Rav. VII, p. 56.

105 Sév. VI, pp. 366–7.

106 Rav. VI, p. 144.

107 Beurain, pp. 84–5, 53.

108 Ibid., pp. 60–1.

109 Ibid., p. 63.

110 BN Mss Clairambault 986, fo. 191; Sév. VI, p. 408.

111 Beurain, pp. 65–6.

112 Ibid., p. 68.

113 Ibid., pp. 71–3.

114 Ibid., pp. 74–5.

115 Sév. VI, p. 408; Bussy V, pp. 118–19.

116 Ibid.

117 Ibid., pp. 282, 287–8, 282.

118 Segur, *Tapissier*, p. 142; Primi Visconti, p. 296; Segur, *Tapissier*, p. 145.

119 Sév. VI, p. 433.

120 Beurain, pp. 88–9; Segur, *Tapissier*, pp. 133–4.

121 Ibid., p. 131.

122 Rav. VI, p. 211; Sév. VI, pp. 433, 408.

## 8: Accusations Against Mme de Montespan [pp. 242–268]

1 SS (Norton) I, p. 413.

2 SS (Truc) III, pp. 48–9; Saint-Maurice II, pp. 174–5; SS (Norton) I, p. 413.

3 Rav. VI, p. 19.

4 Ibid., pp. 47–8.

5 AN 1127, fo. 138.

6 Rav. VI, pp. 211–14; BN Mss Français 7608, fo. 288.

7 Rav. VI, p. 225.

8 Ibid., pp. 217–18.

9 Ibid., p. 400; ibid., V, p. 252; ibid. VI, pp. 173, 63; AN 1127, fo. 29.

10 AN 1127, fo. 29.

11 AN 1127, fos. 29, 119.

12 BN Mss Français, 7608, fo. 307.

13 Rav. VI, pp. 215–17.

14 Ibid., p. 232.

15 Ibid., pp. 249–52, 255–9.

16 Ibid.

17 Ibid., pp. 273–6.

18 Ibid., pp. 283–4.

19 AN 1127, fo. 29, repeated 3 September; BN Mss Français 7608, fo. 302; see also Colbert VI, p. 414, Rav. VI, p. 306.

20 BN Mss Français 7608, fo. 301.

21 Rav. VI, pp. 281–2.

22 Ibid., p. 433.
23 PRO SP 78/140, fo. 146; Rav. VI, p. 288.
24 Ibid., p. 287.
25 BN Mss Français 7608, fos. 295–6.
26 Colbert VI, p. 409; Rav. VI, p. 299; BN Mss Français 7608, fos. 297, 304.
27 Ibid.
28 Rav. VI, p. 305.
29 BN Mss Clairambault 986, fo. 315.
30 Colbert VI, p. 415; Rav. VI, p. 303.
31 Ibid., p. 424; Colbert VI, p. 420.
32 Rav. VI, pp. 304, 37, 140, 194–5.
33 Ibid., V, p. 330.
34 Ibid., pp. 271, 448–9; ibid., VI, pp. 30, 167–76.
35 Ibid., V, pp. 265–6.
36 Sourches I, p. 214n; see also Ormesson II, pp. 529–30.
37 Lough, *France Observed*, p. 147; Grandet I, pp. 498–500.
38 Rav. V, p. 485.
39 Ibid., VI, p. 319.
40 Ibid., p. 179.
41 Ibid., pp. 194–8.
42 Ibid., pp. 234–7.
43 Colbert VI, p. 417.
44 Rav. VI, pp. 241–5.
45 Ibid., pp. 321, 265, 198, 425–6.
46 Ibid., pp. 263–8.
47 Colbert VI, p. 419.
48 Rav. VI, pp. 288–91.
49 Ibid., pp. 294–8.
50 Ibid., p. 262.
51 Ibid., p. 276.
52 Ibid., pp. 306, 319.
53 Ibid., pp. 319–22.
54 Ibid., p. 321.
55 Ibid., pp. 312–13; Colbert VI, p. 412.
56 Ibid., p. 413.
57 Ibid., p. 410; BN Mss Français 7608, fo. 299.
58 Colbert VI, p. 410.
59 Rav. VI, p. 315.
60 BN Mss Français 7608, fos. 278–9; BN Mss Clairambault 986, fo. 331.
61 Rav. VI, pp. 326–7.
62 Colbert VI, p. 411.
63 Rav. VI, pp. 368–9.
64 BN Mss Français 7608, fos. 284–5.
65 Rav. VI, pp. 183, 369.

## 9: The Chamber is Suspended
[pp. 260–290]

1 Rav. VI, pp. 330–1.
2 Ibid., pp. 327–9.
3 Ibid., p. 334.
4 Ibid., pp. 335–6.
5 Ibid., p. 335.
6 Ibid., pp. 420–1.
7 Ibid., p. 337.
8 Ibid., p. 429.
9 Ibid., p. 456.
10 Ibid., pp. 337–40.
11 BN Mss Français 7608, fo. 237.
12 Rav. VI, pp. 372–4.
13 Ibid., p. 436.
14 Ibid.
15 Ibid., p. 381.
16 Brunet I, p. 443; Primi Visconti, p. 304; see Maintenon, *Lettres* II, pp. 292–3.
17 Rav. VI, pp. 421, 393.
18 Ibid., pp. 393–4.
19 Ibid., p. 395.
20 Ibid., p. 393.
21 Ibid., pp. 349–52.
22 Ibid., pp. 375–6.
23 Ibid., p. 376.
24 Colbert VI, pp. 419–20.
25 Ibid.
26 Rav. VI, p. 384.
27 Ibid., pp. 395–6.
28 Ibid., pp. 419–36.
29 See Fouquier, *Causes Célèbres IV, Les Assassins de Henri IV: Ravaillac*.
30 Rav. VI, pp. 426–7.
31 Ibid., pp. 428–9.
32 Ibid., p. 421.
33 Ibid., p. 434.
34 Ibid., pp. 398–9.
35 Ibid., p. 402.
36 Ibid.
37 Bussy V, pp. 211, 176–7.
38 Decker, p. 177.
39 Montpensier IV, pp. 424, 439; Bussy V, p. 229.
40 Rav. VI, p. 346.
41 Ibid., pp. 419, 459.
42 Primi Visconti, p. 278.
43 Colbert VI, pp. 67–8, 422–3.

44 Clement, *Mme de Montespan*, p. 233;
Rousset, part one, II, pp. 437–64;
Primi Visconti, p. 213; Bussy IV,
p. 386.
45 Primi Visconti, p. 210; Montpensier
IV, p. 515.
46 Colbert VI, p. 415; for Colbert's
memo, see Colbert VI, pp. 414–22;
for Duplessis's memo see Colbert
VI, pp. 407–14.
47 Colbert VI, pp. 67, 423.
48 See e.g. Rav VI, pp. 356, 191,
254–5, 311.
49 Ibid., p. 384.
50 Colbert VI, p. 418.
51 Ibid., pp. 417–18.
52 Choisy I, pp. 90–1.
53 Colbert VI, pp. 423, 68.
54 Ibid., p. 424.
55 Rav. VI, p. 347.
56 Ibid., p. 458.
57 Ibid., pp. 454–9; also BN Mss
Français 7608, fo. 364.

**10: The End of the Affair** [pp. 291–313]
1 PRO SP 78/143, fos. 82v–83v.
2 Clement, *Mme de Montespan*,
pp. 402–4.
3 Rav. VI, pp. 486–7; Laulan, p. 840;
Petitfils, *Mme de Montespan*, p. 217;
Laulan, p. 840.
4 Primi Visconti, p. 210; Bussy V,
p. 259.
5 Brunet I, p. 199; Caylus, p. 32;
Spanheim, p. 82.
6 Rav. VI, p. 496.
7 Ibid., V, p. 469; Colbert VI, p. 429.
8 BN Mss Français 7608, fos. 392–3.
9 Rav. VI, pp. 462, 481.
10 Ibid., p. 246; ibid., VII, p. 64.
11 Ibid.; ibid., VI, pp. 465–7, 460–1.
12 BN Mss Clairambault 986, fos. 457,
461; Rav. VII, pp. 80, 238–9, 168.
13 Ibid., pp. 64–70.
14 BN Mss Clairambault 986, fos. 262,
267; Rav. VI, p. 496; AN 1127, fos.
147, 149.
15 Rav. VI, pp. 413, 403.
16 Ibid., pp. 406, 482.
17 Ibid., pp. 467–9, 485.
18 Ibid., pp. 471–9.

19 Ibid., p. 495.
20 SS (Truc) II, p. 294; Sourches I, p. 88.
21 Rav. VII, p. 17.
22 Ibid., pp. 17–18.
23 Ibid., p. 83.
24 Ibid., pp. 51–4, 62.
25 Ibid., pp. 44–5.
26 Ibid., p. 12.
27 BN Mss Clairambault 986, fo. 179;
Rav VII, pp. 23–7.
28 Ibid., pp. 28–9.
29 Ibid., p. 32.
30 Ibid., pp. 34–41.
31 Ibid., p. 80.
32 Ibid., pp. 83–8.
33 Ibid., p. 88.
34 Ibid., p. 92; Sourches I, p. 88.
35 Rav. VII, pp. 20, 7–8, 34.
36 Sourches I, p. 88.
37 SS (Truc) II, p. 294.
38 Rav. VII, pp. 98–100.
39 Ibid., pp. 102, 105.
40 Ibid., pp. 109–10.
41 Ibid., pp. 106–8.
42 Sourches I, p. 125.
43 BN Mss Français 7608, fos. 392–4,
376.
44 Rav. VII, pp. 113, 116.
45 Ibid., p. 388.
46 BN Mss Clairambault 986, fo. 257;
Rav. VII, pp. 7–8.
47 Ibid., p. 134; Lemoine, *Les des
Oeillets*, p. 42; Petitfils, *L'Affaire des
Poisons*, p. 177.
48 Rav. VI, p. 436.
49 Lemoine, *op. cit.*, pp. 42–3.
50 Rav. VII, pp. 111, 96, 149.
51 BN Mss Clairambault 1192, fo. 22;
Rav. VI, p. 389; AN 1127, fo. 107.
52 Rav. VII, pp. 150, 164, 169.
53 AN 1127, fo. 31; Rav. VII, p. 126.
54 See Rav. VI, pp. 465, 470.
55 BN Mss Français 7608, fo. 384; Rav.
VII, p. 97.
56 BN Mss Français 7608, fo. 378.
57 Rav. VII, pp. 112, 115, 115–16.
58 BN Mss Français 7608, fos. 402–9;
Rav VII, pp. 118–19.
59 Ibid., pp. 112–13.
60 Ibid., pp. 122, 120, 186.
61 Ibid., pp. 136, 116, 149.

62  Ibid., p. 119.
63  Ibid., pp. 122–3.
64  Ibid., p. 124.
65  Ibid., p. 127.
66  Ibid., p. 138.
67  Ibid., pp. 128, 131, 136, 149.
68  Ibid., p. 187.

## 11: Conclusion [pp. 314–339]

1  Clement, *Mme de Montespan*, p. 413;
    Rav. VI, p. 457.
2  Maintenon, *Lettres* II, p. 389.
3  Spanheim, p. 87; Maintenon, *Lettres*
    II, p. 395.
4  Clement, *Mme de Montespan*,
    pp. 264–5.
5  Dangeau I, p. 88; Spanheim, p. 80;
    Choisy I, p. 208.
6  Maintenon, *Lettres* II, pp. 401, 380.
7  Forster, pp. 40–41; Montpensier IV,
    pp. 498–9; Caylus, p. 141.
8  Cordelier, p. 146.
9  Spanheim, p. 88; Lavallée II, p. 486;
    Maintenon, *Lettres* V, p. 377.
10  Dangeau I, p. 265; Maintenon,
    *Lettres* III, p. 102; Scott-Stevenson II,
    p. 19.
11  Spanheim, p. 87; Caylus, p. 176.
12  Dangeau I, p. 77; Sourches I,
    pp. 385–7.
13  Ibid.; Dangeau I, pp. 337–40.
14  Sourches II, p. 91; Dangeau III,
    p. 276.
15  Sourches III, pp. 365–6.
16  Dangeau III, p. 325.
17  Ibid., p. 483; Caylus, p. 176.
18  Clement, *Mme de Montespan*,
    pp. 331, 286; Sév. X, p. 384.
19  Dangeau XI, p. 284; SS (Norton) I,
    p. 321.
20  SS (Truc) II, pp. 862–4; Clement,
    *Mme de Montespan*, p. 348.
21  Ibid., pp. 344–5.
22  SS (Truc) II, p. 863; Clement, *Mme
    de Montespan*, pp. 226–7.
23  SS (Truc) II, p. 866.
24  Dangeau XI, pp. 378–9; Clement,
    *Mme de Montespan*, pp. 337, 325;
    Decker, p. 229.
25  Saint-Germain, *La Reynie*, p. 338.
26  Sév. VII, p. 90; Primi Visconti,

p. 282; SS (Truc) I, pp. 647–8.
27  Colbert VI, p. 424.
28  Rav. VII, pp. 182–3.
29  Ibid., VI, p. 486; Sourches I, p. 80.
30  Rav. VI, p. 399; La Fare, p. 209.
31  Colbert VI, p. 428.
32  Segur, *Tapissier*, p. 10; Primi
    Visconti, pp. 292–3; Bussy V, p. 69.
33  Ibid., p. 173.
34  Sourches III, p. 40.
35  Trevor-Roper, pp. 15, 47; Briggs,
    *Witches and Neighbours*, pp. 8, 363.
36  Ibid., pp. 390, 57; see *Daily
    Telegraph*, 23.03.02; *Mail on Sunday*
    20.10.02.
37  Gibson, p. 137.
38  Coynart, pp. 273–80.
39  Voltaire, *Works*, ed. Morley XII,
    part ii, p. 167; Sourches III,
    pp. 110–11.
40  Dangeau III, p. 360.
41  Cabanes & Nass, p. 177; Dionis,
    pp. 86–7; Sourches III, pp. 436–7.
42  Scott-Stevenson I, pp. 100–1;
    Forster, p. 174; Brunet II, p. 25.
43  Scott-Stevenson II, p. 42.
44  Ibid., p. 51; Amiel, p. 317; Kroll,
    p. 154.
45  Coynart, pp. 274–5.
46  Colbert VI, p. 407.
47  Cruysse, *Lettres Françaises*, pp. 136,
    138.
48  Mandrou, *Possession et Sorcellerie*, p.
    279.
49  Ibid., pp. 285–6, 290, 306, 325,
    285–6.
50  Coynart, pp. 149, 155–6; Mandrou,
    *op. cit.*, p. 308.
51  Ibid., pp. 280–1.
52  Sév. VI, pp. 225, 272.
53  Feuquières, *Lettres* V, pp. 175–6.
54  Montpensier IV, p. 419; Sév. VIII, p.
    483.
55  Rav. VI, p. 181; Berryer, p. 175.
56  Griselle I, pp. 504–5.
57  Lough, *Locke's Travels*, p. 255;
    Dangeau I, p. 2.
58  Maintenon, *Lettres* II, p. 523.
59  Ibid., III, p. 454; Scott-Stevenson I,
    p. 78; Amiel, p. 175.
60  SS (Norton) II, p. 282.

61 Ibid., p. 320.
62 Ibid., I, p. 239; Primi Visconti, pp. 300–1.
63 Kroll, pp. 43–4; Primi Visconti, p. 46; Kroll, pp. 44, 47.
64 Spanheim, p. 288.
65 Sourches I, pp. 110, 284; Kroll, p. 67; Scott-Stevenson I, p. 182; Brunet I, pp. 29–30.
66 See Lemoine, *Mme de Montespan et la Légende des Poisons.*
67 Primi Visconti, pp. 278, 299; Feuquières, *Lettres* V, pp. 175–6, 180.
68 La Fare, p. 212; Choisy I, p. 224; Saint-Maurice I, p. xxxvii.
69 Primi Visconti, p. 178.
70 Ibid., pp. 292, 294.
71 Feuquières V, p. 192.
72 La Fare, p. 214; Primi Visconti, p. 300.
73 Ibid., p. 277; Sév. VI, pp. 232, 226.
74 Primi Visconti, p. 282.
75 La Vallière I, p. 52.
76 Mandrou, *op. cit.*, p. 453.

# BIBLIOGRAPHY

—⦿⦿⦿—

**Note**: unless otherwise stated, all books in English were published in London and all books in French were published in Paris.

## UNPUBLISHED SOURCES

**Bibliothèque Nationale François Mitterrand**

4-FM-15043, *Factum pour Dame Marie Vosser, Veuve de Pierre de Hannyvel, Sieur de Saint-Laurens ... Contre Maistre Pierre-Louis Reich de Pennautier, Receveur-General du Clergé et Trésorier de la Bourse des États de Languedoc,* 1677

4-FM-29352, *Deuxième Part de Factum pour Dame Marie Vosser ... Contre ... Pennautier,* 1677

4-FM-29355, *La Qualité de Ceux Qui Étaient du Commerce de Sainte-Croix,* 1677

FP 2662, *Requête Présentée par la Dame de Saint-Laurens à nos Seigneurs de Parlement,* 1677

FP 2662, *Réponses du Sieur Pennautier aux Deux Requêtes de Mme de Saint-Laurens,* 1677

4-FM-27378, *Factum pour Monsieur Pierre-Louis Reich de Pennautier ... Contre Dame Marie Vosser, Veuve du Sieur de Saint-Laurens,* 1677

**Bibliothèque Nationale Richelieu**

Mss Clairambault 1192, *La Diablomanie de Monsieur de Luxembourg ou Histoire de la Prison de Monsieur de Luxembourg*

Mss Clairambault 986, *Inventaire des Papiers et Interrogatoires Faits par M. de La Reynie aux Personnes Détenues dans le Château de Vincennes pour les Poisons, Rangés par Ordre Alphabétique*

Mss Français 7608, *Recueil des Piéces Originales et Copies Concernant le Procès Instruit par M. de La Reynie et Jugés par la Chambre d'Arsenal 1679–91*

**Assemblée Nationale**

Mss 1127, *Chambre Ardente 1679–82, Extrait fait par M. Brunet, avocat, des Procès Criminels Instruits et Jugés Pendant Lesdites Années Contenus en Douze Cartons qui ont été Remis entre les Mains de M. la Garde de Sceaux par les Héritiers de M. de La Reynie*

**Bibliothèque de l'Arsenal**

Mss 10,338 to 10,359. Mostly printed by Ravaisson

## PRINTED SOURCES

Amiel, Olivier (ed.), *Lettres de Madame, Duchesse d'Orléans, née Princesse Palatine*, 1981

Antin, Duc d', *Mémoires*, 1822

Aumale, Mademoiselle d', *Mémoire sur Madame de Maintenon*, ed. Comte d'Haussonville and G. Hanotaux, n.d.

Barker, Nancy Nichols, *Brother to the Sun King: Philippe Duc d'Orléans*, Baltimore, 1989

Beaupré, J. N., *La Belle de Ludres*, Saint-Nicolas de Port, 1861

Beaussant, Philippe, *Le Roi Soleil Se Lève Aussi*, 2000

Belin, Camille, *Nicolas de La Reynie*, Limoges, 1874

Bely, Lucien, *Dictionnaire de l'Ancien Régime*, 1996

Bernard, Leon, *The Emerging City: Paris in the Age of Louis XIV*, Durham, North Carolina, 1970

Berryer, *Leçons et Modèles d'Éloquence Judiciaire*, 1838

Bertière, Simone, *Les Reines de France au Temps des Bourbons; Les Femmes du Roi Soleil*, 1998

Berwick, James Fitzjames, Duke of, *Memoirs*, 1779

Beurain, Chevalier J. de, *Mémoires pour Servir à l'Histoire du Maréchal-Duc de Luxembourg Depuis sa Naissance en 1628 Jusqu'à sa Mort en 1695*, The Hague, 1758.

*Bibliography Annuelle de l'Histoire de France*

Bluche, François, *Louis XIV*, translated Mark Greengrass, 1990

———— *La Vie Quotidienne au Temps de Louis XIV*, 1984

Boiteau, Paul and Livet, C. L. (eds) *Histoire Amoureuse des Gaules (by Bussy-Rabutin) Suivie des Romans Historico-Satiriques du XVIIième Siècle*, 1856

Bossuet, Jacques Bénigne, *Oeuvres Complètes*, 1841

Bottineau, Yves, *Versailles, Miroir des Princes*, 1989

Braux, Gustave, *Louise de La Vallière de sa Touraine Natale au Carmel de Paris*, Tours, 1981

Briggs, Robin, *Communities of Belief: Cultural and social Tension in Early Modern France*, Oxford, 1989

———— *Early Modern France, 1560–1715*, Oxford, 1977

———— *Witches and Neighbours. The Social and Cultural Context of European Witchcraft*, 1997

Brunet, G. (ed.), *Correspondance Complète de Madame, Duchesse d'Orléans*, 1886

Burke, Peter, *The Fabrication of Louis XIV*, 1992

———— *Popular Culture in Early Modern Europe*, 1978

Bussy, Roger de Rabutin, Comte de, *Correspondance de Roger de Rabutin Comte de Bussy avec sa Famille et ses Amis*, 1858

Cabanes, Dr and Nass, L., *Poisons et Sortilèges. Deuxième Serie*, 1903

Campbell, Peter R., *Power and Politics in Old Regime France 1720–45*, 1996

Cartwright, Julia, *Madame*, 1894

Castelot, André, *Madame de Maintenon. La Reine Secrète*, 1996

Caylus, Marthe Marguerite, Marquise de, *Souvenirs de Madame de Caylus*, ed. Lionel Peraux, 1908

Chassiagne, Marc, *La Lieutenance-Générale de Police à Paris*, 1906

Choisy, Abbé de, *Mémoires de l'Abbé de Choisy pour Servir à l'Histoire de Louis XIV*, ed. M. de Lescure, 1888

Clark, Stuart, *Thinking with Demons. The Idea of Witchcraft in Early Modern Europe*, Oxford, 1997

Clement, Pierre, 'La Chambre de l'Arsenal' in *Revue des Deux Mondes*, 15 February 1864

—————— *Mme de Montespan et Louis XIV*, 1868

—————— *La Police sous Louis XIV*, 1866

—————— *Trois Drames Historiques*, 1857

Colbert, Jean-Baptiste, *Lettres, Instructions et Mémoires*, ed. Pierre Clement, 1866

Cordelier, Jean, *Madame de Maintenon*, 1955

Corneille, Thomas and Visé, Donneau de, *La Devineresse*, ed. P.J. Yarrow, University of Exeter, 1971

Cornu, Maître Marcel, *Le Procès de la Marquise de Brinvilliers*, 1894

Cortequisse, Bruno, *Madame Louis XIV. Marie-Thérèse d'Autriche*, 1992

Corvisier, André, *Louvois*, 1983

Coulon, Marcel, 'Racine et la Mort de la Du Parc' in *Mercure de France*, 1 June 1940

Courtois, Afred de (ed.), *Lettres de Madame de Villars à Madame de Coulanges*, 1868

Couton, Georges, *La Chair et l'Ame. Louis XIV Entre ses Maîtresses et Bossuet*, Grenoble, 1995

Coynart, Charles de, *Une Sorcière au XVIIIième Siècle. Marie Anne de La Ville 1680–1725*, 1902

Cronin, Vincent, *Louis XIV*, 1964

Crousaz-Cretet, P. de, *Paris sous Louis XIV*, 1923

Cruysse, Dirk van der (ed.), *Madame Palatine, Lettres Françaises*, 1989

—————— *Madame Palatine, Princesse Européenne*, 1988

Dangeau, Marquis de, *Journal du Marquis de Dangeau avec les Additions du Duc de Saint-Simon*, 1854

Danjou, F., (ed.) *Archives Curieuses de l'Histoire de France Depuis Louis XI jusqu'a Louis XVIII*, 2nd Series, vol. XII, 1840

Davis, Natalie Zemon and Farge, Arlette (eds), *A History of Women in the West. Volume III: Renaissance and Enlightenment Paradoxes*, Cambridge, 1993

Debus, Allen G., and Multhauf, Robert P., *Alchemy and Chemistry in the Seventeenth Century*, Los Angeles, 1966

Decker, Michel de, *Madame de Montespan, la Grande Sultane*, 1985

Dewald, Jonatham, *Aristocratic Experience and the Origins of Modern Culture. France 1570–1715*, Berkeley, California, 1993

Dionis, M., *Dissertation sur la Mort Subite*, 1710

Drevillon, Hervé, *Lire et Écrire l'Avenir. L'Astrologie dans la France du Grand Siècle, 1610–1715*, 1996

——— 'Magie et Raison d'Etat: L'Affaire des Poisons' in *Histoire*, Number 216, December 1997

Duclos, Charles Pinot, *Mémoires Secrètes sur les Règnes de Louis XIV et Louis XV*, 1804

Dunlop, Ian, *Louis XIV*, 1999

——— *Versailles*, 1978

Duchêne, Jacqueline, *Bussy-Rabutin*, 1992

Elias, Norbert, *The Court Society*, translated Edmund Jephcott, Oxford, 1983

Erlanger, Philippe, *Louis XIV*, translated Stephen Cox, 1970

Esmein, A., *Histoire de la Procedure Criminelle en France*, 1882

Fabre, Dr Jean, *Sur la Vie et Principalement sur la Mort de Madame, Henriette-Anne Stuart, Duchesse d'Orléans*, 1912

Felibien, André, *Description Sommaire du Château de Versailles*, 1674

——— *Les Divertissements de Versailles Donnés par le Roi à Toute sa Cour au Retour de la Conquête de la Franche-Comté en l'Année 1674*, Paris, 1674

Fenélon, François Salignac de La Mothe, *Écrits et Lettres Politiques*, ed. C.H. Urbain, 1920

Feuquières, Antoine de Pas, Marquis de, *Lettres Inédites de Feuquières*, ed. Etienne Gallois, 1845

——— *Memoirs Written for the Instruction of his Son, Translated from the French*, 1737

Forster, Elborg (ed.), *A Woman's Life in the Court of the Sun King. Letters of Liselotte von der Pfalz 1652–1722*, John Hopkins University Press, Baltimore, 1984

Fouquier, Armand, *Causes Célèbres de tous les Peuples*, vol. IV, 1861

Funck-Brentano, Frantz, *Princes and Poisoners*, translated George Maidment, 1901

——— *La Cour du Roi Soleil*, 1937

Gibson, Wendy, *Women in Seventeenth-Century France*, 1989

Glaser, Christophe, *The Compleat Chymist*, 1677

Goldman, Lucien, *Racine*, Cambridge, 1972

Goubert, Pierre, *Louis XIV and Twenty Million Frenchmen*, translated Anne Carter, 1970

Gould, Cecil, *Bernini in France. An Episode in Seventeenth-Century History*, 1981

Grandet, Joseph, *Mémoires de Joseph Grandet. Histoire de Seminaire d'Angers*, ed. G. Letourneau, 1893

Griselle, Eugène, *Bourdaloue. Histoire Critique de sa Predication*, 1901

Guitton, Georges, *Père de La Chaise, Confesseur de Louis XIV*, 1959

Hamscher, Albert N., *The Parlement of Paris After the Fronde 1653–73*, University of Pittsburgh Press, 1976

Hatton, Ragnhild, *Louis XIV and his World*, 1972

—— 'At the Court of the Sun King' in A.G. Dickens (ed.), *The Courts of Europe*, 1977

Hilton, Lisa, *Athénaïs, the Real Queen of France*, 2002

Horric de Beaucaire, Charles, *Recueil des Instructions Données aux Ambassadeurs et Ministres de France Depuis les Traités de Westphalie Jusqu'à la Révolution Française*, vol. XIV: *Savoie-Sardaigne et Mantoue*, 1898–9

Isambert, F.A. (ed.), *Recueil Général des Anciennes Lois Françaises*, 1822–33

Iung, Theodore, *La Vérité sur le Masque de Fer (les Empoisonneurs)*, 1873

Jaeglé, Ernest (ed. and translated), *Correspondance de Madame, Duchesse d'Orléans*, 1890

Kenyon, John, *The Popish Plot*, 1972

Kieckhefer, Richard, *European Witch Trials*, 1976

King, James E., *Science and Rationalism in the Government of Louis XIV, 1661–83*, New York, 1972

Krailsheimer, A.J. (ed.), *Letters of Armand Jean de Rancé, Abbot and Reformer of La Trappe*, Michigan, 1984

Kroll, Maria (ed. and translated), *Letters from Liselotte*, 1970

Labatut, Jean-Pierre, *Louis XIV, Roi de Gloire*, 1984

La Batut, Guy de, 'Mademoiselle de Fontanges' in *Les Oeuvres Libres*, 152, 1934

La Baumelle, Laurent Angliviel de, *Mémoires Pour Servir á l'Histoire de Madame de Maintenon*, Amsterdam, 1755

La Bruyère, Jean de, *Les Caractères de Théophraste*, ed. Robert Garapon, 1962

Lacretelle, Pierre de, *La Vie Privée de Racine*, 1949

Ladurie, Emanuel Le Roy and Fitou, Jean-François, *Saint-Simon, ou le Système de la Cour*, 1997

La Fare, C.A., Marquis de, *Mémoires et Réflexions sur les Principaux Événements du Règne de Louis XIV*, Rotterdam, 1716

Lafayette, Mme Marie Madeleine de, *Histoire de Madame Henriette d'Angleterre*, 1925

Lagarde, Henri, *L'Apothicaire-Chimiste Christophe Glaser*, 1891

Lair, Jules, *Louise de La Vallière and the Early Life of Louise XIV*, translated Ethel Colburn Mayne, n.d.

Langlois, Marcel, *Madame de Maintenon*, 1932

—— *Louis XIV et la Cour, d'après Trois Témoins Nouveaux: Belise, Beauvillier, Chamillart*, 1926

Latruffe-Colomb, Dr., 'Quel était le Principe le Plus Actif des Poisons Qu'Employait la Brinvilliers?' in *La Chronique Médicale*, 15 October 1908

Laulan, Robert, 'Un Diagnostic Retrospectif sur la Maladie Mortelle de Mademoiselle de Fontanges' in *La Presse Medicale*, 4 June 1952; also in

*Mercure de France*, 1 April 1952

Lavallée, T. (ed.), *Lettres Historiques et Édifiantes par Mme de Maintenon*, 1856

La Vallière, Louise de, *Réflexions Sur La Miséricorde de Dieu. Suivie de ses Lettres*, ed. Pierre Clement, 1860

Lebigre, Arlette, *L'Affaire des Poisons*, 1989

———— *La Justice du Roi*, 1988

———— 'Le Grand Siècle des Empoisonneuses' in *Histoire*, Number 37, 1981

Le François, A.B., *Les Mystères des Vieux Châteaux de France*, 1865

Lemoine, Jean, *Les Des Oeillets: Une Grande Comédienne; Une Maîtresse de Louis XIV*, 1938

———— *Madame de Montespan et la Légende des Poisons*, 1908

———— *L'Affaire Montespan. Réponse à Messieurs Sardou et Funck-Brentano*, 1908

———— 'L'Enigme Montespan. Le Requisitoire de Monsieur Armand Praviel' in *Revue des Questions Historiques*, vol. 122, 1935

Lemoine, Jean and Lichtenberger, André, *De La Vallière à Montespan*, 1903

Levron, J., 'Louis XIV's Courtiers' in Ragnhild Hatton (ed.) *Louis XIV and Absolutism*, Ohio State University Press, 1976

Levron, Jacques, *Daily Life at Versailles in the Seventeenth and Eighteenth Centuries*, translated Claire Etiane Engel, 1968

———— *Les Courtisans*, 1960

Lewis, W.H., *The Splendid Century. Some Aspects of French Life in the Reign of Louis XIV*, 1953

Locatelli, Sebastien, *Voyage de France 1664–65*, translated Adolphe Vautier, 1905

Lossky, Andrew, *Louis XIV and the French Monarchy*, Rutgers University Press, New Brunswick, New Jersey, 1994

Lough, John, *France Observed in the Seventeenth Century by British Travellers*, 1985

Lough, John (ed.), *Locke's Travels in France, 1675–79*, Cambridge, 1953

Louis XIV, *Oeuvres*, 1806

Luxembourg, Duc de, *A Letter from a Trooper in Flanders to his Comrade Shewing that Luxembourg is a Witch and Deals with the Devil*, 1695

———— *The Bargain which the Duc de Luxembourg...Made with the Devil to Win Battles*, 1692

Magne, Emile (ed.), *Lettres Inédites du Grand Condé et le Duc d'Enghien à Marie-Louise de Gonzague, Reine de Pologne, sur la Cour de Louis XIV*, 1920

Maintenon, Françoise, Marquise de, *Conseils et Instructions aux Demoiselles*, ed. T. Lavallée, 1857

———— *Lettres*, ed. Marcel Langlois, 1935

Mandin, Louis, 'Racine, le Sadisme, et l'Affaire des Poisons' in *Mercure de France*, 1 April 1940

Mandrou, Robert, *Magistrats et Sorciers en France au XVIIième Siècle*, 1968

———— *Possession et Sorcellerie au XVIIième Siècle*, 1979

Marchesseau, Dr Robert, *Une Urgence Abdominale. La Mort de Madame Henriette d'Angleterre*, Bordeaux, 1947

Marie, Alfred and Jeanne, *Mansart à Versailles*, 1972

Marion, Marcel, *Dictionnaire des Institutions de la France aux XVIIième et XVIIIième Siècles*, 1923

Marshall, Peter, *The Philosopher's Stone. A Quest for the Secrets of Alchemy*, 2001

Masson, A., *La Sorcellerie et la Science de Poisons au XVIIième Siècle*, 1904

*Mercure Galant*

Mettam, Roger, *Government and Society in Louis XIV's France*, 1977

―――― *Power and Faction in Louis XIV's France*, 1988

Meyer, Jean, *Bossuet*, 1993

Michael of Greece, Prince, *Louis XIV. The Other Side of the Sun*, 1983

Michelet, J., 'Decadence Morale de XVIIième Siècle' in *Revue des Deux Mondes*, vol. XXVI, 1 April 1860

Mitford, Nancy, *The Sun King*, 1966

Moine, Marie-Christine, *Les Fêtes à la Cour du Roi Soleil*, 1984

Mongredien, Georges, *La Vie Privée de Louis XIV*

―――― *La Vie Quotidienne sous Louis XIV*, 1948

―――― *Mme de Montespan et l'Affaire des Poisons*, 1953

―――― 'Une Intrigante à la Cour de Louis XIV. Mademoiselle de Montalais' in *Mercure de France*, CCCII, 1 March 1948

Montpensier, Anne Marie Louise d'Orléans, Duchesse de, *Mémoires de Mademoiselle de Montpensier*, ed. A. Cheruel, 1891

Mossiker, Frances, *The Affair of the Poisons*, 1972

―――― *Madame de Sévigné. A Life and Letters*, New York, 1983

Motteville, Marquise de, *Memoirs*, translated Katherine Prescott Wormley, 1902

Mousnier, Roland, *The Institutions of France Under the Absolute Monarchy 1598–1789*, translated Brian Pearce, University of Chicago Press, 1979, 1980

Muchembled, Robert (ed.), *Magie et Sorcellerie en Europe du Moyen Age à Nos Jours*, 1994

*Narrative of the Process against Madame Brinvilliers and of her Condemnation and Execution for having Poisoned her Father and Two Brothers*, 1676

Nass, Dr Lucien, *Les Empoisonnements sous Louis XIV*, 1898

Newton, William Ritchey, *L'Espace du Roi. La Cour de France au Château de Versailles 1682–1789*, 2000

Nicholl, Charles, *The Chemical Theatre*, 1980

Noel-Williams, H., *Madame de Montespan*, 1903

Nolhac, Pierre de, *Histoire du Château de Versailles*, 1911

Norton, Lucy, ed. and translated, *Saint-Simon at Versailles*, 1958

―――― *The Sun King and his Loves*, 1983

Noyer, Mme du, *Correspondence of Madame du Noyer*, ed. and translated, Florence L. Layard, 1890

Ojala, Jeanne A. and William T., *Madame de Sévigné*, Oxford and New York, 1990

Oresko, Robert, 'The House of Savoy in Search for a Royal Crown' in *Royal and Republican Sovereignty in Early Modern Europe*, ed. R. Oresko, G.C. Gibbs and H.M. Scott, Cambridge, 1997

Ormesson, Olivier, Lefevre d', *Journal*, ed. M. Cheruel, 1860

Patin, Gui, *Lettres*, ed. J.H. Reveille-Parise, 1846

Petitfils, Jean-Christian, *L'Affaire des Poisons. Alchimistes et Sorciers sous Louis XIV*, 1977

———— *Lauzun*, 1987

———— *Louis XIV*, 1995

———— *Madame de Montespan*, 1988

Pirot, Edme, *La Marquise de Brinvilliers. Récit de ses Derniers Moments*, ed. G. Roullier, 1883

Primi Visconti, Giovanni-Battista, *Mémoires sur la Cour de Louis XIV*, traduits et publiés Jean Lemoine, 1908

Racine, Louis, 'Memoires … sur la Vie et Ouvrages de Jean Racine' in Jean Racine, *Oeuvres Complètes*, ed. Raymond Picard, 1950

Ravaisson, François, *Archives de la Bastille*, vols IV–VII, 1870–4

Renée, Amedée, *Les Nièces de Mazarin*, 1858

Ricotti, Ercole, *Storia della Monarchia Piemontese*, 1861–9

Robert, Henri, 'La Marquise de Brinvilliers' in *Les Grands Procès de l'Histoire*, 2nd Series, 1923

———— 'Racine et la Du Parc' in *Les Grands Procès de l'Histoire*, 5th Series, 1926

Rouben, C., (ed.) *Correspondance de Bussy-Rabutin Avec le Père René Rapin*, 1983

Roujon, Jacques, *Louvois et son Maître*, 1934

Rousset, Camille, *Histoire de Louvois*, 1862

Rowlands, Guy, *The Dynastic State and the Army Under Louis XIV. Royal Service and Private Interest 1661–1701*, Cambridge, 2002

Ruggieri, Eve, *L'Honneur Retrouvé du Marquis de Montespan*, 1992

Sackville-West, Vita, *Daughter of France*, 1959

Saint-Germain, Jacques, *La Reynie et la Police au Grand Siècle*, 1962

———— *Louis XIV Secret*, 1970

———— *Madame de Brinvilliers*, 1971

Saint-Maurice, Thomas Chabod, Marquis de, *Lettres sur la Cour de Louis XIV*, ed. Jean Lemoine, 1910

Saint-Simon, Louis de Rouvroy, Duc de, *Historical Memoirs of the Duc de Saint-Simon. A Shortened Version*, ed. and translated, Lucy Norton, paperback ed., 1974

———— *Memoires*, ed. Gonzague Truc, 1953

Scott-Stevenson, Gertrude, *The Letters of Madame. The correspondence of Elizabeth Charlotte of Bavaria, Princess Palatine, Duchess of Orléans, called*

'Madame', at the Court of King Louis XIV, 1924

Segur, Pierre de, La Jeunesse du Maréchal de Luxembourg, 1900

————— Le Maréchal de Luxembourg et le Prince d'Orange, 1902

————— Le Tapissier de Notre-Dame. Les Dernières Années du Maréchal de Luxembourg, 1903

Sévigné, Marie Chantal, Marquise de, Lettres de Madame de Sévigné, ed. M. Monmerque, Paris, 1862

————— Correspondance, ed. Roger Duchêne, 1972

Shelmerdine, J.M. (ed.), The Secret History of Henrietta Princess of England with Memoirs of the Court of France for the years 1688–89 by Madame de Lafayette, 1929

Solnon, Jean-François, La Cour de France, 1987

Soman, Alfred, Sorcellerie et Justice Criminelle: le Parlement de Paris, XVIième à XVIIIième Siècles, Hampshire and Vermont, 1992

Sonnino. Paul (ed. and translated) Louis XIV. Memoirs for the Instruction of the Dauphin, 1970

Sophia, Memoirs of Sophia, Electress of Hanover, translated H. Forester, 1888

Sourches, Louis-François, Marquis de, Mémoires du Marquis de Sourches sur le Règne de Louis XIV, ed. le Comte de Cosnac et Arthur Bertrand, 1882

Spanheim, Ezechiel, Relation de la Cour de France en 1690, ed. Emile Bourgeois, 1900

Stead, Philip John, The Police of France, 1983

Stokes, Hugh, Madame de Brinvilliers and her Times, 1924

Thiers, Jean-Baptiste, 'Traité des Superstitions' in Superstitions Anciennes et Modernes: Prejugés Vulgaires, Amsterdam, 1733

Thomas, Keith, Religion and the Decline of Magic, 1982

Treasure, Geoffrey, France in the Seventeenth Century, 1966

————— Louis XIV, 2001

————— Mazarin, 1995

Trevor-Roper, H.R., The European Witch Craze of the Sixteenth and Seventeenth Centuries, 1969

Vallot, Antoine, Journal de la Santé du Roi Louis XIV écrit par Vallot, d'Aguin et Fagon, ed. J.A. Le Roi, 1862

Voltaire, 'The Age of Louis XIV' in Works, ed. Lord Morley, translated William F. Fleming, vol. XII, New York, 1927

————— Le Siècle de Louis XIV, 1985

Walton, Guy, Louis XIV's Versailles, 1986

Warolin, Christian, 'La Vie Fugitive de Mlle de Fontanges'. Memoire posthume de Maurice Bouvet in Revue d'Histoire de la Pharmacie, volume 48, number 326, 2000

White, Michael, Isaac Newton. The Last Sorcerer, 1998

Wolf, John B., Louis XIV, 1968

Ziegler, Gilette, The Court of Versailles, translated Simon Watson-Taylor, 1966

# INDEX